[STR

The Siege of Sadr City

Sgt. Konrad R.K. Ludwig (Ret.)

A book by
Roland-Kjos Publishing

Stryker: The Siege of Sadr City
by Sgt. Konrad R.K. Ludwig (Ret.)
First Edition Trade Paperback (Rev. 2)
September 2013

ISBN: 978-0-9853398-0-7

Published by Roland-Kjos.LLC
P.O. Box 804
La Cañada Flintridge
California 91012, U.S.A.
http://www.roland-kjos.com

Names and identifying information of certain people depicted in this book have been changed to protect their privacy. All actions and dialogue are offered in good faith as the author's own recollection of events.

In some cases this book describes conversations in which the author was exposed to second-hand information, conjecture, and hearsay. These events have been introduced as such and included in the narration with the explicit and limited intention of accounting for the opinions, beliefs, and rumors common among the men regarding public figures, events, and decisions. The author makes no endorsement of their accuracy.

Please submit feedback, corrections, and reviews to:
feedback@roland-kjos.com

In Memory of:

SGT. Randell Olguin – KIA September 30th, 2007

SSG. Joseph Gamboa – KIA March 25th, 2008

CPL. Steven Candelo – KIA March 26th, 2008

CPL. Joshua Molina – KIA March 27th, 2008

SGT. Michael Lilly – KIA April 7th, 2008

CPL. Jason Kazarick – KIA April 7th, 2008

CPL. Justin Mixon – KIA June 1st, 2008

...all men of the 1st Squadron, 2nd SCR.

This book is not for mothers.

Table Of Contents

Stryker - M1126 Infantry Carrier Vehicle

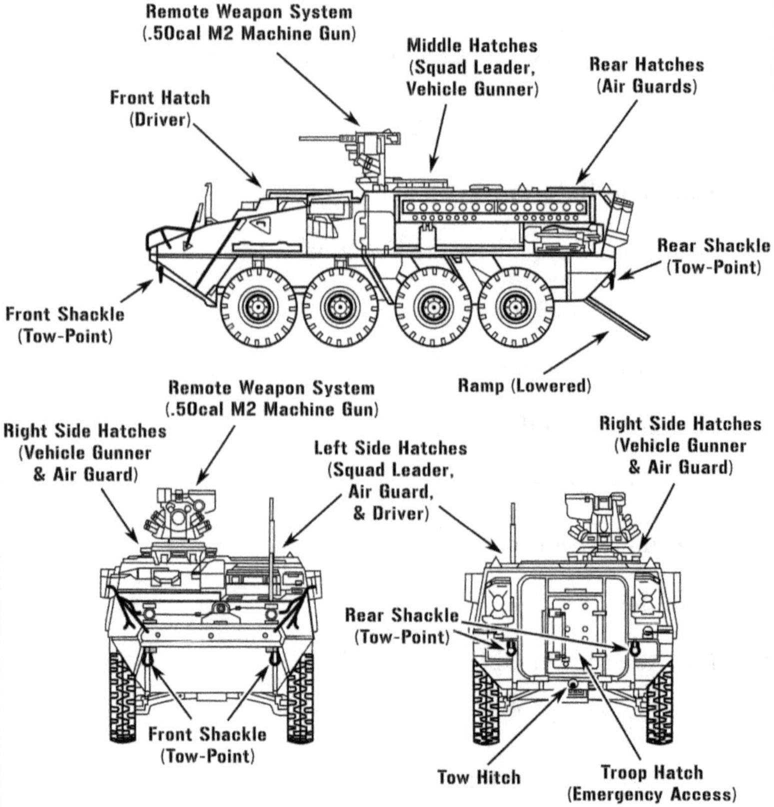

Type:	Armored fighting vehicle
In service:	2002 - Present
Used by:	United States & Canada
Weight (ICV):	16.47 tonnes
Length:	6.95 m (22 ft 10 in)
Width:	2.72 m (8 ft 11 in)
Height:	2.64 m (8 ft 8 in)
Crew:	(Driver / Gunner)
Passengers:	Crew + 9 (Infantry Squad)
Armor:	7.62 mm/14.5 mm/RPG Resistant
Main Armament:	M2 .50 cal. Heavy Machine Gun
Secondary Armament:	MK19 40 mm Grenade Launcher
Targeting System:	M151 Remote Weapon Station
Suspension:	8×8 wheeled
Operational Range:	500 km (310 mi)
Top Speed:	100 km/h (62 mph)

Baghdad (MAR 2008)

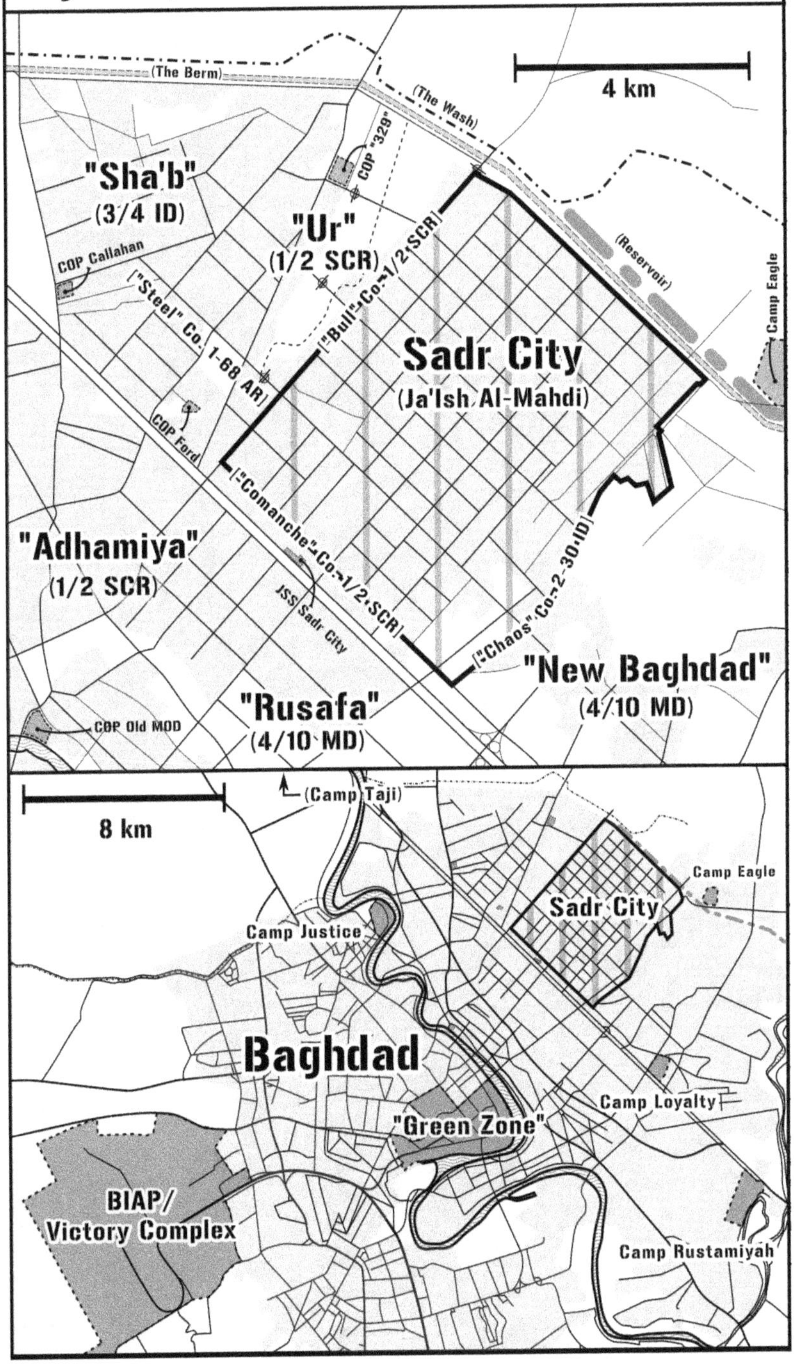

- Prologue -
"Here There Be Dragons"

We had a mantra in Bull Company: "Twenty minutes from flash to bang." It was the countdown by which we ran our lives. The deadline of every raid. As soon as we crossed over into the militia stronghold of Sadr City, that twenty minutes was all the time we had to hit our objective, grab the target, and get the hell outta' Dodge. After that, the hornet's nest was stirred. When that time ran out, every breath we took had to be earned with a fight. Any longer and we'd be surrounded by a swarm of insurgent fighters who were frothing at the mouth to eat us alive. Back then, Bull Company was the only conventional taskforce assigned to do high-profile kill-or-capture missions into the heart of Baghdad's most feared district. Our enemy, the Jaish al-Mahdi, was among the most expertly trained, well organized, and fully supplied insurgent militias in the world. All it took was twenty minutes for them to rally an army of untold number and fill the streets with a bloodthirsty mob. Once that happened, all bets were off.

The clock started as soon as they saw us coming. Jaish al-Mahdi lookouts littered along the edge of town woke up their lieutenants with the information they needed to stage an effective response. Those lieutenants then shot reports up to the highest levels of command, and the militia's reaction would already be in the works. As soon as we hit the border, we were running out of time.

We had five minutes to make it to our objective. That's five minutes to navigate through a maze of road-blocked avenues, four-story buildings, and shanty houses. Five minutes to memorize the route and take a mental note of how we'd get out of there alive. Five minutes — at top speed — to be on-site and through the door. Meanwhile the militia kept track of our positions from the rooftops. On every block, intersection, and hurried turn, they shot off bursts of gunfire into the sky to make sure everyone in the city knew exactly where we were. By the time we got to our objective the element of surprise was long gone: the militia knew exactly what to expect.

After five minutes we kicked down the doors and flooded into our objective. A mosaic of violence and chaos followed. There were screams and shouts. Anybody stupid enough to pick up a weapon was gunned down. In a flurry of panic and pandemonium, we stormed through the rooms until the entire building was clear. While the assault teams inside the objective shifted gears to prep the suspects for exfiltration, the men outside on the perimeter began preparing for the worst. From that point forward we were at the mercy of our enemy. They were hiding in every major city block and in less than fifteen minutes they'd be out in the streets. That's the moment the tides turned.

Just five minutes into each raid, women and children had already teamed up with their sons and brothers to set the stage for our demise. They lit tires on fire and rolled them into the middle of the street to white out the infrared cameras of our heavy air-support and overhead reconnaissance. Massive diesel generators spun up to feed juice into the streetlights all around us to black out our night vision goggles. At that, we were left out in the open with nowhere to hide. It was us against them — flat-out. No thermal cameras. No night-vision advantage. No snazzy tricks and no backup. Just grunts with guns, standing in the middle of the street, and lit up like Christmas. With each passing minute, we became the underdogs in a force-on-force engagement — so we stuck to the timeline no matter what.

We had ten minutes on-target. That's ten minutes to work through a laundry list of action items that would take your average team an hour or more to accomplish. We had to round up the suspects, swab and inspect them for explosive residue, and double-check them for a positive identification. Meanwhile, special exploitation teams combed through each room for intelligence materials and evidence. Contraband was confiscated and cataloged into little plastic bags. Every action was double and triple checked to perfection. The only reason it ever got done in time was that we knew our lives were on the line. A single screw-up and it was all over.

Fifteen minutes into the raid, every man in Bull Company broke like hell for the exfiltration, no questions asked. The suspects were zip-tied and blindfolded, the exploitation teams abandoned their search and packed up their gear, the detainees were loaded into vehicles, we pulled off of the objective, and every soldier on the perimeter flipped their selector switch from 'safe' to 'fire.' That far into the operation, the militia's special groups of snipers and RPG teams were already on their way, and the random pot shots from down the street shifted into focused and deliberate attacks. It only took fifteen minutes for the quiet midnight streets of Sadr City to become a spawning pool for the impending fight — a fight we knew we couldn't win. So when our Strykers' ramps slammed shut, it was time for us to move. Every soldier was accounted for, the vehicles called up their status, and we got the hell out of that city before the militia could swallow us whole. It was just a matter of time before they killed us all. The only question was how long we might hold out.

That much we had learned the hard way.

It was moments past midnight in the fall of 2007 when I rolled out with the rest of Bull Company on our first high-profile raid into Sadr City. Intelligence from higher up the chain of command placed a large group of militia leaders at a meeting in the middle of town. It was a sterling opportunity: a chance for us to round up key players in the local insurgency and strike a solid blow to their organization. If we could pull this off, it would prove our worth as a high profile combat unit and set the tone for the entire deployment to come. After all, we'd only been in Iraq for about a month, and we had yet to make good on our name.

As far as the mission was concerned, it was a fairly standard raid. In fact, it was exactly the kind of operation we had been trained to carry out. With the high mobility and built-in stealth of our eight-wheeled, light armored "Stryker" infantry fighting vehicles, it was going to be an easy task to sneak in, hit them where it hurt, and get back to our base with the suspects before they even knew what hit them. When the call came down the chain for us to suit up and get ready, I ran over every detail in my mind. I thought back to the countless hours we'd spent in shoot-houses and scenarios, duking it out with simulated bad guys. I went over the basics we had learned during hundreds of mock-up firefights. I reminded myself that I was ready for this job. I told myself that we were elite. I lied to myself like a pro.

"It's alright," I said. "You're ready for this."

Truth be told, my stomach was churning. I had no idea what to expect. There I was, getting ready for some hardcore shit — a high-action raid into one of the most dangerous cities in the world — and I couldn't even remember the last time I threw a punch in anger. This would be the first time in my life I had ever been in a direct, two-way, live-fire situation against real bad guys who were actually shooting back. The thought of what could happen if anything went wrong was sobering to say the least, but that would happen whether I was ready for it or not. All I could do at that point was sit around at the combat outpost and wait for the green light to go. After an hour or two of standing-by, our platoon sergeant stepped out into the hallway of the barracks to "spin us up," and we got ready to roll.

"Let's go!" he shouted. "Everybody downstairs. Ready condition one! Move it!"

In a single sweeping motion, we donned our gear and raced out the gate on our way to the target. As the platoon radio operator at the time, I was up in the lead vehicle with our platoon leader, Lieutenant Savage. He was standing up in one of the front two hatches next to the vehicle gunner and commander, Specialist Wallace. As we raced to the objective, they pored over maps and satellite imagery of the mission. With every passing mile they barked directions up to the driver, Specialist Pfister, who was sitting in the "driver's hole" with a thin partition between him and the massive super-diesel engine of our Stryker.

As we tore through the streets, the acting squad leader on the truck, Sergeant Brasel, was standing watch out of one of the back hatches of our Stryker. Beside him was one of the squad's acting team leaders, a good friend named McKeever, who we all called "Smiley." I was among one of the half-dozen guys sitting on the bench seats down below in the troop compartment. Next to me was the other team leader, Sergeant Lilly; my good friend, Gonzo; our buddy, Wilson; and the platoon special-ed case, "Leroy." Together we made up the under-manned tag-team that would be known as 2nd Squad for the night, since outpost guard duties and kitchen patrol had stripped everybody else from our platoon. Not counting Lieutenant Savage, the vehicle crew, and myself, the only dismounted firepower we had on that truck was a six-man squad, three of whom were carrying light machine guns into the raid.

We listened intently to the chatter on the radio loudspeaker as the convoy raced through the highly contested eastern districts of Baghdad. Those of us who were below tack-welded our eyes to the navigational computer in the front of the troop compartment. A long string of pale blue dots marked the positions of every vehicle in the company. These were projected over a satellite map of the operation, and every refreshed image blinked us closer and closer to the point of no return. I was glued to the screen, waiting for the action to begin. As we banked around the last corner on our way to Sadr City, Lieutenant Savage called up our status to the commander.

"Bull-Six, this is Bull-One-Six." The loudspeaker crackled in my ear. "We have just passed Route Copper West and are turning onto Route Miller. Time-now. Over."

"This is Bull-Six. Roger." The firm reply of our company commander snapped back.

"That's it." I said to myself, checking over my own radio for the fifth time. "This is what we trained for. It'll be slicker than shit. No problem. In-and-out."

As I muttered the words, I was filled with doubt. What can I say? I was nervous. This wasn't like anything I had ever done. Nothing even came close. If I fucked up the smallest thing I might get one of my best friends killed, and that was all I could think about. So I went over the timeline, checked my watch, did some quick mental math to ballpark when the countdown would begin, and went over my own role in the mission. Our platoon was tasked with holding the perimeter while the main effort cleared the objective.

Simple enough, I figured.

At least we weren't the first ones through the door. In some ways, there wouldn't be very much for us to do out there besides sit in a Stryker and listen to everything unfold around us. Then again, who knew? This was our first time in.

I glanced over at Gonzo, who was seated across from me in the troop compartment, and I could tell that he was going over the mission in his head like me. We could only expect what we had heard in the briefings — but that doesn't count for shit when you're out there on the ground. Besides, Sergeant Lilly and Sergeant Brasel were the only ones who had any idea what we were getting into. Hell, Sergeant Brasel was an Army Ranger — this is what they *do.*

I stopped to think about that for a second and felt a calm wash over me.

"No." I muttered. "This is what *we* do."

After two years of training, I was as ready as I could ever be. At a certain point, all you can do is suck down the fear and get it done. After all, experience comes from action — and action is what we had coming. It's the whole reason I had signed up to be a grunt, and now I was sitting in the lead vehicle of a high-speed kill-or-capture raid on some of the most wanted men in the world.

When our Stryker whipped around another corner, Lieutenant Savage jumped back on the radio. "Bull-Six, this is Bull-One-Six. We are turning onto Route Maryland and approaching Sadr City. Over."

"This is Bull-Six. Roger." The radio stayed hot for a few moments as our commander considered his words. "Stay alert."

With another blink of the screen, our dot jumped over the border of the city and into the territory of the Jaish al-Mahdi. Now that the clock was ticking, Lieutenant Savage checked his watch.

"Bull Six, Bull-One-Six. 1st Platoon has passed Route Grizzlies and is entering Sadr City at 00:26 hours. Over." He let go of the transmission switch and turned his attention to everybody in the truck. "Alright guys, keep your eyes open. Ludwig, keep track of the time."

"Roger."

I pulled up my sleeve to put a marker on my watch at the very moment we'd hit the line. Not a second later, a burst of gunfire tore off into the sky and my heart screeched to a stop.

"Whatcha' got?" Lieutenant Savage called out to the crew.

"Shots fired from the rooftops." Sergeant Brasel replied. "No visual."

"Alright. Let me know if you see anything."

"Roger."

We passed through the second intersection on the infiltration route and another small burst rang out. Looking up through the front hatch, I could see the flash of tracers soaring high into the sky.

"Well now they know we're comin'." Gonzo looked at me with a grin.

"Sir, that's signaling fire," Sergeant Brasel said.

"That's what I'm thinking too."

Lieutenant Savage flipped on his radio and called it up to our commander. "Bull-Six, this is Bull-One-Six. It looks like the militia is marking our positions with sporadic tracer-fire from the rooftops."

"This is Bull-Six. Good copy. Are you taking fire?"

"Bull-One-Six, negative."

"Alright. Continue mission. Bull-Six, out."

Wallace dropped down below to scan the road ahead of us with his fire control system, and zoomed in on a cluster of shanty structures.

"Sir!" He smacked Lieutenant Savage on the leg. "I think our route is blocked up ahead!"

"What?"

"It looks like a market to me."

"Alright, let me see this..."

Our platoon leader dropped down beside him to check it out. There was no way we were getting through: a barricade of concrete barriers, piles of rubble, and tangled concertina wire blocked the entire road from wall-to-wall, and beyond it was a sprawling collection of tents and cheap shacks.

"Pfister!" Lieutenant Savage shouted up to the driver. "Take a right up here!" He glanced over at Wallace. "Good job. Keep scanning the roads and take the first open left you can find."

"Yes, sir."

The Stryker spun around the corner and Lieutenant Savage jumped back on his radio. "Bull-Six, this is Bull-One-Six. The primary infiltration route is blocked with a market. We are now turning right onto Route Fox and looking for a detour. Over."

"One-Six, Bull-Six. Roger. Get us back on track."

"This is One-Six. Wilco." He paused to look at his color-coded map of the known and suspected locations of roadside bombs, and keyed up for another transmission. "Should I be avoiding Black Routes?"

I felt my heart sink as I realized the gravity of what he was asking. On the whole, almost every route in Sadr City was confirmed to have a dozen or more collections of roadside bombs. We called them "Black Routes" — routes that nobody was stupid enough to drive on — and every infiltration route was carefully chosen to pass them up. But there we were, about to do the exact opposite just a few minutes into the operation.

"One-Six," our commander called back. "Screw it. They're all Black Routes. Take the next left and stop wasting our time. Bull-Six, out."

"Alright," Lieutenant Savage said to the crew. "This doesn't change anything. Keep scanning for IEDs and keep your eyes on the rooftops."

"Roger." We shouted back in a cluster.

"Ludwig." He turned to me. "What's the time?"

The hair on the back of my neck stood on end as I realized how quickly things were moving.

"We're just under five minutes, Sir."

"Shit." He stood back up in his hatch. "We should've been on-target by now."

Another long burst of rounds rang out through the city. The militia was gearing up. Their network of spotters and signal fires were already hard at work. I could almost feel the city rumbling into consciousness. By now they knew we were coming — and they were ready for us.

"Pfister!" Lieutenant Savage shouted. "Punch it!"

The engine revved up as the driver hit the gas, but another field of shanty structures and roadblocks spanned every turn we came across. Our detour was growing, and with each extra mile we pushed our luck that much further. When the militia got up and running, it would only take one well-placed trigger to blast a hole in the side of our truck. In that city, a vehicle recovery was the last thing we needed to handle, so when another route passed us by, our commander jumped on the company net to check on our progress. From a quarter mile behind us in the convoy, he was flying blind and along for the ride. The radio was his only source of information.

"Bull-One-Six, this is Bull-Six. What the hell is going on? I'm looking at my map and it's telling me that you're still driving down Route Fox. I told you to take the first left you could find. Over."

We whizzed through another intersection. Wallace checked it over and there was still no way through to the other side.

"Jesus," he sneered. "Do they have this whole fucking place walled off?"

"Bull-Six," Lieutenant Savage called back, "this is Bull-One-Six. Every turn we've come across is blocked. Break—"

Our commander didn't wait for him to finish. Before Lieutenant Savage could key up his handmic for the second half of the transmission, our commander cut him off.

"One-Six, this is Bull-Six. I don't see how this is an issue; these are major routes we're talking about. Take the first road you can find and get us back on track. Out."

It was a cold decree but as Fate would have it, Wallace spotted another avenue — this time with an opening to the other side.

"Pfister," he said without hesitation. "Hard left!"

"What do you see?" Lieutenant Savage asked.

"I think there's a way through."

With mechanical precision, Pfister tapped on the brakes and jammed the wheels to one side. Everybody held on to whatever they could find as the inertia sent us flying into the walls of the Stryker. When the turn was over, Lieutenant Savage jumped back on his radio to call it up.

"Bull-Six, One-Six. We have found a way through to Route Echo. We are now back on track and closing in on the objective. Over."

As we approached the barricade, a wide-open clearing spread with plenty of room to our left and right. We weaved through the market and got back on course. For a while, it even seemed like Lady Luck would be coming over to our side. But as soon as we hit the final drag, Pfister punched his foot on the gas and she cashed in our chips. Without warning, the asphalt underneath our Stryker gave way and every ounce of our twenty-ton, armored chariot crashed to a bone-shattering halt. At top speed we had fallen into a trench about as wide as a car, and deep enough for a man to stand.

All I remember from the crash was being hurtled forward into the firewall of the troop compartment, and buried by all of the other soldiers piling up behind me. I was slammed against a metal plate, and our whole world turned over onto its end. Without hesitation, the second vehicle in the convoy picked up the lead and the company drove on with the mission leaving us stranded and alone about a half-mile away from the target.

Nursing a fresh bruise on his hip, Lieutenant Savage dropped down out of the hatch. "What the fuck was that?!" he shouted.

"I don't know sir." Wallace was dazed, but he jumped right back into his seat and got to work. "Pfister, you okay?!"

A voice cried out from the driver's hole. "I'm good!"

"Make sure nobody's hurt!" Lieutenant Savage shouted back to Sergeant Lilly.

Those of us who were down below struggled to unpeel ourselves from the mess and climb back onto the benches of the truck. Thankfully, nobody was critically injured, but our Stryker was practically flipped onto its side.

"Sir," Wallace did a scan with the thermals and got back to Lieutenant Savage with the news. "It looks like we're caught in some kind of trench."

"Pfister!" Lieutenant Savage cried up to the driver. "Try to back out!"

The gearbox shifted into reverse and Pfister punched the accelerator, but the snapped rods and twisted bearings of the drive train slammed hopelessly against the undercarriage of the hull.

"I'm not getting any power to the wheels!" Pfister called back.

"Sir." Wallace turned to Lieutenant Savage. "That sounds like it's either the drive train or the transfer linkage. Either way, something down there is totally busted."

"Goddammit!" Lieutenant Savage slammed his fist against the hatch above him. He took a moment to gather his thoughts and keyed up the radio. "Bull-Six, this is Bull-One-Six. My vehicle has run into some kind of ditch and it's completely disabled. I'm going to need another vehicle over here for the recovery. Over."

It was a desperate plea that went completely unnoticed. As soon as Lieutenant Savage pulled his finger off the transmit switch, another voice rang out over his.

"—we are in the building and clearing the objective. Over."

There was nothing we could do. The raid was now in full swing. The company was decisively engaged and everything else would have to wait.

"Sergeant Brasel!" Lieutenant Savage shouted. "Prep the recovery equipment. I want to be ready-to-roll when they get here to pull us out."

Wallace made a break for his gear bag. "Pfister!" He ripped open the zipper and searched for the right tool. "Put the truck in neutral. I'm going to disengage the transfer case."

"On-it!" Pfister snapped back.

The gears rattled as he struggled to shift out of reverse, but something was clearly wrong. There was a loud clunk, a grinding moan, a hard slam, and the engine stalled out completely. A cold shiver ran down the back of my spine.

The truck was dead.

"What the hell just happened?!" Lieutenant Savage shouted.

"I don't know, sir." Wallace brushed him off and got back to work. "Pfister, start the truck back up and try it again."

"Ludwig," Lieutenant Savage turned his attention to me. "What's the time?"

I glanced at my watch. "We're twelve minutes in."

There was nothing else to say: we were running out of time and nobody knew for sure what would happen when those twenty minutes were up. I had asked a squad leader in the unit we replaced once. All I got was a thousand yard stare and a cold shoulder.

"You'll see," he sneered.

Well there we were, less than a week later, and his prophecy was about to come true.

In preparation for the recovery, Gonzo and Smiley dismounted the truck through the troop hatch in the ramp so they could fold the "Rhino," one of or our IED countermeasures, into its towing configuration before bullets started flying. Through the driver's hole, I could hear Pfister working his magic at the controls. Wallace was running him through the procedures to get the Stryker started. One by one, the two of them cold-booted every system in the vehicle, hoping to track down the issue and work around the obstruction. As they worked, the clicks and whirs of flickering servos fired off in rapid sequence all around me, but there was only so much we could do from inside of the vehicle. They worked as fast as they could, but it was clear that our Stryker was out for the count. If we were going to get that thing out of there, it was going to take a lot more than some switches and crossed fingers. After a couple of minutes of bashing their heads against the wall to fix the problem, Lieutenant Savage turned back to the rest of the men in the troop compartment.

"Sergeant Brasel, where's that recovery equipment?"

Sergeant Brasel looked up from his search. "It's not here, sir."

"What?!"

That was bad news. The recovery equipment was what we needed to hook up our vehicle for a tow — and now it was missing.

"We looked in both benches. Twice. There's nothin' here."

"You've got to be kidding me."

Lieutenant Savage shifted his focus back to Wallace. As the most experienced man in the crew, Wallace was in charge of the Stryker. Before we rolled out, it was his job to make sure the truck was ready to roll and fully stocked to the mission standard.

"Where the hell is the recovery equipment?!" The words came out of Lieutenant Savage's mouth like a hard right-hook.

"What?" Wallace balked at the question.

"Did he fucking stutter?!" Sergeant Brasel echoed the question. "Where the hell is the equipment, Wallace?!"

With his attention focused entirely on getting our truck started again, Wallace hadn't wasted any time worrying about the equipment in the back of his Stryker. After all, it had been there every day since the start of our deployment and every day in the years of training before tonight — so why bother? But now that he was thrust into the spotlight with everybody's eyes on him, he remembered all too well why we couldn't find any of the gear.

"We don't have any, sir." He spoke with a flat tone.

"What?!" Lieutenant Savage was stunned.

"The call came down from Squadron Headquarters a couple of days ago. They said the Colonel wanted us to change our load-out and put only one recovery vehicle in each platoon."

This was a huge transgression from the norm. For years now, two trucks in every platoon maintained a full set of equipment in case anything went wrong.

"So what happened to the rest of the gear?!" Lieutenant Savage demanded.

"They made us hand it over."

"Why?!"

It took one look in Wallace's eyes to see that the answer to Lieutenant Savage's question was nowhere to be found. Who knew why these things ever happened? They just do. You can complain about it all you want. What was done was done and we had no control over the situation to begin with. The only thing Wallace could do about it now was shrug.

"So who's got a fucking set?" Sergeant Brasel cut in.

"In the company?" Wallace asked.

"In our platoon."

"3rd Squad, Sergeant. They should have all our gear."

"Yeah, sure." Sergeant Brasel scoffed. "And we're just supposed to sit here and wait for them to show up, huh?"

It was a rhetorical question. 3rd Squad was on the totally opposite side of our objective, pulling double-duty now that we were caught in a ditch. There was no way they were getting pulled of the line to come back to our position and hook us up for a tow.

Our truck settled into an uneasy silence as everybody pieced together the implications of what had happened. The militia was well into overdrive by now. There could be hundreds of them pouring down on us in the time it takes to brew a hot pot of coffee. And if that wasn't enough to stir our nerves, there were fewer than ten of us in that Stryker and nobody was coming to our rescue any time soon.

Somewhere nearby, the militia kicked on a generator and the streetlights all around us lit up. We were bathed in light. You could see twenty meters in every direction, and not an inch farther. I couldn't help but laugh at the timing: it was right on the mark with the intel. Right when we should've been up with the rest of the company, balls-deep into the objective, setting up a bulletproof perimeter. But we weren't at the objective; we were caught in a ditch a block or two away and basking in the heat of high-wattage floodlights.

"Ludwig," Lieutenant Savage turned to me. "How much time do we have left?"

I glanced down at my watch and my blood went cold.

"We've got five more minutes, sir."

Before anybody could react, a hard metallic thud slammed into the outer hull of the truck.

"Well," Pfister chuckled hopelessly. "I guess they know we're here."

For the next five minutes Lieutenant Savage did everything he could to get in touch with the commander. He called over and over, but nobody responded to our hails. Much to my surprise, Wallace and Pfister had continued troubleshooting the problem with our truck and somehow got it started — but given that our entire drive train was still shot, it wasn't much of a relief. The entire time, Sergeant Brasel had been up in the back hatch with one of his men, returning fire into the darkness as more and more rounds snapped by. As for the militia, nobody in our truck knew what the hell we could do to stave off the tide. The numbers just didn't add up. It was obvious that we were screwed.

Finally, our company commander broke the silence and called us back during an idle break in the radio chatter. "Bull-One-Six, this is Bull-Six. I copy your vehicle is disabled and you are in need of a recovery. Break." He let up the handmic to clear the net for any emergency transmissions that might come through. "A section from 2nd Platoon is en route to your position to begin operations. Hold fast and stand by for their arrival. Out."

It was a simple transmission with a single point: the tactical equivalent to "Yeah, I heard you. Now shut up." But at least it was something. I leaned back with a sigh of relief, trusting that some reinforcements were on their way and felt my nerves relax, but Lieutenant Savage was hardly at ease.

"We're not out yet." He shot me a hard look.

I could see that he was still chewing over the situation in his mind. It was a hard one to deal with, that's for sure. No matter what we did, every decision he could make looked like it was guaranteed to get somebody killed. If we hunkered down to wait, a single well-placed RPG could end us all; but if we got out to fight, we'd be out-numbered with no cover and zero concealment. It's simply a fact that six men with a platoon leader, his radio guy, and a downed Stryker isn't much to work with. But that was the call he had to make: to die or die trying. So he took a second to himself and considered the options before jumping into action and committing us to our destiny.

"Sergeant Brasel! Prepare to dismount your men!"

We all stopped what we were doing to listen.

"I want you to get the truck ready for the recovery and provide security until 2nd Platoon shows up. Make sure you've got at least one light machine gun facing north around the front of the vehicle and put the rest of your team on the far side of the road. Got it?"

"Yes, sir."

"I want everybody on the ground. Ludwig, you're up in the back hatch. We're going to have to hold out here until those trucks show up, and I don't know how long that's going to be — so watch your ammo."

Sergeant Brasel turned to his men. "Alright, you heard him! Gonzo and Smiley, you're up north! Everybody else, conserve your fire and watch your ammo! Let's go! Dismount!"

In a flurry of commotion, the troop compartment cleared out and everybody dove behind whatever cover they could find. When the last man stepped off, I made my way to the back hatch, jammed up the ramp control and plugged my headset into the communication console beside me. As the men outside were pelted with fire, I flipped the input switch over to the company frequency so I could tune into another wash of chaos. I could barely understand what was going on over all the commotion. A dozen voices competed with one another for the commander's attention, the twenty-minute benchmark had run out, and the entire company was settling in for whatever was in store. I did my best to keep track of the situation until a single voice interrupted the flow, standing out above the rest. It was one of the pilots overhead, referring Lieutenant Savage by his call sign.

"Bull-One-Six, this is Skyhawk-Two-Three. I'm on your platoon net. Over."

It wasn't exactly protocol for them to drop down to a platoon frequency, but Lieutenant Savage called him back anyway.

"Skyhawk-Two-Three this is Bull-One-Six. Go ahead."

"Yeah, listen you've got two large groups of – *ahh* – looks like twenty or thirty military aged males. They are well armed and closing in on you from the north. Be advised. Over."

I couldn't believe what I was hearing. Lieutenant Savage wasn't any less surprised. Our single, split-up, and undermanned squad was about to face off with a platoon's worth of insurgents and had no idea it was coming. With a flip of his handmic, Lieutenant Savage called the pilot back.

"Skyhawk-Two-Three, this is Bull-One-Six. I copy your last. Can you engage?"

There was a short pause as the pilot looked over the scenario unraveling below him. "*Ahh* – Negative. Those targets are way too close to your men. I can't risk it."

I tried to imagine what that must've looked like from above and the thought of it made me shudder. I wasn't in a helicopter, I was on the ground. I wouldn't know what the mobs of Jaish al-Mahdi looked like until they started shooting at us for real — but he had a bird's-eye view on exactly how bad it was going to get. He could see it all happen from a couple hundred feet in the sky, and he was looking at men so close to us that he couldn't even shoot. I looked at the screen of Wallace's thermal targeting system, but I couldn't see a single gunman.

They must be coming at us from the rear, I thought.

To confirm my suspicions, a loud prattle of gunfire rang out from down the street, whizzing right over the ass of our truck and the hatch I was about to stand up in.

"Bull-One-six," the pilot called us back. "Did you get my last?"

"Roger." Lieutenant Savage was stunned by what he had said. "Thanks for the heads up. Keep us posted, I guess."

What else could he say? $38 million dollars went into building the most advanced attack helicopter in the world. A few more were spent training the pilot in the hot seat. We knew full well he was sitting up there on top of thousands of 30 mm rounds with a space-age targeting system that can read a newspaper from a quarter-mile away — but he couldn't do anything about fifty insurgents with knock-off assault rifles and flaming car tires?

I glanced down at my watch to check the time. We were 22 minutes into the mission: right on time for the militia to start closing in on us for real. Deep down I could tell that I really started to feel the fear, but Lieutenant Savage just picked up his rifle and shot a glance right at me.

"Well," he said. "Let's do this."

He jumped up in his hatch and picked up a sector of fire. With a nod and a grunt, I flipped on the red-dot scope of my rifle and followed suit. The militia would be right on top of us any minute now. If that was the case, I figured I might as well die standing up.

We held our ground for another fifteen minutes before the entire company lost control of the situation. The two Strykers that had been designated as our recovery team were still nowhere to be seen. They had been ambushed just a few meters away from the objective and pinned down by a stiff pocket of resistance. To move any farther off the line would've not only opened a gaping hole in the perimeter around the objective, but also created a third unsupported element which the militia could envelop and destroy.

The worst part of all this were the developments on the objective. Our infiltration teams had trouble with some of the detainees, which had slowed down the exfiltration process. To make matters worse, a second search effort had spilled over into the neighboring apartment building to the north. From what I could gather, one of our targets had narc'ed out his buddy next door, who turned out to be the highest ranking commander in our end of town. It was the only chance we'd get to nab him, so our commander made the call and took the risk. Usually that's no big deal, but under the circumstances it had become a precarious situation at best. Following through on that intel had cost us precious time.

By then, the militia's random pot shots had become a steady rhythm of concentrated fire. It was a beating pulse that I had heard about before but hadn't wrapped my mind around. It was almost a dance. A kind of tango that can't be measured with a metronome but fell into a rhythm regardless. I could feel it and I knew that it was just barely getting started. Everything was up for grabs and we had little hope of getting back out of there unscathed, so I stared out of the back hatch of our Stryker, maintained my sector of fire, and prayed.

The pilots called us again with news of a second mob closing in from the west and a third large group was seen racing around to close off the engagement from the north. At that point, there were literally hundreds of insurgents on the ground engaged in a synchronized effort to envelop the entire company and take advantage of our disabled vehicle. From the back hatch of the truck, however, I couldn't see a damned thing. A streetlight right in front of me draped a curtain of darkness across the road barely fifty meters out. Beyond that our battlefield was only visible to my buddies on the ground. They had worked their way into the most dominating firing position they could find, taking cover behind a car and some rubble on the far side of the street. From where they stood, the city was teeming with insurgents — and based on what I could hear, they were fighting for their lives.

Thanks to the aid of a good position, what little they could see with their night-vision optics, and Sergeant Brasel's dismounted thermal scope, they could spot a mob of insurgents spanning wall-to-wall, pushing women and children in front of them as cover. Doing his best to avoid hitting the innocent civilians the militia had thrown into the crossfire, Sergeant Brasel marked every target of opportunity he could spot with his tracers so his men could engage. When a target went down, they used Sergeant Brasel's thermals to make sure he stayed dead — other than that, any sense of a "confirmed kill" was just a myth. It was obvious that there was no hope of keeping track of who-shot-what with all the gunfire going on. They just pumped out a steady stream of bullets down the street to keep our enemy at bay. Come to think of it, that was probably the only thing keeping my buddies alive the whole night, because Lord knows there wasn't any cover for them to hide behind. Of course, that only counts if you have rounds left to shoot, and Brasel's team was running out of those with a quickness.

Preparing for that panicked cry of "Need more ammo!", I cracked open a fresh box of rounds that we had stored on the top of the truck and got ready to toss it down to my buddies. We had two full boxes on our Stryker. At the rate they were shooting, I figured that would give us about forty more minutes before the militia could simply stroll right up and kill us — at that point we wouldn't even have any rocks to throw at them. But as I thought about these finer points of exactly how and when we'd all die, a strange silence gripped the battle. It rolled in like fog and lingered just long enough to resemble a dream. I have no idea why everything stopped in that moment, but I've since come to realize that shit like that just happens sometimes and when it does you take it for everything it's worth.

The two Strykers that had been selected to help us out finally broke through their ambush, raced down the street and met up at our location. Once on-site, they pulled into a base of fire and reinforced the perimeter. As soon as they got into position, two of their squads dismounted to join our fire team on the ground, but the militia knew exactly what was going on. When that last boot hit the street and their men were exposed, all Hell broke loose. This time, the militia was zeroed in on our position and every one of them had good cover and a clear shot. We were right in the middle of an ambush and they weren't going to let up until every last one of us was dead or dying.

"One-Six. Two-Seven." The other Stryker's platoon sergeant called Lieutenant Savage on the company net. Over the chaos of the moment, his calm voice seemed unreal and unfit for the situation. "We are on-site at your location. I've dismounted two squads and we are hooking up a tow-cable, time-now. Over."

Lieutenant Savage called him back. "This is One-Six. Good copy. Be advised: we have taken heavy damage. We cannot disengage our transfer case for a recovery. Over."

"Two-Seven, Roger. We'll see what we can do."

While they spoke, a rapid shower of gunfire littered the background noise of their transmissions. Rounds flowed in from every direction. Our return fire was wholly insufficient, yet despite the overwhelming threat of mortal danger, every man on the ground held fast. Whether that was out of courage or fear I can't say, but I've learned that sometimes the difference is semantic.

One of their Strykers pulled up behind ours and kicked into its lowest gear. As soon as it was ready, a five-man team from down on the street stood up and got to work. Their first challenge was to unstrap the ten foot, heavy-duty tow-cable — the kind of cable you'd typically see on a suspension bridge or a crane — from the outside of their own vehicle and split into buddy teams to hook shackles up to the back corners of both Strykers. When the shackles were bolted down, the two teams fastened the cable to both trucks and gave the signal that the job was done.

That night, every ounce of their mettle was tested. These men were completely exposed to the enemy's fire that was hammering into the scenery all around them. Rounds landed within an arm's reach of where they worked and they still carried on with the task at hand. Only after everything was tied up and double-checked could they dive back down to the earth, and hide behind the safest rubble they could find. It was the bravest thing I'd ever seen in my life.

As soon as the job was done, the other vehicle got to work pulling us out of the hole. They used caution as a benchmark at first, but it was clear that we weren't going anywhere with just a gentle tug. The entire front-end of our vehicle had been thrust underground by the crash. It was jammed all the way up to the axles in mud, and our drive train was mangled beyond function.

"Fuck this!" Their gunner shouted over the radio. "Hang on!"

His driver gave up on the pretense, flipped their transfer case over to "all-wheel drive," and slammed his foot on the gas. With a loud jerk the cable snapped tight and both trucks were rattled to the bone. Our metal hull moaned under the stress as twenty tons of armor and heavy-duty machinery came head-to-head with the brute force of their engine — but our wheels bit deep into the soft clay and refused to budge. Completely unfazed, their driver dropped off the throttle and slammed it back down for another go. A loud crack of snapping metal parts rang out through the chassis of our Stryker. Whatever it was that had bound up our transfer case and locked our wheels in place finally broke free with a heavy lurch. A fourth violent and gut wrenching heave of unregulated torque ripped us out of our shallow grave and dragged us back onto level ground.

I cheered with excitement. For the first time all night it seemed like something was actually going our way. We sent up a status report to the commander and he came back with an order to prepare for an immediate exfiltration. The five-man team on the ground jumped back into action and disconnected the heavy metal cable with the same courageous abandon as before. They unscrewed the shackles, pulled off the gear, and strapped it back in place on the side of their truck. The ramp dropped, they loaded up, and their Strykers rolled into position to join up with the rest of the company — but our trials were a long way from over.

"Pfister," Wallace was back in action. "Try to kick the truck into neutral."

This time the gears worked, and for whatever reason the truck didn't die.

"Got it!" Pfister shouted.

"Alright." Wallace got to work on the transfer case and ran him through the checklist. "What about the steering?"

Pfister spun the wheel through its entire range of motion, but there was zero feedback on the road. I could hear the whir of fluid spurting out of the shattered steering pump as he turned it from side to side.

"I got nothing," Pfister grunted. "It's totally fucked."

Lieutenant Savage jumped back on the radio to call up our new status to the commander. Now our commander was furious. Precious time was pissing into nothingness and we still had men at the objective. What was supposed to be a quick recovery had blown into a balls-out rescue operation – which is significantly more complicated than yanking a Stryker out of a ditch. As if that wasn't enough, our entire company was still decisively engaged with no reason to believe our enemy would ease up any time soon.

"Bull-One-Six, this is Bull-Six!" he shouted. "I'm here to command a raid, not a fucking towing service! I want anybody involved with the recovery of the crash site to drop down to 1st Platoon's net! I'm putting Bull-Seven in charge of that operation! Get it done!"

Deciding he had better things to do than deal with the commotion, our commander put First Sergeant Williams in charge of the operation. As the second recovery operation got organized, I held my position in the back hatch, still staring at darkness and listening to the madness unfold. Now that we were almost an hour into the raid, the assault elements were finally wrapping up their search of the second house. More and more problems were streaming out over the radios. I couldn't help but wonder how the hell I was still alive.

"What are they waiting for?" I muttered quietly to myself.

It seemed to me like the Jaish al-Mahdi had the perfect chance to strike. We were split up, free for the taking, and our odds of survival were diminishing with every second that we stuck around. All they had to do was sack up and charge. At least that way I'd have something to fight. But that's when it hit me: they had probably done this a hundred times before. They had surrounded our predecessors and closed in for the kill every time a mission went south. It wouldn't have taken a military genius for one of them to figure out that we would always have the better shooters and the bigger guns. No, that lesson would've been learned with a shit-load of casualties right off the bat. As the saying went, "We killed off all the dumb ones." That far into the war we were fighting people who knew how to stay alive. People who know first-hand that nobody goes toe-to-toe with a full company of American Strykers and expects to win. Not unless we had a broken wing. Not unless we were out for the count. Not unless we had nothing left to shoot. Well, we had walked right into their trap and all they had to do now was bide their time until we ran out of bullets. The rest was up to us.

"Reloading!" I heard Wilson shout out to his teammates.

"I gotcha' covered!" Sergeant Brasel shouted back in reply.

At that point they had already boxed us in. They were already throwing together roadblocks and machine guns on every avenue out of there. So what were they waiting for? They were waiting for us. Our time was up. Now they got to pick when and where the fight would go down. From that point forward, all we could do was react. In the military, we call that "losing the initiative." Once that happens, the battle is all but lost. If that was the case, I was already dead.

As it turned out, nobody in our company actually had a fully functional set of recovery equipment on their vehicles. By the time Squadron Headquarters had finished up their "layout" just a few days prior, they snatched up all of our best equipment and left us to deal with the aftermath. So now it was up to us to track down a complete collection of recovery gear right in the middle of all that shit and discover that we had been well and truly fucked. But after much longer than I'd like to admit, the company-wide search finally managed to assemble a completed set, which was loaded up onto First Sergeant Williams' vehicle so he could haul it out to the crash site and finish the job.

As soon as it arrived, the second Stryker in First Sergeant William's formation pulled right up in front of us and dismounted their squad for the hookup. In the middle of what sounded more like a hailstorm than a battle, they set out to unstrap both of the heavy-duty tow bars from the sides of our Stryker and maneuver them into position at the front of our truck. It was agonizing work by any measure — pushed to the extreme now that they had to get it done in the middle of a firefight — and once the two steel bars were in place, they had to be bolted onto the front of our vehicle, one after the other. While most of the squad was busy doing that, one of their men also had to break off from the group to screw the tow hitch on the back of their own Stryker so it would be able to tow us to safety when all the bolts were in place. After both tasks were completed, the lead Stryker could finally be visually "ground guided" into place so the crew could lock down the tow-bars and the "recovery" could get underway.

We often joked about how insane that process would be in combat, but I never really thought I'd see the day. Ever since that night it's been impossible to shake the image of that squad standing right out in the open as they worked, while Hell rained down on them from two directions. On more than one occasion, bullets ricocheted right off the equipment they were handling, and left deep scars and gouges on our gear — but it wasn't until the tow-hitch could be locked shut and the rest of the equipment was double-checked that the job was finally done. And they stuck it through to the bitter end. Those men faced more perils that night than anybody else I know, and while that was about to become a record-breaking recovery time, it hardly felt like it in the middle of all that shit.

"RPG!" A voice cried out.

"Fuck it!" Somebody else shouted back. *"Keep working! We need to get this fuckin' truck outta' here! Let's go!"*

The rocket fired up and tore through the air, missing us completely for a building down the street.

"See! They can't shoot worth a shit! Now grab that tow-bar!"

I was in a daze. The world around me was coming apart at the seams. I stared down the road. I listened. I stood in awe. Then a loud snap of a bullet cracked over my head and I realized with horror that somebody was finally shooting at me. My training kicked in and I sank as low as I could to scan for the shooter, but I still couldn't see anything from where I was standing — let alone a well placed gunman in the darkness.

"Come on," I whispered.

The snap of another bullet whizzed by. It ripped through the camouflage netting over my head with a foot or two to spare, and I peered even harder into the darkness. Another crack rang out, this time slapping my face with a puff of air. This time I flinched and tried to hide my face from the unknown shooter. There was nothing else for me to do. When the fourth and fifth rounds flew by, my heart fluttered out of control.

I knew exactly how this was going to end: I'd be standing in the back hatch of a Stryker, cowering like a bitch until some hot lead tore into my face and my lifeless corpse dropped to the floorboard. My hands clung to the cold metal of my rifle.

I don't want to die like this.

That was all I could think about. I pictured the men running rooftop-to-rooftop with packs of rocket propelled grenades, itching for the right moment to pop one off on our truck. I closed my eyes and imagined a thousand foot soldiers flooding in from every direction to overtake what couldn't have been more than 25 men, set into a bullshit perimeter around a fucked up Stryker. Another round cracked by overhead, and for the first time in my life, I was truly and deeply terrified.

"Drop the fucking ramp!" I heard a voice cry out from down below.

I broke out of my trembling panic and glanced down at the street. What I saw caught me totally off guard: while I was cowering in fear, Sergeant Brasel had simply walked up to the back of the truck like it was no big deal, hauling Leroy along for the ride. Disregarding the steady flow of gunfire from down the street, he just stood there with his hand clasped tight around the carrying handle of the kid's body armor and waited for my reply.

"Hey! Ludwig!" He shouted again. "Drop the fucking ramp!"

"Clear the ramp!" I shouted back.

"Ramp clear!" He confirmed there was nobody in the way.

I pieced myself together and slammed down the toggle switch of the ramp control. As soon as it hit the ground, he tossed the panicked soldier into the troop compartment like a sack of dirty laundry.

"Keep this motherfucker on the truck before he gets somebody killed!" he shouted.

The next moment he disappeared around the side of the truck, as fearless as he had seemed before, running back to his men who were still fighting.

Wondering how Sergeant Brasel could've mistaken the severity of the situation at hand, I looked back down the road to see if there was anything I had missed. As I peered out at our enemy, another few rounds snapped by the outside of our Stryker. The hairs all over my body stood straight up. I felt my heart race at the thought of a shooter who could see me clear as day and take a well-aimed shot at my face — but when another few rounds popped off, I realized the shots were still far too inaccurate and undisciplined to have an effect. I was positively in danger, but it was also clear that if I actually did get hit it would most likely be a matter of dumb luck and not my enemy's design. I took a deep breath and stared down at the road. Another burst of rounds rang out, and all of a sudden it was like I couldn't care less about some towel-heads taking pot shots at our Stryker.

So that's how it works, I thought.

Without wasting any more time I jammed up on the ramp controls and closed off the outside world. I took a few more breaths and got a grasp of the situation. I turned my attention to the kid in front of me and checked him for some kind of wound or disability. As far as I could tell, nothing was wrong with him — that is to say, he wasn't shot or anything — but there was nothing going on up in his brain. In fact, I had probably looked like him in the hatch just a few moments earlier: totally dumbstruck.

"Hey, Ludwig!" Lieutenant Savage jumped down to see why the ramp had gone down. When he saw the two of us sitting there, he chimed in with a quick command and got back to the fight. "Put him in the hatch! I need you up here on the radios!"

"Yes sir!" I smacked Leroy on the arm and echoed Lieutenant Savage's command. "Hey, get in the hatch!"

"What?!" he shouted back.

"Get in the hatch!"

"What?!"

He looked back at me with wide eyes and no idea what in the hell was going on.

"Jesus Christ, are you deaf? Get in the fucking hatch!"

"I can't hear you sergeant!"

I knew immediately why Sergeant Brasel didn't want him on the ground: he was totally deaf and useless. Later I would find out why. Out there on the street, Sergeant Brasel was marking targets for his men to engage. When he made his way around to Leroy, a lone gunman ran right out into the street and our boy lit him up exactly as he was ordered. In theory that's no big deal, but it was also the kid's first kill. That's not something you can take lightly. For all the training and grunt mentalities, we're still human beings. It's still a big deal to kill another man. It takes something out of us — especially the first time. So he froze up. He drifted off into his own world. It didn't help much that a few moments later, Wilson unloaded a long burst of automatic fire right next to the kid's face and mowed down a group of combatants who had run out from behind cover.

With all that chaos, Leroy went into shock and Sergeant Brasel knew right away he had to get his soldier out of there before it was too late. Sergeant Brasel had to put that kid somewhere safe where he could gather his thoughts and recover from what had just happened. I guess a Stryker was as good a place as any. The only problem is that I had no idea how to coach him back to snuff now that he was sitting there in front of me oblivious to the outside world. Hell, I was just as scared as he was. A Stryker's armor might be made out of bulletproof materials, but that doesn't mean it's a sanctuary. I could tell he wasn't coming back to reality any time soon, so I just spoke as loud and clear as I could and hoped to God he'd understand.

"I'm not a Sergeant, Leroy! I'm a Specialist! Now get in the fucking hatch!"

I grabbed his vest and shoved him skyward until he rallied to his feet. Before I could crawl up to Lieutenant Savage, another few rounds cracked by overhead. Now, I realize that I wasn't exactly the model for a universal soldier that night, but at least I could hear what the fuck was going on — he didn't even have that much going for him. As soon as I heard the gunshot I realized that I couldn't just let him stand there and die like an idiot. I wasn't ready to have that on my conscience, so I turned back, jumped up in the hatch next to him, and tried to give him some advice that I hoped to God would keep him alive.

"Hey! Keep your fucking head down!"

Without waiting for him to reply, I grabbed his helmet, yanked it down to eye-level with the armor skirt, and gave him the hand-signal for taking cover. I met his gaze to make sure he understood what I was saying. He nodded back at me with wide-eyes.

"Roger, Sergeant!" he smiled.

"Don't get shot!" I smacked him on the back with a laugh.

"Okay!"

He nodded back at me and turned his gaze out to the street. A few more rounds whizzed by and I wondered if it was the wisest decision to stick Leroy up in the back hatch when it was about time for the militia to come out of the woodwork – but deep down I felt my heart crack.

Like I'd do any better?

The thought caught me off guard. I dropped back down into the Stryker, hit with the realization that even if he wasn't the best choice for the job, it wouldn't matter for very long. My buddies on the ground would be out of ammo soon and I wasn't half convinced that the luck of all these near misses would hold out on a night that had otherwise gone to Hell in a matter of minutes.

"Ludwig!" Lieutenant Savage was getting impatient. "What are you doing?!"

"Just checkin' on Leroy, sir!"

"Well get up here!"

I crawled up to the front of the Stryker near his hatch.

"What's up, sir?!"

"I need you on the radios! Let me know as soon as Bull-Six starts the ex-fil!"

"Roger!"

I plugged back in and flipped over to the company frequency. The radio was full of reports of the militia throwing together hasty roadblocks on all of our primary exfiltration routes. At that point, the Apache pilots had given up on trying to keep track of all the mobs, and only one thing was for sure: the stage was set and we were quickly coming up on our last chance to get out of there alive. Now that the hookup was almost done, all we had left to do was pull our boys off the objective, link up at the crash site, maneuver into formation, and break out of the kill-zone before every road we could take was blocked. With any luck, we'd be out of there in less than thirty minutes — but we all knew that it would hardly be that easy.

"Bull-Seven this is Two-Four-Victor" one of the vehicle gunners called up to our First Sergeant. "We are missing the retaining pin on our tow-hitch. Over."

The words cut through the traffic as everybody on our frequency listened in. Just as I had expected: there was more bad news in the hopper.

"This is Bull-Seven. Say again?!"

"This is Two-Four-Victor. I say again: there is no retaining pin on our tow-hitch. Over."

Without the retaining pin, the tow-hitch can't lock down on the bars. If the tow-hitch can't lock down on the bars, the slightest tug or bump would disconnect them from the lead vehicle. We weren't going anywhere without that damn pin, but that wasn't what caught me off guard. What didn't make any sense is how the little steel retaining pin that locks down the tow-bars is connected to the tow-hitch by a small yet very heavy-duty metal chain — a chain that can support the full weight of a man. A "missing pin" didn't happen in real life; you had to cut the thing off with a pair of bolt cutters first.

"What the fuck do you mean you don't have a retaining pin?!" First Sergeant didn't even bother with radio etiquette.

"This is Two-Four-Victor." Their gunner called him back, sticking to the facts and taking the ass chewing in full. "Our recovery crew just now noticed that it was missing. They say the chain is broken. Over."

Like I said, the recovery equipment across our entire company was in shambles. Even though they had finally tracked down the parts in the middle of a firefight, it was hard to notice a missing retaining pin until it was all too late. After everything that had happened that night, that was the point everybody finally started losing their cool.

"Well, who's got a fucking pin?!" First Sergeant's question came over the radios like a hot sear.

The silence that followed was unnerving to say the least.

"I swear to God!" he shouted. "When we get back to base, I'm having everybody's ass for this! I ain't dying over no fuckin' pin!"

By then, the main effort on the objective was finally wrapping up, and the search for missing recovery equipment spread out into their ranks. A tow-hitch retaining pin was tracked down and set aside for the recovery, but they couldn't bring it over until the job on-target was finished, so we just had to sit there and wait some more.

After a few minutes of unwavering contact, they finally pulled off the objective and rallied on the crash site to hook-up our Stryker. Once they were on site, they handed off the functioning tow-hitch to the recovery crew and got into position with the rest of our company to roll out of the city. Again, that squad who had already faced more than their fair share of gunfire had to gather around the back of our towing Stryker and bolt in a new tow-hitch for the ride home. For the last time, we had to ground-guide the other Stryker into position for the recovery. When it was done, the crew gave their signal to the Stryker and fell back into their firing positions in the street.

"This is Bull-Seven to all Bull-Elements!" Our First Sergeant called out over the company net. "The hook-up of One-One-Victor is complete! I want all dismounts back on the trucks! Let's get this show on the road!"

"Hey, sir!" I smacked Lieutenant Savage on the leg to get his attention. "That's us!"

"On it!" He used his short-range radio to get in touch with Sergeant Brasel and Sergeant Lilly, who picked up their team and got back on the Stryker.

As the ramp rose shut, a single militia foot soldier ran out into the light and clear into view for the first time all night. It was a signal that their final push was about begin. Before I could react, however, somebody in the truck muttered a cold phrase.

"Wrong move."

A burst of rounds flew in from out of sight and hit the man dead center in the chest. He stumbled, his legs gave out, and he collapsed facedown into the asphalt road. He was the first kill I had ever seen.

When the ramp slammed shut Sergeant Brasel jacked in his headset and shouted up to Lieutenant Savage. "Sir! These guys are right on top of us! We need to get the fuck out of here!"

"I know!" Lieutenant Savage snapped back.

Adrenaline was the only fuel we had left. Still hopped up with excitement, the men around me were oblivious to exactly how bad the odds had been. To them, it was just a street full of insurgents pouring out of the woodwork, coming down like Hell; but those of us who had stayed on the vehicles, we knew that everything they had seen was barely a fraction of what had been unleashed throughout the city. That was made clear, however, when a burst of heavy-caliber rounds fired off from one of our Strykers nearby. It caught our attention by the balls. The next moment, another vehicle followed suit.

That was the final straw: up until that point we'd had strict orders to hold our fire with the .50 cal machine guns unless we absolutely needed them. Considering what we'd been up against all night, I didn't want to know what set them off — I was just happy they were still fully stocked and we were throwing caution to the wind. By now, they were unloading ten to fifteen round bursts into whole crowds of armed insurgents, trying desperately to clear a path through their ranks. It was like swatting at a swarm of flies: a hail of lead would chop down a half-dozen people and a dozen more would step up to fill in the ranks.

One by one, the vehicles of Bull Company called up their status to the commander as our dismounted elements maneuvered back onto their vehicles in what was now a steady and unrelenting fire. Everybody in the convoy was ready to go, our vehicle was hooked up, the targets were in custody and — thank God — there weren't any casualties to report. Once everything was set, our commander laid out the exfiltration plan and gave the order to move, but as soon as the truck in front of us kicked into gear, a new problem was thrust into light. Our front-left wheel was jammed into position by the crash, jackknifed outward and locked firmly into place. Since our steering column was shattered we had no way to point it forward again, and after a few feet of dragging along, the convoy stopped dead in its tracks.

The gunner of the Stryker towing us called it up over the net. "Bull-Six, this is Two-Three-Victor! Short halt! One-One-Victor's wheels are turned all the way to the side! They need to straighten those out or we're gonna' do some serious damage to that Stryker! Over!"

In a hail of gunfire, Lieutenant Savage keyed up his handmic to call him back. "Two-Three-Victor this is Bull-One-Six! Our Steering column is broken! There's nothing we can do about that wheel!"

"Hey, this is Bull-Seven!" First Sergeant cut in, "Fuck it! Drag the motherfucker back to base! I don't care! We gotta' go!"

Again, the convoy kicked into gear and yanked us forward down the road. The sound of screeching rubber and knocking steel echoed through the troop compartment. It was all I could hear, like it was a living creature, breathing in life and screaming out pain.

"Hang in there." I whispered, patting the battery pack of our wounded Stryker like it was a pet. "We'll get you out of here soon, babe."

But nobody had any delusions: there was a long road ahead of us and one wrong turn could add a lifetime to the journey. Worse yet, a well-placed roadside bomb would end it all. That's exactly what I was hung up on: somehow I managed to tune out the continuous gunfire and deafening shriek of our Stryker until the only thing going through my mind was a single moment where the entire engagement would end in fireball — and take me with it. One fatal blast and we'd all be dead. I sat there on the bench, staring at the radios and waiting to die.

It was all I could do.

When we rounded the nearest corner, I could've sworn we hit the sidewall of a hurricane. Close-range, small-arms fire was coming from all around us and the response from our own convoy was to hurtle bullets into every crevice we could find. We dragged forward through it all, bit by bit, until our front left tire was ripped apart by the asphalt into flakes and shreds. Within a matter of minutes we were riding on nothing but the rim. A few more and we had ground deep into the hub, smearing a trail of oil behind us like a bloody stain in the earth. A new chorus of violent rumbling marked that transition — from rubber to forged steel —, which I can only imagine resembles the sound of being swallowed whole by an industrial shredder.

The jagged undercarriage of our Stryker carved into the pavement and slowed the convoy down to a crawl. Where we would've typically blown through an ambush at high-speed, this time we had to take every one of the shots, and each new turn was packed with fierce resistance. The men up in the hatches had their balls to the wind. Up there you're exposed to the elements, and all you can do is shoot back with the vain hope that if you fire off enough bullets, you can keep your enemy in the shadows. From the sound of it they were succeeding gloriously, but when the lead vehicles came face-to-face with an unexpected roadblock, the entire operation once again crammed into a full stop.

"Come on!" Lieutenant Savage cried out. "We need to get moving!"

A gunman stuck his head out of a nearby window and took advantage of the blocked convoy, shooting right down at the lieutenant from point-blank range.

"Fuck!" Lieutenant Savage ducked behind the small sheet of ballistic glass beside his hatch to fire wildly back at the shooter.

Now facing his own torrent of incoming fire, the man in the window ducked back out of sight. Within a few minutes, the lead platoon managed to push the barricade out of the way using the jerry-rigged plow on the front of their truck. After a slow crawl back to the original exfiltration route, we finally caught sight of our salvation.

The border of Sadr City was just a few hundred meters away. Hell, we could've seen the end of the road with our own two eyes if anybody was paying attention. But bullets were spewing out of — and into — every window in that city. The only thing I could hear above the gunfire was our own disintegrating Stryker, thinking at any moment it would fall apart around us. The sheer volume of incoming rounds was so extreme that it was impossible for our boys to aim. Instead, most of my buddies would freely admit that they had been reduced to shooting blindly at the shadows and praying to God they hit something bad.

It wasn't even fighting anymore. It was expenditure. Pure and simple. Nameless bullets flew around like rice at a wedding. All I could think about was death. I waited for that final blow. I closed my eyes. I did my damnedest to accept what was coming. It was a straight-line drag to the finish — just a few hundred meters of open road — and I didn't believe for a moment that we were going to make it out of there alive. Yet somehow, mixed up in the madness, all that combat started fading back into silence. We pushed farther down the road and closer to our salvation with every minute. The wild and chaotic drum-line of bullets melted away. The downpour of a torrential rainstorm passed us by and faded back into the distance. By the time we hit the edge of town, any evidence of a battle was gone. There was nothing left of the fight. Nothing but the sound of our shattered Stryker eviscerating itself out on the open road. Nothing but heavy breathing and whimpers of prayer. Nothing but a mural of bullet holes on every Stryker in the line. All I could hear was my wildly convulsing heart and the sound of shivering muscles that'd grown tired after hours of clenching down with fear. I opened my eyes and looked at the map: we were finally out. After a Hail Mary race for the border, it was all over.

We dragged around the first turn that led us back onto friendly terrain and after a few hundred feet, the convoy crumbled to a halt by the side of the road — still well within sight of the city. In the silence that followed, we stopped to take a breather, called in some reinforcements, and checked over our buddies for the fatal wounds that were expected. Much to our surprise, nobody on our Stryker was hit, and we had somehow made it out of there without getting blown up by a roadside bomb or taking a single shot from an RPG.

"This is Bull-Six to all Bull elements," our commander called out to the company. "I want an update on your status."

Each platoon leader and vehicle in our company called him back with similar news. Despite everything we had been through, we made it out of there without a single casualty.

"I don't believe it," Lieutenant Savage dropped out of his hatch and fell down onto the seat next to me. "We made it."

The thought was still working its way into my conscious mind when he said it. I didn't know how to respond. He gazed around the compartment like a shell shock victim struggling to count fingers — like he was impressed by the unexpected tangibility of everything he touched. We made it — sure, but the words had yet to make it into some kind of meaningful realization in my mind.

How?

I couldn't stop asking the question.

There was a long pause in the Stryker when he said those words. A painful silence. I was still waiting for an ambush, and nobody could believe we were still alive — but it was over. We crossed back over the border and it was done. There was a hurricane and then quiet. Screaming and then silence. Like I was overcome with an acute and frightening deafness. As if vibrations themselves as a physical concept had ceased to exist. The whole Earth was standing still. It was pure, painful, and unbelievable silence. We could've been ghosts and I would never have known. Every one of us should've been dead, yet there we were — limbs intact. But I guess that's war.

I did one final check of the time: what was supposed to be a thirty-minute snatch-and-grab raid had spiraled into a full two hours of balls-out brutality. What was supposed to be a "bread-and-butter play" was really a fight to the bitter end. That was the first time I had ever watched a man die. The first time I had ever been in a real fight for my life. The first time I had ever been faced with my own mortality, knowing all too well that somebody had done everything they could to kill me.

We pushed our luck right up to the razor's edge that night. To this day I have no idea how we survived. But one thing was for damn sure: there was no way in Hell we would ever let a sloppy mission put everybody's life at risk again. From that moment onward, we learned, we adapted, and we trained, until everything that had happened that night became little more than an introduction to the Jaish al-Mahdi and barely a glimmer of what they had waiting for us in the months to come. That spring we'd charge back into the heart of Sadr City to face down the full force of our new enemy — only then, nobody expected to make it out of there alive.

- Chapter One -
Needs Of The Army

When I joined the Army, a single phrase on my contract stood out above the rest: "...a period of no less than five years and 22 weeks." That's what I signed away to the service. 65 months of my life. 1,980 days. More than half a decade.

I was seventeen.

I suppose if I could still remember all the shit that was going on in my head, I'd know why the hell I fought so hard to be a ground pounder. All I know for sure is that I told those bastards to pack me onto the first bird outbound to the war. I begged them for a front-row seat to combat. I *demanded* to see some action.

Ironically, it was my recruiter who was the one with a level head.

"Are you sure this is what you want?" He had asked me that a hundred times. Now, right before we walked into the office where I would sign away my rights to the Army, he asked me once more — just in case.

"I'm sure." I nodded.

"Absolutely positive? This is big, man."

"I'm positive."

"You don't have to do this all in one shot. Five years is a long time."

"I know."

I had no idea. Five years earlier, I was twelve. What the hell did I know when I was twelve? A smart man would've thought about that. But I wasn't a smart man. I was seventeen.

"And the Infantry?" He waved a copy of my aptitude exam in my face and compared it to a list of occupational specialties I could choose from. "Listen, I can get you anything you want with these test scores. Anything. Medic, Psy-Ops, Computer Technician. Hell, I can get you workin' in the Pentagon. Swear to God. You name it. We can make it happen." He paused for a second and poured his heart into the final phrase. "There's no reason for you to be a ground pounder."

As he spoke I leafed through my own thick packet of papers and looked around at the other recruits in the waiting room. Every one of them was holding out for a reservation to a nine-to-five desk job of administrative bullshit.

The idea made me cringe.

I didn't want some cushy job in the rear. I wanted to be on the ground and see it for myself, without the filters and bias of brand name news corporations. I wanted to make a difference. I wanted to go somewhere I could never go on my own. I wanted to do something people never get to do in their life. I wanted to get pushed to the extreme and see for myself what was happening "over there." I wanted to see if I had what it takes to make it through real world combat and find out what it's like to be one of those hardened vets on the far side of oblivion. The military offered all of those things to me in spades. All I had to do was say "yes." The only problem was that I kept insisting on getting shot at and my recruiter was on a quest to set me straight.

"Seriously, Ludwig. You don't have to be a grunt. Just say the word."

"Yeah," I looked up at him with a smile. "But that's what I want."

He shook his head at the thought of what I had coming.

"I don't get it, Ludwig. You're a smart kid — and you're *motivated.* I don't want to see that go to waste."

I took a second to gather my thoughts into words. As I gummed it over, I could see the hope in his eyes. A hope that evaporated as soon as I set out to make my final stand.

"Sergeant Jones, why would I join the Army to do something that I can do as a civilian? I don't need to join the Army if I want to work with computers. I'm here to go to war. And if I'm gonna' go to war, I want to fight."

That was the last time he asked.

By the time my graduating class in high school showed up for their first day of senior year my head was already shaved clean and Uncle Sam had handed me a thirty-pound rack of body armor. Before their teachers could master everybody's name I was belly-down in live-fire training. By the end of the first ball game in the season I had mastered the craft of shooting, led a squad of fellow soldiers, and memorized the capabilities of every small-arms weapon used on the ground by the United States Army. The night before their first semester finals, I marched twelve miles with a dead-man's weight on my back. When basic training was finally over, at two in the morning on some idle night in December, I stood atop a military relic of piled-up dirt named "Victory Hill." The jagged pins of my infantry crossed-rifles insignia were stabbed into my bleeding chest and pounded in place by each one of my drill sergeants. It was a barbaric ritual dating back to the dawn of Rome — and up until that point it was the best night of my life.

Basic Training only lasted for three months, but it felt like a lifetime. Every day of it was a fifteen-hour montage of physical activity and combat training. By the time Senior Prom was announced, I was already shipping off to my first duty station. I was cleaning a light machine gun before I was allowed to smoke a cigarette. I had been groomed to kill before I could legally fuck. When it was time for me to go off to war, I wasn't even old enough to buy a beer back home — so my dad took care of the tab and we called it even.

People forget that when I tell them about the war. They don't realize how young I was. They'll ask me about a memory and I'll watch their eyes glaze over. They'll fit me to the stereotype whenever I try to paint the picture of what happened. They take one glance and mumble, "Yeah, that fits," because it's easy to imagine a 6'4", 215 pound combat veteran on the far side of the world, wielding a four foot long, belt-fed machine gun. But it wasn't like that at all. Back then, I was still a child. I was still a boy. I was a scrawny little goof ball named "Konrad," who grew up in the bubble of an upper-middle-class suburbia. Somehow I got the idea into my thick skull to join the Army instead of finishing high school. Two years later, I was nineteen years old and staring death in the face. I had grit in my teeth and a belly full of fear, and maybe if I knew back then how it would all turn out, things would have been different. Maybe I would've waited a little while before running off to be a soldier. But that's not how it went down. Not for me, at least.

Most of the guys I know joined the military as soon as America went to war. September 11th hit, President Bush gave his speech, they quit their day jobs and the Infantry got some new recruits. Simple as that. No questions asked. I was in the eighth grade when it happened. Hell, I didn't even know what the World Trade Center *was* until it crumbled into pieces. I woke up on the morning of September 11th to find my family huddled over the television in the family room with slack jaws. I came out just in time to see the first tower fall.

"Are you guys seriously watching a movie?" I asked. "It's like six o'clock."

"No," my dad said. "This is really happening."

I didn't know what I was looking at. Two buildings were burning down and nobody had any answers. At that point we didn't even know it was a terrorist attack. So I watched both towers fall, packed up my lunch, and rode my bike to school — after all, that's what eighth graders *do* — but it wasn't even ten o-clock before the administrators sent everybody home. Our campus was right down the street from the Jet Propulsion Laboratory in Pasadena, California. That put us barely a half kilometer away from the heart of NASA's off world, unmanned operations — a fact which led many of our faculty to believe it was high on the list for a run-in with a 747. It didn't take long for the panic to spread from there.

As the facts unraveled, the true gravity of the situation crystallized in my mind. America had been attacked, terrorists had taken the credit, and motives once far away from the public eye were suddenly thrust into view. Less than a month passed before we put boots on the ground in Afghanistan. Within a matter of weeks, the Taliban was in full flight. By the time the invasion was over, I had barely gotten back to sack lunches and morning bike-rides to school.

After everything that had happened, the biggest effect the war had on my life could still be measured in inches of displacement where previous headline issues had crawled below the fold on the front pages of newspapers I didn't read. If you had asked me at the time, I couldn't even point to Afghanistan on a map. But one thing was for sure: the fall of 2001 was a triggering event. It was the first time I opened my eyes as a child to look out across the world to places I had never heard of. The first time I paid attention to America's influence around the globe. The first time I truly faced the fact that sometime in the last century American soldiers had gone everywhere I could think of, to fight and die for people like me. Little did I know, America would be at war for the rest of my adolescent life.

Barely one year after the invasion of Afghanistan, more than 35 countries declared war on Saddam Hussein. Overnight, 190,000 American, British, and Australian troops poured into the wastelands of modern-day Mesopotamia. Nine days later — on the eve of my sixteenth birthday — American troops made their final push up to Baghdad. By the end of the following week the Iraqi army was in shambles and the capital was ours. A week after that, Marines rolled into Saddam's hometown of Tikrit and we accepted the total surrender of his remaining Imperial Guard.

All told, it took us 26 days to conquer the entire country. Given a footprint of about 166,859 square miles, we averaged a staggering 6,418 square miles of conquered territory a day — equivalent to about 267 square miles an hour. Now, of course we didn't span every corner of the country. But even if you measured straight up the 500 mile highway from our beachhead landing at al-Faw to Saddam Hussein's last stand, the invasion of Iraq averaged a startling pace of about twenty linear miles a day. That's 0.8 miles an hour. In other words, you could've driven a steamroller from where we landed on the beachhead to where the final battle took place in the time it took us to crush one of the most dominant military forces in the world.

But the invasion of Iraq wasn't just war. I was watching prime-time, international American Gladiators with a front-row, low-bandwidth satellite feed of the action. Reporters practically crawled over each other to get a picture in front of something burning. We cheered as a nation when Saddam's two sons, Uday and Qusay, were hunted down and killed by the mysterious warriors of "Taskforce 20." We came together as a culture over holiday meals to cry for the lynching of the despot himself. And when there was nothing left to kill, we touted the dollar value of reconstruction stimulus like tallied points on the high-score list of Pac-Man, negotiating the finer issues of American imperialism as we waited in line for morning lattes.

It was absurd really, and like everybody else I swallowed it whole. Gallup polling in late March showed that 72% of Americans favored the war in Iraq, while fewer than a quarter of the sample group felt the war was a mistake. Even a full two weeks after the invasion was officially over, only 172 Coalition troops had been killed in action, and it was in the face of those numbers that I became convinced as any that we had won the war. But soon enough that infamous corporate entertainment industry we all call "the news" declared their own war on public approval for the sake of some cash at the bottom line.

With shocking speed, reporters across the country were ripped from their front line posts and crammed into five-star hotels where they could "mitigate bias" and sniff out "the truth" over complimentary peanuts from the lobby down stairs. With these new watchwords of media spin, it wasn't long before juicy snapshots of American heroes were muscled out of the mainstream media and replaced by horrid photos of the human cost of war.

Naturally, the approval ratings tanked.

By October of my tenth grade year of high school, a widely cited and peer-reviewed anti-war study suggested more than 9,000 enemy combatants had been killed in the invasion, with at least 3,200 civilian deaths in the struggle to depose Saddam. Given those numbers, we could figure for every one of "ours" who died in the campaign, at least 53 of "them" were killed outright, with 19 civilians who never made it out of the crossfire alive. These were startling figures by any measure — most notably for the one-sided and relatively low cost of what we had accomplished. But it was the last of those statistics that became the cornerstone of the political discourse. Nobody in their right mind was about to step into a public forum to say any number of innocent civilian deaths could be "justified." Since casualties from the occupation were ongoing, the hunt for controversy practically dictated that journalists throw together any numbers they could find to amass highly speculative "death tolls," and inspire doubts about our noble cause.

It didn't help that in that same month, during a series of attacks nicknamed the "Ramadan Offensive," the first major outbreak of insurgent violence foreshadowed the brutal reality of what was to come. With the uniformed members of Saddam Hussein's military wiped out, Sunni loyalists had picked up the will to fight, and our new enemy revealed itself as one who hid among the civilian population and didn't give a half-flung shit about collateral damage. Now there was no telling who was or was not a combatant in a sea of civilians until some bomb went off, and the horrid snapshots of innocent looking victims lying dead in the street — shown without context or explanation — was all America needed to grow weak in the knees.

Then came the media spin: a heartfelt fiction that American soldiers were over there murdering innocent Iraqis for the hell of it. Due in no small part to this shock-and-awe journalism, Gallup polling showed a startling drop in American approval of the war. In a single month, just 54% of the population remained firm in their opinion of what was happening in Iraq. By the end of the year, a widespread "feeling" that it was all a "mistake" had risen by 82%. Despite definitive and major landmarks of progress, calls for an immediate withdrawal from Iraq became a legitimate point in the collective discussion barely nine months into the conflict. We hadn't even been fighting for a year and the debate was already turned on its head. For a time, all I remember hearing about were widespread reports of wanton destruction, civilian casualties, and corrupted intentions. As for me, I simply couldn't understand how such a clear-cut element of war could be spun into the "unforeseen" and "unacceptable" — especially not when they paled in comparison to the bloodshed of conflicts past. It was strange to me that so many people could've rallied behind the cause without realizing the obvious repercussions of the act.

This is war, I thought.

We went there to defeat a dictator. That means tanks and bombs and guns. It means killing and collateral damage. Acceptable losses. A fair trade for what needed to be done. And that job wasn't over — so the war carried on.

Towards the end of my tenth grade year of high school, in the spring of 2004, a group of insurgent forces ambushed a convoy of food supplies in the city of Fallujah and killed the Blackwater security contractors who had been hired to protect it. Hours later, the mutilated the bodies of four American men were hung from a bridge outside of town. I knew exactly what it was: a bloody middle finger to the Marines right down the road. It was a battle cry behind which both the insurgents of Fallujah and its neighboring suburb of Ramadi would rally. And with the new digital age upon us, photos and videos spread instantly to every news organization in the world, and the nation was gripped with heated public outcries for revenge.

On both sides of the political aisle, representatives in our government demanded a response to the killings. Within days, American troops followed through with an attack. The expectation was that our boys would make quick work of the enemy in Fallujah. Instead, what would later become known as "the First Battle of Fallujah" turned into a bloodbath of unmatched proportion.

Due to extensive organization among the insurgent armies of both al-Qaeda and the Sunni loyalists of Saddam Hussein, violence quickly erupted across half the country in response to the attack. Within days, insurgent forces in Ramadi, Mosul, Husaybah, Samarra, and Baquba followed suit. After a month of heavy fighting, the entire country had slipped into chaos. American troops had taken heavy losses, and their assault into Fallujah had secured barely a quarter of the sprawling city.

It was in the shadow of these events that a powerful organized crime syndicate, led by a man named Muktada al-Sadr, fielded its own ruthless paramilitary force known as the "Jaish al-Mahdi." As Coalition troops began their assault into the North, al-Sadr's militia rose to power in the south and began a widespread uprising throughout the country. While this act was politically unrelated to the insurgent efforts in the North, it was the perfect time to successfully assert his militia as one of the leading paramilitary forces in the country. More importantly, he had successfully ushered in a new phase of bloody conflict that would become iconic of the war in Iraq.

From the Coalition's perspective, the results of these coordinated uprisings were devastating. Within a matter of days al-Qaeda and Sunni Loyalists in the North confirmed their dominance over most of the major cities, including the strongholds of Fallujah, Ramadi, and Husaybah. At the same time in the South, the Jaish al-Mahdi managed to capture the cities of Najaf, Kufa, al-Kut, Nasiriyah, Amarah, Basra, and the entire eastern half of Baghdad. In the many weeks that followed, Iraq was torn apart by some of the hardest fighting of the war. When the first day of summer came, American troops had yet to capture the original targets of Fallujah and Ramadi, the city of Mosul had been abandoned, and ongoing battles with the Jaish al-Mahdi in the south showed no end in sight.

This "Spring Fighting of 2004," as it is now known, came to a head in the city of Najaf, where thousands died in a fierce battle between Coalition troops and the Jaish al-Mahdi. After a bitter loss at the end of a bloody fight he could never win, Muktada al-Sadr finally agreed to a general ceasefire. For the first time since the fighting broke out, Coalition forces were able to give their undivided attention to the al-Qaeda strongholds in the North.

Within weeks our troops embarked on the Second Battle of Fallujah — a bloody campaign that would quickly become the most famous engagement of the Iraq war. This time, American Marines embarked on some of the heaviest urban combat of their history since the battle of Hue City in Vietnam, capturing the entire city outright. Rather than mark an end to the Spring Fighting of 2004, however, the invasion of Fallujah only led to another uprising of insurgent forces in the North, causing a second firestorm of violence to break out across the country. By Christmas of my junior year in high school we had already seen the bloodiest and most brutal fighting of the Iraq war.

Recruitment and retention for the United States military reached an all-time low in January of 2005. At that point, scandals like the prisoner abuse at Abu Ghraib had done a great deal to damage the public image of foreign conflict, and it didn't help much that neither war showed any sign of ending soon. As for the troops who signed up when it all began, they had been fighting in both Iraq and Afghanistan for nearly half a decade with rolling deployment cycles and limited manpower. A large majority had already been forced into their second or third rotation out to the front lines already. For them, reenlistment was nothing more than a blank check to get blown up a few more times or get killed in the process. For everybody else, there was hardly an inclination to volunteer. Two years of fighting had left a field of human debris to serve as an example of what can happen overseas.

Nearly 1,700 soldiers had already died, and an additional 10,843 had been critically wounded. But the rate of growth for these statistics was the most disheartening factor of all. By the time I turned seventeen in March of 2005, another 149 names were added to the list of killed in action. In May alone, suicide bombers killed more than 700 Iraqi civilians and 79 American soldiers as sectarian violence reached its bloodiest point since the war began. And it was right about then I looked up the nearest Army recruitment office and tested out of high school to join the Army.

So why did I enlist?

For starters, I was in it for the kicks. I wanted to do something nobody else had the balls to do. I wanted to be physically and mentally challenged in ways I could never imagine. I wanted to try something undeniably tangible and incredibly dangerous. To embark on something that could very well kill me if I didn't do it right, because everything up to that point in my life had been double-wrapped and cordoned-off with caution tape.

But I also wanted to be a part of something *big*. I wanted to go out into the world and carve my place in history. I wanted to do something that mattered, instead of sitting at home and watching it all unfold on TV. It wasn't good enough to pin yellow ribbons on my backpack and wave a flag on the weekend. Not when I met every requirement to serve. Not when so many men had signed up as soon as they could, when we first invaded Iraq and Afghanistan and all this shit kicked off. Staying at home to "show my support" for sending young men like me to go fight and die for what I believed in was USDA approved, stamped and sealed, pure, shameless hypocrisy.

So what if people were dying over there? It's war. That's a given. It didn't matter if we were lied to about why, if it was all for naught, or if the whole thing was a bad idea. What was done was done. We still had a job to do. Now more than ever. And that's why I joined: because at the end of the day I had no good reason *not* to. I was the textbook recruit. I was physically fit, mentally tough, ideologically driven, hell-bent on the adventure, and I believed in the cause.

So if I didn't go, who would?

That was the question I couldn't shake. Thousands of people had given their lives for something *I* believed in, and they were sent there because people like *me* thought it was the right thing to do. But it's easy to point your finger and say that something needs to be done when you're not the one who has to go there and do it. So the way I saw it, it was my turn to carry the burden of suffering I had demanded from countless others. It was my turn to put my life where my mouth was and actually fight for what I thought was right. It was my turn to step up and serve — even if it was the last thing I ever did.

Without hesitation, I picked up the digital pen on my contract counselor's desk and squiggled my name across the dotted line of servitude. It was the steady hand of a young man who knew exactly what he was doing. Right at the top of the page, printed in big bold ink, was the time I agreed to spend "in service." After that came a reminder that when my five year stint of active duty was up, I'd have another two and a half years in the "Inactive Ready Reserve" — a period of time when Uncle Sam would be free to call me up whenever he saw fit. In the middle of the page, a short block of finely crafted legal print explained that at any time and for any reason the conditions of my contract were subject to change according to the Army's whim. None of that mattered to me. I let my eyes drift down to the only thing they couldn't change, and beamed with pride at the sight of three highlighted cash-bonuses for a "priority seat to combat." I didn't care about the money. I was just stacking the deck.

Two weeks later I shipped out to Basic Training. I was gone so fast they had to white out the dates on my paperwork. I was on the road before I even really knew what happened. At 04:00 in the morning they stuck me on a bus in LA and 24 hours later I was corralled into a formation with a few hundred other recruits at the 30th Adjutant General Reception Battalion (aka: 30th AG) of Ft. Benning, Georgia. My whole life had been reduced to little more than a seven-day heap of monochrome clothing, which I had hastily shoved into an olive drab duffel bag at the behest of an unfriendly drill sergeant. My feet were numb from the hard, unpadded leather in my boots. My skin chafed from the chemically flame-retardant, rip-stop fabric of my uniform. Out in front of us, a single man stood proud and tall with a wide-brimmed hat, and revealed himself to be the drill sergeant in charge of "in-processing."

"Listen up Privates!"

He shouted with a clear diction and hard tone of discipline. His steady and collected voice echoed through the woods behind us, and deep into the night sky.

"The Infantry has one mission!" he continued. "To close with and kill the enemy by means of fire and maneuver!"

As the phrase sank into our thick skulls, he walked back and forth from one end of the massive crowd to the other.

"*That* is your job! And it is *our* job to show you how!"

I looked around me to take in the sea of eager Privates, as giddy as I was to be a part of history. Hundreds of them, from every corner of the country. I had never seen so many races, religions, and creeds stand together under a single cause — yet there we were. And what that drill sergeant was telling us was exactly what I wanted to hear. Something real. Something intense. Something in the now. It was everything I had signed up for and nothing less. So I stood there shivering in the cold, with tingling toes and a great big smile carved into my face.

"Make no mistake about it," he cried out. "We are at war! And I can assure you that sometime soon your life will depend on what you learn in the next few months! So we will push you! We will threaten you! We will hurt you, if we have to! You will suffer more than most of you have ever known! You will be cold, tired, and exhausted! But you *will* learn these skills, Privates! You will master them as you have mastered nothing else in your life! And, God willing, you will use them to kill your enemy. This is no bullshit, Privates! This is the Infantry! Now, *sound off!*"

All together, as a massive, bumbling formation of civilians, we cried out our broken recollection of the Infantryman's Creed. In just fourteen weeks it would become a unified voice – one so loud your ears rang when it was over. Even if I had wanted to, there was no turning back now. I was about to become a shit-eating, ground-pounding grunt. Everything else was up to the Man.

I got my assignment orders when Basic Training was finally over. Thanks to the conditions of my contract, I was expecting a clear-cut assignment with a front line role. A "priority seat to combat," as the Army had put it. With great effort, I muscled my way through the two-page document of acronyms and administrative jargon to decipher the language of my fate. At first I thought I had missed something. My copy of instructions said nothing about an impending trip to the Sandbox. Much to the contrary, the papers in my hand spoke of a future where I'd be shanghaied off to Washington State and kept as far away as possible from any likelihood of an explosion.

"There's gotta' be a mistake." I pleaded with my drill sergeant.

"Take it up with Branch." He smirked.

That was the typical cue to fuck off, seeing as "taking it up with Branch" means you bust your ass for some face-time with an apathetic paper-pusher. Typically those administrative types don't give a shit about some grunt and his orders, especially not if he's a freshly pinned private with a gripe about his duty station. But it was all I could do, so I followed through with my drill sergeant's suggestion and walked clear across the base to get the low-down on what the hell was going on. Surprisingly, I made it all the way up to the corner office of the head-honcho in the building before I hit the wall and couldn't go any farther.

"Sorry, Private." He shook his head. "There's no mistake: you're seventeen. The Department of Defense won't do it."

"But I've got my contract right here!" I said. "It clearly states that I have a priority seat to combat!"

I handed him my wrinkled sheet of paper, slashed up with streaks of highlighted ink. Across the bottom was a solid paragraph explaining their obligation to put me in the path of some angry bullets. It was clear-cut and spelled out, with no room to wiggle.

At least, that's what I thought.

He scanned over the contract and chuckled before setting it lightly back on his desk to explain to me what was going on.

"Yeah son, listen... Recruiters can tell you whatever the hell they want. The fact is that you're not going over there unless you're eighteen years old. And if you've got nothin' else in your contract, you go wherever the hell they need you."

"Yeah, but—"

"No buts, Private. That's how it works."

"Fuckin' recruiters," I mumbled.

"What's that!?" He snapped.

"I was just pissed at my recruiter, Sergeant." I motioned to the contract with an angry hand.

"Now hang on one second, *Private!*" The Branch officer slid the wrinkled contract back over to my side of the desk. "This isn't your recruiter's fault. He hooked you up, so stop complaining."

I tried to mask my snarl as I reached up to handle the piece of paper on his desk and scan it for whatever it was that I had missed.

"What are you talking about?" I protested.

The Branch officer was hardly amused.

"Look at the bottom there." He tapped his finger on the line of text spelling out the dollar value of my signing bonus. Highlighted in yellow was the magic figure: *$20,000 CASH*. He let that sink in before he continued. "It's not like your recruiter didn't *know* you couldn't get deployed; he just didn't *tell* you. But here's the deal, Private: you got those priority combat kickers anyway."

"Yeah, but I'm not going to combat," I interrupted.

Making no attempt to hide his restraint, he shook off my comment and continued on with the explanation.

"*Exactly,* Private. But that doesn't matter now. I don't know what these bonuses were doing on your contract in the first place, but you signed on the dotted line and you don't even have to go. That money's in the bag and there ain't shit we can do to get it back. Hell, if it was worth my time I'd call this up the chain and get his ass relieved. So you want my advice? Take the twenty grand, kid. And stop being in such a god-damn hurry to die."

He had a point. And that was that. There was nothing else I could do. I got on the plane, they flew me to Washington State, and I reported for duty at the Ft. Lewis Welcome Center like my orders commanded. A week later I became a bona fide member of the 1-5th Infantry Battalion (INF) of the 25th Infantry Division's (ID) 1st Stryker Brigade Combat Team (SBCT), a mangy band of miscreants living in the forgotten backwaters of the base.

As it turns out, there's only one good way to greet a private...

- Chapter Two -
THE DEATHMASTERS

"Who's that?"

The non-commissioned officer in charge of the Battalion Headquarters stood up from behind his desk and walked over to our side of the room with a snarl.

"This is the new Private." My escort chuckled.

"Is he any good?"

"He looks alright."

Even as I stood at parade rest, I could hear the faint, disproving growl form in the back of the man's throat.

"We'll see about that," he said.

On the last day of in-processing, a soldier from my new unit was sent to pick me up from the Ft. Lewis Welcome Center and drive me into the dregs of the base. Right before my eyes, the standard living conditions of the various units on the base were stripped away until there was nothing left but condemned buildings and decomposing training equipment. There, in the slums of a massive bureaucracy, my future loomed all around me. Of the billions of dollars the Army had spent on upgrading barracks facilities around the world, he explained, none of it had gone to the Infantry. Every last dime had been spent on "people other than grunts" — who were refereed to with loathing as "POGs."

I tried to empathize with him, but he shut me down with a quickness as soon as I opened my mouth.

"That's how we like it," he snapped.

It was clear that I wasn't there for small talk and he wasn't interested in whatever it was that I had to say, so for the rest of the ride I elected to keep my mouth shut because the last thing I needed was to burn a first impression.

As we neared our destination and got out of the car, it became clear to me that I had stepped into a world of its own. One that had been separated from the rest. Quarantined, even. In and amongst the men in my new neighborhood were dozens of baby-faced privates doing push-ups or crawling in the dirt. There wasn't a single smile to be seen. And hovering over their sorry faces were men much harder than any I had ever seen before, shouting at the top of their lungs like it was a natural form of communication.These sights were not unfamiliar thanks to the diluted rigors of basic training, but here they were different. Here it was personal. It was *these* men who would die if anybody failed, and *these* men knew that more than anybody else.

At the sight of it, I couldn't help but imagine a strange species of man who feeds on innocence and shits out pain. The kind of person who has been welded together like steel. Men who could be trusted to do what needs to be done. These were those kinds of men, and together they formed a rabid pack of wolves that had been kept in a cage and far away from the everyday people of America. Wolves who could be counted on to walk away from everything in their life, seek out the enemies of America, and kill them. For these men, war and killing was anything but an abstraction. It was their profession. One that they had carried out with remarkable ferocity.

More than a year before my arrival at the gates of Ft. Lewis, the entire 1st Stryker Brigade Combat Team, of which my new unit, the 1-5th INF, was a part, shipped out to Iraq and embarked on one of the most notable tours of duty up to that point in the war. During the very first month of their deployment, they were thrown into the Second Battle of Fallujah and fought side-by-side with the Marines who had been dispatched to retake the city. Without pause or reflection, they were then thrust into the Battle of Mosul where they took the lead role in another outbreak of fierce, close quarters urban combat. And it was in those streets that they spent the majority of their deployment hunting down insurgents until every major al-Qaeda cell in Mosul had been killed, captured, or disbanded.

No matter how you cut it, the men of 1st Brigade, and with it their 1-5th INF Battalion, earned their stripes in Hell. It was the aftermath of those two battles that proved their character beyond a doubt. Without hesitation they got to work, rebuilding the city and offering relief to refugees who had been caught in the crossfire of the fighting. By the time they were done, every commander in Iraq knew their unit by name.

Upon returning to America, the entire unit was promptly recognized with a Valorous Unit Award for their service in the war. Not only had they participated in two major battle campaigns and restored order to the streets of Mosul, but in the final days of their deployment they were also dispatched to protect the very first free Iraqi elections after Saddam Hussein was deposed. And all this had happened while I was sitting back at home getting drunk with friends on the weekend and riding my bike to school during the week.

So there I was, barely a month after their return, walking through the door to the Battalion Headquarters of the 1-5th INF to get looked over by the non-commissioned officer in charge (aka: NCOIC).

"We got a fuckin' new guy!" My escort announced as we stepped into the office.

With everybody's eyes on me, I snapped to the position of parade rest and stood as tall as I could. The NCOIC simply walked over to where we were standing, glanced at my escort, scoffed lightly, and got back to his scowl. He might as well have had a technical manual and inspection checklist in-hand. The process was no different from any other piece of equipment.

"What's your name?" He barked.

"Private Ludwig, Sergeant."

"Oh!" He glanced at my escort. "Listen to that! You hear how he said Sar gent?"

"Fuckin' cherry." My escort chuckled

"You from the city, Ludwig?"

"Roger, Sergeant."

"Yeah? Which one?"

"Los Angeles."

"L.A., huh? What, you from fuckin' Beverly Hills?"

"Negative, Sergeant."

"You sure? 'Cus you sound like a rich kid."

"How so, Sergeant?"

They both laughed.

"Well you sure as shit ain't from Alabama. Here, repeat after me: *Saaarn't*." He dragged out the vowels, smearing the entire word into a single syllable.

"*Saaarn't*," I mimicked the phrase.

"There you go! 'Roger, *Sarn't*.'" He motioned for me to repeat it one more time.

"Roger... *Sarn't*," I obliged.

He cracked a smile and drove on with the evaluation. "Good job! Now, can you shoot? 'Cus most city boys can't shoot worth a shit."

"Roger, Sarn't. I can shoot."

My escort leafed through my packet, reading over what little I had accomplished. "It says here he's an expert marksman."

"Yeah... in Basic." The NCOIC chuckled. "You ever get in trouble, Ludwig?"

"Negative, Sarn't."

"No Article-15's?"

"Negative, Sarn't."

"Drugs?"

"Negative."

"You drink?"

"Sometimes."

"It says here he's seventeen." My escort glanced up from my paperwork.

"That's unsatisfactory, Private! Drinkin' under age?" The NCOIC shook his head back and forth in an almost cartoonish manner. "You better set your shit straight if you want to get by around here."

I nodded in response, defaulting to the proper pronunciation of the word. "Roger, Sarn't."

Without a trace of recognition that I had replied, the NCOIC stepped up close to get a better look at the goods. It was hard to miss the fact that his eyes barely made it up to my collarbone but he still had an easy twenty pounds on me in muscle. As I glanced around out of the corner of my eye, I could see that went for everybody else in the room. For the first time in my life I was surrounded by a bunch of guys who made me feel like a pencil-pushing geek.

"Man, you're a fuckin' sky scraper!" My inspector leaned in close to see if I'd flinch at the proximity of his terrible breath. "I bet you suck dick at push-ups."

"Pretty much, Sarn't." I kept my composure and slapped a smirk across my face.

"Well don't worry." He smiled back. "They'll work that outta' you. With an attitude like that, you'll look like Dolph Lundgren up in this motherfucker in a week or two for sure." He snatched the packet from my escort and dropped it down onto another desk, turning back at us to make his decree. "Give him to Bravo. Let 'em have some fun."

Everybody in the office chuckled at my plight. As for my escort, he just gave me a pat on the back and smiled.

"Well there you go, Private. Welcome to the Deathmasters."

I muscled my gear alongside him, taking in the decrepit buildings all around me.

"Hey," he chuckled. "Look at the bright side. At least you have a whole weekend to get ready."

That was Friday. I spent the weekend settling in. At 05:45 in the morning of the following Monday I was torn awake from a deep slumber to discover that my door had been kicked in and replaced with a pissed off non-commissioned officer. From what I could tell, his defining traits were clenched fists and a lip full of tobacco.

"So you're the fuckin' new guy?!" He barked. "You're the fish?!"

I crawled out of bed and sprang to my feet, overcome with shock and still groggy from the rude awakening.

"Well?!" He drove on.

Realizing what was about to go down, I locked into parade rest and stared straight at the wall.

"Roger Sarn't," I said. "I'm the new guy."

"No, you're the fish."

"Um... Roger."

"It's not *'um roger.'* It's just *'roger.'* What? Are you some kind of fuckin' pussy?"

"Negative Sarn't."

He looked me up and down, then shoulder-checked me out of his way to inspect my room. I could hear deep breaths of rage as he walked past.

"I'm Sergeant High. I'm gonna' be your fuckin' team leader. That's Alpha Team, of 2nd Squad, in 1st Platoon. From here on out, you're my bitch. Got it?"

"Roger, Sarn't."

"Let me see your gear."

I jumped into action and tore into my wall locker, grabbing the two duffel bags I had shoved inside. He flipped them over and dumped everything out. Kneepads, Kevlar, uniforms, socks, boots... they went everywhere. My personal effects were mixed in with the mess. He had canned my entire life onto that floor and didn't give a damn. He just glanced it over and turned his belligerent gaze right back to my eyes.

"That's it?!" He shouted. "You haven't set it up?! What the fuck is wrong with you?!"

I looked down at my pile of jumbled equipment and froze. Nothing was put together into a cohesive "kit." It was just a heap of equipment. My pouches floated around in the pile without reason and my body armor fell bare to the bone. Nobody told me I had to have it set it up. I didn't even know how they did it here. But who gave a shit? That was my first mistake: waiting for instruction instead of figuring it out myself.

"Well?!" He shouted.

"I— uh—"

"Do some fucking push-ups!"

He hadn't skipped a beat. I dropped to the ground and started pumping them out.

"What's your battle roster?!" He shouted.

"My battle roster, Sarn't?"

I had no idea what he was talking about.

"Yes, dipshit! Your fuckin' battle roster number. Don't tell me you don't know what a battle roster number is!"

"Negative, Sarn't."

"Negative what?!"

I sighed with frustration.

So much for first impressions.

"I don't know what a battle roster is, Sergeant."

"What the fuck! Didn't I just say *'don't tell me you don't know what a battle roster is?!'*"

"Roger, Sarn't."

He snatched my helmet up from the ground and gave it a closer inspection. At least I had the camouflage cover strapped down right.

"On your feet!" He shouted.

When I stood back up and locked into parade rest, he held it right in front of my face so there was no question if I could see it. "See your camo band?" He grabbed the elastic strap tied to the helmet and flipped it over with his finger. "Right side. Underside of the band. Black sharpie. Write the letter Bravo, the last four digits of your social security number, and the first letter of your last name. No spaces. Got that?!"

"Roger, Sarn't!"

"That's your battle roster number."

"Roger, Sarn't!"

"Now, on the outside here," he flipped it back over. "Write your blood type. Same deal. Black sharpie. And don't fuck up!" He dropped my helmet back down to the ground and looked back at the jumbled state of my quarters. "Clean up this fuckin' room! I want you downstairs in two minutes! Got that?!"

"Roger, Sarn't!"

For a second I stood there waiting for him to give the order to get to work. He held his watch up in my face and showed me the cover plate. The time was already ticking.

"What the fuck are you waiting for?!"

He let the question hang in the air and I vaulted towards my gear, frantically attempting to shove everything I owned back into two bags which had been over packed as it was. I already knew I was doomed — but that was the point.

"That's right," he chuckled. "You're my bitch now."

He walked back out of my door with a smirk to check on the rest of his team. I could hear him laughing all the way down the hall. When he got to the far end, he shouted his final command for everyone to hear.

"Don't be late, *fish!*"

I heard it echo through the barracks. It bounced off the walls and into the stairwell. A string of dirty cheers followed. That was my introduction to the Deathmasters. It was the first day at my unit and I was already suckin'.

"We got another cherry!" I heard some unknown voice cry out.

"Hands off!" Sergeant High laughed. "This one's fuckin' mine."

I didn't make it downstairs in time. I was never supposed to. I spent the rest of that day sucking in pain and doing everything I could to play catch-up with the clock. I was a "virgin cherry" at the bottom of the food chain. A single mistake and he'd jump on it like a hawk. The tiniest screw up and I was in a world of pain. My only entitlement, he explained, was four intermittent hours of sleep and a single square meal in a day — a fact of life that he was determined to prove. It was cold-blooded meritocracy. As the saying goes: I could either get smart, or I could get strong.

For that entire day and every day after, I spent my waking hours cranking out excruciating physical exercises and getting humiliated as a rite of passage. It went on like that for weeks. Sergeant High would storm into my room at the crack of dawn and drag me out into the hallway for some early morning Jiu-Jitsu. I'd fight back and he'd win. I'd tap out and he'd have me crawling up and down the halls, shouting every step in the troop leading procedures of the Army. Surrender wasn't even in the cards. If I so much as thought about giving up without a fight, he made sure I suffered even more.

My life had become a montage of shouting, fighting, sweating, and suffering every day, for weeks on end, until the day I could prove to Sergeant High that I was more than just a steaming heap of "maggot shit." One day, I finally lashed out in anger with an open-handed choke. The next thing I knew, he lodged his fist into my solar plexus, knocked the wind right out of my chest, and used every ounce of his body to slam me down into the freshly buffed floor.

"Yes!" He stood over me with a cheer as I coughed on my own spit and heaved for a lungful of air. "That's what I fucking want from you, you goddamn piece of shit!"

I wrestled myself back into a defensive posture and started picking myself up off the floor.

"Do you want to kick my fuckin' ass?!" He shouted for the world to hear. "You wanna' fuckin' kill me yet?!"

I steadied my breathing and answered him straight up. "Roger, Sarn't!!"

"I want to hear you say it!"

"I want to fucking kill you, Sergeant!"

"Then what the fuck are you waiting for?! Get the fuck up! On your feet! I'm not fuckin' done with you!"

I inhaled through the pain of a freshly bruised rib and crawled to my hands and knees. Still coughing from the pain, I rose to my feet, shored up my footing and lunged for his neck. All it took was a quick flash of his wrist before I was getting choked out with my own collar and slammed into the corner of a nearby wall. By the time I regained consciousness, he had dragged me all the way down to the end of the hall and the entire platoon had gathered around to watch the show. There was no escaping his wrath, and the only way this was going to end was in a knockout fight to the finish.

For all my talk about front line action, one of the hardest lessons I had to learn in basic training was that I wasn't raised to be a fighter. I never sought out violence. I don't like inflicting pain. Most of all, I never understood how somebody can think that beating the shit out of another person is "fun." My brain just never worked like that. Sure, I played football and took a shot at wrestling, but there was something different about a real fight. Something that bothered me deep down. All throughout Basic, I had gone through the motions, learned all the moves, and choked out my fair share of opponents thanks to my own size and strength. But never once did I enjoy it. Never once did I look forward to it. Even when I was fighting Sergeant High, some deeply rooted restraint refused to give in to the act of violence.

But something inside of me cracked that day. It broke right in the middle of my heart. I could feel the pop. The extra surge of adrenaline. The rough timing in my breath. When I got back on my feet I went balls-to-the-wall on that asshole. I gave him everything I goddamn had until I had nothing left. He beat the living shit out of me. Every minute of it I was lost in a blackout rage. Every time I landed a solid hit or got the upper hand for the slightest moment, I did my best to break his fucking neck. When it was over, I could barely stand on my own two feet.

I hated every minute of my life with Sergeant High, but he was teaching me something I could have never learned on my own. He was teaching me how to turn off my emotions and become a disciple of violence. To "flip a switch" and be ready to fight. To let rage consume my entire being, until I enjoyed inflicting pain. I had to want to hurt him like he wanted to hurt me. Until then, I had reacted to his attacks. I had fought back when he struck first. I had put up a defense for as long as I could. But that wasn't good enough to win. If I wanted to win, I had to be ready and waiting for him to kick down that door. I had to abandon all the civility that had been programmed into my head by society and give myself completely to all the rage that I could muster. I had to set the conditions and attack him first. And once that happened, my days as a "fish" were numbered. It was only then that my welcome into the unit was complete.

Eventually, there were enough new Privates rolling in that I became one among many. Together we realized that all we had to do to avoid special treatment was fuck up less than anybody else. For some of us, that was an easy task. For others, not so much. Most of all, it was made clear to all of us that we had a job to do and a bunch of newborn privates isn't a good enough reason to gum up the works.

A few weeks after my arrival, one of our squad's team leaders was swapped out with one of the machine gun team leaders who had served in Iraq, a man by the name of Sergeant Lilly. The explanation I got was that he'd moved over to get some time in a standard "line" squad, because in the Infantry every month we spent "off the line" counted for jack if we wanted to get promoted. Sergeant Lilly had been a team leader for quite a while, but the only way he was going to get promoted was if he was leading a real four-person fire team. Thankfully, he turned out to be exactly what we were missing.

Don't get me wrong, Sergeant High made plenty of headway hammering in the mindsets, skills and discipline necessary to be a grunt. But when it came time for a calm and collected mentor, that was where Sergeant Lilly staked his claim. I learned pretty much everything I needed to know about moving, fighting, and killing from Sergeant High. It was Sergeant Lilly who picked me up when I was down and taught me how to soldier. That isn't to say he wouldn't smoke the shit out of us just the same for falling out of line. Those two guys were like the yin and yang of industrialized violence, and our squad leader, Staff Sergeant Hailestock, was the glue that brought it all together. Back then, there wasn't a single squad I'd rather be a part of than 2nd Squad, in 1st Platoon.

In a few more months, the ongoing stream of new recruits got so big that a reshuffling of the roommates was in order. At first I had been paired with a guy named Waite, who was regarded as one of the "universal soldiers" in our platoon. That worked out well enough, with the two of us egging each other on to greatness, until some nineteen year old fuckwad got piss-drunk and kissed a light-pole with his car at ninety miles an hour. The very next day, every officer at Ft. Lewis was on a crusade to reel in the "pandemic" of under age drinking, and at the top of the list of "action items" was the segregation of age groups in the barracks.

Coincidentally, that was the same weekend Waite stocked up on a 24 rack of beer.

"What the fuck?!" Sergeant High was furious when he found out about my age. "You're fuckin' seventeen?!"

"Roger, Sarn't."

"But what the fuck?! What are you even doing here? Shouldn't you be in diapers or something?"

I laughed. "Probably, Sarn't."

"Man, fuck!" He pounded his fist into the cinder-block wall. "Here I've got my two strongest guys quarantined in a room n'shit, and you go fuck it up by bein' under age! Seriously?! Seventeen?!"

He stopped, sighed, and turned to look at my roommate.

"Waite, how old are you?"

"21, Sergeant."

"Alright." Our team leader took a deep breath and tried to stifle his growing rage, but Sergeant High was never one to be calm and collected. "It looks like you two are changing rooms."

The news was a shock to me. I didn't even know that's why he was there until he asked about my age. I just thought we were musing about some retard with a drinking problem.

"Come on, Sarn't!" Waite wasn't happy about it either. "I can move the beer into a different room! It's not that big of a deal!"

"Yeah, I know. But this one's from higher. I can't afford to have this shit coming back to bite me in the ass down the line." He turned his head out the door and shouted down the hallway.

"Peterson!"

"Yeah?!" A smarmy voice cried back.

"Get the fuck in here!"

Peterson jumped to his feet and ran down the hall, weaseling into the room to join Waite and me in a line.

"How old are you, Peterson?"

"Twenty, Sergeant."

Sergeant High clenched his teeth.

"Alright. That'll have to work. Say hello to your new roommate, Ludwig. Waite, you're moving in with Hooch."

When he dropped the line, it caught us all off-guard. Waite was pissed, I was pissed, Peterson was dumbfounded, and Sergeant High looked like he was going to "skull fuck a baby" – as he liked to put it. Hooch wasn't exactly the most popular soldier in our Platoon, and the first time I met Peterson, Sergeant High made me do a hundred push-ups on account of some registration fuck-up with his car. Despite our overall dissatisfaction with the call, however, the changes were made and Peterson settled into my room. After that, we got on with life, and to my surprise he turned out to be an awesome roommate. Better yet, he became my new best friend. A few days later I knew him as "Ian" and he knew me as "Konrad" – which, in the military, is the highest badge of honor.

Best of all, he was a fellow Californian.

"I knew you were cool for a reason," he laughed. "It's like a fucking super-power, you know? Californians can always tell if somebody else is from California."

That's how we got to know Gonzo, another private who had shown up with the rest of us.

"I swear to God he's from California," Ian nodded.

"Where at?" I asked.

"Down by you, in L.A."

When we confronted Gonzo, he confirmed the suspicion and we moved on to finding our next target.

"Did you guys know that First Sergeant Williams is from California too?" He asked.

"No way!" Ian said.

"I don't know," I said. "He's got that thing to him, you know? I can totally see it."

The next time we cleaned our room for an inspection, we hung a large California flag over Ian's bed and confronted First Sergeant Williams who cheerfully admitted he was from our state.

"The Sergeant Major's gonna' love that shit." He pointed at the flag.

Just a few minutes later, our Command Sergeant Major walked in to inspect our room with a similar reaction.

"Hey, are you guys from California?" He pointed at the flag.

"Roger, Sergeant Major!" We both shouted at the same time.

"Good shit! So am I! Where are you from?"

"Los Angeles, Sergeant Major!" I said.

"Mendocino, Sergeant Major!" Ian said.

"Mendocino? Hey I've been up there! That's badass, dude!"

He didn't even check the room to see if it was clean. We had a quick chat about how awesome it was growing up in California and he moved on to hassle our neighbors.

"Carry on, dudes!" He threw up his hand.

"Roger that, Sergeant Major!" We both shouted.

The next month, Ian turned 21. It turned out that nobody bothered looking at a calendar when he told them about his age. Then again, nobody really cared about that anymore anyway. Like most middle management crusades, the crisis of underage drinking was long forgotten. By then our commanders were back to preaching about safe sex and the inherent dangers of payday loans. Besides Ian's birthday, the most eventful thing that week was meeting a guy named Heithold. He walked right into our room like he'd known us for years. Without asking or introduction, he just plopped down on my bed and asked a simple question.

"Hey, what's up?"

It was the first time I had ever seen the guy and he was up in my space before I knew what happened. I must've called him by his last name all but twice before he felt obliged to make a correction:

"You know what? Just go ahead call me Bryce."

Ian mocked him with a scoff. "Okay... *Bryce.*"

"Yeah, '*Specialist Heithold*' is my slave name," he continued.

"So, what?" I asked him. "Is Bryce your first name?"

"No, just... Call me Bryce. Please."

"Alright."

"So you guys don't mind if I hang out in here, do you? My roommate literally smells like dog shit and I can't stand to be in my own room. I don't even know how he does it."

"Sure," I said with a laugh. "Come over any time."

I wasn't lying when I said it. I just didn't know he would stick around for the duration. Every day after that his visitations became a routine. Whenever there was some downtime, he'd come in and bullshit around for hours. When we got off work, he wouldn't bother going "home." Eventually, the three of us became a trio. To this day, I consider them my closest friends in the world. Together we became inseparable.

That didn't go unnoticed by our leaders, who insisted that I stay away from the "likes" of "those types." To be frank, Ian and Bryce didn't give a flying fuck about service or promotion. Ian was there because he was bored, and Bryce had originally signed up for an entirely different specialty. After catching his Sergeant Major in a scandal, however, Bryce was quietly, forcefully, and illegally "re-classed" into the Infantry without a say or defense. Naturally, that kind of run-in with a corrupt bureaucracy can leave a sour taste in one's ideologies and Bryce made it clear to our leaders that he wasn't in "the mood" for their "shit."

As for me, that ideology was still thick, pure, and pumping through every inch of my veins. The way I saw it, my friendship with the two of them was a purely personal matter, but to Sergeant High I might as well have been peddling heroin out of the back of a shady van. One day he brought me down to the platoon command post to have a chat with our acting platoon sergeant, Staff Sergeant Dukes. Before Sergeant High brought me in, I could hear their conversation from out in the hall.

"What's the big deal?" Staff Sergeant Dukes asked.

Sergeant High did his best to keep his cool. "He's spending all his free time hangin' out with that Peterson motherfucker and their little butt-buddy, Heithold!"

"Isn't Peterson his roommate?"

"Yeah, but that doesn't mean they've gotta' be goin' out together and shit! I only put him there because the two of them were underage!"

"So what's the big deal?"

"These motherfuckers are bad news! They're total shit-bags! I don't want them fuckin' with one of my best guys!"

There was a short silence before Staff Sergeant Dukes made his decision. "Alright, bring him in."

The scolding I got was far less than I expected — more of an act of solidarity than anything else. But in the end, it amounted to little more than a "don't fall in with the wrong crowd" kind of speech. To my credit, I hadn't done anything wrong — but to Sergeant High, the emphasis was on "yet." In either case, it was made clear that I had no business "hanging out" with either Ian or Bryce during the workday, unless it was in an official capacity and mission-essential. More importantly, I realized something that day which would stick with me for a long time to come – and it had very little to do with either Ian or Bryce.

Those of us who had just shown up? We were the young guns who had been raised on a war. For various reasons, we waited four or five years before joining up to be all that we could be. It was the team leaders like Sergeant High, who signed up as soon as the war started. For them, soldiering was a crusade with an ideology and a conflict. There wasn't a single moment in their careers that America wasn't at war. They had made an act of conscious will to serve their country as soon as they were needed. Yet for all the platoon sergeants and higher, the Army was just a way of life. It was an institution that had been with them for a long, long time. And it was only in this latest chunk of their career that America had been at war.

I don't imagine Sergeant Dukes gave a single shit about some deadbeat friends of mine, but for Sergeant High it was a big deal. He was afraid they'd poison me with their apathy and strip me of my resolve. But the thing was that I had bought in to the life much too hard to be corrupted that easily. If I was going to give up on the system, it was going to take a lot more than the likes of Bryce or Ian to turn me. And after I was set free from my short ass-chewing, I went right back to playing video games with my friends. The next morning I'd wake up as I had done every day before, and bust my ass on the morning work out. I'd head out to the range with the platoon and give it everything I had. Why? Because I *believed*. And nothing was going to change that.

By the end of summer, everything I'd looked forward to since my first day in the Army flew right out the window. With little warning, our entire Brigade was renamed and reflagged with a completely different title, for a completely different cause. Our new mission was to fly off to Europe and spend four years showing our allies in NATO what a Stryker can do. Within the span of a single ceremony, nearly 700 men in 1-5th INF became the "1st Squadron" of the "2nd Stryker Cavalry Regiment." As for the Bravo Company "Deathmasters," we were now the "Bulls." As it turned out, some orders from the Pentagon had drifted their way down the chain of command selecting our entire Brigade to conduct a flashy show-and-tell operation off in Europe.

According to NATO regulations, each participating nation of the alliance is required to field any new technology in a series of joint training operations within a year of its development. As for the Stryker, it had not only been developed but actually employed in real-world combat before the rest of our allies could take a look. Now it was a well-known asset in the field of urban combat and the joint chiefs wanted the best of the best to be the ones to show it off. Who better than a well-known brigade that had just come back from one of the hardest tours of the war?

As far as I was concerned, every misguided aspiration of mine to become the next incarnate version of Audie Murphy died as soon as I found out what we were in for. I knew exactly what it really was: a circle jerk for some high level generals where they could shake each other's hands and pin more stars on their lapels. With a job like that, getting shipped out to the sandbox was pipe dream, at best.

After barely a year in the military I had already noticed that hypnotizing higher-ups with shiny antics, political posturing, and flashy lingo was as good as doctrine. Every once in a while, with the wrong commander, it ranked even higher than keeping good men alive. This was a brigade level operation of international pomp and circumstance. Nothing in the world was going to pull us off that detail. Least of all another chance to fight and die in the desert.

From the looks of it, I was going to be stuck in Bavaria for the rest of my short-lived career. My only hope was that I could "re-up" when it was all over. But then I'd be one of those bastards in a Tactical Operations Center somewhere, with all the rank of a man who had served and none of the experience that you earn "down range." If all that wasn't enough to suck the pride out of my very bones, our new name hit a low blow to the esprit de corps across the unit.

I mean, *Cavalry?*

We were the Infantry, not some slapdash Cavalry unit. That's a rivalry that dates back literally thousands of years, to the first time in human history some pompous douchebag jumped on a shiny horse to go ride into combat in the middle of a giant battle, only to run away later while the boots pressed on.

"The 2nd Stryker what?!" I protested.

I was up in arms at the news. I thought it was some kind of fake-out, or one of those practical jokes you learn about when you get punked – like grid-squares, headlight fluid, and elbow grease. Out of the entire brigade, only one part of a single battalion was even a cavalry to begin with.

"We're the 2nd Stryker Cavalry Regiment." Sergeant Dukes tried to get back to his briefing.

"Yeah, but we're not Cav', Sarn't. We're the Infantry." I looked at him like he was killing my cat.

"Yeah. I know, Ludwig. But we're called the '2nd Stryker Cavalry Regiment' now."

"Wow, this is bullshit." Ian was on my side.

"What about our flag?" I pressed on. "Are we keeping the crossed rifles? I mean, this is still an infantry unit... Right, Sarn't?"

"Yes, we're still an infantry unit."

"So what's with the name?"

It was a big deal to me, though apparently not so much to him. I suppose after a decade and a half in the service, you get used to these things.

"I don't know, Ludwig. It's just a fucking name. It's the same goddamned unit as yesterday so shut the hell up."

Yeah, but it was *Cav'*. It couldn't get worse than *Cav'*.

For the sake of the feud, I teamed up with Ian that weekend to find a cowboy accessories store in Tacoma. We beelined to the "insignia and hats" section and got our hands on some props. By the time we got back to our rooms, it was a quick task to assemble our very own pseudo windswept cowboy hats, complete with "2nd Cavalry" insignia stabbed right through the brim. It looked just as ridiculous as it sounds, especially on two young men who were running around town in street clothes and slippers. We made an ass of everything Cav'. We ran through stores and fast food joints and stood in the heart of society to shout things like "Cav ho!" and "Little Big Horn!" Hell, it was a wonder we didn't get arrested and brought up on charges for the show. That was our last hoorah in America – and it didn't last for long.

In just a few weeks time they packed us up and shipped us off to Nuremberg, where we would serve out the rest of our careers as proud members of "Bull Company," in the "1st Squadron" of the "2nd Stryker Cavalry Regiment."

Nothing was ever the same after that.

We spent a year in Germany. It was a year of garrison duties. Of early mornings, bad food and long foot-marches. We mastered the idolized flag ceremony. We memorized hollow chants of motivation. Yes, they were the very same ones you see in the background of a war movie. And yes it gets hard to think up and memorize a new one every week. But each month we embarked on another string of field problems and every day it was the same old news. We'd get up at 05:00 for a room inspection. By 06:00 we were out the door and waiting in the freezing cold for a formation that wouldn't start for another thirty minutes. We'd do an hour and a half of physical training until chow. Finally, when our bodies were bathed, rooms cleaned, and uniforms donned, the day began.

We cleaned floors and scrubbed walls. We wiped down windows and desks. We conducted inventories on gear that'd been checked a day or two before. When there was nothing left to clean, we sat around in the open awaiting another random task. Usually that just meant we'd clean it all again for the sake of looking busy.

On the upside, our training regimen was anything but routine. In the months that had passed, the 2nd Stryker Cavalry Regiment built a solid reputation within NATO. For a while, it seemed like every time we went out into the field for maneuvers we got kudos from on high. Better yet, Bull Company and the rest of 1st Squadron pulled ahead of the pack with a pleasant shine. The more we trained, the more they paired us up with a new high-speed unit from another allied country who were eager to have their guys along for the ride.

It wasn't magic. It was hard work, and we had a solid set of sergeants to guide the way. As I quickly came to relish, nearly every leader in Bull Company was a combat veteran. Most of our squad leaders and platoon sergeants had even served on the line for two or three deployments in a row. When one of the squad leaders in our platoon was selected for Special Forces, his replacement turned out to be a former Ranger School Instructor by the name of Staff Sergeant Benjamin.

Sergeant Benjamin wasn't just a Ranger, he was also an ex-body builder. In a past life he would've been referred to as a giant who could crush your skull between his fingers. His bicep was about as big around as my neck and he was even taller than me. But all that meant was that Sergeant Benjamin fit right in beside the rest of our company's leaders, with his own time clocked-in at war.

There were nearly three decades of direct combat experience between the twelve leaders of 1st Platoon. On average, they'd spent more time down range since the start of the war than back at home with their families. If you asked me, that was the biggest reason why we did so well in training. We never lacked a dose of wartime wisdom. Sometimes it seemed like everything we did could be linked back to a story of war and violence.

We trained urban combat tactics every day. We filed around in entry group 'stacks' and talked to each other with hand signals in lieu of spoken words. We broke off into teams and conducted high-stress drills in the middle of the night. Whenever there was a chance, we put live rounds in a target until every man among us was an expert marksman. When there wasn't any way to get out into the field, we'd study the craft of modern warfare between everyday chores and garrison details. It wasn't long before we could clear an objective without a single spoken word, and not long after that before we could do it in the dead of night.

It was across those rolling Bavarian hills and pines I became an expert infantryman — and that goes for every other cherry in Bull Company. That was the best training I could have ever had. And we had some of the best teachers in the world. After months of waiting and knowing that nothing would be coming over the horizon, I could feel the remnants of whatever morale I had left wearing down into shreds.

I couldn't help but think that I'd never get my shot at the war — at least not with these guys. If I wasn't going off to war, why had I signed up for the military in the first place? I had it in writing that I'd be getting shot at within a year, but a year later I was freezing my ass off in the snow with a couple of "hooah's" from the British Army. If we ever got called up to take a crack at the Middle East, chances were good that there'd be nothing left for us to fight.

From what I had seen on TV, the war in Afghanistan was allegedly down to its final days. The going theory at the time was that our efforts had brought the Taliban to its knees, and everything else had been a waste of money and effort. From the look of things, all we had left to do was pull our troops out of the mess and go home. If you were in uniform back then, a trip to Afghanistan was essentially seen as a second-rate tour in the Suck. To us, the "real" action was in Iraq. Ironically, public outcry to end that war was just as strong for the opposite reason.

By the end of 2006, the situation in Iraq had spiraled into a full-blown civil war. Over the course of the winter months, a new record of civilian deaths had been reached. Since the Spring Fighting of 2004, car bombs had revealed themselves to be the favored method of political discourse. Far from playing a role as outside observers to these discussions, Coalition troops were right there in the middle of it all. The number of killed and wounded had risen steadily throughout the year, despite the obvious progress of ratifying a new constitution, establishing a permanent government, and electing public figures into democratic office.

According to the majority of opinions and editorials I had seen, Iraq was little more than a gaffe. It was a quagmire of unrivaled proportion. Whatever good had been accomplished was already lost, and there was nothing we coud do now but walk away and call it quits. I had been told repeatedly by every veteran I had met not to trust what I saw on the news, but I still knew that public opinion had the power to end both wars if enough people changed their minds about the cause. In fact, I wouldn't have been surprised at all to see us out of the country by the end of the year. It was a notion that tore me right down the middle with dismay. Sure, I would've been happy to see peace, but I wasn't happy at all about the prospect of defeat. It was contrary to one of the most fundamental rules I had learned as a child:

Don't start a fight you can't finish.

But that was just part of my frustration. The biggest factor in my waning motivation was that I had been stuck in a bogus position, handling the radios for our lieutenant. The job wasn't all that bad, and in real terms I had little reason to complain, but that was exactly what I had joined the Infantry to avoid.

A week after arriving in Germany, my squad leader pulled me aside to let me know about the upcoming change in my assignment.

"Hey, Ludwig," he said. "We're losing you to the platoon leader."

The words came out of his mouth boiling with empathy and frustration. It was obvious that he had just gone toe-to-toe with whoever came up with the order and lost.

"What?" I balked.

"Yeah. They need a radio guy. You got picked for the job."

It took everything I had not to blurt out, "That's bullshit!" and storm into somebody's office to pick a fight. I busted my ass for eight months to get ahead and what I got in return was a handful of disappointment. I took a few breaths. I tried to remember that this guy had my back and I made a plea to his better senses.

"Come on, Sarn't..."

"I'm sorry man."

He stared back at me matter-of-factly. There was nothing we could do. Nothing anybody could do. Orders were orders, and these were mine.

"Are you fucking kidding me?!"

I didn't even notice the words slip out until it was too late to take them back. It was pure sympathy that he didn't bust my ass for the informality.

"Hey!" He barked. "I don't like it either but I can't help you, man. This one comes straight from the Platoon Sergeant. There's nothing I can do."

As soon as I heard that rank, I knew he was right. On the day we showed up in Germany, the Department of Defense decided to bump our acting platoon sergeant, Staff Sergeant Dukes, back down to a squad leader position and make room for somebody else with the proper rank to fill the role. I guess it wasn't good enough to have a Staff Sergeant in charge of a platoon in the highest-profile unit in Europe. The only problem was that our new platoon sergeant was sorely lacking in all the fundamental qualities of a leader — shortcomings that were clearly apparent in his overweight stature and overabundance of bite-size clichés.

In any case, I reported for my new assignment with all the discipline I could muster. With a blank face I knocked on the door to the platoon command post, entered the room, and snapped to parade rest in front of our platoon sergeant's desk. With a familiar scoff he sized me up and laid out the specifics of my new position.

From that day forward I would be the right hand man to our lieutenant. For the most part, that meant I'd be fixing radios, drawing map overlays for every mission, and wading through a mountain of paperwork to keep our platoon running smoothly. On the battlefield I'd be a brain-on-loan. In the office I'd be a personal assistant. My days would be filled with brewing coffee, loading encryption data into our radios, tracking serial numbers of all our expensive gear, writing down notes during each mission, and serving as the messenger for the leaders of our platoon. And when it was time to go to the range, I'd walk up the line, shoot my fair share of bullets, and get back to scanning the "net" for a call from Squadron Headquarters.

It was a full-access gig, he said. Part of the "big picture." According to him, the most important part of my job wasn't even in the field. It was to keep my eyes and ears open. To know everything about anything that was going on "upstairs." He told me it would be my job to keep us one step ahead of the game. In that respect, at least, he was right on the money. What I didn't believe for a second, however, was that getting stuck behind a radio would be the best thing that could happen to my military career.

"Do you know why I picked you?" He asked.

"Negative, Sarn't."

Calling on every motivational bone in his body, he spewed out a line that was made for a movie.

"I picked you because from what I hear you're quick, you're smart, you're not afraid to talk to officers, you're loud as hell, and you know your shit."

He let the words sink in. I made it clear with my body language that I wasn't convinced. After a few moments of silence he finally conceded the point and leaned forward to level with me "man-to-man."

"But more than any of that," he continued. "I picked you because you're a friggen' computer genius and that's like 99% of the job."

So that was it: I could type. It was a skill the Army forgot about when they threw together the enlistment aptitude exam, one that was mastered by my entire generation because of AOL Instant Messenger and IRC chatrooms. Now he had used it against me as an excuse to clear the spotlight, so some other unmotivated shit-bag could take my place on the line. To hell if I could smack a target dead center at over 300 yards; I could type. Who cared if I knew how to stabilize a casualty with no arms or legs and eviscerated intestines; I could type. And gods be damned if I could fit a fully-automatic, belt-fed grouping into the torso of a man on the far side of a football field — I could still type. Like all my buddies who become drivers because they could drive, or got stuck in the supply chain because they had legible handwriting, I got stuck as the platoon secretary because I knew how to use a computer.

So much for "Be all that you can be."

A few months later, our old platoon leader finished the end of his rotation and I found myself hoping that I'd get released from my term on the radios and put back on the line. But when another officer rolled in and took his place, my assignment was extended to an indefinite term. Aside from the company communications clerk, I was the only "radio guy" in Bull Company with a full tenure and no hope of getting fired.

"Listen," our platoon sergeant tried to smooth it all over when the official order was given. "I know you think it sucks, but this is bigger than you. This guy's never run a platoon before and he's got no idea how it's done. If I switched you out now, we'd have two little newbies calling the shots — one jacked up radio guy and a cherry-ass platoon leader. I can't have that. You're sticking around until he's on his feet. Until he's broken in. Period."

At least he had a decent point. To be fair, the job didn't come without its own special list of perks. I was getting pretty good at sifting my way around the hierarchy and I had plenty of friends in important places. Not only did I know more than the average Joe about what was going on in the boardrooms of our commanders, I had freedom – and freedom was a luxury that I enjoyed. In any case, that's how I got to know our new platoon leader, Lieutenant Savage. It took no time at all for us to become a tight-knit team. Far more telling was that I actually started liking my tenure on the radio.

At the end of the day, I really did learn more about leadership, planning and operations by working with Lieutenant Savage than I could've ever picked up with a machine-gun or a scope. He knew all the military theory you could imagine and he was committed to being the best leader that he could possibly be. Whatever he may have lacked in experience could easily be harvested from our squad leaders, with whom I ended up spending the majority of my time on account of my elevated position. By the end of Lieutenant Savage's so-called "break-in" period, I was one of the most senior Radio Operators in the company. I knew all the tricks, I'd been to all the schools, and I was synced up tight with our new platoon leader. Yet in the back of my mind I still couldn't shake the notion that all of this was for nothing. All those months of "playing Army" would end up being all I'd have to show for five years of military service. The closest I'd ever come to combat was on the make-pretend battlefield of Bavaria.

In due time I was called back into our platoon sergeant's office to hear for myself that I'd be stuck on the radios for as long as he could swing it. After that I just had to accept that it would be a cold day in Hell before I'd ever get back to my old squad. From that point on, I was biding my time for something else to come along. I was just punching the clock until the days were up. Sooner or later I'd be free of my military service, and I vowed to myself that on that day I would never look back.

By the end of the year, Sergeant High's worst nightmare finally came true. I gave up. I tapped out. I let my uniform go slack and I shammed out of duty. But it wasn't because of Ian and Bryce that I finally caved in; It was because I had done everything I could to serve my country and got nothing in return. And the more I thought about it, the more it seemed silly of me to have expected anything else in the first place. After all, I had my chance to sign up for some cushy job in the Pentagon. So to hell with my signing bonus — the only way I was going to see a fight was if I started one at a bar.

- Chapter Three -
To The Gates Of Babylon

A year into my enlistment, the situation in Iraq had gotten so bad that little hope remained for a successful occupation of the country. In the middle of a global cry for a withdrawal, President George W. Bush opened 2007 with an executive order for more than 20,000 soldiers to pack up and ship off to Iraq. This was in addition to the 140,000 who were already there. It was the antithesis of the American will. It was the opposite of whittling down the numbers. As if it wasn't enough to start a war, now he had to rally the battle cry after five long years of fruitless struggle and kick off a desperate push to the finish line — at least, that's how it was explained on the news.

Within a few weeks of the announcement, and still months before the first new units would set foot in the country, media outlets on both sides of the line dug in, firmly establishing their stance on the surge. And that stance, no matter what, was to label it a failure. What nobody heard about were the underlying justifications, or why the surge was the only option on a street-by-street basis.

That far into the war, despite hundreds of thousands of soldiers already devoted to the cause, Coalition forces barely controlled half of the country. And it had been like that for years. After the ceasefires with al-Qaeda and the Jaish al-Mahdi in 2005, a large portion of the country was still under the control of various militias and criminal organizations.

Instead of spreading themselves out across a massive country with over 30 million inhabitants, the Coalition forces turned inward to focus on those areas with the most critical roles: areas of high commerce and political function.

The "Green Zone" (also known as the "International Zone," or "IZ") in Baghdad was a perfect example of one of those places. When the war began, coalition forces walled in a huge chunk of the city with a barricade and security grid around the Iraqi equivalent of Washington D.C. Inside that wall, American and Iraqi civilians with positions of authority over the entire country drew up plans for the future. Meanwhile the reporters of the world compiled briefs for the nightly news over peanuts back at the hotel bar — far away from any real danger from the war.

It was inside of that wall that most of the backdrops were framed behind forty-second clips of current events, pulled right off the daily reports of "serious incidents" without ever leaving "the wire." Whenever some reporter was brave enough to face that outside world, it was typically well within the boundaries of American control, right in the heart of Baghdad where actual "fighting" had been more-or-less unheard of for years.

Of course, where the voids of authority left gaps in the state, the rise of criminal organizations was inevitable. The Jaish al-Mahdi was the best example of that ascent to power. They had started as a neighborhood watch in Sadr City to secure the town after the fall of Saddam and had quickly grown into the strong-arm of Muktada al-Sadr's very own paramilitary mob. After the end of the spring fighting in 2004, they remained a well-organized force with strong numbers in every city they seized. In fact, the ceasefire had only blessed them with credibility. In the years that followed they grew into a full-blown army, operating with a more-or-less free hand. After five years, they numbered in the hundreds of thousands, most of whom lived and worked within the confines of Sadr City and its surrounding neighborhoods.

Baghdad, as with many other regions of Iraq, was split right down the middle between "us" and "them." All we'd done was cordon off secluded little sections of the city. The rest had been left to ruthless criminals like the Jaish al-Mahdi. We drew a line past which no soldier would tread, and they laid claim on whoever lived on the far side of that line. Even while the very heart of their dominion was right across the Tigris from our own world famous installations, they might as well have been living in another country.

By then, it was a well circulated fact among the front line troops of Baghdad that the total number of militia fighters operating within the Jaish al-Mahdi's half of the capital was estimated to outnumber the multi-national occupation force by the thousands. That figure, however, didn't even do justice to the overwhelming odds they really faced. In 2006, the total number of American soldiers stationed in Baghdad barely topped 13,000 troops, with little more than 10,000 poorly trained Iraqi soldiers loyal to the cause and fighting alongside them. What's more, the tiniest minority of both figures were ground-pounding, war waging grunts who actually lived and fought outside of the wire. The rest lived back in the rear, far way from the front lines.

For years the Jaish al-Mahdi and various other criminal organizations had been free to terrorize the people of Iraq into submission, using corrupt politicians to protect their interests in government while spiritual leaders in mosques across the city preached a message of hate and revenge. On the streets, their power was reinforced by a thick atmosphere of apathy and fear, while the leaders of al-Sadr's movement raked in millions of dollars and all the power they could grab. As long as that continued, the nation could never be free, so the goal of the surge was to cross into those uncontrolled areas and liberate the millions of people who lived in a lawless world of murder and extortion. Our goal was to push back into territories that had been off-limits for years, and put an end to the corruption that had been eating the country alive.

What stood out the most to those of us in uniform, however, wasn't even the fact that President Bush had increased the number of soldiers getting shipped off to war. It was that he had extended the duration of an Army deployment by leaps and bounds. Now, instead of spending a twelve-month tour overseas, soldiers were ordered to pull fifteen-month rotations in the sandbox. That's a year and some change in the Suck. Five whole fiscal quarters of combat. More than twice as long as a seven-month deployment with the Navy or the Marines and almost four times longer than that of the Air Force.

Overnight, the entire Army was put on edge. It might as well have been a certified guarantee that every "limp-dick" in the service was about to get his shot at the Shit. For the first time since we arrived, I caught myself thinking that something might have actually come along that really was big enough to blow our entire mission in Europe. Something big enough to rock the boat on the entire theater of war. Something that would give me my chance to pound some dirt in the Suck. For a few months, there was nothing on the wire. Not until some private heard the news for himself and spilled the beans on the whole thing. According to the rumors, our unit was next on the list for a rapid deployment to Iraq. And best of all, we were in for a proper fight.

As the legend goes, just a few short months into setting up for the troop surge, General Petraeus himself had requested our unit by name. Apparently, our past reputation as the former 1st Stryker Brigade Combat Team had made a dent on the collective memory of the Pentagon, and it was decided that a full brigade of mounted infantrymen would be essential in the months to come. Whether that's really the case it's hard to say, since I didn't have the clearance to find out for myself. But whatever led to the sudden change in plans, those orders were substantial enough to override an entire pan-national, long-term training operation that was originally intended to be the climactic forte of our entire Regiment's mission in Europe — and at that, I took the rumor at face value and drove on.

For the first time in years, I felt a fire under my ass. All of a sudden the training and war games were real again. It didn't matter if I'd be running the radios; we were finally going to war. It was in the cards. It was in the bag. Once everybody's "dwell time" was up in just a few short months, we'd be shipping out to kick some ass. Simple as that. Just like I wanted. All we were missing were the details. For all the talk, nobody really knew what was going on behind the closed doors of the men in charge. We were just drawing lines between the random chunks of information that could be scraped together in transit from point-to-point.

Still, there's a private in every office, and you can always count on the "Joe Network" to pull through with the facts.

We teamed up as a squadron and tuned in our ears to listen. After a while, the truth was known in full. More than one credible source put us landing in Kuwait by the end of the year. Damn near all of them said we'd be heading off to Iraq when we got there, which meant that we were in good shape to see some shit. When I met up with one of my buddies who was stuck on a detail in the Regimental Headquarters, he told me everything I wanted to hear about the documents they were shredding, and the passing phrases overheard in the latrine.

"That's not even the good part," he said. "The word going around is that we've got a special mission."

"Yeah? What's that?" I egged him on.

"No idea. That one is still tied up with the Colonel. All I know for sure is that we're going to Baghdad, that we've got a special mission, and whatever that is, it'll be sick as hell."

When the officers caught wind of what we were up to, they did everything they could to shut us down. That was all the confirmation we needed. We could ask them anything in the world but if we so much as barked about Baghdad and some special orders from Petraeus, they'd run our ass into a solid stone wall of denial.

"We're not going anywhere," they'd say. "Stop asking."

It was the party line. They said it again and again. No matter how we weaseled in the questions, they'd shut us down when we got too close to the truth. After a few weeks of dealing with the rumors, the commander finally brought us all together so he could put our inquisition to rest.

"Listen," he said. "I know that there are all kinds of rumors going around about us going to Iraq. There's no point in pretending like you haven't heard it by now. Well, you're going to hear it from me: We're not going anywhere. Got it? There's nothing on the blotter. Nothing is coming down the chain. I can't even imagine a single reason why anybody would think there is. So the rumors stop here.

"If I hear so much as another word about some non-existent deployment, about General Petraeus asking for us to go on some special mission, or about us being boots-on-the-ground by August, there will be repercussions. That's it. From this point forward, I don't want to hear a single word. Stop acting like a bunch of teenage girls and get back to work. We've got a major training op coming up, and we need everybody's head in the game."

That was it. It was the golden ticket. The nail in the coffin. He might as well have spelled it out with a Lite-Brite. Of all the rumors going around, there was only one that made it into his concession. There was only one that stuck his ass on a silver platter if it got out. He didn't even realize what we were looking for, and after his speech there wasn't a single doubt in my mind.

We were finally going to war.

Everybody else was quick to come to the same conclusion, but we all stayed quiet and whispered in the shadows. Nobody was excited to become an example of his wrath. After months of loading up boxes, inventorying equipment, filling out leave forms, and running through weeks of training in the woods, the powers that be finally deemed it time to let us in on the big secret. At the closeout formation of an early morning four-mile run, the Colonel gathered our whole squadron together to spread the word.

Most of it we already knew, but this time it was official: the squadron was breaking off from the Regiment and heading to eastern Baghdad for a high-profile mission. What we hadn't pieced together ourselves were the mission specifics. Squadron Headquarters and Apache Company were going to be assigned to their own battle space in an active neighborhood of eastern Baghdad, while Bull and Comanche Companies were specially selected to hold the line on the western flank of a place called Sadr City. After going over the general play-by-play of what to expect from the deployment and how the squadron would be laid out across the capital, we broke into smaller groups so our own company commanders could give us a tighter breakdown of the mission. For Bull Company, that secondary briefing unveiled a whole different story all together.

"I'm telling you right now, this place isn't pretty."

Our company commander glared at us with his lips tightened and fist in a knot. He was wearing his "I'm dead serious and you better listen" face – and we knew it well. He strung out a pause between the critical points to glue down our attention and get the nature of the thing across.

"As you heard from the Colonel, the 82nd Airborne has had a hell of a time securing the eastern half of the city. They're running into some fierce resistance by a well-trained militia called the Jaish al-Mahdi. The 'JAM,' as we also know them, is operating out of their stronghold in Sadr City, and nobody's been able to bust them out.

"Now, some of you may have heard about the place – others, maybe not. I know the Colonel skimmed over it pretty quick, so I'm going to lay it out for you in detail: Sadr City is the real deal. In the last five years, the Jaish al-Mahdi has rigged it from top to bottom with roadside bombs and special weapons engagement areas. They are well organized and out for a fight. That's our new home, men. Sadr City."

Sadr City.

I had heard about it in a headline somewhere and now I was going there to see it for myself. I was going to beat the streets with the men to my right and left and finally take part in the making of history. While I was taken aback by the sudden change of pace and detail, our company commander carried on with his briefing.

"As soon as we hit Baghdad," he looked around at everybody there, "Bull Company will be taking over as the conventional, high-impact raid element into the city. That means we'll be doing hardcore snatch-and-grab raids on high value targets and intelligence opportunities as they present themselves. It's an around-the-clock mission, men. Trust me, it's not going to be a walk in the park. We're talking real, hardcore shit. To give you an idea of what I mean, the only other group of people who have anything to do with this place is a collection of Special Forces, Ranger, and Delta units called 'Taskforce 17' – and I'm not even allowed to tell you anything more about them.

"The point is this: there are more than two million people living in that city – and none of them are on our side. The whole place is bad news. It's still too active to build a legitimate forward operating base there, so the 82nd Airborne had to set up their own combat outposts on the front lines of the conflict.

"I'm talking old-school, 'kick in the door and call it home' kind of places, men. From what I've been told, every one of them gets a daily dose of indirect fire, small arms contact, and random sniper engagements. In addition to these regular attacks, they also have daily run-ins with roadside bombs and ambush positions along every major route in the area – mostly on a route called 'Grizzlies,' which to my knowledge has been off-limits to Coalition Forces since the fighting began."

Every one of us listened closely as he described the nuts-and-bolts of our mission. Back then, Sadr City was the darkest neck of the woods. Nobody patrolled there. Nobody drove through there. Nobody even cleared the surrounding routes. And most of all, nobody ever ventured into it unless they had a damn good reason to be there. It was a stain on the map of Baghdad. A massive urban slum. It was a checkerboard of shitty avenues and bad-times, east of the Tigris and far away from the comfort of America's mighty Forward Operating Bases and Logistical Supply Areas in Iraq. For most people it was just a myth, but for those of us standing there in Bull Company, it was likely to be the last place many of us would ever see.

As for the Jaish al-Mahdi, they truly were a force to be reckoned with. Not only did they command thousands of zealous foot soldiers, but they had built up a limitless arsenal of weapons to fight us with. I'm not just talking about the typical stores of AK-47's, Dragunov sniper rifles, and older model Rocket Propelled Grenades – or RPGs. The JAM had special-ordered a unique laundry list of modern weaponry to hit us where it hurt. On that list were state-of-the-art RPG-29's, which are specially designed warheads capable of blasting through the armor of any modern battle tank. There were Iranian made 12.7 mm DShK heavy machine guns, which are older model Russian anti-aircraft guns placed in strategic overwatch locations on rooftops and balconies so they could hammer down on unsuspecting victims. Every once in a while, the militia would hit a passing convoy with semi-automatic .50 cal sniper rifles, using armor-piercing rounds to punch through our ballistic glass and kill the man sitting on the other side. Somewhere in the heart of the city was at least one ZPU-4 – a quad-barrel, fully-automatic 14.5 mm anti-aircraft cannon which had been acquired during the invasion. According to legend and a growing number of battle damage assessments, that thing reared its head every once in a while to ward off nearby Blackhawks and catch the occasional Apache by surprise. But last on the list, and by far the most feared, was an endless minefield of Explosive Form Penetrators called "EFPs." Those are a special kind of roadside bomb that flash-melts a liquid stream of molten copper and hurtles it off at three times the speed of sound to slice through whatever it finds and kill whoever is standing in the way.

All of that meant one thing: as soon as we crossed into their realm, we played the game by their rules. For starters, there were no airborne medivacs, because any attempt would be shot down well before one could land. In addition, there would never be an opportunity for a ground-level reconnaissance or first-hand description of what we'd find on-target because nobody could go in ahead of time to scope it out. Exfiltration routes and infiltration routes would have to be different and ever-changing. We'd have to come up with tactics and maneuvers on the spot. And every time we went into that city, we'd have to fit a massive margin of error into a twenty-minute deadline. If anything went wrong, there would be no back-up call. The closest thing we'd have to a recovery unit was a nearby battalion of Humvees, which had never set foot on the far side of the red-line. So even if they could get out to us, it was likely by that time that there wouldn't be very much to do besides pack up a bunch of body-bags and ship us home in little pieces.

That was what we were up against: an entire city that was out for blood. Over two million people living in close-quarters with an unlimited arsenal of lethal force. They were the world's largest and most disciplined militia, pitched against a single squadron of about 700 American soldiers. As for us, when the going got tough, we'd have little more to our name than some high-speed light-armored vehicles and outdated maps of the city.

"The point is," he continued. "This isn't going to be your average deployment. We're not going to be dicking around at some FOB and running missions whenever we feel like it. We're going to be on the ground, in the streets, and doing high-profile shit. We earned this mission, men — and we're going to follow through with it."

I had waited two long years for my shot at the war. I studied and trained with the best of them. I gave the Army every ounce of motivation until there was nothing left for me to give. Now I was finally heading to the front lines of some serious shit. The only question was if I was really ready for what I had bargained for.

The rest of the briefing was just a blur. They let us go and told us not to come back until Tuesday. "Go spend this time with your families," was the standing order of the weekend. For those of us who had yet to tie ourselves down with a wife, we took it as an invitation to embark on a four-day bender of booze and bar fights. Not five minutes after I had made it back into my room and stripped out of my PT uniform, Bryce barged in with a beer and a smile.

"Berlin!" He shouted bluntly.

It was a call to arms. An affirmation of action. It was everything I needed to hear.

"Berlin!" I shouted back.

"Exactly!" He laughed. "I'll be back in an hour."

There wasn't anything else to discuss. He got the tickets and I set out to warn the locals. Fifty minutes later he was back in my room with a fully loaded bag on his shoulder.

"I looked at the train schedule to the airport and got us the earliest flight available." He said. "We have three hours."

"Awesome!" I cheered, thinking about all things we were about to do with our freedom.

I had lived in Berlin before as a kid. I knew exactly what to expect. Besides, I still had a couple friends to show for my time there, and as soon as we got back from the briefing I had shot them a quick message – to which they replied on short notice. The news was good, and I was eager to share it.

"Phillip told me that we can stay with him," I continued. "Laura and Julia said they can squeeze in a visit too, but we'll have to be quick since they have stuff planned for the weekend."

"Awesome. Want to go?!"

"Now?"

"Well, yeah. Unless you want to sit around here and wait for all these shit-heads to get piss-ass drunk and get us put on lockdown."

I took a moment to consider it, realizing that the world was my oyster and I could do whatever the hell I wanted.

"Good point. Let's go."

We didn't even file the paperwork for a four-day pass. Not that I cared. With news of the deployment now out there and official, nothing could stop us from going off to war. Not unless we found our way into a jail cell or the morgue. I'm sure arrangements would've been made in either case.

By nightfall we had arrived. Minutes later, we had a fresh bottle of whiskey in-hand. Within the hour it was gone. There's not much else I can say about that trip. We got drunk as hell and that's how we stayed, paying it forward for every shitty day to come. It wasn't until the tail-end of our adventure that I was forced to face the reality looming over my horizon. In a brief moment of respite, while a half-dozen locals with a bushel of weed did their best to smoke Bryce stupid, I wandered out onto the balcony of my old German buddy's flat and took a breather to myself.

"Man..." Phillip was already outside when I started hanging over the balcony to wrestle with the contents of my stomach. "I can't believe this shit."

He looked sober as a bell, but I knew he was trashed. Still, there was a pale gasp of lucid thought in his expression.

"Heh, yeah." I cracked a smile. "He's gotta be high by now. You guys have blown so much weed on smoking him out."

"No man!" He smacked me on the shoulder. "I'm talking about the war. I mean — this could be the last time I fuckin' see you, you know?"

"Yeah." I took a moment to regain my balance and drank another shot of the home-made schnapps in my glass.

"This is for real, man! You're going over there and you might not be coming back."

Yeah, I know, I wanted to snap back at him. But there was something very genuine in his voice that made me think twice.

We were the same age, from totally different sides of the world, with upbringings as similar as night and day. For two years I had it crammed down my throat that death was a part of the job. For him it was like getting sidelined by a freighter. I had worked with German soldiers and knew what it was like for them to be shunned by their own population. They were like a cult of ancient warriors, kicked out and left in the cold as a caste. Sure, they went home on the holidays and lived among the German people, but for a guy like Phillip to know somebody personally who's getting shipped off to war and really might not be coming back? It was like a myth. But more than that, he was right.

Up until that moment, I had been well acquainted with the idea that I could die. In fact, I had done everything I could to ignore it. I had shoved it out of sight and out of mind. I had faced it, acknowledged it, and moved on. It was the unspeakable truth. Something better left alone. But there he was: the first person I knew from the real world to look me right in the eyes and say out loud what I knew to be true.

I might not be coming back.

That's how it stuck, and it never went away. With those words he roused that forbidden idea from deep in some backwater cortex of my brain and it began a merciless campaign on my subconscious. No matter what I did, those words echoed into the foreground and my thoughts became a stage for their madness. I would drink and cheer, saying hails and farewells, but all the while "might not" was turning into "will not," and fear washed over into acceptance. It was no longer a doubt but a fact: I wasn't coming back alive.

The following Tuesday, first thing in the morning, our unit preparations began. For the next few months we embarked on the process of packing up our shit and training for our new mission. And when I stopped to look at it, everything in my life seemed so small in comparison to the war. All those things I had started in in the past had become fruitless in the face of my new fate.

"And what about us?" my girlfriend asked.

What about us? I was giving up on my past. I was coming to terms with my mortality. Accepting what was in store — and there wasn't any time for a long-forgotten squeeze on the far end of the world. With a single phrase, I ended a fling that had become a two-and-a-half year saga.

It was a relationship with a high school sweetheart that'd followed me into the uniform — and I didn't even hesitate.

"We're breaking up."

What else could I say? It was an era of change. Down to my very core, it was punctuated with calculated acts of accepting my fate. I penned out the tattoo that'd been crawling around in my mind for years. I wrote letters to long forgotten friends and locked them up inside my journal. I burned things once dear to me. When the time came for us to fill out the forms of our last will and testament, I made a mockery of it all.

"Is this really what you want them to do with your remains?" My squad leader held the paper in his hand and looked at me with scorn. *"'Put me on a burning Viking ship and send me out to sea, with a broadsword in-hand?'"*

"Roger, Sarn't!" I laughed.

He was even less amused when I pressed the issue.

"We have a $400,000 life insurance policy, Sarn't. I might as well put it to good use."

I couldn't care less what they did with my remains. After all, I wouldn't be around to see it. So instead of lingering on things that were out of my control, I stuck my head in the sand and let it go. I mean if I was right about dying — whatever. Once you get over the notion of non-existence, it's a pretty easy thing to accept your death.

But what if I was wrong?

That's what scared me the most: not dying, but *almost* dying. Becoming one of those poor bastards who got blasted into a vegetative state. Or maybe I'd just spend the rest of my life remembering what it was like to have legs. Boom and then silence? A blast to the brain? That's a piece of cake. It's part of the job. All you've gotta' do is close your eyes and let it happen.

Becoming a disemboweled nugget?

No.

That was something else entirely. That chilled me to the bone. And as the days dragged on and the nights fell silent, the only thought in my mind became the notion of how I *wasn't* going to die. How I'd get stuck in a wheelchair with a broken colostomy bag and a shattered spine. I'd be gurgling on my own drool until it was time for a daily sponge-bath. I might remember having a dick — way back when — and God knows I took it for granted. Every night I struggled with the idea. It became the fear of death, evolved. One night it got so bad I caught myself shaking in bed. I was shaking for Christ's sake. Shivering like a cold puppy in the rain. I was lying there, imagining every horrible thing that could happen, until I took a deep breath and coached myself back to sanity.

"That won't be me," I whispered. "Not me."

After all, I wasn't coming back alive.

I wasn't coming back at all.

That night I retreated into the comfort of knowing for a fact that I was destined to die. I was determined. I was resolved. And in that way, death had become my watchword. My own mortality had became salvation. I coached myself to sleep every night with the comfort of my undoing, and hoped with every ounce of my being that when it was all over I'd be anything but a "survivor."

When I woke up each morning, I buried my head under a pile of work, turned off my brain, and made like everybody else to pack up my shit and get ready for the deployment. When the time came for our final four-week training operation, I played my part to perfection. It was our best field problem yet, with everybody on the top of their game. The next month we went home for a final block of leave to say goodbye to our loved ones — but deep inside I had already left them behind.

Frankly, I don't remember very much of those fourteen days of leave. It's not that I was fucked up or high or anything. I just didn't really care. I know I ate some burgers, I saw some friends, and we had some family dinners. Tears were definitely shed at my expense and there was a final good-bye to the heart I had broken — but my mind was elsewhere. I had waited so long for what was coming that I was blinded with excitement. Sitting there at home felt like somebody had pressed the "pause" button on my life. I felt like I had been dragged off to dinner at the most important part of the movie. All I could think about was the war. In the last few days of my trip back home, I went out with my sister and my good friend Andy to track down a tattoo parlor with a clear schedule and a steady hand. I showed them a ten-inch wide design of interwoven triangles that marked a disciple of Odin — the Norse god of war. It was a symbol called the "Valknut," which is roughly translated as the "Death Knot," or more accurately, the "Knot of Valor."

According to the sagas, the Valknut was a mark that Vikings used to carve into their shields, swords, and skin as a sign of their willingness to die in battle in sacrifice to Odin. Since I had studied Norse Mythology in my spare time, and both my sister and I were the proud descendants of a four-hundred year old family with an intact name and the same farm from way-back in the sixteenth century, it was a matter of pride that I do the same as my ancestors.

"You want this all in one go?" The artist asked me.

"It has to be," I said.

"You can't go and come back in a few weeks to finish it up?"

"Nope. In a few weeks I'll be in Iraq."

"Alright man, but this fucker is big. It's going to take a while, and it'll hurt like hell."

"That's part of the fun." I smirked.

"Ha! That's what I like to hear! Come on over here and let's do this."

It took four and a half hours for him to ink that sucker into my torso. It was a branding for the world to see when all that was left of my body was a heap of skin and bones. The ink wasn't even settled by the time I got back to Germany. I was home and back in the blink of an eye. The next time I'd see any of those people, if I even lived to make it back, was a lifetime away. Yet even then, on the eve of heading 'down range,' I had no idea what to expect. All I had was a ticking clock to that red-letter day when everything was going to change.

The night before we shipped out, I sat in front of a bottle of Yukon Jack with Bryce and Ian and wondered how in the world the summer had gone by so fast. My room was already packed up. My possessions were rotting away in a storage container. My bags were stuffed full of gear and the Spartan sheets on my bed were the only artifacts still serving as décor. We had nothing left to do but get drunk as hell and wait for the morning call. Everybody else in the barracks was in the same boat. We drank, we talked, we took turns making dramatic notes on Facebook, and then we passed the fuck out. It was far less of a climactic adventure than I had imagined.

The next morning, the 1st Squadron of the 2nd Stryker Cavalry Regiment gathered together in their respective Companies to account for their men and say goodbye to loved ones who they were leaving behind on base. They took pictures, distributed hugs, went over countless nuances of combat wisdom, and loaded up onto buses with a vigorous "Hooah!" For many of us, passing through those gates was the beginning of a journey into the unknown. For some, it was going back to something better forgotten. For all of us, it was the beginning of something huge.

The drive to the airport took half as long as the formations on either end, but the Army had reserved its own set of terminals so it didn't take long for us to mount up onto the plane. One thing we couldn't avoid were the friendly faces of the TSA. Much to my surprise, they had traveled all the way to the far side of the Earth just to see us off, scan us over, and pat us down. When I approached the security checkpoint, a bright young lady repeated a familiar line:

"Sir, do you have any lighters, matches, liquids in excess of three fluid ounces, knives, blades, or scissors of any kind?"

I was stunned. 9,000 miles away from sovereign American soil and I still couldn't escape the inquisition.

"Sir?" She repeated.

I laughed and confessed my sins. "Yeah, I have a lighter and a water bottle."

With a straight face she worked through the routine. "Sir, FAA regulations require that I confiscate all lighters, matches, and fluids. If you could please place them in this container here, I can get you on your way."

I gave her a smart-ass wink, threw my half-empty water bottle into the trash container, and blew her off as I made way through the metal detector.

She quickly took a step to the side and barred me from passing with her arm.

"What?!" I was bewildered.

"I need to confiscate your lighter, sir."

"We're not even in America. What are you guys doing here?"

"It's an American charter jet with American soldiers and an American crew, which hasn't been checked through customs. According to international treaties it still falls under American jurisdiction. Please give up your lighter and I can have you on your way."

I scoffed at the entire situation and motioned down to my M-4 Carbine, body armor and fully loaded magazine of force-protection ammo.

"You know that FAA regulations also expressly forbid passengers from carrying semi-automatic assault rifles and thirty rounds of ammunition, right?"

"Yes, sir. The government has made an exception in this case for your weapon. But I still have to confiscate your lighter."

"Whatever. I don't even smoke. Here you go."

I reached into my pocket and threw the lighter into the trash but she continued to block my path.

"Sir, what is that on your hip?" I saw her gesture down to my multi-tool in its sheath.

"It's a Gerber."

"Does it have a blade exceeding one inch in length?"

"Uhh... yeah."

"Sir, I'm going to have to confiscate that as well. FAA regulations expressly forbid any knives, blades, or scissors of any kind."

"I thought the government made an exception for our weapons." I wasn't going to give up an eighty dollar survival tool without a fight.

"Your guns, sir, yes. But we can't let you on that plane with a knife. It's a potential danger to the crew."

"There are over 100 people on this plane with loaded semi-automatic rifles and fully-automatic machine guns. We have hundreds of live rounds of lethal ammunition, and you're tripping out over a multi-tool?"

"Not me, sir. The FAA."

"What's the hold up?!" Somebody with authority shouted up from behind.

She had me in a pinch but this was my goddamned Gerber we were talking about. It's the most useful thing that ever came out of the brains of man.

"Can I stick it in my duffel bag or something when I get down there?"

"No, sir. I can't let you beyond this point with a knife."

I changed my tactics to charm and put on a smile.

"You know I'm about to go to war, right?"

"Yes, sir." she smiled back.

"—and you know, my very life might come down to this Gerber one day?"

She laughed.

"—and if you take this Gerber from me, it'll be your fault."

"It won't be my fault, sir, since the government is the one sending you off to war. But, for what it's worth, I really hope your life never comes down to that Gerber – because it's not getting past this door."

She had me.

I took off my knife, handed it over, and caught up to the line of men stretched out ahead of me. I knew that if I held up the process any longer, a Gerber would be the least of my problems. The file led down a flight of stairs and out onto the open concrete where our private jet was parked. Beside the boarding ladder, a Staff Sergeant of unknown origin explained to us exactly how to line up our weapons when we boarded the plane:

"Place them at your feet! Muzzles pointing towards the aisle! If you're in the middle, point your muzzles to the right! Lay them down from butt-stock to muzzle! Place your body armor under the seat in front of you!"

I couldn't help but laugh at how hard somebody was overthinking the whole process. This was one of those frequent times in a soldier's life when his existence can be effectively compared to cattle. Like everybody around me, I would respond to my superiors with an idle "hooah!" and waddle forward in line until I was given more specific instructions. When I approached the ramp of stairs leading up to the cabin, I took a moment to look around and enjoy the German landscape. From there I was hooked, turning back on every step to get another glance at the scene. When I reached the top, a gentle voice spoke softly in communion.

"It's beautiful, isn't it?"

I faced into the cabin and met eyes with the woman who'd said exactly what I was thinking. She was middle-aged, very attractive, and like me, she was also looking out at the golden leaves of fall and the billowing breath of the gods.

"Every time we fly to Kuwait it makes me appreciate how beautiful the rest of the world really is."

She giggled and melted my heart with a single smile. I was speechless.

"Yeah." It was all I could muster. "That's exactly what I was thinking. Well, I've never been to Kuwait, but... Yeah. It's beautiful."

"Oh," she giggled almost maternally. "You'll know what I'm talking about."

"You have a nice flight." I regained my composure.

"You too," she smiled flirtatiously back. "If you need anything, just come and get me."

As I shuffled toward my seat I realized that I must've been one of a thousand young-buck soldiers she'd seen off to war. Still, she knew the power of a woman's charm. Watching her work, I could see how she lit up the faces of every man she talked to. She was leaving a little wake of fluttering hearts all over the cabin.

"Sir, if you could please return your chair to its upright position that'd just be wonderful."

It was the first time I'd ever heard those words sound like a loving plea.

"Oh!" the victim was caught off guard. "Yes ma'am! Absolutely!"

"Thank you, darling!"

As she made her way, row by row to my seat, I watched her and imagined some alternate universe where I could take her out to dinner — instead of her escorting me off to war. A few moments later, she stopped by my seat on the way to help another soldier and chimed in with a smile.

"Hey there, hon! Can I get you water or anything?"

I still couldn't get over how stunning she looked and how genuine she kept her smile after a thousand repetitions.

"No I'm fine," I said, my heart skipping a beat.

I smiled and she nodded, lightly touching my shoulder as she moved on to help the next man in line.

"Hey there, Sarge!"

"Oh! Hi, ma'am!" I heard the man behind me stammer.

They were stock phrases but she said each one with conviction, not merely as a flight attendant checking on cargo between coffee-breaks.

"How's your back holding up?" She continued.

"Oh it's good," he said.

She wasn't just talking at us, she was talking to us.

"Okay. Well, as soon as we finish loading up I'll come and bring you an extra pillow. How's that sound?"

"Wonderful, ma'am. Thank you!"

It was like she knew us already. Like she'd met us and known us for years. Every time she talked to somebody, it was some special, personalized dialogue — not some manufactured care.

"Can I get you anything, darling?" she said to the next man down the aisle.

"Actually, yeah. Can I have some water?"

"I'll make sure it's sparkling, just like you like it."

How did she know?

I was transfixed. Then I realized it was in moments like the one looking out at the German landscape where she'd registered each of our faces. It was in hearing conversations over the commotion of shuffling into our seats, in handing out mints and blankets. She was good. Plain as that. She was loving and attentive. There must've been fifty or sixty of us in her section of the plane and I wouldn't be surprised at all if she knew every one of us personally by the time we left.

"Here you go darling," she whispered to me just a few hours into the flight.

I looked up to see her handing over my specially ordered mix of orange juice, apple juice and ginger ale.

"I hope I got the mix right."

I must've blushed at the wink she gave me. I don't know how I couldn't.

"Thank you so much," I said.

"Oh, it's my pleasure. You think they want anything?" She motioned to the two men passed out on both sides of me.

"I think they're fine."

"Well, I'm going to bring them some water just in case. You too! I don't like knowing how hot it is down there. It's my job to get you off that plane in Kuwait with a big 'ol smile on your face. It's the least I can do."

She looked down for a moment with sadness, as she thought ahead to where we were going and what we were going there to do. I could see it in her eyes. It was personal to her.

"Do you know anybody down-range?" I asked her.

"Yeah, I have a nephew. He's in the Marines — in Afghanistan."

"I'm sorry to hear that. I hope he gets back safe."

"Oh, no! He'll be fine," she smiled and nudged my shoulder. "He's a POG. Not like you guys. He's not in the Infantry — thank God."

We both chuckled.

"So you know the deal, huh?"

"Hon, you can't do what I do without hearing all about who's got the balls and who sits back in the rear drinkin' Starbucks."

"Yeah, you've got a point there."

"Nothing makes me happier than knowing he'll be comin' home safe. God's truth. I thank the Lord every day that he's not out there in the hills or on the streets getting blown up and shot at like some worthless hunk of meat."

I didn't know what to say. This woman was spilling her soul in the silence between hard snores.

"That's what gets me — every time. Whenever we have to fly another plane full of you boys down to that God-forsaken country. I can't help it. All I can see when I look at every one of you is some poor woman's little baby. I know that every one of you has a mother somewhere, crying herself to sleep at night, knowing she might never see her son again."

"Wow," I said jokingly, trying to lighten the mood. "Well now I feel horrible."

"Don't you dare!" She scolded me. "You be proud of what you're doing!"

"Yeah, but I love my mom. I hate knowing what I'm putting her through."

"You don't even worry about that! Your momma's more proud of you than anything in her life — you hear, me hun? Ain't nothin' she's more proud of than her little boy. You just make sure you give her the biggest hug you can when this is all over, okay?"

Tears welled up in her eyes and I found myself thinking it was more than just a nephew of hers who'd been shipped off to Afghanistan, and that he was anything but okay.

"When you finally come home, you're gonna make her the happiest woman in the world."

Before I could say anything back, she was fighting to regain her composure.

"Ha! Look at me." She reached into her pockets to pull out a handkerchief, and wiped her tears from her eyes. "Like I said, it gets me every time. Every plane-full of you — the way I see it, you're all like sons to me. It's the least I can do for your mothers: make sure their babies get treated right and sent off with a smile."

She smiled through her tears and freshly bleeding mascara.

"I'm gonna' go get you a water, hon. You just sit tight."

As she walked away I had a picture in my head as clear as crystal. It was of a son who'd had been shipped off to war to die. It was of a mother who had lost the most important thing in her world. It was of her becoming a flight attendant so she could save her soul. So she could have a thousand surrogate sons. So she could care for them like she hoped her son had been cared for, give every one of us a glimpse of our own mother, and remind us what we were fighting for.

I wish I could go back in time and kiss her, give her a great big bear hug and hold her while she cried. I wish I could thank her. Not just for me and the men next to me, but for every man shipping off to war whom she had cushioned with love like precious treasures wrapped up with packing peanuts.

The next five hours were just like any other flight. We ate and drank a steady stream of refreshments and endured hours of droning vibrations. Eventually, the batteries of portable DVD players and laptop computers died off and the cabin filled with the quiet air of unconscious soldiers who had been up since well before dawn. If it wasn't for the rifles, body armor, and machine guns littered on the floor and shoved under seats, I could've just as easily mistaken it for a trip to New York or Hawaii. But as I stared out the window, the lush and vividly green earth below us slowly faded into a vast expanse of dirt and sand. It was like watching a time-lapse video of the earth turning to ruin and its surface blasting over with desolation. When it finally seemed like there was nothing left of a living and breathing world underneath us, the pilot's voice came on over the PA.

"Gentlemen, I just wanted to inform you that we will be passing over Baghdad momentarily. If you look out the right side of the aircraft you will see a thick, dark-green river. That's the Tigris. And if you follow that down a ways you can see the city on either side of it."

I joined a few eager eyes and followed his instructions.

There it was: Baghdad. It was a lot smaller than I'd imagined. Having grown up in Los Angeles, I always assumed a world-city would be the size of a small country. I mean, flying over my home town in a commercial jet takes the better part of half an hour. You come out over the mountains to either side of it and all you can see is a horizon full of highways and houses. It stretches out until the earth curves away from you. You can look clear past the downtown skyscrapers to the point where it rams up against the ocean or north to the mountains and south into the hazy landscape.

That's what I expected when I gazed out of the window: the capital city to one of the most influential countries in history. The main stage of modern warfare. The defining conflict of my generation. Something befitting the legend. I stuck my face in that window expecting a sprawling expanse of smoke and fire. But when I finally saw it, I almost missed it. The entire span of Baghdad looked like nothing more than a dark stain on a tan sheet. It was a muddy puddle. Like somebody took a piss in the desert and it never dried. Just a blotchy brown island of mud, in the middle of a vast sea of sand.

"That's it?" I muttered with disappointment.

CNN had painted the place to be a melting pot of chaos. They made it sound like any other American capital, like New York or San Francisco. After all, it was Baghdad — the heart of a whole foreign country. The largest city in a thousand miles. For the bulk of human history it had been the epicenter of the ancient world and the birthplace of human culture. Baghdad: the beating heart of a mystic Arabian land that was mythical, legendary, and timeless.

And it was just twenty miles from end to end.

I could ride my bike across the whole width of it in about an hour, assuming I didn't get killed somewhere along the way. Beyond the city limits was an expanse of nothingness so immersive that it was unreal. Within minutes, the entire city had slipped behind us into the haze and all that was left of what I had seen was a dark green scar that trailed off into the distance. A scar that marked the poisoned remains of an ancient river that had fed some of the largest empires in history. Literally a river of biblical proportions, now little more than a sewage main, carrying millions of gallons of disease infested waste into the open waters of the Persian Gulf.

The next time the pilot's voice came over the PA, it was a final call to prepare for landing. As he clicked on the handmic, I stirred awake from my catnap to hear the news.

"Gentlemen, we are now on our final approach to Kuwait City. Please place your seat-backs and trays in their upright and locked positions and stow any electronics you may still be using under the seat in front of you. Thank you."

Twenty minutes later we touched down on the tarmac and lined up to deplane.

"Get ready for this shit," somebody said.

When the door opened, it blew my mind. Almost instantaneously, the temperature of the plane jumped a dozen points. As each row of soldiers filed out of the aircraft, the temperature rose still higher. When I reached the threshold of the door, I could see the shimmering of hot and cold gases mixing and rapidly expanding in a chaos of densities, while the cool interior spilled out of the compartment and into the hot air of Kuwait. Until then, it'd been just 70 degrees in that cabin — which was a step up from the 60-something average of the German outdoors. Throughout the duration of the five-hour flight, it never wavered more than a few points away from 75 degrees. But five minutes after those doors opened, the entire cabin was swallowed whole by 112 degrees of sweltering afternoon heat.

"Just wait." Somebody chuckled. "This is nothing. It's already cooling off."

"What are you talking about?" some cherry asked.

"Brother, it's already fall."

We got off the plane and some unknown Major stepped out in front of us to give a speech and let us know what was in the works.

"We're waiting on a couple buses to bring us out to the base." He finished up the briefing with the only information that really mattered. "Just stand by here and we'll let you know when it's time to go."

We took an extended smoking break until they loaded us onto a civilian convoy of chartered transportation and hauled us off into the desert. That was my first introduction to the real and unending sea of sand that is Kuwait. As soon as we passed through the gates of the airport, my eyes were glued to the window and transfixed by the scene.

There was nothing in Kuwait. There was sand, a horizon, and a sky. Occasionally we'd come upon some long forgotten and half-buried artifact of the past, but it would simply buzz by and be lost once again to the sands. I saw an old shack, a rolled truck, a collection of wheels and tires, a farmhouse with no fields, a trailer... I could make out decades of human history, strewn around a desolate wasteland and trapped in the passing slide-show of rusty metal skeletons and cracking plastic trim. On both sides of the highway, a thick margin of roadside trash reached out to some arbitrary point where it was finally consumed by sand, as though the desert was some hungry beast, feeding on memories. But everything there was abandoned, forsaken and lost. It was completely hollow and none of it seemed real.

After an hour or so of driving, my unwavering gaze into the void caught the attention of one of the guys sitting nearby.

"Why do you keep staring out that window, Ludwig?" He chuckled.

But how could I explain what I was feeling?

Time itself had stopped ticking. We were caught in a flux. The laws of physics were suspended right in front of my eyes. We careened forward across the asphalt at speeds in excess of eighty miles an hour, but it still felt like we were getting nowhere. We were stuck on a treadmill, getting swallowed by the sand. We were becoming one with the mirage of the horizon. I half expected a squad of soldiers from some lost battalion of the Foreign Legion to appear with repeater rifles and the reins of their dying horses in hand.

During a short bathroom break at some unknown mile-marker between dunes, the sun vanished behind the landscape and the night sky took over. From that point on, there wasn't anything left to see. No moon. No stars. Not a single trace of light in the distance. We were sinking deeper into the surreal. Lost in a pitch. Surrounded by a nothingness that was traced with invisible features. The headlights of our convoy were the only source of illumination for a hundred miles in every direction. Yet even those bright torches of halogen were swallowed whole by the darkness ahead of us. Were it not for the strips of paint on the road flashing by, I could've just as easily mistaken our journey for motionless suspension within a void.

It went on like that for hours. Sometimes I wondered if I was going insane. For a little while I got lost in a paranoid theory that our drivers were double agents and they had driven us right across the border into a war zone. But we hurtled onward until a warm glow stretched over the horizon and the sky filled up with light. At first I mistook the aura for a sunrise, but it was much too bright to be a force of nature. It was still miles away. An hour's worth of driving at least. But as we drew closer it surrounded us in a cloud of dusty light. Soon I realized that what I had mistaken for the sun was just the backwash of a thousand light bulbs, spilling up into the sky and shining out into space. It was like somebody had constructed a man-made supernova to signal aliens on the far side of the galaxy.

From the back of the bus, the voice of one of our leaders spoke out with authority. "There it is, men! Camp Buehring."

Camp Buehring was one of the largest staging grounds for troops flowing in and out of Iraq. As such, it never slept. The commanders of Camp Buehring kept every inch of that base as brightly lit throughout the night as it was during the day. No matter where you went, all around the clock, somebody was working.

When we pulled up to the main gate the vastness of the complex was revealed. It took us more than half an hour to navigate through the network of security checkpoints and blocking positions at the perimeter. Upon emerging from the battlements, another fifteen minutes were blown driving to the welcoming post on the outskirts of the facility. We filed off the buses for an accountability formation and they ushered us into a large, air-conditioned tent, filled with chairs. A projector displayed a map of the entire complex on the wall. Tacked to the poster board behind it I spotted a flier for the "Midnight Marathon" – just three and a half laps around the base and you're done.

We filed in, took our seats, and the briefings began. They gave us a lecture about the base, a Q&A on the theater of war, a finance briefing, and a seminar on standards. They made it clear what was expected of us and what rules we had to follow. We had it hammered into our heads that the non-combat soldiers stationed at Camp Buehring were off-limits to our grunt-like philandering. Moreover, our weapons were to be clear of ammunition at all times and any kind of backpack or bag was an absolute no-go at the chow-hall.

When the list of *dont's* was run aground, a new speaker stepped up and introduced us to the camp facilities. Among them were the many "Morale, Welfare, and Recreation" areas, with phones and computers available for fifteen minute intervals to anybody who had time to wait. The base came fully stocked with a Starbucks, a Pizza Hut, a Subway Sandwich kiosk, and a plethora of Bazzars, falafel stands and "Hajji Marts." All of these were pointed out on the map, along with gems of information like where we were, where we needed to go, and what we could find at the "On-Post Exchange." Most importantly, he signaled to an array of abandoned tents called the "Back Forty" and made it clear that we had standing orders to avoid it. As the man with the laser pointer put it: "There's nothing back there but a bunch of abandoned tents and bad news."

Well that's exactly where they sent us.

We got on our buses with new orders to unpack at our temporary housing area. As soon as we got there, I was quick to recognize the place as the very same "Back Forty" from the lecture. At first I took it personally, but then it made perfect sense. The Back Forty was a beautifully segregated space where the Infantry could hang-out and do their grunt shit without reminding everybody else what their "hazard pay" was supposed to cover. In a way, I guess, the guy at the briefing hall was right. There *was* nothing back there — nothing but an infantry squadron of seven hundred men with a hard-on for war.

For the next two weeks we unpacked our shit, up-armored our vehicles, consumed gargantuan quantities of chow, and sat through dozens of briefings about the occupation of Iraq, the nuts-and-bolts of American tactics, and what to expect when we hit the ground in Baghdad. It was a busy fourteen days. Among the topics were: "Identifying the Ranks and Uniforms of Coalition Forces;" "Interacting with Local Nationals;" "The Structure and Development of Iraqi Security Forces;" and "Staving Off Our First Encounter of the Inevitable Roadside Bomb for as Long as Possible." Okay, I made up the title for that last one — but that's exactly what we learned.

We also learned that three separate attempts had started and failed to create an independent Iraqi security force, each one succumbing to either corruption or terror. First we had tried to build up local Iraqi Police departments by drawing on the population to uphold the law. The problem was that a local police officer and his family were far too easy for the bad guys to find and kill before he could do any good. So the next thing we tried was recruiting local police from all over the country. These "National Police," however, lacked the fundamental loyalty necessary to stand up against organized crime and make a difference against the militias. They were far away from home with few friends and a weak paycheck. All it took to turn them was a handful of petty cash and a few threats about dying in their sleep. National Police lived together at their station, so if you turned one it was an easy task to coerce his entire unit.

Last but not least was the Iraqi Army, who we had raised from the dead, complete with Soviet era weapons and no hope for a twenty-year pension. The problem with them wasn't so much in their formation as it was with the government of Iraq. That far into the war, the militias were such a pervasive authority in the country that they had reverse engineered our fragile little concept of "democracy." To them the voting populace was like cattle. To further their interests in the state they simply bribed, brainwashed and coerced the people into the polls. Nowhere else was this as clear as with Muktada al-Sadr and the Jaish al-Mahdi, who controlled roughly half of the voting population of Baghdad by maintaining an iron fist over Sadr City.

But the Iraqi military wasn't the only military covered those two weeks at Camp Buehring. During our lessons it was made clear that "the Coalition" was just a catch-phrase used by the brass. That American soldiers out-stripped any other service or nationality by tens of thousands, and that few of our allies had ever ventured out of the protective walls of the major Coalition bases to do anything of substance besides jump on a convoy to go home. This was an American war, fought by American soldiers, so it would be the Americans who did the heavy lifting — and that meant us.

Our instructors assured us nobody could be trusted, that the war would be fought with words, that our battle was over the hearts and minds of the people and — above all — that when we got hit, *somebody* was going to die. We went over the latest weapons and tactics on both sides of the fight. We studied past operations and a list of "lessons learned" by those who came before us. They penned out every single sign of how to sniff out something wrong and even gave us some extra tips for when we'd be out there on our own.

These were the realities of the war. They were drilled into our minds, padded with statistics, and braced with first-hand accounts. They even showed us photos and videos to back it all up. During the segment titled "The Cost of Complacency," our instructor stressed the ever-present threat of danger with a cued-up series of propaganda videos that had been captured by our enemy. He showed us countless American soldiers who had been shot, blown up, and eviscerated without ever seeing it coming. Each time, I saw myself in their shoes. Most of the kids in those videos were just as young as me. They might as well have been caught with their pants down and fly unzipped. One moment we'd see a young marine patting a kid on the head with a smile and the next moment they're lost in a cloud of body parts while the chanting voice of the trigger man praised Allah for the grace of bloodshed.

As though deliberately ignoring the first half of our crash-course training bender, however, the next string of briefings was intended to teach us the ins-and-outs of our rules and regulations. These briefings covered hundreds of procedures, dozens of subjects, and thousands of facts. They included detailed reports on enemy dispositions, technical courses on experimental equipment, a dozen or more general orders lined up to regulate the troops, and methodically calculated guidelines for lethal engagement. Each one was described with a fantastically black-and-white scenario of armed combatants versus victimized soldiers, and after seven days of hearing aggregated lists of all the ways we could die, they followed it up with a bullet-point briefing on how there wasn't shit we could do to stop it.

"Death by Powerpoint," as we came to know it, struck me as the ultimate orgy of Pentagon officers washing their hands clean of responsibility for the true grit and consequences of what they'd started. After putting us through that non-stop bender of slides and lectures, they could always fall back to saying, "These guys knew better," and "They were briefed on the official policy." To make sure that the men up-top were absolved of liability, they even gave us pamphlets and flowcharts, pre-laminated for fifteen months of breast-pocket storage.

But the "Rules of Engagement" (aka: ROEs) only exist in the comfort of a courtroom. Out in the real world, all those scenarios get twisted into shifting shades of gray. We knew that all the clear cut guidelines they preached would soon get plastered over with the gritty mosaic of reality.

There would never be a clear shot or a thin line. It was going to be dirty and unknowable and impossible to figure out. But one thing was painfully clear: out there we'd be on our own. If anything went wrong, they'd hang us out to dry in a heartbeat. And it was on the last leg of that final briefing one of our instructors went off-the-record to level with us about everything we had learned.

"Listen," he said. "You do what you've gotta' do."

The words carried out across the crowd and sank in to everybody there who hadn't been and didn't know. To the rest, it was just a reminder of days past.

"At the end of the day," he continued, "you're the only one who can make the call. And the only choice you get might come down to rotting in a prison or getting buried in a coffin. You might end up spending the rest of your life knowing that you could have done something to keep your best friend alive. So when the time comes you *make* the call. Got it?"

We shouted our answer back to him as a group and he got back to the slides in front of us. For the veterans, I'm sure that was just another *spiel,* but to me it was a lesson packed away for the long-haul. Something told me he had learned it through personal experience – whether it was the glaze on his eyes or the harsh tone in his voice. In either case, I would've bet you a hundred bucks he could name a handful of friends who never came home because of a gun-shy trigger finger and a single moment of hesitation.

We marched back to our half of the base cheering the most ruthless cadence in the book. We still had tangible preparations that needed to be done. Things like repacking and reinventorying a dozen or more shipping containers full of equipment and supplies. We drove our Strykers, now fresh off the boats from Germany, to be up-armored and refit with the latest signal jamming, communications, and navigational equipment. We rezeroed our rifles and optics, and every platoon in the squadron ran through dozens of combat scenarios. The latest and greatest knowledge of what we had learned in the classroom was built on top of what we already knew, and for two weeks we touched on every skill in the Infantry Bible. All the while we adjusted to the heat and taught ourselves an important slogan: *hydrate or die.*

"You won't feel it in thirty minutes," the senior medic let us know. "Hell, you won't even feel it in an hour. But I guarantee you'll feel it tomorrow. You need to be drinking constantly, every day. If you don't, you'll fall-out."

So we stuck around in buddy-teams and carried water everywhere. I only forgot that lesson once. It was the first time I ever became a casualty of the sun. On the way back from the firing range, one of our Reefer Trucks got stuck in the sand and we spent all afternoon getting that sucker back on the road. Like an idiot, I didn't have a drop to drink. Needless to say, I spent the rest of that adventure in a feverish daze, wrapped in cold towels and stuck on the verge of a medical evacuation.

After two weeks in Kuwait, with the Strykers loaded up onto trains and everything else packed up to go, it came time for us to get back on the road. Once again, we found ourselves waiting in formation at the Kuwait City International Airport, this time to catch an Air Force cargo plane geared up for a night-time ride.

It was a far cry from the comfort of a commuter jet, but it worked. The lowest-bidder passenger seats into which we fastened our third points of contact were bolted to a flat-rack cargo plate and tied down to the steel rollers on the floor. This time, we didn't get any instructions. They didn't serve us chow or cheap refreshments. No flight attendants came tending to our needs. We piled everything on our laps and wore each item of protective gear we owned. Exactly "why" was still unclear to me, but as soon as they strapped down our duffel bags and raised the ramp to take off we went airborne with a bang. No taxi. No speech. No call for seat belts. Just a sudden roar of turbojet engines and the violent jerk of an up-heaved cargo bay.

I imagine our trip from that point forward was in no way dissimilar to a short session in a large decompression chamber. The only portal to the outside world was a small eight-inch window on the left side of the aircraft, designed purely to convey the hour of the day. Once again, the passage of time became enigmatic, but this time there was nothing to see or hear as we went. I just zoned out on a bulkhead and accepted my role as cargo until some point in the ride when all the white lights switched off and a single red dome-light turned on. It was the only marker of progress since we had taken off — a signal that we had crossed over the border and into the airspace of Iraq.

Of course, none of this was communicated to the pack of rabid Grunts infesting the cargo area of the captain's plane; we were just livestock. We didn't need to know how much longer we'd be waiting to get off that damn plane, just like we didn't need to know a "combat landing" involves a hard bank to one side and spiraling damn-near out of control from cruising altitude to the landing strip in a matter of minutes so that nobody gets the chance to shoot you out of the sky. We didn't *need* anything — but it still would have been nice.

Without any warning at all, our massive chamber rolled hard to the left. Everybody inside had to scramble for their gear to keep it from flying around the cabin and landing on some other sucker's head. Those of us with unfastened seat-belts were quick to clip in, and the men who were fast asleep were jolted awake by a gut-wrenching heave. I realized why our protective gear was necessary right before the pressure in the cabin sky-rocketed to unbelievable heights. My ears swelled shut. My guts twisted and floated weightless inside of my chest cavity. I could swear to God they haven't designed a better ride at a theme park. We were in a free-fall, with no reference or situational awareness, and there was no telling when it was all going to end.

After a few more heaves, my equilibrium went mad. I tried my best to stare at one point on the cabin wall, but it didn't help. I tried rotating my head to compensate for what I thought was down, but that made it even worse. The combining forces and lacking frame of reference cast me into a discombobulated vertigo. One moment the world would be right and I would be sitting on the "floor." A second later it felt like I was glued to the ceiling. In the height of the maneuver, I found an island of relief by imagining I was floating halfway between the wall and the floorboard, with my back somehow pointing to the earth and my face floating on an imaginary axis of rotation. But as soon as I got used to that direction of pull, another wiggle on the stick shot all my best efforts to Hell. That continued on for longer than I'd like to remember, until we leveled out with an unmistakable jerk and came in contact with the ground. The lights flickered, the cabin rumbled, somebody cheered, and after a quick taxi with a short maintenance check by the crew, the loading ramp dropped and we were hustled back off the plane.

"Let's go! Let's go! Down the ramp! Check your weapon! Check your gear! Helmets on!"

I grazed a hand over all of my vital equipment and grabbed my assault-pack, staggering to my feet as fast as I could.

"Let's go! Go! Go!" The yelling continued.

Between the noise of the aircraft and the shouting from its crew, I was caught up in excitement.

I don't believe it, I thought. *I'm finally here.*

My foot stepped off the ramp and slugged the warm asphalt beneath me. I scanned the horizon and filed through to the passenger holding area. With every step I searched around for a place to get behind cover. When we got to safe territory, I took a knee and picked up a random sector of fire. I was all-ears. 100%. Every fiber in my body was getting ready for a fight. I swear to God, it was the most embarrassing moment of my military career.

"Ludwig!" One of our squad leaders, Staff Sergeant Moore, saw what I was doing and waved me down. "What the fuck are you doing?!"

"Uhh..." I stammered.

There wasn't a single reason for me to be pulling security in the middle of another airport. Not a damn one. So I went with the first thing that popped into my head.

"I'm just... Just fuckin' around... Sarn't."

It was barely a half convincing lie, but at least I was enough of a screwball that he bought it.

"Cut that shit out! Get over here!"

"Roger!" I stood back up and got in formation with a million-dollar poker face. "Where are we, Sarn't?"

"This is BIAP, man."

"Oh...?"

I wasn't sure what that meant, but a quick look around led me to believe it was well out of harm's way.

"Yeah man. *The Baghdad International Airport.* Ain't nothin' goin' on around here. You might as well put on some clubbing shoes and go pick up some honeys."

"Hey Sarn't Moore!" One of the team leaders in the company, Sergeant Walter, made his way over from the far side of the holding area. "You remember the last time we were here?"

"Yeah man," Sergeant Moore turned to greet him with a smile. "That was some crazy shit."

I tried to imagine what it must've looked like back in 2004, but all I could see was a patchwork of fifteen-foot blast-walls and the occasional high-rise office building in the distance.

"Dude," Sergeant Walter said. "The last time we were here, this place was still goin' nuts."

"Really?" I asked.

"Yeah, man! That was, what?" He turned to Staff Sergeant Moore. "Back in '03? '04?"

"Yessir! They took this airfield in '03. We showed up right after that. Man, back then, this place was like the wild fuckin' west."

"Now it's like a fuckin' playground," Sergeant Walter shook his head with disdain.

"You got that right, brother."

"What's so different?" I asked.

"This is 'Camp Victory' now," Sergeant Moore explained. "It's the largest Forward Operating Base in the country, Ludwig."

Sergeant Walter continued. "Yeah. The war's over, man. I don't care what the commander thinks we're in for. All we're gonna do here is sit on our ass and work out at the gym."

"You got that right." Sergeant Moore threw up his fist for a pound. "Time to get *swole.*'"

As they reminisced on old memories, I prayed to God they were wrong. The more I opened my eyes to what was going on, however, the more I realized how unremarkable everything around me looked. Sure, the nighttime air had a heavy musk of burning trash and there was a steady hum of generators no matter where you tried to hide, but nothing else was different from what you'd expect from any other airfield.

My inner monologue was interrupted when our First Sergeant got up in front of the entire company to order us into neatly organized "chalks" — groups of 45 to 50 men apiece that would fly up to our next way station and get that much closer to the end of the line. I took my cue to get back to my gear and plopped down next to Lieutenant Savage. As we sat there in silence, it dawned on me that Sergeant Moore and Sergeant Walter really were spot-on with their assessment. The more I thought about it, the more I realized everything we had been told about Sadr City and the Jaish al-Mahdi could very well have been a bunch of smoke and mirrors to motivate the men and snap us into disciplined shape. After all, the days of Fallujah, Mosul, the Debecka Pass, and Nasiriyah were long over. Other than weekly updates of political misguidance, I hadn't heard a goddamned thing about a major battle in Iraq for a year or more.

No matter how I shuffled the cards, I couldn't ignore the quiet backdrop or the peaceful scene of it all. I found myself caught between two extremes of what the next fifteen months would be like. Though our commanders made it clear that some "old-school shit" was in the works, I couldn't find a scrap of evidence to refute the obvious assertion that all we had waiting for us was a whole lot of nothing. We just sat around the airfield and waited for a long time while I pondered the fate unraveling in front of me.

We were in the heart of occupied Iraq. The capital city of a conquered country. What could I have possibly expected? Tracer-fire off in the distance? Nightly mortar attacks? Hell, there wasn't even a column of smoke in the sky. Baghdad was just a city, and BIAP was just an airport. Unless I was missing something big, there was no way we'd see all the action we had been promised. From the looks of it, I had gone all the way overseas just to sit around and pump iron like a prison inmate.

"Sir," I asked Lieutenant Savage. "What are we waiting on?"

"A flight," he laughed.

"What?"

I thought I misheard him at first, but he repeated the word.

"A flight. We're waiting for seats to open up so we can head over to

Camp Taji and move into the housing area." It was strange to hear him refer to our next airlift as a "flight," and even stranger to hear the calm disposition of the phrase "housing area" in his sentence. I was confused by the situation as a whole. As far as I knew, the entire deployment had been scheduled out to the day.

"Don't we already have a flight?" I asked.

"Nope."

"Aren't we the military?" I continued. "I mean, this should be pretty simple... right? We just call up a bird and go."

I gestured over to the half-dozen CH-64 Helicopters parked on the strip. Whatever the issue, there had to be a pilot somewhere who could shuttle us up to our next stop.

"Apparently not." He shook his head.

"You're kidding me, right?"

"Nope."

Caught up in the thought of how placid the war seemed to have become, I threw my bearing out the window and cracked an open-handed joke. "What, did we forget to book a flight or something?"

"No," he said with a straight face. "We booked it. But our connecting flight got here too late so they gave away our seats to the 'stand by' passengers in the terminal."

I thought he was bluffing at first. The casual use of civilian terminology seemed completely out of place, given the backdrop of military hardware and "war-fighting" mentalities, but I knew that he was just telling me exactly what he had been told himself — and that his reaction had been much the same as mine.

"So how do we get a flight?" I asked.

"We have to book new seats at the Air Travel Office and wait for something else to open up."

Again, the words came out of his mouth with a straight face and only the slightest acknowledgment of how ridiculous it all sounded when he put it into words.

"And...?" I egged him on.

"And the next flight doesn't leave until tomorrow evening, so until then we're on the standby list."

As he embarked on an explanation, I learned that the Army's pilots moved so much living cargo across Baghdad every day that it was impossible to call up a specially-ordered bird for each trip. Instead, they elected to kick-start a civilian model for air traffic control. According to that model, nothing went airborne without a stamp and some paperwork, and there was a contingency in place for when guys like us missed a 'connecting flight' to a nearby 'hub.' As you might imagine, American service members are remarkably punctual creatures, so our 'stand by' ticket was never called. By the time the Air Travel Office closed down for the night, our company First Sergeant had enough time to work out a crash-pad for his men. We packed in, took refuge until morning, and after a 24-hour stint at BIAP we got back on the road to the front lines.

I had every hope that our next stop might look a little more like it was built during a war, but Camp Taji was just another one of the largest Forward Operating Bases in the country. It struck me as more like a theme park than anything else — with all the fly-boy amenities I never expected to find "down range." During our first expedition to the far corners of the base we found a plethora of fast-food restaurants, coffee shops, wi-fi hotspot access, a first-run movie theater, a public swimming pool, and even a salsa bar with cheeky events like "Hawaiian Shirt Tuesdays" and "Near-Beer Fridays." I also had one of my first run-ins with the legendary gourmet chow halls of Iraq, of which Camp Taji was blessed with two. In case you're wondering, the stories are true: I haven't had a better buffet-style meal to this day. But my adventure brought with it the mixed discovery that only some of these amenities were put there for the likes of us. More than half of them weren't even close enough to our housing area for us to use. It took an hour long bus ride just to get some socks and a cheeseburger. Who knew when I'd find the time for the monthly poetry reading.

As soon as our Strykers rolled off the train from Kuwait, Bull Company was ordered to get our trucks set-up to a mission-ready standard and roll out of the wire for our first patrol of the deployment. In the week it took us to set everything up, our secondary task was to understudy the men in the unit we were replacing, who had been doing our new job for the past year or more. I was still the radio guy at the time, so that meant I got the added luxury of rolling out on their last mission with the rest of our leaders — a rite of passage referred to as a "right seat ride." It was part of the hand-off of responsibility from one unit to the next.

"Here's the deal." Lieutenant Savage briefed me when it was time. "These guys have had a long tour and this is their last mission — so it's nothin' big. We're just gonna head on down to one of the combat outposts Captain Bradford's been talking about, get to know the place, and tag alongside these guys for the rest of the night."

In the first few days of hanging out with these guys, I was confronted with the knowledge that we were filling in for hardened veterans who had been fighting the Jaish al-Mahdi since before the troop surge began. I recalled the vivid memory of what their blast-riddled trucks looked like after fifteen months in combat and became a little shaky at the idea of rolling out on my first mission as part of a ride-along during a high-speed raid.

"Okay." I nodded blankly. "Any idea what they're doin', sir?"

"Yeah. One of their civilian contractors had an incident with a sniper yesterday and we're going out tonight to question the locals to see if they know anything about what happened."

That was hardly a reassurance — but at least it wasn't a raid. In fact, our first order of business was strictly administrative in nature: we had been ordered to check-in with the brigade commander of Combat Outpost (aka: COP) Callahan, so we could set up a new cycle of 24 hour shifts as back-up for his men and get a five-star tour of the facilities out on the line.

I had every confidence in the men with whom we rolled out, but I still knew that the only route we could take into our battle-space traversed some of the most dangerous roads in the city. Furthermore, our destination was supposed to be right in the middle of contested territory. Thanks to the briefings in Kuwait, I knew exactly how easy it would be to get hit with a roadside bomb on our way to the outpost. I had goose bumps for the whole drive. To me, every pile of trash on the side of the road was just another reason to be scared.

When we got to the outpost, I marveled at the sight of it. A double-layered concrete barrier skirted the perimeter of the outpost. The outer gate of its only entry control point — or "ECP" — was a hand-painted, tack-welded four inch steel pipe. Beside it, a bi-lingual sign announced the immediate dispatch of unwelcome patrons with lethal force. Only then could we navigate through the serpentine path of concrete barriers, which led up to the hardened guard post at the inner threshold of the base.

The main structure of COP Callahan was built out of the corpse of a charred and desolate four story shopping mall. Long ago, it was burned down from a terrorist attack. Now it was an outpost for the American Army. Since then, its "personality" had only improved with time. All around the outside of the structure, the wall was smeared with blast marks and craters from hundreds of rockets, mortars, and heavy missiles. Chunks of concrete rubble surrounded the entire foundation and the perimeter walls were painted with a patchwork of holes where explosions had punched through to the inside.

The place was totally tactical — it had to be. COP Callahan was the kind of place where men had to wear body armor just to take a shit, and if you spent too much time thumbing your poop-chute it was an accepted risk that you could catch a bullet to the face. Its windows were sealed shut with bricks and mortar. Thick curtains concealed the doors and bays around the first floor of the building. Its insides were even lit with red fluorescent lights so you couldn't make out the details from far away — assuming for a moment you got a straight shot at the inside of the structure. I tried to keep track of all the places where a hole had carved through to the men inside, but halfway around the nearest corner of the building I lost count and gave up.

"Sir," I asked Lieutenant Savage. "What neighborhood are we in again?"

"This is Sha'ab," he whispered. "Keep your voice down. We have to maintain strict noise and light discipline whenever we're here."

"Roger." I changed my tone to a quiet rumble.

"And if you see anybody smoking, tell them to put it out. This place is crawling with snipers."

I followed him inside to link up with the outpost's commander who gave us an updated briefing on the situation. As it turned out, everything I heard about the outpost was true. Since the day it was christened, COP Callahan had taken every kind of barrage the militia could get their hands on. When we got the official tour of the outpost, our escort stopped by the aid station not just to show us where it was, but to boast about the skill of their medics. I could see by the bloodstains on the trim that it had been earned with experience.

Our standing orders laid it all out in the end.

"Be ready for the worst at a moment's notice," the outpost's commander snapped.

"Anything else?" Lieutenant Savage asked.

The commander nodded his head as though considering some future fate. "I'll let you know if anything comes up, but you better be there when I need you."

Two days later, I was back at the outpost with the rest of my platoon to see that their commander had stayed true to his word. He worked out a place for us to crash and we settled in for the night. It was practically a broom closet — but what the hell. It's not like I was about to complain. It even came with a shitty copy of "Oceans Thirteen" and a free TV.

Sergeant Benjamin was hardly impressed by the scene. As another Army Ranger in our unit, he had seen conditions much worse than anything we had been exposed to on our trip. Compared to Taji, I imagine he probably thought COP Callahan was exactly the kind of place where we belonged.

"Make yourselves at home." He gestured to the cots and rubble. "I bet a hundred bucks that we end up living here."

Our company ran daily convoys back down to Combat Outpost Callahan for about a week before his prophecy came true. Some officer finally realized that a regular trip from all the way out at Taji was a bad idea. Even if we changed up the schedule, there were only two or three variations for the route. With an hour long drive, it was a roll of the dice each way. So barely a week into the patrol matrix we were ordered to pack a bag and move in for good. The rest of our equipment would just have to be left behind for the remainder of the tour.

On the first night of living at the COP, a couple of my buddies grabbed their shit to shuffle downstairs for a smoke. With nothing else to do, I tagged along for the sake of conversation. To my surprise, the smoking area in COP Callahan was one of the few places where I didn't have to wear body armor to get a full view of the sky. For that, it was nestled into a dark corner right outside the main building, and surrounded by a heap of protective battlements to keep us safe from anything but a direct-hit. It seemed silly to me that the smoking area was better protected than the porta-shitters. Then again, I guess you don't need access for a sewage truck to empty the butt-can of a thousand smokers.

This was all new to me, but the vets took it in stride. To them, COP Callahan was an artifact of the war they remembered. It was a symbol of how the entire country used to be. We set off on a long conversation that worked through everything we had seen, and soon enough our wit got the better half of discipline. In fact, I was laughing so hard I completely missed the first explosion.

"Hey!" Somebody shouted. "Shut the fuck up! Something's going on out there!"

I stifled my laughter and tried to find out who was talking. My eyes caught a couple tracers flying up into the sky and a few mortars followed suit. Just a few kilometers away from us, a full-on fire-mission kicked off and I finally got to hear the sounds of war I had wanted to experience for so long.

"Sounds like the JSS," another voice offered from the shadows.

I could tell right away they were natives to the outpost, but what caught me off guard was that I hadn't noticed them at all until the rounds came in.

"You mean JSS Sadr City?" I asked.

"Yeah."

I stopped to think for a second and realized why I knew the name so well. It was an outpost of similar circumstance to Callahan but with even less to its name. For our brothers in Comanche Company, that meant living in shipping containers right on the border of Sadr City — right in the very base where those rounds were landing.

"You know somebody over there?" he asked.

"Yeah," I said. "We've got a whole company out at the JSS."

Another blast echoed as the mortars zeroed in. The voice I was talking to stepped out into the moonlight and revealed himself to the group. He took a long drag off his cigarette. The bright orange glow of burning tobacco underlit the jaded features of his face. When his lungs were full of smoke, the cherry glow died out and he exhaled a heavy cloud into the air.

"Welcome to the war."

I suppose it was one of those dime-a-dozen clichés that are in every soldier's story. Hell, I've probably heard the line a hundred times and I don't care. When he flicked that butt into the ash container and turned on his heel to disappear into the shadows of the outpost, my blood went cold. There was no soul in what I heard. No caring or concern. Not even a single scrap of empathy for the men who were dying on the other side of town.

The final string of mortars rang out and I tried to imagine what it's like to run for my life as random explosions tear into everything around me. I tried to ready myself for what it was going to feel like when it was my turn to get hit by the blasts. I felt a sharp pain in my heart for the men who were in the middle of it all — a pain that clawed its way up my throat and swelled into a ball of emotion right where the air gets through to the world. If I had tried so much as to utter a single word, I'd have broken down into tears. Not tears of sorrow or loss, but of abject terror. Tears of missing home, and being so scared of what's coming that you can't imagine what it'll be like. Tears I held back and swallowed whole, because I was just as afraid of these men I had met.

There was nothing I could do for the guys out at JSS Sadr City. Nothing any of us could do. We could only listen to the explosions and pray that nobody got hit. But some day that was going to be us, and we all knew it. It was simply a matter of time. Sooner or later, we'd all get a chunk of it. And for the first moment in years, I finally asked myself if this is what I really wanted all along or if I was just high on some lofty ideal that had landed me right in the middle of something very real — and very bad. But I got my wish that night. I got to hear the booming voice of war. I heard it laugh and cry. Heard it hammer fear into hearts and scar memories. And it was all too real. Real bombs. Real bullets. A real enemy who really wanted to kill me. Real life with a real death. A real war with no do-overs. I stuck around to hear the silence that followed in the wake of the attack. I wondered more than once what the hell had I gotten myself into. But it was too late for second guesses. I was already there. That was the end of the line. I was out in the Shit playing tag-team Russian Roulette with loaded rifles and steel bombs. There was no running away from what we had coming, so I bit my tongue and ate my doubts.

Of all the things on my mind, only one stood out above the rest: that no matter what I still believed in or what I thought about the war, my journey was just getting started.

1st Platoon of "Bull" Company posing for a photograph on the day they shipped out to Iraq in August of 2007.
[Photo credit: James Flemming]

For two weeks the men of the 1/2nd SCR lived in "the Back Forty" of Camp Beuhring, Kuwait, as they prepared for a 15-month tour of combat.
[Photo credit: Ian Peterson]

The men of Bull Company throw up the unit hand signal in celebration of their final flight to Baghdad.
[Photo credit: Chris Landry]

A view of Camp Taji from the window of a Blackhawk Helicopter. (The perimeter of the base is not visible in this photograph.)
[Photo credit: Ian Peterson]

A photograph of the north-eastern slums of "Ur." Due to the complete lack of infrastructure, exposed sewage was a common sight throughout the city.

Though much of Bull Company's battlespace was a slum, the majority of the local population lived in densely packed neighborhoods like the one visible in this photograph overlooking the Copper West Checkpoint.

A photograph of what lay beyond the "northern berm" of Sha'ab and Ur. [Photo credit: Ian Peterson]

A typical house in Ur. Most of Bull Company's time was spent walking door-to-door, interviewing locals and searching for weapons caches belonging to the Jaish al-Mahdi.

An early morning photograph of COP Callahan. Throughout their deployment, the men of the 1/2nd SCR lived in rudimentary combat outposts like this along the border of Sadr City.

Inside of COP Callahan, men lived in cramped conditions with few amenities, rotating between three 12-hour shifts of combat patrols, quick reaction force details and "rest." [Photo credit: *James Flemming*]

Explosive Form Penetrators (EFPs) *were the deadliest threat to Strykers in and around Sadr City.*
[Photo credit: Ian Peterson]

After Bull Company's first raid, 1st *Platoon's lead Stryker* (B-11) *required a complete rebuild of its suspension, hydraulics and steering.*

3rd Platoon, Bull Company, during a 12-hour dismounted patrol through the districts of Sha'ab and Ur.
[Photo credit: Chris Landry]

(From left to right) Sgt. Tuioti, Sgt. Holsker, Lt. Savage, *an interpreter and* Ssg. Bitolas *discuss the next leg of their day's patrol inside the troop compartment of 3rd Squad's vehicle* (B-13).

An early photograph of COP #329 taken during its "construction." The sheet metal roofing seen in this photograph was the only free-standing structure before the project began. [Photo credit: Ian Peterson]

The majority of the people who lived in the districts surrounding Sadr City were receptive to Coalition efforts against the Jaish al-Mahdi.

After six months of daily operations, the men of Bull Company had earned the trust and confidence of the locals.

(From left to right) Cpl. Kazarick, Sgt. Lilly, and Spc. Ludwig enjoy a warm cup of tea during an interview with a local community leader. [Photo credit: Ian Peterson]

A photograph of Spc. Peterson and his M-240B machine gun taken on the first morning of the battle as they rolled out to recapture the checkpoints in Ur.

Due to the relentless nature of the conflict, each platoon in Bull Company was only afforded a single "rest" cycle during the entire five day struggle to retake Ur. [Photo credit: Chris Landry]

On the morning of the "Thunder Run," Spc. Ludwig, Spc. Peterson, Sfc. O'Brien, and the Bull Company sniper team set into position in the highrise building seen in this photo at the Florida/Charlie intersection.

By the end of the day, the landing zone of JSS Sadr City was filled with disabled and destroyed vehicles. Most of the squadron had barely made it out of the city alive.

The following morning, Bull Company assaulted Objective #608 in order to put a stop to the Jaish al-Mahdi's relentless mortar and rocket attacks raining down throughout the city. [Photo credit: Chris Landry]

On the 30th of March, Jaish al-Mahdi troops began a 36-hour counterattack to recapture what had been the cornerstone of their defensive posture. [Photo credit: Ian Peterson]

(Top) Spc. Ludwig takes a quick breather to eat some chow during a lull in the fight. [Photo credit: Ian Peterson]

(Right) The battlements at Outpost Gumby underwent consistant improvement throughout the week.

(Bottom) Spc. Peterson and Ssg. Moore can be seen here, engaging their enemy from the safety of a well-prepared emplacement.

By late afternoon on the 2nd of April, the neighborhood immediately surrounding Objective #608 was in ruin and the Jaish al-Mahdi's counterattack had failed.

Throughout the week spent at Outpost Gumby, special convoys like the one pictured here ran nightly operations to clear a path out to the objective and and carry supplies out to the men. [Photo credit: Ian Peterson]

After abandoning Outpost Gumby, Bull Company settled into a new patrol base back on Route Florida, quickly dubbing it "the Fortress." [Photo credit: Chris Landry]

Throughout the battle, the Iraqi Army played an increasingly crucial role, augmenting American troops in Sadr City, eventually filling-in to hold the frontline for themselves. [Photo credit: Ian Peterson]

On the 17th of April, the Jaish al-Mahdi launched a massive indirect fire-mission onto the main structure of JSS Sadr City, leaving it crippled and uninhabitable. [Photo credit: Chris Landry]

Sandstorms brought with them heavy outbreaks of fighting due to the crippling limitations of American technology and the dynamic nature of urban combat. [Photo credit: Unknown]

A photograph from the gunner hatch of a Stryker during heavy fighting along Route Bravo. [Photo credit: Ian Peterson]

After nearly a month of construction under constant enemy fire, the Gold Wall still covered a total span of less than two kilometers in length. [Photo credit: Chris Landry]

Ssg. Contrerasbaez and Ssg. Benjamin mourn the loss of Cpl. Kazarick, Sgt. Lilly, and Ssg. Gamboa during an emotional memorial to their friends. [Photo credit: Unknown]

In the months following the battle Bull Company maintained a constant presence south of the Gold Wall, earning the favor and support of the local population. [Photo credit: Unknown]

- Chapter Four -
GROUND POUNDING

"Come on, sir... Call it."

Staff Sergeant Benjamin, like the rest of us that morning, was exhausted.

"You know I can't do that." Lieutenant Savage muttered, brushing him off and turning back to his map with heavy eyes.

"Sir... This is ridiculous."

"I know."

We'd been up all night — again. First thing in the morning, at the ass-crack of dawn, some Humvees were hit with a string of roadside bombs out by the edge of town. There were no casualties, but it was still our job to escort Explosive Ordinance Disposal (aka: "EOD") out to the blast site so they could take some pictures and analyze the scene. That first analysis rolled right into a second one when another convoy of Humvees was hit on the other side of town. When one of our own platoons took the third hit of the day, we turned around to escort EOD out to them as well. After nine hours in-sector, it then fell on us to drive some douchebag big-wig out to COP Callahan for a schmoozing session. That wouldn't have been that big of a deal if we hadn't already spent the lion's share of our morning cleaning up the aftermath of a couple blast sites. The fact that the roads still hadn't been cleared of IEDs didn't help much.

Thankfully nothing happened, but we weren't even done with that job before our orders changed, and as soon as our cargo jumped off the truck at COP Callahan we set off on a short notice cordon-and-search to look for some schmuck named "Ahmad." It was a total bust, seeing as how that's one of the most common names in the Middle East, but we did manage to waste the rest of our day interviewing a dozen families to see if they had ever heard of the guy. So after fourteen hours in sector, it was our turn to take over the company battle-space for a twelve hour patrol, which had turned into a long chain of dismounted movements and back-breaking work.

By the time we pulled into the most recent house for a quick break, we had already spent more than 24 hours in sector and Sergeant Benjamin was on a crusade to get us some sleep.

"Sir, come on," he beckoned.

Lieutenant Savage made a few marks in his notepad and tried to ignore what he was hearing.

"What else could we possibly do out here?" Sergeant Benjamin continued.

"Another foot patrol," Lieutenant Savage muttered.

It was clear to me that they were trying to keep the discussion at a low rumble, but after a full day of operations, it's hard to keep your cool.

"Are you kidding me?!" Sergeant Benjamin shouted through his whisper. "We've walked across this sector three times already!"

Lieutenant Savage looked up from his work with a stern glare.

"—And we're going to do it again."

He called out for the rest of his squad leaders, making it clear that he had come to a decision about what to do with the remainder of our patrol. They shuffled into the room to hear the news and everybody else listened in to get a bead on what was next.

"Alright," he struggled to keep his eyes open as he spoke. "We're going to do another foot patrol. Hopefully we can push this one out a bit longer so it'll be the last."

There was a string of uneasy sighs.

"Yeah right," Sergeant Benjamin muttered under his breath.

"What's that!?" Lieutenant Savage snapped.

"Sir, how much longer are we going to stay out here?!"

"Until our patrol cycle is finished, Sergeant Benjamin."

"So that's it?! Gotta' get the last click outta' Joe, huh? We've gotta' work 'em right into the ground?"

"Sergeant Benjamin!" Lieutenant Savage shouted. "Can it!"

I had never seen that kind of insurrection get so far — especially not in front of the men. Sergeant Benjamin dropped silent and Lieutenant Savage turned back to his map.

"Here's the deal, we're going to head back up Route Rolling Rock to Route Maryland, and do a quick run through this shanty-town right here." He traced a circle on the map with his pen. "From there we'll hike over to Checkpoint Grizzlies, come back down this road — here — and sweep through these junkyards one more time."

His pen glazed over the same worn spot that he must've pointed to a hundred times before. With each pass, the ballpoint tip had left a faint mark on the page. After hundreds of iterations you could barely see the terrain under the river of ink. At that point, however, the map was just a prop. We had long ago memorized every rock on the ground where he was pointing.

"That should take us right up to 07:00 or 07:30 hours," he continued. "Questions?"

"Yeah. What are we doin' after that?" 3rd Squad's leader, Staff Sergeant Bitolas, spoke up.

Lieutenant Savage looked out at his men. He could see that we were exhausted and strung out. All we had going for us was force of will — and Lieutenant Savage was no better off. He'd been right there with us the whole time, walking every dismounted mile, talking to every disgruntled local, and humping the same load of gear. Even he was on the verge of saying 'Fuck it.' But we had a mission, and he had a responsibility, so everybody's eyes were on him.

He let out a long sigh. "After that we can mount-up and do an overwatch of Copper West or something."

"Can the boys get some chow?"

"Yeah," Lieutenant Savage answered.

It was a small gesture, but it was enough to keep me going. An overwatch from the Strykers meant anybody who wasn't stuck up in a hatch could catch a cat-nap until our relief rolled in. Just a few more kilometers and it would all be over.

"When do we step off?" Staff Sergeant Moore asked.

Lieutenant Savage looked at his watch. "Let's head out at six o'clock. That'll give 'em another five or six minutes to relax."

I'm not about to say it wasn't good news, but five minutes is hardly time to settle in and take a load off. I couldn't even take a piss before it was time to get up and fall in line. When it was over, Sergeant Benjamin came over to those of us in his squad and let us know what was coming.

"Get ready to move," he said. "We're heading out."

"What's next, Sarn't?" Gonzo asked.

"Another foot patrol."

"Figures."

"Yeah, well we work to-time and not to-standard. You know the deal."

"Yeah, I got it."

"Sergeant Benjamin!" Lieutenant Savage shouted up to us when the rest of the platoon was ready to move. "Go ahead and lead the way! Order-of-march will be 2nd, 3rd, Weapons, and 1st!"

"Roger!" Sergeant Benjamin shouted back.

We filed into the streets and spread out without saying another word. Nobody needed to be told where we were going, everybody knew either by premonition or by routine. There were only so many streets in a town and we had been at it all night.

Our long walk dragged us up the dirt path of Route Rolling Rock, across the dusty pavement of Route Maryland, and spread us out into the fields of boulders and rubble to the west of Checkpoint Grizzlies. On the way, we came into heavy contact with a pack of rabid dogs and passed a couple piles of rotting sheep guts leftover from the holidays. Nobody spoke a word. Not even a muffled complaint. We were too tired for that kind of bullshit.

One more foot patrol.

I clung to the idea for everything I was worth.

When we hit the end of our northward journey, it was time to turn around and double-back. An hour later we crossed over the starting point of the patrol. Pushing even farther to the south, we trudged through the worst parts of the neighborhood slums and came out at the front gate of the first junkyard on our route. After another hour of crisscrossing through endless piles of discarded I-beams and rotting bus frames, we got orders from the brass to fold our patrol into a higher-level search for caches and contraband. With a single set of instructions, our idle "walk-through" became an exercise in manual labor.

The key to an effective search was to find the hardest possible place to hide a cache, and go look in that spot. As the joke went, we had already killed off all the idiots. That far into the war we were fighting the ones who had a knack for staying alive. An effective search usually meant we had to relocate a mountain of hub-caps and wade through a knee-deep reservoir of human waste just to find a twelve ounce Zip-Lock bag of Composition-B or a dozen magazines for an AK-47. By the time we called it quits, the morning sun had peeked out over the rooftops and a new day dawned. All told, we clocked-out that day with 26 hours of the hardest work I've ever known — and that was just another day in the Suck.

When we mounted back onto the Strykers, I plugged in my headset and got ready for the drive back to base. Sergeant High had already climbed up into the hatch next to me while Sergeant Benjamin made his way to the squad leader hatch next to our vehicle commander, Biaz. As soon as the ramp went up, we got the call that our relief was in-bound.

"Finally!" Sergeant Benjamin shouted to the driver, "Scalzitti, let's roll!"

"What? We're going back already?!" Biaz, coughed up a tired laugh.

"Well, you know, we just had to get the last click outta' Joe."

We had been in-country for more than six months. In six months a lot of things changed. Things like heavy eyes and evaporating boyhood. Like humor turning darker than tar. Like our boots wearing down to the nub. In six months, every shred of cherry was picked clean from our bones. Dust had made it into the corners of our souls, and we were broken in like hard leather. We had long ago grown numb to the routine.

In order to maintain our Strykers at a more forward location and cut down on refit operations back to Taji altogether, a new home was carved out for us at a place called "Combat Outpost Old MOD," which was the former campus of the Iraqi Ministry of Defense. When the war was won, we had repurposed the whole thing into a joint combat outpost for American and Iraqi Army personnel. The irony here was that everybody knew our Iraqi Army cohabitants were really double agents for the militia, so even at "home" we had to keep a watchful eye out for the shadows. The trade off was that we never got mortared — the militia didn't want to hit their own guys.

There were manpower changes too. After a long string of malfeasance, our old Platoon Sergeant was finally relieved of his duties. His replacement, a man named Sergeant First Class O'Brien, turned out to be exactly what we needed. That arrival was just the first step in a new era of Bull Company's leadership. In January our old company commander had finished up his run in office, and a new one was brought in to take over. Since that transition, we'd been fighting under the command of a hot-shot leader by the name of Captain Bradford. If you could say anything about him, it's that he took the reins and ran. After that, we were like a whole new unit.

For the past 180-something days, Bull Company's area of operations was marked on our map as a place called "Ur" — a depraved slum spanning the north-west border of Sadr City. If I hadn't seen it with my own two eyes, I wouldn't believe a place like Ur could exist. It was an ant-farm of abject poverty. The very bottom of a rotten barrel. Its people were either starving, destitute, or mutilated with disease. At best, you could say they were dirt-poor. As for the worst of them — I'm simply at a loss for words. Those people lived in a jungle of junk yards, brick shelters, shanty structures and trash heaps, intermixed and infested with the lowest standards of human existence. Thick rivers of piss, shit, and trash snaked between shoddy buildings and tacked-together shelters, gathering into great lakes of sewage wherever the ground was low. These creeping bodies of dark green filth engulfed whole regions of the neighborhood.

As the months ticked by, they grew even larger until they had swallowed entire communities under the muck.

If you flew in from overhead, you could spot the place out in a second: Ur was a four kilometer long, "V"-shaped pit of desolation, cut right into the eastern half of Baghdad. Across the open end of that "V" shape, the northern flank of Ur was capped with a massive berm of dirt and trash. According to the satellite imagery — and what we could gather from the locals — the only thing we'd find on the far side of the berm was an empty canal.

"Well," Lieutenant Savage shrugged. "We might as well go check it out."

That was back when we didn't know.

On one of our first patrols, we ventured over the berm and down into the basin on the far side, thinking it was solid ground. Instead, it turned out to be a deep, muddy wash of chemical waste. The entire channel was filled with a syrup of oil and dust. The only reason it looked solid was because a thin layer of dirt rested right on top of the muck. Those of us who didn't slip and fall right over sank into it like quicksand — so we turned around and crawled back out as quickly as we could.

"Call Bull-Base." Lieutenant Savage scraped the gunk off his shoes. "Tell them we don't have to worry about anything coming over the berm."

"Roger." I keyed up my radio to relay the message.

"Let's get the hell out of here."

When I got back to the top of the berm, I turned around to look out at the desert. There was nothing but a flat expanse of dirt and sand trailing off into the distance, with tiny specks of human life spread out like crumbs on a marble floor. Beyond that vast field of nothingness. A wall of dust blurred the line between the earth and sky. It was like we were stuck inside of a snow-globe of dirt and sand.

Our friendly border in Ur was to the west, marked by the major avenue of "Route Miller." Beyond that was the suburb of "Sha'ab," where the 82nd Airborne Division's 2/325th AIR Battalion of "White Falcons" were on the beat. Because it was regularly cleared and more-or-less secure terrain, Sha'ab was our only real chance of getting to Ur without taking contact on the way — but that's not to say it never happened.

There were only three roads leading into Ur from Sha'ab, and every one of them converged at a little gem of an intersection we came to know as "the Triangle of Death." Now, that's not the most creative name in the world, and I didn't come up with the line, but it was certainly appropriate to the situation. 3rd Platoon got hit practically every time they rolled through. When it was our turn, I tried to make peace with another wrong I had committed to the world. After six months, there wasn't that much left for me to atone for, so I just shrugged it off and hoped for the best.

Our hostile border was on the eastern side of Ur and marked by what many people considered to be the most dangerous road in the city. "Route Grizzlies," as it was known, might as well have been a force field: the entire length of it was lined with hundreds of roadside bombs and rocket firing positions to ambush whoever tried to traverse its length. At one point, a daring attempt was made to clear the route from end-to-end using a heavily loaded convoy of mine-resistant vehicles. In less than an hour, they were hit with more than a dozen high-powered, armor-penetrating EFPs, and fought through a series of coordinated ambushes carried out by the militia. At the end of the second hour, every vehicle in the convoy was heavily damaged and — needless to say — the mission was scrubbed. What I didn't expect to hear was that they'd barely traversed 300 meters of the road before turning back and calling it quits.

300 meters.

That was it.

Beyond Route Grizzlies was the stronghold of Sadr City. Since it was put together as a massive housing development back in 1959, it was the only part of Baghdad with evenly spaced roads and clearly marked blocks of apartment buildings. To this day, that's the most defining characteristic of the district, and probably the best reason why the Jaish al-Mahdi was so well entrenched for a fight. The regular spacing and overall design of Sadr City allowed the militia to put together a virtually plug-and-play strategy for their insurgency. Each of the city's 84 major blocks were interlaced with dozens of back-alleys and footpaths that were the same as every other. In short, they had fully concealed access to every inch of the city while the major routes we'd take to get around were lined with ambushes and bombs. In addition, each block was built with its own mosque, and long ago they had converted these holy structures of peace into military outposts to serve as command centers for their men.

The Jaish al-Mahdi were fully aware that our rules of engagement strictly prohibited us from returning fire at a mosque without approval from on high. More importantly, they knew that we knew they knew that. It was a P.R. nightmare to explain why American soldiers would ever dream of attacking a house of peace, and rather than face down the gauntlet of cameras every time, our standing orders were to avoid them at all costs. In the end, that was just another bullet point on the list of factors that came together to tip the scales. An organically engineered chain of command with a full battalion of militia regulars was run out of each mosque in the city. There was nothing we could do to stop them and, just in case we ever came looking for trouble, they had the whole place rigged to blow.

This was the Sadr City I came to know.

By the time Bull Company showed up, all the pieces of infrastructure that had come with the original development of Sadr City were crumbling after decades of neglect. In their stead, the residents of Sadr City had cobbled together a makeshift power grid and water service, which the Jaish al-Mahdi now controlled at the muzzle of a gun. Like Ur, sewage disposal was still an issue in Sadr City, but the paved streets were enough to consolidate most of the waste, and channel it off to a park or playground nearby. So at the end of the day, I suppose you could say that Sadr City was like any other ghetto in a war-torn Third World country.

Come sunrise, the streets were packed full of vendors and haggling shoppers, while cars fought their way through traffic that resembled more of a battle royal than a daily commute. Donkey-drawn carriages carted boxes of Sony DVD players next to the butchered carcasses of gutter-fed livestock and rotting produce. Fancy sports cars of mafiosi crimelords dotted the landscape between mangled 1980's sedans and rusty Japanese pickup trucks. The whole place was a storm of shouts, honks, and commotion, riddled with ad-hoc improvements and built upon a latticework of jerry-rigs. Life there carried on with its own downtrodden, chaotic sense of stability, which seemed to coagulate just outside the gates of madness.

The only weakness of the militia's holdout in Sadr City was that it survived on imports — just like every other city in the world. Each morning, hundreds of thousands of cars and trucks siphoned rivers of goods into the city to feed its ravenous need for consumption. In exchange for what? I don't really know. But whenever the sun was up, every road into Sadr City jammed up with commuters, many of which doubled as supply convoys for the militia. Gas, guns, and explosives were the staple products of their trade. The first was just a source of income. The other two were the meat and potatoes for the cause. All three were shipped in from Iran using the northern highway as a primary supply route, on trucks that had to cut through Ur to make it anywhere near Sadr City.

That was where we came in.

Three main roads led into the heart of Sadr City from the north. Each one sliced right across Ur, and we knew them from north to south as Routes "Maryland," "Copper West," and "Gold." If a large shipment was going to make it into the city from our area of operations, it was going to happen on one of those roads.

"We need to plug those damn holes," the Colonel said. "We're gonna' starve these bastards out until they have nothing left to fight us with."

Armed with the new doctrine, we built up a string of checkpoints and manned them with platoons from the Iraqi Army. Their job was to search the passing vehicles for explosives and small-arms. Our job was to stop by every day to check on them and show them how it's done. If you had asked me, I would have said it was a total waste of time. I can't even tell you how many man-hours I've blown on trying to get one of those lazy bastards to do a basic pat-down for his own safety. For the most part, the only thing my Iraqi counterpart would have to do is escort the passengers to-and-from the holding area, and feed them instructions as we went along.

We were supposed to be "teaching" them how to do it, but you can't teach somebody who doesn't care about learning. It didn't matter how many times we ran them through the motions, they always gave us the same dumb smirk and did their best to fuck it up. One time, my counterpart at the checkpoints spent an hour shouting false commands to the locals and herding them through before I could pat them down. It took everything in my power not to punch the guy in the face. Instead, I backed him up against the wall and gave him a piece of my mind.

"You're fucking worthless," I spat the words into his face. I was so close to him that could feel my own breath reflecting off his brow.

"Hey," Lieutenant Savage said. "Give him a break! They haven't had the same kind of training we have. You're gonna' have to deal with a little lack of discipline, alright?"

"I don't know, man." Sergeant Benjamin blew off his own special-ed case and came over to join us before the next car rolled in. "We've shown them how to do this – what – a hundred times? It's not like they don't know how to search a fucking car. This is a total waste of time."

"No," Lieutenant Savage protested. "This is the heart of the mission. It's the most important part of why we're here. Our job is to train these guys so they can take over the fight, and we can go home."

"And when is that, sir?" Sergeant Benjamin's incredulity was unmistakable.

"When you can finally show these guys how it's done."

He had a point, but it wasn't because they didn't know how to do it that it never got done. The cold truth was that if they started searching cars, the militia was going to kill them all – and their families too. If they arrested a single "bad guy," their life was over. So who were we, a bunch of infidels that'd be gone in a year, to tell those guys at that checkpoint what was and wasn't worth dying for? The militia wasn't going anywhere, and these soldiers had better things to do than fuck with the food chain. All the way up to the top, their commanders were on the take. Every one of them was working for the militia in one way or another. Nobody was safe. Besides, an example had already been made in the past.

Somewhere along the line, one of the commanding officers of one of the checkpoints elsewhere in town had been promoted and some new-school, young-buck graduate of the Baghdad equivalent to West Point had taken his place. I have to give him credit for showing up and whipping those bastards into shape, because after settling into his new command, he had a laundry list of bad-guys cuffed-up and prepped for a prison cell. The very next day, however, he got lined up with the bulk of his men against the outer wall of the checkpoint and gunned down by a militia firing squad. They were left out in the open to rot as a message to those who got in the way of the Jaish al-Mahdi. The story was a legend. Understandably, it was twice as hard to get their replacements to do the job.

When we weren't training Iraqis on pat-downs, we spent the rest of our time running the beat in Ur. The "streets," however, were little more than a tangle of muddy back-alleys and strips of unpaved earth. They wound around buildings and doubled-back on one another in a web of footpaths and tire-tracks. It appeared to me those streets had been thrown together as thoughtlessly as the houses on either side, but to my surprise it was actually rather official.

After a month or two of trying to map the whole place on our own, we stumbled into a real estate office and made friends with the guy whose business it was to know where the lines had been drawn in the sand. When we asked for a copy of the map posted on the wall over his desk, he gladly handed it over. The event was followed shortly by a long string of revelations.

"Look at that," Lieutenant Savage mumbled to himself, "this place isn't even called Ur."

"What?!"

"You know how we've been having all that trouble asking the locals where things are?" Lieutenant Savage asked.

"Yeah?"

"That's because we're not even in 'Ur' — we're in Qouds. 'Ur' is actually up in what we call 'Sha'ab.'"

I was surprised at first, but then it all started to make sense. Our maps were probably based on some random, half-assed interview conducted years before we got there by somebody who had probably never set foot in the neighborhood.

"No," our interpreter clarified. "Ur *is* Sha'ab."

"Exactly! Man, we've got this all wrong."

"Well, good thing we've got that map." I laughed.

We spent all of our spare time patrolling that shoddy excuse for an infrastructure. Thanks to our updated knowledge of the area, we had a better idea of what was where and how to get around. In any case, we still called it Ur, because if we didn't, nobody else in the Army would have any idea what the hell we were talking about.

Thanks to the map, we also discovered that whenever we needed to go from one end of Ur to the other, we could stick to a route we later named "Rolling Rock." Rolling Rock wasn't so much a single road as it was a series of dirt pathways and tire-tracks snaking along a bunch of junkyards and open fields across the middle of town. If we followed the right set of tracks like the map said, Rolling Rock ran from the northern edge of the berm all the way down to the southern checkpoint on Gold. One wrong turn, however, and we'd find ourselves chassis deep in muck or caught up on a tangle of power-lines in no time.

Despite its widespread squalor, the neighborhood as a whole was not completely barren of a resemblance to the western world. Many of the more defined dirt roads were lined with two- or three-story "houses," and the few appliances we found inside were all adorned with the same iconic logos of the Fortune 500 back home. The differences of course, were in the details: instead of measuring out a floor-plan and carefully stacking materials in accordance to a design, their homes were thrown together with low-grade, tan colored brick, and glued in place using cheap, pulverized mortar. The floors and structural supports were reinforced with hand-bent rebar that was eye-balled into place without measurement or correction. The structure was then filled-in with an alchemist's version of concrete, which they mixed with bare feet in holes in the ground, like grapes at a vineyard. Upon closer inspection, what appeared at first to be a classic trim formed around the windows and doors of higher-class buildings revealed itself to be nothing more than poorly tack-welded strips of aluminum glued to tinted plastic sheets and hollow-panel doors.

The thing was that no matter how destitute the family might've been, it was unheard of to go without a hacked satellite receiver and old-school television set, tuned to pick up every channel in the world. We found Playstation gaming consoles, BOSE 5.1 surround-sound stereo systems, and cutting-edge HP desktop computers with stacks upon stacks of DVD-RW discs in some of the most disgusting hovels you can imagine. We'd see kids listening to music on first-class cellphones not even ten feet away from a "kitchen" with a dirt floor. And in some places, right in the middle of the ghetto, we'd come across marble-clad mansions with gilded handles and vaulted ceilings. Who cares if they looked like a five-year-old put them together, it was still a freaking mansion.

"How much does a house like this cost?!" I asked one of our interpreters.

"Oh... Maybe a couple hundred-thousand — maybe a million Dinar."

"What?! That's like... a thousand bucks! You're telling me I could get a two story mansion with marble floors and shit for — like — a grand?!"

"Ludwig!" Waite laughed. "Are you thinking of buying a house here or something?"

"I don't know. Maybe. But the utilities look like a real ball-buster."

"Yeah man, and the commute? You saw the traffic on the way in."

"At least the neighborhood is pretty nice."

"From what I hear the school district is getting better by the day."

Waite motioned to the man speaking to Lieutenant Savage and our Interpreter. Our mission that day was to conduct a neighborhood-wide survey of past improvements to the area. Education was on the top of the list. Apparently one of our schools was the envy of eastern Baghdad.

A loud explosion rang out in the distance and my radio went nuts. I linked up with Lieutenant Savage and filled him in on the situation.

"Sir, 3rd Platoon just got hit escorting EOD. Bull-Base wants us to take over."

"Roger. Let the squad leaders know we're moving out."

That was the end of the social calls for the day.

When we showed up in-country, Bull Company was supposed to be an "above ground" unit. That meant we were only there to run high-speed raids and stand by at COP Callahan as local reinforcements. But after a few weeks of taking it easy, the White Falcon's commanding officer put us to work.

"No point in having you Stryker boys sittin' around doin' nothin'!" He said. "Let's get you in the fight! Let's see what you can do!"

He put us to work alright. That's how we got Ur. Back then it was part of the 'no-go' zone of Sadr City. It was a hot-bed of conflict. The border-town to oblivion. It might as well have been a mine-field. The word on the wire was that the 82nd Airborne didn't even bother patrolling it anymore because it always became a shit-storm whenever they tried.

"Yeah, they've been hit pretty hard," Lieutenant Savage told me early on in the deployment. "This place isn't a joke."

Since then, we had combed over every inch of Ur with a fury. We did a dozen or more high-speed raids on key targets of opportunity and searched hundreds of houses. The Iraqi Army might not have been doing their jobs at the checkpoints, but at least their presence was keeping the militia from rigging those streets with IEDs. And in six months we'd crammed a lifetime of work into that mud. It took six months, but we had finally forced the militia out of hiding. We had pushed them back across Route Grizzlies and changed the face of Ur. The work was agonizing, exhausting, and unending, but after six months we had earned the right to take our helmets off and play patty-cake with the kids. We went from guns-drawn to hand-shakes, and now it was tea and cigarettes in every home.

The clearest sign of what we had accomplished came during an overwatch operation of the Copper West Checkpoint. The idea was to set up a firing position on some key piece of terrain, and keep an eye open for enemy activity in the area — which we had been doing on a daily basis. The problem was that there was only one piece of useful terrain anywhere near the checkpoint. It was a three-story apartment building inhabited by a single family, right on the corner of Rolling Rock and Copper West.

From the top of that building we could see clear across town. It was the only building in the area with such a wide field of view. Obviously, that also made it a hard opportunity to pass up, so every platoon in Bull

Company went back there daily. Thinking back now, the owner of that house must've had soldiers knock on his door two or three times each day at random intervals to hang out on his roof for hours at a time and drill him on the local happenings in his neighborhood.

After abusing his generosity for six months straight, however, we started getting worried that we might have drawn too much attention from the militia. The last thing we needed was for an entire family to get murdered for helping us out. In response to that threat, Captain Bradford put out the order for us to use some other building from that point onward. Our platoon was sent in to apologize for the prolonged inconvenience and conduct our final overwatch from the apartment.

Like we'd done countless times before, the majority of our men went upstairs to the top floor and pulled security out of the windows. A single fire-team was left by the front door, while the rest of us – six or seven in all, stuck around in the living room to drink chai and socialize with the family. As soon as we settled in, Lieutenant Savage went about the task of letting the man know that we'd be taking a break from using his house so he wouldn't have to worry about getting hit by a militia kill-team. No sooner had the interpreter said those words and the man was on his feet, throwing up his arms with anxiety.

"*La! La!*" He motioned for us to stay in our seats, then rambled off something in Arabic I couldn't understand.

"He is saying *'No! No!'* He wants to thank us," our interpreter translated. "He is saying every morning before we come, the militia was using his house as place to leave dead bodies after they kill them."

"Exactly," Lieutenant Savage continued talking to the man. "And we don't want those men to come after you for helping us."

The interpreter struggled to explain the situation to the man, but he teared up with emotion and continued his rant.

"No, no..." The interpreter continued. "He is saying every morning, he would have to pick up the bodies and move them somewhere else so his daughter would not have to see them."

Our interpreter struggled to keep up.

"He says every day he was waking up before prayer, sometimes three or four bodies there. They are murdered by the militia. He says ever since we come here, the militia stopped. He saying we have stopped militia from doing this, and we are always welcome. He is begging us to stay."

Lieutenant Savage was shocked. He smiled and the man caught a glance of his expression, rambling on with excitement.

Our interpreter laughed and gave us the news.

"He says we can even move in if we like!"

The man called his wife in to bring us more chai and looked around at all of us with a desperate expression on his face. Lieutenant Savage had him sit tight until we could get in touch with Captain Bradford to explain the situation. As we took our leave, the rest of the guys chatted with him and the interpreter.

"Are you serious?" Captain Bradford called us back.

"Yeah," Lieutenant Savage laughed.

"Alright. That's fine by me. Go ahead and maintain your overwatch for another hour and then carry on with the mission as planned. Bull-Six, out."

Lieutenant Savage turned back to the interpreter. The man sat there with wide eyes, waiting for the word. When he saw Lieutenant Savage smile, his own face lit up with a cheer.

"Alright, we're not going anywhere," Lieutenant Savage reassured him. "We'll be coming back here every day to check on you and your family, and I thank you for letting us use your home to fight the militia."

The man kissed his hands and threw them up to the sky. He got up to shake every one of ours, rambling incoherently with tears swelling in his eyes.

"He says 'thank you.'" The interpreter said. "Thank you very, very much."

I was speechless.

The first time we showed up at that house that same man had glared at me with more contempt than I had ever seen in my life. I'd be lying if I said it wasn't mutual. There was no love in that house. We spent an hour and a half sitting in awkward silence, fuming with anger. Ironically, he was probably mad at us for the same reason we were about to leave. But six months later, that same man was shaking my hand with tears in his eyes and begging us to stick around.

"It's my pleasure." I nodded back with a smile.

It was a genuine phrase.

I would've spent another year in that Shit just to know that his family was safe. To this day I wish we never left that house. I was willing to die for every single one of them. And not just them, the whole neighborhood. Everyone we were fighting for. Everyone who'd suffered since the war began, eking out a life under the shadow of the militia. Everyone we had promised to help, and signed up to serve.

That's one of the things people never heard about when they read through the headlines of the war — about how deep we worked our way into that world. How it became a part of us. How we had nicknames for every kid on the block and a personal oath to each family out in-sector. We weren't just over there, we were a part of it. We were fighting for their lives as much as ours, living in a fucked up world and doing everything we could to make a difference. And no, I don't know what the hell that has to do with America, but at least I could point at some place on the map and say for sure that I made a difference. That I did something right. That I had something worth dying for and it was something that mattered — as unheard of as it might've been. For that alone it was worth it, but that fight was the fight of our lives.

"Persistence is key." Those were the magic words. If we had any hope of victory we couldn't afford to give the militia time to fester. We had to be out in the streets, pulling security and schmoozing with the locals during every hour of the day. In order to keep that kind of constant presence in Ur, Bull Company had to go all-out. We ran a 36-hour cycle between each of the three platoons in our company. That's a 36-hour day: 24 spent working outside the wire and 12 spent back at base, getting ready to go out again.

First on the list was a 12-hour patrol. That's 12 hours in the Suck. 12 hours of walking, talking, searching, and fighting. 12 hours of non-stop, back-breaking work, knowing at any minute that we could be hit with a roadside bomb or take a dead-on shot by a sniper. You'd be amazed at what a group of men can do in 12 hours. We could sweep through our whole area of operations, conduct a series of searches at all three checkpoints, and finish up a four kilometer foot patrol before it was time for chow. We set up cordons and talked to dozens of families to get a picture of what was going on in the area. We settled into high-side positions and overwatch locations to look over half the city until our eyes bled. And after all that, we'd still have time on the clock.

Next up was a 12-hour cycle of "rest." That's 12 hours of "holding down the fort" – of guard, mail-call, maintenance, and sleep. The "rest cycle" was our time to recharge batteries and get some rack, but "rest" is the wrong word to use. The Infantry doesn't really "rest." That was just our time to hack out the vehicle maintenance, clean all our weapons, re-program and inspect the radios and equipment on every Stryker, straighten up the barracks, run through our post and pre-patrol personal hygiene rituals, chew through a stale plate of hot chow, plow through a relentless pile of paperwork, inventory all of our equipment, load and unload a convoy of supplies, finish our outpost guard duties, and pick up trash around the COP. Essentially, that 12-hour rest cycle broke down into two three-hour shifts of hard labor, with about six hours of sleep crammed right in the middle. Our sheep-counting time shrank even farther if we planned on doing something extra for ourselves like call home, watch a movie, or grab a quick session on the Internet.

But sooner or later, the "rest" cycle was over, and that's when we set out on another 12-hour shift as the designated "Quick Reaction Force" (aka: QRF) in-sector. Another word you could use for QRF is "reinforcements" – although that term meant a lot more than simply swooping in when shit hit the fan. It was also picking up the slack for everything that might need doing while somebody else was out on patrol. Usually QRF missions were limited to not-quite-combat operations, things like escorting EOD or playing taxi-driver for some high-ranking officer. There were times we spun up for no better reason than a 12-hour babysitting gig for Route Clearance, guiding them around the city or stepping in as their body guard when they got hit. Sure some missions were a lot of fun, like when we'd roll out on a short-notice snatch-and-grab raid to kill-or-capture a time sensitive target in a secret compound. But even then, there was no escaping a neighborhood-wide "cordon and talk" that would follow up the raid in order to keep our standing with the local population.

That was the worst part about QRF: knowing every hour we spent on one of those slapdash missions pushed us that much closer to the start of our next patrol. Regardless of rank and file, it was a recipe for high-tension outbreaks of anger.

"I don't believe this shit!" Lieutenant Savage tried to muffle his outbreak, but it was hard to miss the sound of headphones smacking up against hard steel.

Typically, he was the last person in our platoon to lose his cool, but it was already midnight and for the past week QRF had been packed with busywork. They were the kind of missions that are just long enough to suck, and spaced just far enough apart for us to set down our gear and crawl into bed before getting called back up to roll out of the wire for another go.

This time we hadn't even made it off the trucks.

"What's up, sir?" I asked,

"We've got to go back out. Route Clearance just got lost again."

"You're kidding me, right?"

"No."

"What the fuck?!" Sergeant High overheard the outbreak and felt obliged to chime in. "They're clearing Route Pluto! How can they possibly get lost?! The motherfucking road is like eight lanes wide! It's got big-ass walls on either side of it!"

"Yeah, I know. And now they're somewhere north of Gold."

He jumped on the radio to call it up to the rest of the platoon and a few minutes later we rolled out of the gate. As you can imagine, I wasn't left with a very fond impression of Route Clearance by the time it was all over.

But QRF was give-and-take. Another week, it was all quiet. For the first time in months, we found ourselves blessed with some downtime to chill out and relax. In about seven days I sat through the better half of the IMDB top-50 list, including almost every science fiction classic starting from 1982.

"You know what?" My buddy Kaz put down his controller and took a break from his game. "I'm actually pretty fuckin' bored."

I looked over at Kaz. Just a few years ago I had met him during a squad competition when I was lumped in with the snipers and tankers. It wasn't until he was moved over to 1st Platoon a few weeks prior that I really got to know him. At this point, he was one of my closest friends.

"I know what you mean," I said.

As we got back to our mind-numbing hypnosis, Doc stuck his head in the door. "Hey, you guys got any new movies? I've watched all of mine like a dozen times already."

"Sorry Doc," I shrugged. "I've got the same collection you do."

He looked over at the other guys in our room, neither of which had anything else for him to watch.

"Check out 3rd Squad," Kaz said. "I think they just came back from the Hadji-Mart. I'm sure they've got something."

"Cool! Thanks!"

Doc spun around and disappeared. The rest of us got back to the mind-warp of modern entertainment. I have no idea how my grandpa's generation passed the time, but it was probably a hell of a lot more constructive than what we were up to over there. I think I watched more consecutive hours of film and television that week than I spent out in sector. I'd logged so many fifteen minute Facebook sessions there wasn't anything new to see. But it wasn't very long before things got back to the way they were, and we started longing for some rest again.

For the most part, nothing ever changed. We had the same battle-space with the same patrol cycle, the same bad chow, the same unending fatigue, and the same shitty weather. We made the same preparations for the same missions. The same ambiguous Middle Eastern faces shouted the same guttural bursts of broken language. We used the same hand signals to tell them slow down, stop, get against the wall, put their hands up, and turn off their car. Every day. Every week. For months on end. It was so relentless that we didn't even notice our lives tick by after a while. We got lost in a never-ending now, and lived for some death-defying raid to break up the routine.

But in subtle and powerful ways, it was also never quite the same.

Like staring out at the ocean: the bigger picture was painted with an unwavering and daunting expanse of tiny little details that were choppy and ever-changing. At random intervals we stirred up the patrol matrix, the hit-times, and the schedules. Every day we took a different route into our area of operations. We varied the patterns of what kinds of operations we ran, for how long we ran them, and where. One day we'd do foot patrol by the water treatment facility, then checkpoint ops down on Copper West. The next day we'd open with an overwatch of Route Grizzlies, and follow it up by a joint operation with the Iraqi Army in Sha'ab. For a whole week we'd drive with the flow of traffic while the week before had been a clusterfuck of weaving back and forth from "flow" to "counterflow." One day we found a roadside bomb that hadn't gone off yet and backed up to a 400 meter stand-off. A few days later we pulled right up next to it. Next week?

Nobody knew.

Down to the pattern of our footsteps, we avoided crossing each other's paths so a sniper couldn't get a lucky shot. We learned that one when Sergeant Brasel got shot in the back. We also learned that body armor works, even though it's heavier than shit. The most terrifying lesson was that our lives really did depend on the small things, so each passing second became a conscious effort and a deliberate variation in an attempt to simulate "random." It was mind-wracking work to keep up a show of the ever-changing. Even then, we were still at the mercy of the random chaos of war. One day we'd run into a gun battle and the next day we'd get hit with a roadside bomb. Or maybe, for no reason at all, we'd catch a long stretch of quiet for days on end. Sometimes the worst neighborhood in the world was filled with smiles while our go-to place to chill was rigged with mines.

There is a myth that is war. It's of archetypes and automatons blasting away at each other during every second of the day. It's a Hollywood picture of men getting in brutal firefights that drag on for hours. But out there on the ground, the real war isn't with the enemy at all; it's with complacency. It's with yourself. It's fighting the urge to zone out and go through the motions. It's keeping on your toes until your tendons snap.

You can let your guard down a thousand times and nothing will happen – but it only takes one to get you killed. And then you're dead. Forever. Right when you least expect it.

If we set up a routine or reacted the same way every time something happened, the militia would be there waiting for us. They were looking for cracks in the armor. They were counting on us to let our guard down. Daring us to do anything twice. Even at our damnedest, we were only men. So, yeah, we got hit. We got hit hard. It was only by some slip of Fate that none of us died. It came down to a matter of inches every time. Each one should've been the last, but they weren't. So we learned. We got better at our job. We got tighter, faster, and hit them harder than they hit us. In six months we were as natural to that world as the locals. We were as foreign to that land as the dirt on the ground. After six months of living, breathing, and sucking down the real face of war, I could barely remember home.

Somewhere in the middle of all this white noise, the 82nd's deployment ended and a new breed of Army flew in from Ft. Carson to replace them. As the tradition went, our squadron commander, the departing 82nd Airborne commander, and a bunch of battle-captains from both of our intelligence wings sat down with the incoming 4th ID commanders to give them a break-down of the battle-space and everything we knew about how to survive. It was more than a courtesy; it was a basic necessity. It was everything we knew about how the enemy thinks and operates, what works and doesn't work, what to do, and where to go if your primary goal is anything other than getting fucked up and killed. It was hard-fought wisdom, earned not only by us, but those who came before us. And from what I heard of the murmurs and mutters sifting through thin walls of meeting rooms on our outpost, they had blown us off entirely.

Over the course of the following weeks, posters and fliers flew up all over the outpost proclaiming new and improved "Ironhorse" standards. Practically overnight, dozens of Sergeants Major showed up at Old MOD and chewed us out for every little thing they could find. They balked at the extra armor strapped to the outside of our vehicles. They mocked our scruffy appearance. They forbid us from wearing basic, Army issued desert apparel like boonie hats and sweat rags. They even showed up to inspect our bedrooms when we were out on patrol, looking for anything to flip out about when we couldn't be there to defend ourselves. When we finally got back from hours in the Suck, they dispatched us in hordes to mop down balconies and scrub every ounce of dust off of the banisters and sidewalks of the Outpost. After a few weeks of getting shoved around like a bitch, I was convinced that every douchebag with a 4th ID patch had a chip on his shoulder, and I could feel my skin crawl every time we saw one of their squeaky-clean vehicles driving around in our sector.

It was infuriating. An anger externalized by our own mockery and insult of everything about them. We laughed at their convoys when they drove by, scoffed at them in the chow hall if we crossed paths, and segregated ourselves in every way we could. Back then, as far as I gave a shit, the 4th ID was as much of an enemy as the Jaish al-Mahdi. Maybe even worse, since it was impossible for us to fight back. All we could do was fall in line and stand by. They were the bosses and we were the underlings. We just had to sit there and watch them roll out of the wire in freshly scrubbed vehicles, carrying on with the mission using unchanging, textbook tactics. Meanwhile, we couldn't take a shit without a new standard getting shoved up our ass.

Nevertheless, as the days carried on, we got used to the routine. More importantly, I realized I was in no position to look down on our new companions. Just a few moths prior I was just another fucked up "Joe" who had never seen a gunfight, and after a half-decade of warfare it was a rare thing to find a unit that was devoid of two-time veterans. The majority of those guys had nothing to do with the high-level bullshit that was coming down the chain. Hell, they'd probably been putting up with that shit for years. Besides, in fifteen months none of our bullshit about lessons learned and hard knocks would really matter. By then, they'd know it all just like us, and some other new kid on the block was going to show up and repeat the cycle.

Soon enough, those same men I had scoffed at became no different from the likes of us — as we had become no different from those men in the 82nd Airborne who I had met out at the smoking area of COP Callahan on my first night in Baghdad. Those guys were back home with their wives now, waiting for another shot at the Suck, and doing their damnedest to get by. But soon enough their dwell time would be up, and they'd jump back on a bird to the Middle East with a full complement of freshly shaved, wide-eyed cherries. And those cherries would be wide-eyed cherries like me — like I had been. And like I had done, they would be strip-mined of their innocence and forged on the frontlines of a war. So who the fuck was I to talk shit? There wasn't any extra credit in bitching about the war. We had bigger things to worry about with the tasks at hand. I might as well have complained about the weather.

On that note, the first time I watched a uniform stand up on its own, starched with the salt of my own sweat, I learned exactly what it meant to be in Hell. Every breath I took felt like inhaling exhaust out of a jet engine. When I walked outside it was like diving into fire. With each step I could feel the hot asphalt below me, blistering through the half-inch soles of my combat boots. When the sun seared my skin, it was like karma's retribution, demanding I repent for all the millions of ants and slugs that have been burned alive throughout the years by little boys with magnifying glasses.

But these things, these semantics, they are meaningless. It's impossible to truly grasp that kind of heat until you're in it and to appreciate its power until you're facing it with a dead-man's weight on your shoulders. When the surrounding air is consistently in excess of 110 degrees, the only thing you can notice is that it's fucking hot. There's no greater truth in three-digit figures. Inside or outside, on a Stryker or on the streets, there is no difference. It's a hotter heat than you can imagine. Stuff like self-erecting uniforms just let you see it with your own two eyes.

But as the months ticked by we also got to see the Suck change its face. The summer heat disappeared. A biting cold rushed in. With a snap of the fingers the whole country became a meat locker. Summer was over, and nothing had ever prepared me for what was coming next.

"NCO's, make sure you check on Joe!" Our new platoon sergeant, Sergeant O'Brien, put out to our leaders. "We all know how much he loves to wrap his dick up in snivel!"

That was on the first bitingly cold day of winter — the first of many to come. As we geared up and loaded the trucks, our leaders made their rounds to check us over for winter gear. Thanks to our years of training in Germany and Washington state, we all knew the deal about fighting in the cold: no matter how much it sucks to freeze your balls off, the last thing you need in a twenty minute sprint-for-your-life firefight is to be caught wearing long-johns and warm-toasties under eighty pounds of gear. So when the dials dropped below freezing, we still walked around with nothing but a neck-gator, gloves and a long-sleeve t-shirt. Body armor and a rip-stop blouse was the closest thing to a jacket I can remember.

"Get me the Hooligan Tools!" Sergeant Benjamin called back to the squad, fighting off the shiver in his bones.

"Right here, Sarn't!" A voice cried out.

One of the men in our squad ran up to him with the heavy pack of sledgehammers and crowbars, with sweat beading from his brow and blood pounding through a bulging vein on his forehead. Benjamin grabbed the pack of forged steel, threw it on his back, and fell into formation with rest of the patrol.

"What's up, Sergeant Benjamin?" Lieutenant Savage laughed as he witnessed the hand-off of grunt-weight to one of his squad leaders. "What are you doing humping the hooligan-tools?"

Sergeant Benjamin looked back at him with a big smile and laughed, "What can I say, Sir? It's fucking cold! No point in letting Joe be the only one who gets to enjoy my squad's portable heater."

From that point on, the Hooligan Tools became a kind of luxury in our platoon. It was the first time anybody actually wanted to carry the extra forty pounds of hard weight, but at that point it was just another way to stay warm.

As far as I can remember, the thermometers bottomed out at thirty degrees. That might not sound like much to a corn-grown kid from South

Dakota, but in the span of just two weeks the dial had dropped more than eighty points. I watched the mercury fall to the very bottom of the scale in the middle of the night during a 24 hour shift at the front door of the Tactical Operations Center. I thumped it a couple times to make sure it wasn't lying. Sure enough it stayed like that until the sun rolled in and I collapsed into my bed.

Yet even though it was officially "freezing" from that point on, nothing ever really froze. It snowed once — the first time in eighty years that snow fell down on Baghdad — but it melted as soon as it touched the Earth. It was almost like the ground was still warm from soaking up the summer sun. Like the heat had sunk in just a few inches below the surface and never cooled. But it wasn't because of some strange geological phenomenon that there wasn't any ice on the ground. Everything was saturated with too much dust, salt, human waste, and bacteria for the water to crystallize.

"How are you holding up?" Lieutenant Savage asked me one night as we lay belly-down on a rooftop in the pouring rain.

"Me, sir?" I turned to face him.

"Yeah, you. Are you hanging in there?"

"Yeah. I'm good, sir."

"You sure?"

Of course I was shivering to my bones and soaked with mud, but so was everybody else.

"Yep. I'm solid." I smiled.

"Alright, man. Hang in there."

Truth be told, that night I was hitting a low point — and it wasn't because of the Suck. By then I'd been the platoon radio guy for almost a year and a half. Sure it had its perks, like having friends in high places and making nice with the lieutenant, but I was sick of it. My peers were passing me up in rank and position because I couldn't get any time on "the line," and this far into the game the job was getting old. Every morning I'd wake up with the crews to do a check on the vehicles, and at random intervals I had to go out when nobody else was awake to "refill" the communication equipment with new cryptography data whenever anybody in the country was stupid enough to lose a radio — or it was just that time of the month.

Still, that's not the kind of thing you go off about when there's a job to do — especially not when you're belly-down on a rooftop, fifty meters away from a confirmed militia IED lab — so I didn't bother bringing it up, like I hadn't bothered for months. But when the operation was over and we crawled off the rooftop he pulled me aside for a little pep-talk.

"You know, when I asked how you were holding up I wasn't just talking about tonight."

"What do you mean, sir?"

"I know you're pissed that you're still my radio guy," he cut right to the bone. "And I know you think I'm holding you back — and I'm really sorry about that."

Here we go, I thought. *This is where he gives me the speech that he's just gotta' keep me on for another month or two.*

"The fact is that I've been so reluctant to let you go because you really are great at your job and I don't know what I'd do if I didn't have your help."

Exactly.

It wasn't the first time he pulled me off to the side for a pep-talk about the wonders of being a radio guy and a promise that it would all be over soon, but what got to me was how long it took between sessions. The last time was almost four months ago, which started me thinking that I had at least another six months of duty at least. It was hard for me to keep my bearings straight. We'd been working together, side-by-side, for almost a year, and by then a comfortable informality had grown between us. Despite our mutual attempts to maintain a professional relationship, I actually considered Lieutenant Savage to be one of my closest friends. In fact, I still do. But I knew my place. There wasn't any room for us to drop the formalities, and I did everything I could to keep myself from lashing out. Here he was, giving me a compliment, and I was practically rolling my eyes.

"It's not that I don't like being your radio guy, sir. I actually really like working with you. It's just that I've been stuck in this position for so long and I joined the Infantry specifically to avoid doing this kind of stuff. I mean, I'm at the point where this is actually screwing up my ability to get promoted, you know — sir?"

I could see sympathy scrawled across his expression. It was one of those times I felt more like I was talking to a friend than a superior.

"Yeah, I understand," he said. "And again, I'm sorry."

I fought back the urge to sigh with frustration, but something told me I wasn't doing very well. At times like these, I tried to remind myself there was a job to do and that it was more important than my own feelings. But rather than bust my ass like an NCO, he brushed off my body language and continued on with what he was saying.

"That's why I wanted to let you know that I'm going to be swapping you out."

The words smacked my face like a cheap whore.

"What?!"

"Yeah, I'm switching you out with Flemming. He's going to shadow you for the next couple of days so train him up and help him out. But after that you'll be in 2nd Squad with Sergeant Benjamin."

A smile stretched across my face from cheek to cheek.

"Roger sir!"

That was my old squad, and Sergeant Benjamin was one of my favorite squad leaders in the platoon. I couldn't have been happier to hear the news.

"Thank you, sir."

"No problem, Ludwig. Oh and hey..."

"Yeah?"

"Thanks for hangin' in there."

"Of course, sir."

"Alright. Let's get moving."

By the end of the week I was back on the line with a gun in my hand and my very own sector of fire.

After about a month of biting cold, our patrol cycle became a rolling dismounted foot-march, just so we could stay warm. As for the militia, they were nothing more than hibernating. It's hard enough to rally a bunch of people to fight in a real army — even more so if it's freezing cold — but those guys were straight-up part-time thugs. They weren't coming out for shit, and for a while it felt like we had free rein on the nation. In the absence of a fight, our QRF cycles became a flood of escorting Route Clearance to sniff out all the roadside bombs in the city while the militia wasn't looking. So instead of catching some shut-eye here and there before a mission, we rolled out every day for a twelve hour escort of Route Clearance, brought them all the way back to base when our QRF cycle was up, and rolled right back out into sector for a twelve hour foot-patrol, totaling 24 hours of back-to-back operations. Frankly, it was burning us out, and I was at the end of my rope, so I didn't even bother with the luxuries when we got back to base anymore. I still remember what it felt like to come back one day and not even change. I just cleaned my weapon, skipped my shower, gummed down an MRE, dropped down on my bunk and passed the fuck out.

"At-ease!!!" Somebody screamed at the top of their lungs.

I was torn right out of my slumber and locked up at parade rest before I could focus my eyes.

"Hey there, men!" I heard a chipper voice reply.

Some dude was standing in front of me, clean shaved and all-smiles. He wore a camouflage Santa hat, and as I eyed him over from head to toe I noticed the Sergeant Major rank on his chest. Immediately I flipped over to disdain.

Who is this fucker? I thought.

I tried to process the face because I knew him from somewhere, but I couldn't put my finger on it, and my first notion was that he was just another Sergeant Major from the 4th ID. It was just – well there was something *else* about him.

"Merry Christmas!" He said.

Our eyes met and I could see my perplexed look and disapproving scowl was agitating him. Before it got too far, I placed the face and knew who I was looking at. He was our very own Regimental Sergeant Major, flown over from the other side of Iraq so he could say "hi" to the men and troop the line, but I wasn't very impressed.

"It's Christmas, Sergeant Major?" I muttered with a grunt.

For the record, it was an honest question. I wasn't trying to be a smart ass; I genuinely had no idea. If you'd asked, I probably wouldn't have even been able to ballpark the month. The holidays came and went without any more notice than some colored paper décor and the occasional serving of half-decent chow. It was a montage of cheesy paper pumpkins, turkey patterned plastic tablecloths, and Christmas candy-cane trim every time a red-letter day came around. I never noticed either way. Who gave a fuck about Christmas anyway? What the hell did that mean to me? All I wanted was to get some fucking rack.

Seeing my brain crumble along on its own, he chuckled and looked over the other guy in my squad. "Yeah! It's Christmas! How's your day been? You boys get any of that good chow down at the DFAC?"

"Negative, Sergeant Major," my squad mate replied.

"What about you?" He turned back to me.

"Negative, Sergeant Major. We were on patrol. We didn't get back until after chow."

"Oh..."

He was clearly annoyed. At first I thought it was just because of me, but I realized that everybody else in the platoon was either still down at the trucks or cramming in a session at the MWR for a Christmas phone call. Other than that, both 2nd and 3rd Platoons were out in sector, and wouldn't be back any time soon. The two of us in that room were probably the only two people he'd managed to find all night: one half-asleep shit-bag and another short, lanky dude with bad teeth and a speech impediment.

So much for an impromptu Christmas visit.

"Well, there's always tomorrow!" He said. "We're goin' to have a real feast down there at the dining facility! We ordered up a special menu just for you guys! How about that! Huh?!"

It was right about then that my higher functions kicked in and I started to realize what I was hearing.

Wait, it's fucking Christmas?! I stumbled over the idea for a second and my gaze wandered down to a random artifact on the floor. *How did I miss that?!*

I did some mental math and figured out that we'd be rolling out for our next mission right about the time the turkey stew got warm. So it turned out we were going to miss that, too.

"Actually, Sergeant Major," I grunted. "We'll be back out on patrol tomorrow before Christmas chow. I doubt we'll get any of it."

"What?!"

"Roger, Sarn't Major." My squad mate backed me up.

The man looked surprised at what I'd said, but I realized that the rest of our regiment was probably living on a FOB somewhere — like most of the Army — complete with 'Salsa Nights' and a chow hall that's half the size of the White House. On our COP, the only people that got to enjoy the holiday meals were usually the cooks. They didn't even clean the dishes; that was our job. But before he got too upset, I realized I had to give him something, because too much truth has a way of pissing off the higher-ups. In all, they'd rather live in a fantasy world where everything is always "hooah" and they're always right. After all, enough people are paid to lie to them every day, it's always the little guy who gets fucked for speaking up. I ran the odds and figured the longer I talked to him, the closer I'd come to becoming one of those little guys getting fucked. What I needed was to find some way to get him out of my hair without pissing him off. We stood there for an awkward moment while he thought of a way to cheer us up. At least he was a grunt at heart.

"Well," he paused. "Fuckin' hooah! Earnin' that paycheck — eh boys!"

"Roger that, Sergeant Major." I straightened my back up and maxed out on the false-motivation. "Don't you worry about us, Sergeant Major! I'd rather be in-sector, showin' these fuckin' towel-heads who's boss! Close with and kill — *hooah!*"

As soon as I saw his awkward chuckle I knew it worked. Rank requires too much politics to entertain that kind of brazen intolerance — but you can't light a guy up for being motivated. That's just bad leadership.

"Yeah—" he hesitated. "Yeah, men! That's the spirit!"

He forced a smile in place and got back to his agenda.

"I just came down here to let you guys know you're doing some great shit, hooah?! So, keep up the good work. Heart of the fight!"

When he backed up to the door, I pumped the motivation angle for all it was worth, shouting out the Regimental motto just a little to loud for comfort.

"Fuck yeah, Sergeant Major! Always ready!!!"

"Always first!" He cheered back.

It took me twenty seconds to fall back down onto my bunk and pass out for the duration.

All that was in the past now. By the time we had embarked on our latest 26 hour marathon of daily operations, I could hardly remember what had happened. The thought hit me as we walked the length of Ur a half dozen times.

"How could I forget that?" I muttered to myself.

I was beat tired. Doing my best to stay awake, I worked out the numbers in my head and realized that we had completed a thirty kilometer ruck march with interspersed activities along the way. I don't think I was the only one to figure that out either, because as soon as we got back to Old MOD it was decided by the men that we deserved some rest and relaxation. Our leaders were right there with us. That morning, every man in our platoon half-assed the process of "coming off-mission" to run through their after action rituals and make out with a pillow. By the time I was done with my own chores, Gonzo was already waiting for me on the porch of our platoon's barracks.

"Man, they really cashed-in this time," he said to me as I sat down on my fold-out chair. It was hard to overlook the exhaustion in his voice.

"You're telling me," I sighed.

"26 hours! Can you believe that shit?"

As he spoke, I held out a tin cigar tube filled with forty minutes of rest and relaxation. Keeping one for myself, I looked out at the scene before us, relishing the fact that I had nothing at all going through my head. Inside those two tin tubes were the best mid-range Dominicans in the country — the very last of my stash. As the fact of it crossed my mind, I wondered when I'd get the chance to buy another one.

Who knows, I thought.

I was way too tired to give a shit about any of that.

"Well, look at the bright side," Gonzo leaned forward in his chair to make a point. "We're pretty much pickin' up right where we left off, you know? So if you think about it, it's kinda' like we never even rolled out."

"How do you figure?"

"Well, we rolled out at like – what? Six in the morning? It's just after nine now. If you think about it, you can kinda' trick yourself into thinking it was just a three hour patrol. Like the whole day didn't even happen."

At first I was a little to tired to catch onto what he was saying, but it made sense as I gave it a go.

"You know," I said. "I think you're onto something."

"Yeah. So essentially we just scored a free rest-cycle."

It was an amazing twist of logic, exactly what I needed to believe.

I slapped my knee and cheered. "Outstanding work!"

"Thank you," he bowed.

I was still dog tired, but I pushed it out of my system. At least I could fight off sleep for another hour. After all, it was the most important hour of the day: the after-action smoke. It was sacred.

"You got a lighter?"

"Yeah man."

He flipped out his Zippo and smacked it into my palm. Like I'd done a hundred times, I opened the tube and slid the cigar into its natural home in my hand, separating it from the thin wooden lining in which it'd once been wrapped. With a flip and a snap, the wood lit on fire, and a couple of puffs later I was billowing smoke into the air.

After five years in the Army I never started smoking cigarettes, but I took to cigars like candy. It wasn't so much the flavor, not any more than an alcoholic likes the "taste" of a hard drink. Sure, I could tell the difference between a good cigar and a bad one. I enjoyed the complex aroma on my tongue and it was definitely a taste I had acquired, but to say I smoked it for the flavor would be a stretch. It wasn't for the nicotine high either. What I really needed was the tiniest ounce of civilization in the middle of all that shit. Forty minutes of class. The better part of an hour to just sit down and appreciate something.

Cigars were a social experience. My smoking buddy, Gonzo, was the man I shared it with. "Cigar aficionados," as we'd say. Our chosen subjects were numbered and listed: cigars, sex, beautiful women, fine drinks, and zombies. We'd step outside, pull the stogie from its tube and take a moment to ritualistically sniff and snip it to perfection before lighting off the brushwood blanket. At the start of the ceremony, we were heathens; but when those cigars were lit, we became gentlemen through and through.

"Well, here's to the mission, fine sir!" I held my cigar up high.

"To the mission!" he cheered back.

Interestingly enough, when I started smoking cigars I learned something about smoking cigarettes, too: it's a culture in and of itself. It's a fine science of five minute conversations. Intense conversations. Real conversations. Five minutes of debate, five minutes of bitching, and some of the greatest five minute stories you've ever heard. But five minutes is all you get. They never last longer, and they never spill over into that world outside the finite realm of a smoking area — unless it's to be brought up during the next five minute smoke break. If you're a smoker, you know exactly what I'm talking about. If you're not, you'll have to take my word on this one: there's more to smoking than sucking in smoke.

All that goes ten-fold for a cigar. A cigar is that same experience drawn out across the better half of an hour. But the best part was seeing how those two tobacco-based cultures came together. Gonzo and I would engage for more than half an hour about Dominican vs. Haitian, blond or brunette, Cognac or Scotch, head-shots or shotguns; and all the while these cigarette smokers would stop by, one or ten at a time, and give us five minutes of the most meaningful contributions a man can give. We focused their power. We turned those quick-snap bullshit sessions into something. We'd be caught up in some of the greats like "Shakira vs. Jessica Biel," or "Who's the bigger fag;" then some *wunderkind* with a pack of Marlboros would chime in to set us straight and settle the whole goddamn thing. Or maybe we'd already solved something, like the best melee weapon for the apocalypse. There we'd be, running the topic aground, and one of these guys would chime in with a ball-buster.

"Sure a machete is the weapon of choice against the zombies themselves," he'd say. "But what about all the obstacles you're going to run into? You can't exactly pry open a door with a machete."

Then what do you know, he'd give us a five minute rant that blew our entire preconceived notion out of the water.

It was a crazy social alchemy. These two features of human nature, both powerful in their own right, happened every day and saved us from insanity. But on days like today, when Uncle Sam was at his worst, all we really needed was a forty minute break to ourselves. After I took a puff or two from my own log of cancer, Gonzo ran the cigar across his nostrils.

"A fine cigar." He spoke in a mockingly educated tone.

"A fine cigar indeed," I said. "A light, sir?"

"Indeed!"

I handed over the Zippo as he had done for me.

"Your lighter, sir." I tipped my hat.

"Thank you, sir." He lit up the stogie and for a few moments of silence we puffed away at our cigars and took in the scene.

Down below us in the alleyway, the cooks vacated the kitchen and a group of Iraqi soldiers played soccer around their trucks. The sun was low in the sky, silhouetting a pair of Blackhawks sweeping over the Tigris. I couldn't help but feel at ease in this world of temporary living and war.

Exactly as we left it, I thought.

Maybe I could just forget about that patrol, but that didn't mean I was going to take my sweet time crawling back into bed to get some rack. And when I did, it wouldn't be as a pissed off and worn out grunt, but as an honest man with some well-earned rest.

We neared the end of our cigars with barely a word spoken between us. The silence ended only when Gonzo exhaled a soft pillow of smoke and spoke right from the heart.

"A gentleman's leisure."

Looking at him, listening to him, you'd never know he was from East L.A.. That's the best thing you learn in the service: people are never what you expect.

"Truly, sir." I nodded. "Truly."

"Until next time?" he asked.

"'Till next time," I said.

We gave each other a nod, ashed out our cigars, and before my eyes reverted back into the true form of tired apathetic grunts.

"Alright, motherfucker." I stood up and yawned. "I'm gonna' get some fuckin' rack."

"You got that right. I'm gonna' go take care of some business."

He put his hand down by his junk and stroked an invisible cock, marking the official transition out of character and back to his former grunt self. As I stood, my legs began to shiver. All the hours I had been awake hit me at once. I went inside and fell right down on my bunk, without bothering to strip down to my shorts. I wasn't getting up for anything. At the very least I can say that I owe that place for the best sleep of my life.

"Get up!" Sergeant Benjamin shouted out to the whole room.

I was already awake. I woke up as soon as his sandal hit the cold tile. My heart sank with every tired stagger he took towards the door, and when he finally flipped on the lights, I knew what was coming. But I just couldn't do it. I couldn't get up. I couldn't move my muscles. I couldn't open my eyes. As everybody stumbled to their feet and pawed at their hygiene kits to take on another day in the Shit, I lay there with my eyes clasped shut, and tried with every ounce of my soul to unravel reality and crawl back into my dream. I felt like a boy getting wakened for school.

Maybe they won't notice, my tired mind was caught in the memory of my childhood. *Maybe mom and dad will forget.*

I could've sworn I was almost there. Back in the memory. Back at home as a kid with my whole life ahead of me. Far away from that fucked up place that had become my home.

"Hey! Ludwig!" Sergeant High smacked my boot. "I know you're up! What the hell are you waiting for?!"

"Moving!" I heard myself shout.

I was on my feet, with my hygiene kit in-hand and out the door to the bathroom before I had time to accept the task. It was a totally unconscious act. Before I knew it, I was counted among the morning migration to the holy sacraments of shitting and shaving before a patrol. It took all of five minutes for me to get back to my bunk and start inspecting my gear.

"What the hell was that, Ludwig?" Staff Sergeant Benjamin chuckled. "Did you hope we wouldn't notice or something?"

"Heh. Yeah, something like that." I rubbed my eyes and threw on my gear.

We filed out the door in ten minutes. Another ten and the Strykers rolled through the gate. In less than 45 minutes, my entire platoon had gone from unconscious to action. In just under an hour we were back in the Suck. We were out all day yesterday. We'd be out all day today. We were going to be out all day tomorrow — that's just the way it was. Ground pounding is an endurance sport.

That patrol was slated to be another dose of the same-old. We'd open with a long dismounted patrol. After that we were scheduled for some other shit up by the water purification plant. That would take all night and the plan was bound to change anyway, so I didn't even bother thinking about it. I lived in the moment. I put one foot in front of the other and followed orders. I walked alongside my buddies and subconsciously scanned for snipers. Eventually, the sun came back around to our side of the world and we came upon a familiar corner from a day or two before.

"Hey!" Kaz waved back at me as he rounded the bend. "Check this shit out!"

He pointed to the side of the road at a rotting carcass. It had been a donkey in a past life. Now it was just the dead husk of a thing once living. Over the course of the past few days it'd been slowly devoured by hounds and flea-bitten sheep until its legs were nubby and strings of its guts spilled out around it.

Then it wiggled.

"What the fuck?!" I waved at Gonzo. "Hey! Check this shit out!"

I fixed my eyes back on the carcass just in time to see it rustle and move one more time.

I swear to God it looked alive.

"Dude," Gonzo laughed. "Man, I think this is it! This is the outbreak man! It's finally happening!"

Kaz laughed along with him as I turned to face it with my rifle. In the back of my head, I felt a fear that it might actually be exactly what they were joking about: the zombie outbreak. The end of the world. The spawning, walking undead — right there in Ur. I couldn't think of a better place for it to start.

"Watch out man," Kaz came in closer as the entire squad looked on. "You don't want to become patient zero, man."

"Yeah, man." Gonzo laughed. "You know the deal. I swear to God I'll fucking shoot you."

A scratching sound echoed from inside the dead beast. It rocked and wiggled, almost flexing and moaning as it reanimated from the dead. Its head convulsed and we heard a raspy growl muffle from out of its chest cavity.

"Okay, seriously though—" I took a step back.

I could see their stances change like mine, thumbing safeties and getting ready for the worst.

"What the fuck are you guys doing?!" Sergeant Benjamin shouted.

"This fuckin' thing is moving, Sarn't!"

"What?!"

"Yeah, check it out!"

Again we heard the growl as the scratching grew louder and louder. The corpse was now convulsing, twitching, and moaning right in front of our eyes. There was no trick. It was really alive.

"Okay, get the fuck away from it — for starters," he said.

"Sergeant Benjamin, what's the hold up?!" Lieutenant Savage called up from the rear.

"Sir, check this shit out!" I replied.

"What? A fucking donkey? That thing's been there all week."

"Yeah, but check it out! It's fuckin' moving!"

Just as I said the words, it stopped cold.

Lieutenant Savage was not amused.

"What are you—"

I cut him off and pointed with anticipation. "Just wait for it, sir!"

After a few tense seconds it growled, wiggled, and growled again.

"Alright." He said. "Back up. Slowly."

As the twitching and rocking of the carcass grew even more frantic I switched the safety of my rifle over to "fire," thinking at any moment it would crack open and reveal some kind of twisted alien, or stand up and charge.

Out of nowhere, a bloody creature burst through the chest cavity of the corpse and gazed right into my eyes. At first I didn't know what it was, but then I realized that I was standing face-to-face with a rabid dog, smeared all over with guts and blood until it was barely recognizable. Strings of rotting flesh hung from its teeth and dangled down its twitching face. The dog was shivering like a tweaked out meth addict. It had crawled inside of that dead corpse and got lost in a rotting cavity of flesh until its only hope was to eat a way out. Now it was staring me right in the face, like I was next in line, and all I could do was meet its gaze and hope it didn't attack.

Sergeant Benjamin broke the silence.

"Wow, that's some disgusting shit."

"Alright," Lieutenant Savage waved us on. "Let's get moving, guys. Stay the fuck away from that thing. I don't want it to bite anyone. Ludwig, fall-in."

I backed away from the dog and it got back to its early morning meal. We carried on with the foot patrol and a few minutes later, Kaz came up behind me.

"Can you believe some of the shit we've seen in this fuckin' place?" He said.

"No man," I said. "This place is fucking crazy."

I looked around at the city and took a moment to consider what it had once been. It was the pinnacle of Eastern society. A modern capital born out of the ruins of an ancient civilization. As recently as my childhood, Baghdad was a "world city." You could still see the remnants if you looked close enough. Now? Now it was in ruin. Now, like that donkey in a way, it was little more than a rotting husk. It was convulsing posthumously, infected by a foreign creature, wrestling inside, and swimming with disease.

All around us, children played in burned down houses and desolate junkyards. At the occasional intersection you could spot battered road signs nodding to the order that once was. Modern tour buses lined up in open fields to rot. Ancient water mains and sewage pipes dared never again to fulfill their function. High-tension power lines hung silently over our heads, held aloft by great metal frames that once stood as a marker for industrial success.

None of it worked anymore. Like the bones of some rotting monster, human inhabitance had become the bacteria feeding on its remains. With the death of our host we'd turn parasitic in nature. Like that dog, the war we waged hastened Iraq's destruction with ravenous outbreaks of hunger. Our violence, as sure as consumption, was eating Iraq alive, and for a moment I wondered how much more it would take before the entire country was reduced to a puddle of blood. I wondered if mankind could sink back into the desert, becoming a corpse like that one on the ground.

This is war, I thought.

Abject chaos, lost within madness. The darkest side of man. Something that has to be seen to be understood, and once grasped can never be forgotten.

"Watch out, Ludwig!" Sergeant High shouted up at me from behind.

I glanced down at my feet and instantly shuffled my step to avoid a perilous fate. I had almost walked straight into a ditch of shit and piss.

"Thanks!" I shouted.

"Keep your head in the game, man."

"Roger, Sarn't."

I shook it off and flipped my rifle back to "safe." He was right. We had a job to do. And thinking too much about it could be a costly mistake. Besides, I had scored an early dose of mid-tour leave thanks to a Squadron screw up with the schedule. In just a few long weeks I'd be back in the states eating gourmet burgers, taking warm showers and sleeping all day. Best of all, I'd be 10,000 miles away from the nearest roadside bomb.

God bless America.

- Chapter Five -
Fighting With Fire

The last thing I did before jumping on a convoy to go on vacation was a high-action raid into Sadr City. 48 hours later I was standing in one of the baggage claims at the Los Angeles International Airport. The clothes I had on were the very same clothes I had worn on the raid. I reeked of carbon, gun oil and dirty socks. Judging by the island of sand underfoot, my boots had probably left a trail of moon-dust all the way back to Kuwait.

Mid-tour leave was like a dream, and like a dream I had awakened when it was over to find that I could hardly remember what happened in those few weeks away from the guys. It was the first time I got an outside perspective of just how fast paced our lives had really been. From end to end, mid-tour leave was only 22 days long, but when I got back to the guys nothing was the same.

By the end of winter, the effects of the surge were hard to miss. We had already managed to push the Jaish al-Mahdi back to the border of Sadr City. The entire district of Ur was now considered a relatively safe part of town. On the southern flank of the city, Comanche Company had even managed to push into the hostile turf of Thawra, which constituted the lower third of Sadr City itself. On the far side of the district, "Chaos" Company, 2-30th INF of the 3rd Brigade Combat Team, 10th Mountain Division, had taken charge of maintaining the border where the 82nd Airborne had once stalled. Beyond our own little corner of the map, the word going around was that great headway had been made across the Diyala and al-Anbar provinces, where the rest of our Regiment and the majority of the surge had been sent. In Basra, however, the war was hardly going well.

After falling back to their outposts throughout the city and weeks of taking shelter from heavy and prolonged indirect fire, the British troops in charge of Basra were forced to withdraw completely from their front line positions. From what I could gather, they had now taken up a defensive position at the airport a full ten kilometers away from the town. While this seemed irrelevant to me at the time, and indeed I had no true understanding of the greater scheme of the conflict outside of Sadr City, the situation in Basra was critical to the fate of the entire campaign. Basra had long been the heart of black market smuggling and illegal oil trade in Iraq, piping millions of dollars into the hands of the Jaish al-Mahdi. So while the tensions between al-Qaeda and Coalition Forces in Ramadi were precarious to say the least, the situation with the Jaish al-Mahdi across half of the country was on the verge of a total shit storm. With all of our "progress" it was becoming clear that the Jaish al-Mahdi would only tolerate so much before it was time to let the cat out of the bag, and losing ground in Basra was a bad sign of things to come. But truth be told, I couldn't care less about the "big picture." I was just happy to be with the guys.

"Did you hear the word?!" Ian ran across the motor pool as soon as he saw me step off the back of the Stryker.

"No. What?"

"You're in Weapons Squad now!"

"What?"

"Yeah, man! You're the team leader for Gun Two!"

That was fantastic news. There's nothing like coming back from a booze fest to find out you've been bumped up to a leadership position. Best of all, Ian was the other gun team leader, so in a way it would be like the good old days when we were still roommates. Right off the bat they told me to get my gear together and roll out with the platoon. I spent the next twelve hours catching up and getting back into the life. To be honest, I didn't mind the sudden jump into action; I was actually kind of excited to find out what it's like to run a twelve hour patrol with a full night's rest.

In my absence, Bull Company had been assigned to the task of constructing a new combat outpost on the corner of Routes Miller and Maryland. "Mortar-Eater-Ville," as Ian called it, was pieced together by a group of National Guard engineers on the property of an abandoned bus-washing station, not even eight hundred meters away from the northwestern border of Sadr City. According to the higher-ups, "Combat Outpost #329" was going to be our new home — a walled in parking lot without so much as a shelter for chow.

"You'll have to rough it for a while," the Colonel told my buddies in his speech. "But in few months we'll get some amenities out there like showers and mail. Just hang in there and keep up the fight. Hooah?"

According to the Generals, COP #329 was referred to officially as "Joint Security Station Ur" (also known as "JSS Ur"), but on the company level we called it by its functional designation, since the Iraqi Army was nowhere to be seen.

The most important tactical features of COP #329 were not only that it was equidistant to and in-range of every known militia mortar firing point, but it also had absolutely no pre-existing structure to protect us from the indirect fire we all knew was coming. What sealed the deal on living conditions was the complete lack of drainage for any kind of water or sewage. That alone might not have been an issue, but COP #329 was also situated on the bottom of the lowest ground. It took no time at all for the lot to fill up with a never-ending sea of standing water.

No matter where I looked, there was evidence of an ill-conceived plan. I couldn't shake the notion that the whole place was a bad idea. COP #329 was a perfect example of something that looks great on a map to a commander who's never set foot on the ground but is destined to get people killed out in the real world. Anybody who had been there for more than fifteen minutes could've told you that, but nobody asked the grunts when it was time for them to move in.

Our job was to head out there and cover the engineers while the walls, bunkers and living quarters were put into place, since Ur was more or less a non-issue that late in the game. It wasn't long before Headquarters Platoon moved in. After that, our patrol cycle was changed to keep the QRF platoon out at COP #329 instead of back at COP Old MOD where they could kick off their gear and relax. Now the only face-time we got with a real bunk bed was during the measly hours of sleep back at the "rear." The other 24 hours of our 36-hour days were spent out in-sector, either guarding the new outpost or running the usual grab-bag of patrols.

By then I was pretty much convinced that the brass were determined to track down some new and perilous frontier to shove us into so we could earn them another bullet point on their resumé. In the weeks that followed, I caught up with my buddies in Weapons Squad and reintegrated into the cycle until it was like I had never left the platoon. Somewhere in all of that, Lieutenant Savage had gone on leave. This left Sergeant First Class O'Brien filling in as the platoon leader, with Staff Sergeant Dukes back in his age-old role as 1st Platoon's acting platoon sergeant.

By the 23rd of March, Bull Company was five days into a string of public relations efforts and search operations in the neighborhood surrounding COP #329 dubbed "Operation Epstein." Our goal was to reinforce our relationship with the local population, now that we'd be living right in the middle of their neighborhood. In addition, we wanted to search the area for contraband and establish a local intelligence network to mount a more effective counterinsurgency against the Jaish al-Mahdi.

For 1st Platoon, the morning of the 23rd followed an entire night of chasing ghosts around the Maryland Checkpoint. Though it had hardly been a violent month up until then, the Jaish al-Mahdi were finally waking up from their winter hibernation to assault Iraqi Army positions along the border of Sadr City. Often, one or two gunmen would carry out these assaults, but a few times they came out with full squads of ten to twenty men. In response to these attacks, 1st Platoon's mission on the night on the 22nd was to set into an overwatch with the company sniper team and wait for the militia to make another move.

Sure enough, that's exactly what happened.

Shortly after 01:00 hours in the morning, the snipers engaged a few armed combatants maneuvering in on the Iraqi Army unit out on Maryland. We spent the rest of that morning searching houses and clearing the neighborhood to look for the gunmen in question. Although it was clear they had managed to evade our search, it wasn't until 05:00 hours that we finally got back to our regular program of dismounted operations and ground pounding in Ur. By 11:00 hours it was time for us to head back to Old MOD for a much needed rest cycle and I was lights-out by 14:00.

That day, sporadic small-arms engagements broke out in every neighborhood east of the Tigris River with heavy engagements raining down on various checkpoints around the city. At 19:00 hours that evening, just five hours into my blissful slumber, our boys out at COP #329 heard a number of rocket attacks come out of the heart of Sadr City toward some unknown and far away target in the south-west. Within a few hours, official reports trickled down from Multi-National Division Baghdad Headquarters (aka: MND-B) informing us that the Green Zone had just been attacked and that a number of civilians had been killed. By the time I woke up, the militia had retreated back into their stronghold, and the streets were stone-quiet.

It wasn't until 23:00 hours that my platoon drove back out to COP #329 to relieve our buddies in 3rd Platoon for the next twelve hours of outpost guard duty. Despite the rising action, we remained more or less unaware of what had passed during our twelve hour rest cycle. Against all odds Bull Company had barely received a single incoming round. By the looks of it, the morning of the 24th would be little more than another turn at the Suck, and I had no reason to believe it would be any different from the previous day. By 10:00 hours we were already finishing up the final four hour guard shift of our QRF cycle, and it was about time for our first patrol of the day. With that in mind, I took my chance to jump off the truck with Doc to stretch my legs.

It was a peaceful morning. I looked around to take in my surroundings while my boots sank into the mud beneath me. We were all getting ready for the day. Ian was up on guard in one of the back hatches of our Stryker. Our two assistant gunners had taken advantage of the extra space freed up by Sergeant O'Brien's temporary promotion and passed out on the vacant bench seats inside the truck. Sergeant Dukes was listening to some heated debate between our vehicle commander Sergeant Montero, and Pfister, who had long ago been moved over to Weapons Squad as the platoon sergeant's driver. It was amazing to me how close we were to the border between us and oblivion, yet we could still bullshit around like it was no big deal.

"Come on, Ludwig, just try it." Doc held his pack of cigarettes out in front of my face so I could smell the tobacco, expecting me to cave to a chemical addiction that had never formed from all the cigars in my past.

"No Doc. I'm fine. Really."

I thought it was funny that Doc was trying to get me to smoke, since I could still remember the day he started smoking. It happened during one of our first field problems in Germany. It was about forty degrees out and I was walking to the port-a-shitters at "FOB Eagle" of the Hohenfels training grounds. With my baby wipes in one hand and my rifle in the other, I trudged through a lake of mud similar to that in which I was now standing so I could drop-off a log and get back to a good book. That's where I spotted Doc, hanging out with the smokers and bitching about the cold. I was just in time to hear him bum a stick off a mutual friend.

"Hey Thomas," he said. "Let me get a Newport, man. I'm out of Black & Milds."

That was it. I knew right there that 'Doc was getting hooked. First it was the occasional Black & Mild. Then it became a regular deal. Now, he was full-on substituting one for the other.

"Oh shit, Doc!" I shouted. "Don't do it!"

"Shut up, Ludwig!" Doc laughed and hailed me back. "I'm not going to start smoking!"

"You're starting right now! That's how it happens man! Next thing you know you'll be a full-time smoker!"

"No, man, I'm just out of Black & Milds. It's just one cigarette, come on!"

"Okay, Doc. I'm just sayin'..."

It was playful exchange, and when it was over I swung open the door on one of the port-a-shitters, jumped inside, froze my nuts off and took a shit. So there we were, once again ankle-deep in mud, only this time we were drenched in sweat, bitching about the heat, and Doc had long since become one of the most regular smokers I knew.

"Why don't you smoke, Ludwig?"

"I can't stand it."

"What about?"

I had my excuses memorized.

"They taste like shit, the smell gives me a headache, and I'd rather keep the money."

"Heh, yeah. This shit does get expensive. Still, you just haven't had the right brand. I mean, you smoke cigars; this is way cheaper. Come on man, try it."

Firm in my distaste for cigarettes, I grabbed the cancer stick out of his hand and sucked down a quick drag. I couldn't even inhale a full breath before the rough flavor soaked into my spit and infected my glands. I blew the smoke out and handed the cigarette back to him while I hacked up a loogie. Ironically, the first thing I wanted to wash the flavor from my mouth was a fine cigar.

"Yeah... no." I said.

"Come on, man! You didn't even inhale!"

"That's because it tastes like shit."

He lifted his pack to see what he was smoking. It was some Iraqi knock-off brand of American Spirits. We might as well have been smoking wildfire.

"Yeah," he chuckled. "I guess these do suck."

But it was the best they had.

He didn't need to say it. He just shrugged it off and we continued our chat about the weather. I tried to clean my sinuses of the rancid taste by heaving deep breaths of air. It only replaced the mucky flavor of tobacco with the rancid stench of my surroundings. As a force of habit, I scanned the rooftops and windows in my line-of-sight. Thankfully, we were standing behind our Stryker and up against a seven foot concrete barrier. There wasn't much to see, which meant there wasn't much that could see me. That meant we were safe for the time being.

Far off in the east, the sun was climbing through a thick, smoggy haze, as though it was doing everything in its power to escape the never-ending drum-roll of high-powered diesel engines. No matter where I went in that country it was impossible to escape the sea of generators, daily commuters, and military hardware. After two full hours of charging their batteries back to full strength, 3rd Squad's Stryker finally shut off its engine. Now that it was our turn, Pfister spun up our truck to do the same. On the other side of the Outpost wall, the rickety old generator of a local falafel stand had been running for days. Beyond that, a chorus of internal combustion engines and discombobulated traffic honked and shouted endlessly for rights of way.

"What I wouldn't do for some fucking quiet." I muttered.

Doc looked at me with tired eyes that said everything without a single word. We stood there for a minute until a chirp on the radio broke our silence.

"—One-Four Roger." Sergeant Dukes responded. "Hey!" He shouted out to the squad. "Mount up!"

Ian echoed the call from up in his hatch, "Hey! Mount up, guys!"

Doc took a long drag of his cigarette and flicked it into the murky water where it sizzled and died. We jumped through the troop-door of the ramp and locked it shut behind us, just in time to see Sergeant Montero fasten up his vest and put on his helmet.

"Pfister," he spoke into the headset. "Get ready. We're moving."

I looked at my watch and noticed we still had another thirty minutes before the patrol cycle was scheduled to begin.

"Where are we going?" I asked.

"Back to Old MOD."

"What's goin' on, Sergeant?" Doc asked.

"We're doing a raid."

I felt my heart skip a beat. That was the best news I had heard all week. With a rush in my step I jumped up into the other hatch of our Stryker and threw on a headset. Pfister flipped our truck around to fall in line with the rest of the platoon. Soon enough we passed through the barricaded gates of our home base and filed up to our rooms in anticipation. We even had a little time to use the Internet and eat some chow while our leaders got the details for the raid. By the time I was called into our squad's room Sergeant Dukes had the imagery and notes all ready to go.

Our mission was to kill or capture a high-ranking commander of the Jaish al-Mahdi. We had gone after him many times before but never caught him in the flesh. The target, a man by the name of Arkan Hasnawi, was supposedly hiding out in a combination IED lab/militia headquarters/torture chamber, right in the heart of the city. Due to the recent attacks on the Green Zone, MND-B decided to bump up a priority hit and bring him in on charges. Given his location and the heavy resistance in the area, it was Bull Company's job to run the Op.

Intelligence reports suggested that the structure would be filled with documents, evidence of criminal operations, and other tactical goodies for us to exploit along the way. This meant the mission was likely to net us any number of high value detainees, in addition to Arkan Hasnawi himself. As an added bonus, there were a few unaccounted for civilians who may have been held against their will on-site. There was a strong chance that we could also liberate a couple prisoners before they were brutally murdered by the militia.

"Fuck man," Montero laughed. "This is a fuckin' jackpot."

"Yeah, just keep listening." Sergeant Dukes brushed him off.

The bad news was that the aforementioned compound was the deepest target we had ever considered. It was also by far the most dangerous. Every route leading up to it was a confirmed "black" route. It was surrounded by four large garrisons of militia footmen who would be on high-alert while Hasnawi was around. Furthermore, our intel suggested that all the structure's entrances were probably rigged with explosives, so there was a strong chance that simply opening the front door could blow us all to bits. That last little fact was the only one to make me flinch.

The plan was to drive in under heavy contact, with the support of Apache helicopters. Upon reaching the objective we'd set into dominating firing positions and begin a total suppression of the surrounding area. 1st Platoon was going to be the main effort — the first ones in. To breach the perimeter we would drive our Stryker through the outer wall of the compound. Once inside, we'd simply bypass the booby-trap by taking out a whole corner of the main structure with the plow on the front-end of our vehicle. At that point, the infiltrating squad would file into the gaping hole with one of our machine guns in tow. The other machine gun would stick around outside with a pile of ammo and a whole lot of hope.

Our orders were to secure the building at any cost and take no chances along the way. Detainees and intelligence would have to be loaded up as quickly as possible so we could get back out of there alive. The exploitation teams would have to do their thing as fast as they could, but the twenty minute deadline we usually maintained for a typical snatch-and-grab raid would be useless under those conditions. There was only one guideline for this operation: *hit fast, hit hard, and get the fuck out of there as soon as possible.*

"So who goes in?" Ian asked Sergeant Dukes with a smile.

He looked up with a flat stare. "I don't give a shit. You two figure that one out."

I knew as soon as I saw Ian glance over in my direction that we'd be up for a game of rock-paper-scissors to make the call. Then I stopped to ask myself if I really wanted either job in the first place.

The mission had many potential points of failure. If an EFP hit us on the way in, the raid would become a rescue operation in a flash. I couldn't help but think back to that first raid in the fall when our truck got caught in a tank trap and everything went to shit. Even if we made it onto the objective, the entire house was still rigged to blow. Sure we could avoid the doors, but what if there was a trigger man or secondary traps throughout the building? If they saw us coming, it would be quick work for them to bail out Hasnawi and set up an ambush instead. That meant as soon as we got on target — *boom.* And even if we could breach the perimeter wall, take out the back corner of the building, and somehow survive the ensuing firefight, getting our vehicle stuck inside of that compound was a worst-case scenario. Maneuverability within those walls would be limited and a welcome target for incoming RPGs. A single shot with one of those — *boom.* In any case, a vehicle recovery would be impossible with all the rubble in such a confined space. If a Stryker got stuck on the inside of the wall our only choice would be to leave it there and limp home without.

In the face of all this, we were reassured that our contingencies were thought out to the "T" — everything down to issuing incendiary grenades and putting an AC-130 Spectre Gunship on stand by. If shit hit the fan there was no time to fuck around. We'd exfiltrate the casualties with another platoon in the company and destroy any of the vehicles that couldn't drive out on their own. If it came down to it, once the company was clear of the objective, we'd pound it into oblivion by close air support and long-range artillery.

We were going into the heart of it all. Hitting the hive. Punching the giant on the nose. No twenty-minute countdown, just constant and deliberate fighting. An all-out assault. Both insanely psychotic and totally awesome — exactly why young men choose the Infantry in the first place. All we had left to do now was get the green-light to roll. So, like everything else in the Army, we stood-by for the word. By midnight, our entire company had long since conducted the pre-combat checks and inspections for the mission. These days we had it down to a science and nothing was ever left to chance. After hours of waiting, however, we worked our way down to our fatigues while the ready condition was set back minute-by-minute. At some point Sergeant O'Brien called us into the hallway with some bad news and we crowded around to hear the word.

"Listen up!" He announced. "We just got orders to stand-down."

Many of us moaned and sighed with frustration — some of us in relief. He carried on with the explanation as we gathered around to get every scoop of the news. It wasn't uncommon to get all spun-up for a raid, only to be called off at the last minute.

"They've been watching the objective with a UAV, and there is way too much shit going on there for us to go in."

That was new. It was the middle of the night. The militia was usually in bed by now, and given what we had seen already, I couldn't figure out what the hell would keep us from rolling out on the kind of mission we had planned. Regardless, Sergeant O'Brien carried on with the explanation.

"I just came back from the TOC and they're looking at hundreds of people with all kinds of cranes and shit, pulling huge crates out of the ground."

When we pressed him for the details, he shrugged and continued on with what he knew.

"We have no idea what is going on down there, but it's way too hot for us to head in and do a raid. So if shit settles down, we'll be going in. Otherwise, we'll be back out on patrol tomorrow as per the usual cycle. Now get some fuckin' sleep."

I wasn't sad to hear the news. Sure, it might've taken me a while to work off all the excitement I had pent up in my veins and I loved the sexy sound of it all, but as much as I wanted to go out with a bang I was also *way* too young to die. Besides, I was pretty tired and I wasn't about to get pissed over some extra sleep. Best of all, 1st Platoon was about to score a free rest cycle before it was time to head back out on QRF, since our scheduled patrol cycle had been scratched for the raid.

It seemed to me that day was destined to be a rare treat of idle relaxation and easy living, so on the morning of the 25th of March I tracked down Bryce and Ian for a long needed hang-out session. We all caught up over chow and Gatorade. We had resolved to stay there and chat until the devil came looking for us himself. Instead, it was another soldier in our platoon by the name of Dulany who ran into the chow hall, gasping for air with an urgent message.

"Heithold!" He shouted to Bryce. "There you are! We've been looking for you! The whole company is loading up! Come on!"

"Wait, what?!" Ian asked.

All three of us were baffled by the news.

"What are you talking about? We're on our rest cycle," I said.

"Well, they spun us up anyways!" Dulany said.

"The whole company?" Ian asked. "Why didn't anybody come for us?"

"I don't know."

"Weapons Squad too?" I asked.

"Yeah, everybody."

We gathered our rifles and stood up to follow Dulany out the door. As we hustled down the road to our company's building, Ian pressed on with the inquisition.

"Wait — what's going on? We're supposed to be on our rest cycle. Why are we getting spun up?"

"I don't know. I was just supposed to get Heithold."

"That's bogus," I said. "You have to have heard something."

"Listen," he glanced over as we walked. "All I heard was that the militia has taken over the checkpoints."

There was no way that was the case. He must've misheard it.

"What are you talking about?" I sneered.

"That's what I heard! When I went into the CP to look for Heithold, I heard the commander saying something about the militia taking over the checkpoints."

"Which ones?" Ian asked.

"All of them."

"What?!"

"I don't know. That's just what I heard. Like I said, I was just supposed to find Heithold."

"Yeah, you said that." Ian laughed.

It was unreal. We're America. We don't *lose* ground. Especially not every checkpoint on the border of Sadr City. Not to a bunch of sand-clowns with a grudge. But if he was right, that meant we'd be in for a fight. A *real* fight. It meant that things were in the works. That the militia was on the loose.

I looked at Ian and we both laughed in excitement like giddy schoolchildren at the prospect of a battle. We'd dreamed about this kind of outbreak since the start of the deployment. Not a raid or a quick reaction, but a full-blown attack. It was really happening. I had no idea how serious it was at the time, but judging by Dulany's account it had to be a pretty big deal.

Before I knew it we were at the door of our squad's room. I passed through the portal and I could see that everybody else was suited up and ready to go. Somehow, the two of us had fallen way behind the curve. They hadn't even sent a messenger. Brushing it off, I jumped straight to my gear and checked over my machine gun while Ian made his way over to our squad leader and asked him what the hell was going on.

"Just get to the trucks," Sergeant Dukes snapped.

Nothing more was said.

I grabbed the crusty, blackened shoulder straps of my body armor and flung it over my head in one smooth motion. My machine gun was next, and after a quick check to make sure I had everything I would need, I ran down the stairs and out the door to the Strykers. When I got to our vehicle, our squad was already in a flurry of activity. Everybody raced to prep for a mission on short notice. I jumped right into the action, mounting one of the guns on the back hatch. Our assistant gunners loaded up crates of water and food. The vehicle crews pulled the covers off of our .50cal machine guns and ran over the functions of each Stryker's fire control system. The order was given to crack open extra boxes of ammo, and bystanders helped out wherever they could.

When I finished mounting my gun and helping out with the truck, I fastened up my knee pads and did a third and final check of my gear. The ramp slammed shut and a moment later, we rolled out of the gate in broad daylight, loaded for bear. It wasn't until we passed under that Persian arch at the outer gate of COP Old MOD and fell in behind Headquarters Platoon on the way out to the front that our company commander, Captain Bradford, finally explained the situation over the radio.

"This is Bull-Six to all Bull-Elements." His voice crackled with static as he took his time to make each word clear and precise. "The militia has overrun the checkpoints at Gold, Copper West, Maryland, and Grizzlies. Initial reports are that they have also taken control of the Iraqi Army's Armored Personnel Carriers and Tanks. All platoons are to prep anti-tank assets. I want machine gunners in the hatches. Respond in sequence. Over."

Our platoon leaders and platoon sergeants called him back to confirm the report.

"Ludwig!" Sergeant Dukes shouted. "Check the AT-4's."

I dropped down into the troop compartment to make sure the anti-tank rocket was ready to go, but it wasn't even there.

"I don't think we have any." Sgt. Montero cut in before I could say anything. "The Colonel made us give 'em up so they could be replaced, but I don't think we got any back."

"No, we don't have any back here." I said.

"Alright." Sergeant Dukes answered calmly, turning to his radio to call up our status to Sergeant O'Brien. "One-Six, this is One-Four. We don't have any AT-4's. Over."

"Roger." Sergeant O'Brien called back. "We don't either."

As I stood back up in the hatch, I could only think of one thing: don't bring a knife to a gunfight. In this case it was an understatement in every imaginable way. Ian charged the bolt on his M-240B machine gun and slapped the feed-tray shut over a fresh belt of rounds. Our awesome weapon had never looked so feeble. It wouldn't be worth a damn if we ran into a tank.

I leaned over and locked eyes with Ian.

"This shit's about to get real," I muttered.

All he could do was nod.

The truck settled into an apprehensive silence as we tore ass over to the far side of town. We were all ears on the radio, listening to the speaker in our troop compartment that was tuned in to the company frequency. Slowly but steadily, the picture of the battlefield was burned into our minds. Overnight, the militia had unburied every cache, rallied every footman and taken to the streets, igniting the peaceful night into a brushfire of brutal fighting. The general realization was that if we had gone on that raid the night before, we would've hit everything in their army like a fly hitting the windshield of a bus. But the bad news didn't stop there. The night before, the bulk of the Iraqi Army had also deserted their posts, either out of fear or crossed loyalties, and they had left behind everything in their arsenal for the taking. The militia not only held every piece of dominant terrain, but they had acquired a fresh batch of military hardware, and every route into town was laced with a fresh batch of explosives just waiting to go off.

They knew our tactical dispositions, our standard operating procedures, our vehicle identifiers, our capabilities, and they had brought everything to the fight. They had mortars, rockets, "lob bombs," RPGs,

EFPs, snipers, heavy machine guns, anti-aircraft guns, home-made explosives, and even brand-new Iranian import rocket launchers. Little did we know, the Jaish al-Mahdi had risen up across the entire country, and every fighter loyal to the cause was out there in the streets. All we knew at that point was that the militia had somehow overtaken every major hard point in and around Sadr City. So with every passing mile of road we surged forward, pushing farther into Hell with our trigger fingers itching and eyes scanning wide.

As soon as we hit the streets of Ur, the three platoons of Bull Company split up to go one-on-one with each of the three checkpoints in the district. 1st Platoon was sent up north to secure Checkpoint Grizzlies and Route Maryland by COP #329. As we drew closer to the objective, our platoon split further into two sections of vehicles and spread out across the open field nearby for an assault.

The checkpoint itself was on the street level with the rest of Route Grizzlies, but the building used by its occupiers as an office and garrison was situated up on the edge of the northern berm, all the way on the far side of its eastern edge. The building provided ample sectors of fire onto any assaulting force so we approached the checkpoint with caution. From what we could see, it was abandoned outright, but you never really know until the fighting begins.

Two assaulting squads were sent in to clear the objective. Weapons Squad was ordered to fall-in behind them to provide close-range support. Once the building was cleared, our intention was to move in and set up a firing position so we could cover the north face of the structure from a counterattack along our own avenue of approach. While all of this went down, our 3rd Squad would hold the perimeter as a reserve force in case the whole assault went sideways.

When Sergeant O'Brien finished up with the briefing, I grabbed my machine-gun and got ready for the call.

"Old school," Ian whispered.

"Damn right," I whispered back.

Over the radio, we got word that the other trucks had dismounted their men. Sergeant Moore, the acting squad leader for Weapons Squad at the time, looked over at us to shout the command.

"Dismount!"

Ian hit the ramp control and we both ran out into the street. Under the weight of all my gear it was hard to catch up with the rest of the platoon, but we ran as fast as we could and filed into the junkyard next to the checkpoint. Our best option was to approach it under the cover of urban discards and pop out just a few dozen meters away, but it would still be a long haul if we started taking fire from the windows.

With lungs heaving and sweat dribbling down my brow, my adrenaline glands injected a gentle and uncontrollable shiver into my bones. I scanned the wreckage intently and glanced over at Ian. What I saw was a face that was hard and cold — a face I had come to know well. Inside, however, I knew he was feeling exactly what I was: excitement, fear, happiness, and terror all fucked into one big heap. It was a twisted emotion of knowing both that you could die at any minute and that you had spent years training for this moment. This wasn't like some raid in the middle of the night. We weren't going in under the cloak of darkness and getting out before they could rally a fight. They had opened up the floodgates with a massive salvo at our center, and now it was our turn to play catch-up. With white knuckles, I clenched down on my machine gun. Every distant concept that had once made up the vastness of the world disappeared. My entire life was right there, in that moment. There was no room for anything else.

Our approach was steady. We leap-frogged around the corners of derelict junk with our ears tuned-in and our eyes scouring over every scrap of metal for a sign that it might explode. To my surprise, I made it all the way to the far end of the junkyard, passed through the northern gate, and rushed along the final approach to the command post without a single shot fired. As it turned out, the checkpoint was a total ghost town. It was also clear that we had missed our enemy by a matter of minutes. Everything of military value had been looted. Guns, armor, ammunition, RPGs, radios... They had all fallen into the hands of the militia. When the building was secured, I set up facing out a window towards the direction of our approach and sucked down the last of the water in my Camelbak.

"Hey, Ian," I asked. "Do you have any water?"

He shook his head from side to side. "Nope. I'm out."

"Fuck."

I waited for the commotion of searches and situation reports to end before flagging down a squad leader and asking him the same.

"Hey, Sergeant Moore!"

"What's up, Ludwig?" he said, popping his head into the room.

"Is there any way we can get some more water in here?"

"What, you're out?"

"Roger."

"Here," he said, throwing me a bottle. "I'll see what I can do."

I split what was left in the bottle with Ian, but I knew it wasn't enough. Outside, Sergeant O'Brien was talking to nearby residents to find out where the militia had gone and why the checkpoint was empty. From my makeshift stool at the window I could hear one of our regular contacts give him the whole story, which our interpreter conveyed loud and clear. It was a tale of woe, from dawn to the death of a lone Iraqi officer who went down swinging to the very end. One of the shop owners from across the street had seen the whole thing. A few others confirmed the details. The rest was left up to our imaginations as we played "connect the dots" with the bloodstains in the sand.

Earlier that morning, when the sun was still low in the sky, an unmarked white van had approached the concrete barriers of Checkpoint Grizzlies. Oblivious to their surroundings, the occupying platoon of Iraqi Army soldiers went about their morning rituals of drinking, frying up some chicken for falafels, and dicking off. Morale was at an all-time low. The men knew the routine and tried to stay out of the way of the militia, but their young and eager lieutenant was fresh out of the officer training program and hopped up on ideology. He was eager to fight for his country and determined to make a difference, so he personally oversaw every vehicle search on the line. He even had the balls to arrest some of the "bad guys," and nobody was that excited to pay the price for his zeal.

They all remembered what had happened the last time a young-gun got too excited.

The white van came to a stop at the checkpoint and a couple of Iraqi men bearing assault rifles and wearing desert camo pants jumped out. They shouted instructions to the soldiers at the checkpoint, at which a number of them grabbed their rifles, got up and crammed into the back of the van. The rest stood there silently. Nobody spoke up. Sure as shit nobody went to fetch their lieutenant. When the van was full, the two gunmen slammed the door shut and drove off, disappearing into the city behind a cloud of dust. Nobody knew if it was the shouting or slamming of the van's door, but something woke up the lieutenant. When he came outside it didn't take long for him to realize what was going on. The militia had come back for their men.

"Fucking traitors," he murmured to himself in Arabic.

A number of his guys were gone, that was sure. He didn't know exactly how many, but long ago he pieced together that as much as half of his men were probably moles. The other half were a useless heap of bums.

"What the fuck was that?!" he shouted.

Everybody stood around silently as he scanned over the troops, taking note of the absentees he could remember.

"Where the hell did they go?"

Nobody answered him.

Without skipping a beat, the lieutenant hustled over to the senior ranking non-commissioned officer at the checkpoint and grilled him about the van, who had gotten inside, and where they were going. He got nothing in reply. The man simply threw up his arms and shrugged. Nobody dared to speak a word. They were too afraid to talk. Facing blank faces with nothing to respond to his question, the lieutenant barked out his order before turning away to head back inside.

"When that van comes back, shoot them before they get here!"

Within moments he disappeared into the command post — the very structure we had assaulted and now held. As I looked around me, it was obvious that I was sitting in the pilfered remains of the man's office. I tried to imagine what must've happened in the time that he had retreated to gather his thoughts, and filled in the blanks from what I had seen of him in the weeks before. I pictured a dozen scenarios. Each one left me overcome with sympathy for the lone soldier who was staring down his final days.

I always believed that good beats evil. That light beats dark. That right will prevail. Hearing that story unfold, I was finally forced to face the reality that all he could do was die. The only question, I suppose, was what to do with the time he had left.

After all, he had to do *something*.

With the names of those who had deserted still burning into his brain, I'm sure he would have scribbled out a list for safe keeping. I suppose that the list in his hand was that something. As were his pistol and bulletproof vest. They were reminders that justice prevails, that he wasn't alone, that backing him up was an army of commanders who care, that one day Iraq would be free of this criminal menace. But only as long as somebody stood up and fought. These were concepts that were alien to everybody around him, but he had seen for himself that the Americans meant business. He knew they were here to make a difference. More than anything, he *believed* — and that belief was about to be challenged for the last time.

"You're saying there was an argument?" Sergeant O'Brien spoke loud and clear to one of our primary sources who had seen the whole thing go down from his shop just north of the northern barricade.

The interpreter translated the question, to which the man answered with a clear response.

"He is saying yes." Our interpreter clarified. "Yes, there was an argument."

"Ask him what it was about." Sergeant O'Brien turned his attention back to the man. "What was the argument about?"

There was a moment of pause as the man considered the rest of the story. He knew that he was already in danger, talking to us like he had. For all he knew the militia could be just around the corner. At a minimum, he knew they were still watching the checkpoint. On days like today, the Americans were always too busy to look out for the little guy. He spoke up with these concerns and our interpreter made it clear he was on the verge of going quiet.

"It's alright," Sergeant O'Brien reassured him. "My men have already cleared the checkpoint. There's no militia here."

The man looked around to see if there were any windows revealing him to the outside world. There weren't. He was alone and, for the time being, safe. Sooner or later, however, we'd be riding off into the distance, and it was hardly in his interest to be the only person the Americans talked to — especially if we got answers.

"Look," Sergeant O'Brien continued. "We're going to be talking to everybody that was here. Nobody will know you told us anything. I promise. I just want to know what happened here so I can put it in our report."

As our interpreter translated his words, the man glanced around one last time to take in his surroundings. It was obvious we had the place surrounded, and by then he had seen us canvass a neighborhood a dozen times. Besides, we weren't the "bad Americans;" we were the good guys. We stuck to our word. That's why the Jaish al-Mahdi had lost control of Ur to begin with.

He mulled it over in his mind for a little longer while our interpreter and Sergeant O'Brien did their best to keep him talking. Whatever it was that kept him going I have no idea, but he eventually got back to the rest of his story. The details, he explained, came second hand from his shop boy whose job was to hustle the soldiers into overpriced smokes and energy drinks. The rest was pretty hard to miss from where he worked. All of it would be confirmed in due time as we discussed what happened with the rest of the neighborhood.

After walking into the command post, the platoon sergeant confronted his lieutenant on behalf of his men. In a sign of solidarity, he blocked the doorway for a private conversation, but let his words carry across the checkpoint so his men could hear what was about to go down.

"Sir," he said. "Let it go."

He let the words sink in. It was great advice. The lieutenant could just let it go. He could just let it happen. He could put down his weapons and slip into the militia's pocket to become another corrupt official of the new Iraqi Army. Corrupt — but *alive.* For a moment he probably even considered it, but the idea of surrender repulsed him. Not just because it was surrender, but because it was the abandonment of everything he stood for. A violation of his every word and worth. And if he surrendered, what about tomorrow? How could he lead a platoon as the man who showed up proclaiming honor and valor only to surrender in the face of fear?

"Let it go?!" He shouted. "Those men are traitors!"

"Insha'Allah," came the platoon sergeant's reply — *if God wills it.*

"They are going to kill innocent people! Are you just going to let that happen?"

"So what? You can't beat them. Besides, they're fighting the Americans now. If you try to get in their way, they'll just kill you. It's best to just sit back and look out for us."

"Bullshit! We are going to fight! That's why we're here! That's an order!"

"And what about your family?"

For a second the young lieutenant froze in fear. Then remembered that nobody knew about his family — at least nobody there. He wasn't like one of those blabber mouths who chats away about the good life back home. No, he was disciplined. The militia was never going to get to his family. They could only kill him — if only that was as much of a relief as he had hoped.

"I'm not going to sit here and let this happen!" he shouted.

"Then you're going to die."

His platoon sergeant looked back at him with a blank expression. It was a matter of fact. In a burst of anger, the young platoon leader lashed out with both his arms.

"Insha'Allah!"

But his platoon sergeant was unfazed. He spoke in a deliberate tone, still loud enough for his men to hear.

"Do what you like, but none of us are going to die here with you."

At that, he turned around and walked away, leaving the young officer to his thoughts. For a while, all the lieutenant could do was pace around nervously and grope for a plan. He still didn't know what to do, and the list of deserters was growing by the minute. Soon enough he'd be fresh out of troops. They could hear the fighting in the distance and they knew they were out-gunned. Perhaps most of all, word was spreading throughout the ranks about the insanity of their commander who was determined to die a hero. One by one his men put down their weapons and walked away. It was as simple as that. All their lieutenant could do was add a name to a list whenever another soldier walked away and try again, in vain, to get in touch with his commander.

Where is he?!

All he could hear on the other end of the radio was static.

It wasn't much longer before the white van was spotted coming back to the checkpoint. The private who had spotted it first stood up and shouted to the men all around him.

"Here they come!"

The lieutenant ran outside and looked down the road. In the distance, a shoddy van with dented side panels raced towards his checkpoint, assault rifles sticking right out of the windows. The soldier who had seen the van first stepped back from his machine gun while another opened up the blockade.

"What are you doing?!" The lieutenant shouted. "Shoot the bastards!"

"You do it," the young soldier snapped back.

A few men chuckled at the exchange as the van pulled up and the door slid open. Another militia footman stepped out, greeted with a strong embrace by one of the soldiers on the line.

"My brother!"

"Kaseem! It's time. The Americans are coming."

The foot-soldier turned to the lieutenant, then looked out at the soldiers all around him.

"Get in!" he shouted.

More soldiers piled into the van as the gunman turned to face the ones who were left behind. He spoke with a soft but very stern tone.

"If you're not with us," he said. "Go home."

Nothing happened at first. It was as though his words hadn't registered. After a tense moment however, the first solider dropped his rifle to the dirt and walked off. The rest of them were quick to follow. Nobody bothered to stick around and see what happened next. The lieutenant stood there, blank-faced and stunned. He was completely abandoned and left there alone at the checkpoint.

"What are you doing?" One of the militia foot-soldiers barked at him. "Get out of here!"

The words were lost in transit. They didn't even register in the young lieutenant's mind. Inside he was a warp of twisted feelings: fury, terror, exhaustion, and patriotism. They tugged at his bones. They froze his muscles and daunted him with indecision.

I must fight them! He thought.

But he didn't know how.

"That's the officer we were talking about!" One of his soldiers shouted from inside the van.

"Oh! The fucking idiot!"

"Yeah!" The soldier laughed. "Shoot him!"

There was still no response from the lieutenant. He was lost in his own mind, groping helplessly for a plan. He tried to grasp how he had shriveled from an officer of a nation's army into nothing but a lone man with a gun. His mind turned to his gun. He didn't have a plan — just a gun.

A gun and a fight.

"Fuck you."

He raised his arm and pointed the crusty, rusting muzzle of his pistol straight at the foot-soldier. With steady form he squeezed the trigger until the hammer gave way and the recoil of a 9mm casing kicked back on his wrist. The round was well aimed, slugging its target right in the chest. The foot-soldier doubled over and fell to the ground with a sharp grunt. His gasps for air gurgled through the new hole in his lungs as he struggled to breathe. Everybody froze in shock. The lieutenant turned his muzzle to another target and fired. Again, his target was hit square in the chest and fell back against the van. When the officer steadied his aim on a third target, he felt a sudden flash of pain in his gut, but he had already pulled the trigger when the world went dark.

When he came to, the first thing he noticed was the filthy taste of desert sand between his teeth. When he opened his eyes, he was staring at the earth, face down. The pain was next. It started as a dull warmth — the feeling of a hot compress or maybe a fire. When he clenched his teeth down, the pain evolved into a sharp stab. His jaw was broken. Shattered, maybe. His first reaction was to moan, but the flexing of his torso brought another wave of pain. He was shot, too.

When he finally managed to eke out a sound, it was nothing more than faint whimper, lost in a field of short, quick breaths, sucking down mouthfuls of dirt. He rolled to the side to cough up the dust in his lungs. His hands were already grabbing the site of the gunshot wound when he filtered through the noise of the world outside of his pain. There was a frantic blur of yells and screaming. He rolled onto his back to see a man standing over him with a rifle in hand. The man swung his rifle into the lieutenant's skull and the world went dark again.

This time when lieutenant came to his left eye was swollen completely shut. His head was throbbing. His hands were covered with his own drying, sticky blood. When he moved his tongue, he could feel chunks of teeth floating around his mouth. Somehow he was still standing.

No, he realized.

He was being held up.

They dragged him to the top of the hill by the front door of the command post and dropped him down to his knees. He tried to kick, to fight back, but his muscles were sacks of water. With every fluttered breath, every twitch, every tortured moan, his gut wrenched with pain. They held his arms, with his hair clasped between the fingers of one of his captors. His body was shivering uncontrollably.

Why am I so cold?

Through the commotion, he caught a glimpse of the white van at the checkpoint. It was spattered in blood. Some of it a soft spray, some of it in long streaks, and some of it in smeared hand-prints of other men, trying in vain to save the lives of their friends.

Three to one, he thought. *Not bad.*

The thoughts calmed his mind as he turned to the blurry image of an executioner standing before him. The face looked familiar. He'd seen this man before, but he couldn't put his finger on it. Then, like getting hit in the gut, he realized who it was.

"I told you." His platoon sergeant looked down at him with contempt. *"Masha'Allah."*

He watched helplessly as his most trusted soldier raised a rifle to his face and flipped the selector switch to "fire." Looking back with defiance he calmed his mind to accept what was coming. A click and a flash was the last thing he saw. The bullet split his face in two.

With the last of the resistance now dead, the militia foot soldiers at the checkpoint hurried to get their guys in the van. A pair of Apache helicopters appeared on the horizon, and time was running out. The Americans were already on their way.

"We need to go!" the platoon sergeant shouted. "Grab him!"

Two men reached down to pick up the lifeless body of their lieutenant. They dragged him down to the van and shoved him inside with the three other men he had shot.

"Nadim! What's with the tank!" The platoon sergeant shouted to a soldier on the top of the vehicle.

"I can't get it to start!"

Of course not, he thought to himself. *The American's would never give us a decent tank.*

"Come on!" He waved the soldier down from the vehicle. "Get in the van! Let's go!"

After ransacking the checkpoint for supplies, they packed into the van and drove off.

"That's everything you remember?" Sergeant O'Brien asked the boy.

The little hustler who had seen it all up close nodded his head in a sheepish manner. We had saved the best for last — as best we could — and everything came together just like our first informant had said. Some thirty minutes after the lieutenant was killed, we had shown up at the checkpoint to get the story for ourselves. One thing that had become painfully clear was that no matter how little we cared for the Iraqi Army, or how cheap and cowardly we may have thought they were in the past, that one lieutenant had more balls than the lot of us. He went down swinging in the face of it all, and for that alone he deserved our respect. Perhaps more importantly, he gave us reason to hope. Hope that some day, maybe, they could stand up on their own.

After about an hour at the checkpoint, we picked up our stuff to move out and the silence we had enjoyed during the assault was broken. Right as I stepped out the front door of the command post I heard a loud crack.

"Sniper!" Somebody shouted.

Everybody rushed behind cover. I was still up on the top of the hill with nowhere to hide. I had no choice but to run in a straight line down the stairs and out of sight, hoping the second shot wouldn't be aimed right at me. By the time it fired off I had just dodged behind a concrete wall.

"Where's that coming from?!" Sergeant O'Brien called out.

There was another loud snap over our heads.

"He's to the east!" Sergeant Moore shouted back.

A few of us shuffled around to different sides of our cover. The fourth round slammed against a brick wall nearby. Sergeant O'Brien was already on his radio.

"Seven this is Six, we are taking small arms fire from the east! Identify and engage! Over!"

The fifth and final round slammed firmly into the side of one of our Strykers, but the Vehicle commander had already turned his gun to the east and let some of his own bullets fly. From on the ground, they felt like a hammer against my skull. When the bursts ended, Sergeant O'Brien received a hail from his radio and turned to Sergeant Benjamin beside him.

"Benjamin, mount up your squad! Signal to Bitolas as you move!" He turned back to our squad. "Sergeant Moore, did you get that?!"

"Roger! Mounting up!"

"Alright, Let's go!"

We made our way to our Strykers while they suppressed the enemy. Rounding the back end of the last vehicle, I realized just how far away our own Stryker was waiting. It was holding up a blocking position down the road that looked like it was a mile away. I knew it wasn't much more than a couple hundred meters but in that heat with a hundred pounds of gear it might as well have been a fuckin' mile.

"You've got to be kidding me," Ian gasped with dismay.

A burst of rounds snapped over our heads and we broke out running. Another one of our platoon's .50 cal machine guns returned fire. When the third burst of rounds rang out and pierced the air around us, I realized how exposed we really were. I was running down a wide open street with nothing but Fate as a vanguard while somebody took pot shots at me and my buddies. Another burst rang out. I was hustling as fast as I possibly could. Rounds skipped off the ground. Somebody else returned fire. I broke into a full sprint and gave it everything I goddamn had. Another burst of rounds skipped by my feet and my heart felt like it was going to burst. From off in the east, an RPG whistled through the air and hit a heap of scraps in the junkyard. Shortly after the explosion, a maelstrom of fire broke out. Us, them, a burst here, a burst there. I didn't know who was shooting or where. The ramp of our Stryker dropped down to the ground and I hurled myself into the safety of that vehicle for all I was worth. When it sealed shut behind me, I couldn't help but laugh.

"Woo-hoo!" Ian shouted, cracking up himself.

"Well goddamn!" Sergeant Moore smacked me on the back, heaving his chest with every breath. "I think they might've been shooting at us," he joked.

"You think?!" Ian shouted.

We took a moment to ourselves to smile and laugh — but it was just a moment. Just long enough to know we were alive. Long enough to let the fear dissipate and leave us ready to fight. In the front of the troop compartment, Sergeant Montero scanned over the scene with Sergeant Dukes looking over his shoulder to guide his aim. The screen panned across a field of discarded waste until it centered in on a battered building with a tiny, slithering, crawling glimmer of a shooter.

"There! See him?!" Sergeant Dukes shouted.

"Yeah!"

There was no hesitation. Sergeant Montero pulled his finger on the trigger and a burst of .50 cal rounds made their way down-range. They slammed into the brick and mortar all around his victim until whatever was left rolled over dead.

"Ludwig," Sergeant Moore smacked my arm to grab my attention. "I want you in the hatch."

I jumped up beside him. Once I was back on two feet, I glanced at the other Strykers down the road. I don't care how long it was, it still looked like a fuckin' mile.

In short time, an Iraqi Army unit assigned to help us in Ur showed up at the checkpoint to take over the fight. There were other engagements breaking out across the rest of Ur, and we had orders to maneuver south and engage a swath of enemy troops closing in on 3rd Platoon. From the looks of it, the Iraqi Army had brought an entire company to relieve us, since the street was packed full of Humvees and armored vehicles. Of all the things I could say about those men, they weren't lacking in ammunition and supplies by any measure.

The Iraqi soldiers who were sent in to set up their slapdash perimeter had magazines of rounds falling out of every orifice on their uniforms. I saw dozens of RPGs slung over the shoulders of men with no business even holding one. On the top of each Humvee, 12.7mm DShK machine guns swung around with long belts of rounds piled up by the gunners in the top hatch. One Iraqi soldier even pulled out a box of grenades right in front of me, handing them out like water bottles to his buddies. It was like a yard sale of Cold War artifacts.

"Hey, Dukes!" Sergeant Moore said.

"Yeah, what's up?"

"I think we might want to move..."

"Why? What do you see?"

We looked out at the band of soldiers getting ready for a shit show.

"Death blossom. Three o'clock."

The death blossom is what we called Iraqi soldiers in contact. They hear one round, one boom, one single snap, and they'll shoot everything they can see. Sometimes they hit other Iraqi soldiers, sometimes they shoot women, and every once and a while a round will find its way into an innocent kid. We never knew with those guys because they didn't give a fuck. The only sure thing was that they cared less about us than the women and children, so it was a prudent act to get right in the middle of their formation whenever they set off on a rampage. That way they have no excuse to turn around and shoot you in the face. But out there on Route Grizzlies we were in a bad spot. The Iraqi Army had pulled up to the west of us, driving on the left side of the road, and Sadr City was to the east. If anything went down they'd have to shoot past us to hit the bad guys.

It took Sergeant Dukes all of two seconds to stand up and see what Sergeant Moore had pointed out.

"Oh yeah," he said. "Hey Pfister, we gotta' move, bud."

Pfister popped the brake release and with a loud hiss we started rolling. Sergeant Montero guided him across the street and behind the Iraqi troops. As though it had been synchronized with our repositioning, a single round cracked off. Like headless poultry, the Iraqi soldiers immediately took to scurrying and firing aimlessly at everything around them. Another round came in and Sergeant Montero had already got a bead on the shooter.

"You're mine motherfucker."

I ducked down just in time to see the shooter in his sights. He squeezed off another burst and the spent shells from the machine gun right above his hatch sprinkled all around his seat. The heavy gunshots rang out, and that was the end of the man on the screen.

The thing about the .50 cal is this: it's big. I don't just mean the round is a half-inch wide and something like an inch long — those are just dimensions. When I say it's big, I mean it'll kill you even if it doesn't hit you. It'll rip your face clean off your skull if the closest it came was a near miss. This was a dead-on hit. A good clean "ghosting." When the rounds reached the center of the aiming reticle, a puff of blood and body parts was the only thing left of Sergeant Montero's target. "Nothing but a memory," as I heard a range instructor put it once.

Nothing but a memory.

We didn't stick around the checkpoint for very long. Across the entire city, more and more reports of insurgent activity had come in, and it was obvious that we had more important things to do. After linking up with the Iraqi commander on the ground, Sergeant O'Brien got back on his truck and we rolled out to play sudden-death whack-a-mole across the northern half of Ur.

In the hours that followed, the Jaish al-Mahdi organized a deliberate counterattack on Checkpoint Grizzlies. The militia knew full well they had nowhere near the means or motivation to defend themselves for long. Favoring a showdown, the insurgent forces poured everything they had at the checkpoint, ultimately depleting the Iraqi Army of ammunition and eventually overrunning their position.

For the second time that day our platoon gathered up to assault the checkpoint, capture it outright, and clear it once again for bombs and bad guys. Just like before, there was nobody there by the time we got on-target and all we could do was secure the scene. By the time another Iraqi Army unit was moved in to relive us, Captain Bradford called up new orders for us to push south once more through a newly discovered enemy engagement area.

Our task was to reinforce another platoon that was taking heavy contact from an ambush on all sides. As soon as we got there, another firefight broke out at Checkpoint Grizzlies. Air weapon teams across the battle space spotted large groups of hostile forces moving into position for an all-out attack. Captain Bradford passed down a fragmentation order for us to respond in-force, but on the way there we ran into our own small ambush and had to fight our way back to the farthest extents of the Checkpoint.

By noon, the situation was painfully clear: we had lost control of Ur. After hours of fighting, whole swaths of militia fighters were still moving through our battle space with up-to-date intel on our locations and measure of force. As we reacted to their efforts, pre-planned countermeasures bogged us down with gunfire, roadside bombs, and deliberately synchronized ambushes. When we secured something and moved on, they took it back ten minutes later. We were caught in a full blown scrimmage, fighting through dozens of small engagements along an entire flank of Sadr City against an enemy who had superior numbers and endless firepower.

The entire day, our platoon ran back and forth across the northern section of the town, fighting between the Routes Copper West, Maryland, and Grizzlies. Sometimes we made it across and nothing would happen. Sometimes it seemed like the militia was right around the corner. Sometimes we got hit where it hurt and had to fight through the pain. We were sniffing out our enemy like a dog while the other platoons in the company held their ground at the other checkpoints and got shit handed to them in spades. The heaviest fighting in that first string of the battle took place around the Copper West checkpoint, where 3rd Platoon held their ground against an endless stream of assaults and indirect fire.

What you need to know about a platoon is that it's a family — and the other platoons in your company are like a band of your closest relatives. From the other side of the battle, we could hear the endless mortars raining down on them. Thick black smoke billowed into the sky and the radios told tales of fierce resistance. It felt like forever. An eternity of listening to your dearest cousins caught in the middle of some heavy shit. It was a lifetime of fearing the worst.

And then it happened.

Bull Company lost a brother that day: Staff Sergeant Joseph Gamboa. He was killed in action. A mortar fell from the sky and landed right in front of his hatch. He died instantly. He was one of the first people in the company I'd ever met.

"The thing about the airfield run," he told me on my first day at Ft. Lewis, "is to never stop running. As long as you can run the whole way without stopping, you don't need to worry about a thing."

I can't tell you how many times I ran that airfield. I can't tell you how many times I followed his advice. But even now when I go for a run it's his voice that keeps me going. I can't explain it. I'll probably never forget it. It's one of those memories that stuck and every time I think of him, it's of that day and those words. I guess you can say I didn't know him very well — I didn't really. Just in that way you know somebody when you see them every day, when you hear their voice and know they're there, when part of you deep down takes that knowledge for granted. I wasn't in his squad. Not even his platoon. But he was still family. It still hurt just as bad to lose him. It also made me look around at my brothers and wonder: what would I do if they were gone? Sergeant Benjamin? Lieutenant Savage? Sergeant Lilly? Ian? Gonzo? Kaz? What would I do if they got hit?

Reports rang out across the net as the fighting continued. Without hesitation, Captain Bradford ordered 2nd Platoon down to Copper West so 3rd Platoon could race Gamboa to the rear. Now that we had a huge hole in our line, it was obvious that the fight was about to surge into a whole other realm of the Shit. Given the odds against us and the sheer number of men we were up against, losing a single man was tactically equivalent to adding another ten fighters to our enemy's ranks. That was a fact of life we'd all have to face, now that Sergeant Gamboa was gone. But the loss of a whole platoon? That was a full third of our company's dismounted firepower. That was over fifty men, and I had no idea when they'd be coming back. That's what scared me more than anything.

Now that we were unable to hold any ground against the Jaish al-Mahdi, 1st Platoon was ordered to maintain a steady chain of roving patrols well into the night. Our mission was to seek out the fight wherever we could find it. In the meantime, our company Headquarters covered down where they could. We had only two platoons to hold down a front line that spanned roughly four kilometers from end to end. It was impossible to stop the militia from maneuvering through the holes. The rest of that day was a total shit show, with small but effective ambushes waiting for us everywhere we went. Eventually we tagged out with 2nd Platoon out at the Copper West Checkpoint to catch a break, but soon after the sun rose back up in the eastern sky and another wash of violence broke out.

On the second day of fighting, 2nd Platoon was the first element in Bull Company to receive a full blown attack break on their position. While they were settled into an overwatch of the Grizzlies Checkpoint, the Jaish al-Mahdi formed up in a company sized element and surrounded them from all sides. This assault turned into an eight hour firefight, during which the entire front was wide open for the taking.

Meanwhile, down at Copper West, a steady rain of mortars and small-arms fire had been holding those of us in 1st Platoon in place for hours. As soon as 2nd Platoon took contact on Grizzlies, however, the steel rain, which had plagued our day, lifted without a single explanation. It was a textbook bait-and-strike tactic. They were hoping we'd break station and go help out our boys up north so that another element could sweep in and take the checkpoint on Copper West. The only oddity was in the ferocity of the engagement up north. Who knew if 2nd Platoon could hold out on their own? And if our enemy wasn't really clever enough for a bait and switch, what would we do if they failed?

At times like these, when I wasn't in the Shit for myself, all I could do was sit back and listen to the fight unfold. In all the months I had served as 1st Platoon's radio guy, I truly came to appreciate the careful planning and clever wit that's needed to win a war. The fact was that any number of militia fighters could've been forming up around 2nd Platoon over on Route Grizzlies, but folding our center wasn't going to help anybody to overcome those odds. And if 2nd Platoon couldn't hold their own against the Jaish al-Mahdi, whatever was left of our hasty rescue wouldn't stand a chance against the ambush they had waiting. There was even less of a chance that we could regain our hold at either checkpoint and carry on with the fight.

I can only imagine what Captain Bradford was thinking, but one thing I didn't doubt at all was the faith he had in his men. Rather than fall for their sleight of hand, he kept both elements right where they were, and for the rest of the day our company headquarters element filled in for the missing platoon. But it was only then that I truly realized how dire the situation had become. We were running on bare bones with everything out on the table. God help us if we lost another man. If that happened, I had no idea how we could win.

For the rest of the day, 1st Platoon had swapped out for another shift to cover the northern sections of town. As before, our task was to conduct a string of roaming patrols during which we'd take contact at random intervals. 3rd Platoon got back to the frontlines that afternoon, which allowed us a brief respite as we changed our tactics and each platoon settled into an overwatch throughout the town. It was a much needed break after an entire day of explosions and fighting.

Late that night, Grizzlies got hit for the last time. From where I was located at the Maryland Checkpoint, I could see the spray of tracers flying up into the air at random. In some ways it was your typical firefight: loud bangs and booms followed by a string of bright flashes with little pops and prattles mixed in to fill the gaps. But in other ways it was just plain wrong, eerie, and unsettling. I couldn't really put my finger on it.

Apart from the engagement itself, the whole town was silent. It was like somebody had draped a heavy rug over the city and muffled its daily commotion. There were no cars or generators and many of the lights were burned out. It was the first time in six months I had ever heard the city of Ur so quiet. At that moment every civilian had either fled or gone into hiding. Now that we were two days into the fight, the militia troops were the only people still walking around those streets. Everybody else was hiding in their homes, praying to their god they didn't get killed in the crossfire.

I watched and listened from afar as an enemy force that must've been twice the size of their own hammered the checkpoint. While I knew they were in need of reinforcements, there was little we could've done to help. No matter how bad it got, we couldn't simply break station and come to the rescue without some kind of back-up to cover us and patch the line. Doing so would just rip a huge hole in the precarious position we had barely captured in the first place. But after a few minutes, the enemy's assault of the Grizzlies Checkpoint ended with a final burst of gunfire like a period ending a sentence.

A single busted up troop carrier was the only thing to make it out of there alive. At first, I didn't know what it was. All I could see was a flood of sparks and sputtering flame barreling at me. It wasn't until I saw it open up with its main gun at the border behind it that I knew exactly what I was looking at. When the vehicle passed us by, I got a good look at the damage. The right side had two large holes in it from a pair of RPGs that blasted through the armor. One of them hit the engine, causing the sputtering and backfiring ruckus I had heard. The other hit the troop compartment dead-on, leaving a gaping hole and a column of smoke to mark the death of whomever was unlucky enough to be stuck inside when the rocket went off.

Another thirty minutes passed before we heard the news over the radio that the Iraqi Army had once again lost control of the Grizzlies Checkpoint. This time, the place was positively crawling with militia. Eager to catch them flat-footed, we shuffled our manpower for the assault and moved in to strike.

In order to cover the engagement and maintain observation on the target, our platoon was ordered to maneuver wide and flank the checkpoint from the north-west. The main effort approached from the south, backed up with a platoon of Bradley fighting vehicles from the 3rd ID. As soon as we got to a fairly decent staging ground, the militia opened up on us from the checkpoint, using stolen night vision optics and military hardware to spot us and correct for fire. The only problem with their plan was that we were easily three times as far away as the maximum effective range of their weapons.

"What the hell are they doing?" Sergeant Dukes chuckled.

The faint, distant pops echoed through the vast expanse between us. The only thing they accomplished was giving us a clear marker for where they were and how many shooters to expect. With a quick spin of his fire control system, Sergeant Montero spotted a number of shooters scurrying around the checkpoint.

"Bull Six, this is Bull One-Six." Sergeant O'Brien called up Captain Bradford from another truck in our formation.

"Bull One-Six, this is Bull Six." Captain Bradford replied.

"Roger, we are looking at three military aged males. Break—"

Sergeant O'Brien broke the transmission for a split second before continuing on with his report. Before he could key up for another call, Captain Bradford cut in.

"This is Bull Six! Yeah! Hit 'em!"

He didn't need to tell us twice, and it was the last time we called up a kill. All together, the vehicles of our platoon hammered away at the checkpoint while the assaulting element moved in from the south. Everyone on our truck crouched down to watch the show. The steady stream of high caliber rounds slammed into walls, tore apart trimmings, and cut down humans like we were squashing bugs. I don't know how to explain what was going through our heads as we cheered and laughed. It's something I don't think you can understand until you're there. Until you've been so exposed to that kind of violence that you get used to the obscenity. Until you've been engulfed with so much madness that it's *fun* to be evil.

After two straight days of fighting, I laughed. Goddammit, with every bone in my body I cheered. And I was anything but alone. That Stryker filled up with the same electric energy of a thousand soccer fans. With every booming string of .50 cal rounds I sat transfixed with anticipation until the little white dots met the little white blobs and they both disappeared to the sound of a distant pop. They weren't people anymore. They were nothing. A target. The enemy. Call them what you want. At that point they were just a construct of the modern institution of warfare. Anonymous people. Worthless.

And I was happy to see them go.

But in the time it took us to suppress the checkpoint and move into position for a dismounted attack, Bull Six had already called into question the entire purpose of retaking the Checkpoint. After all, its entire existence was predicated on the theory that our enemy would be sneaking in bullets for some kind of final assault and that we could starve them out until they had nothing left to shoot. While it turned out that we were right about the bullets, the battle had already broken out — so there wasn't that much logic in fighting for a checkpoint we had built to prevent it. Somehow, Captain Bradford explained all that to the Colonel and against all odds he actually got clearance to call in a Hellfire missile that would level the entire building. All we had to do then was keep any "squirters" from sneaking out back.

The Bradley fighting vehicles moved in to get a closer look at the checkpoint and continued hammering away at it with massive 25 mm cannons. After a good run on it with the tools at-hand, we painted the target with a laser and the choppers did their thing. By the time our ground troops went through the checkpoint to review the damage, nothing remained but plumes of dust and blood spattered concrete slabs.

Now that we had officially decommissioned the Grizzlies Checkpoint for good, we put it out of our minds.

I think at worst I expected two seamless days of fighting to be enough. The toll on human lives was steadily growing. Hell, the city itself seemed to reek of death. But each day the militia pressed just as hard to send us packing as they had day before. And each day we faced a fresh complement of brand new enemy reserves. There was no end to their number. It was becoming obvious that those who'd fought us the day before had simply settled in to play civilian and wait for an opportunity to hit our backs.

The following day we came across some resistance near the vicinity of Route Maryland. We held out against the attack only to get hit with a string of mortars. When we pushed south, the mortars followed. Try as we might, the militia had our entire battle-space zeroed in and no matter what we did they could put rounds on-target at a moment's notice. The rounds came so close we could feel the flakes of flying debris smack against our skin.

Eventually we managed to shut them down in the north despite fierce resistance. When it was obvious the militia wasn't going to retake our position up on Maryland, they shifted gears to attack our boys just south of Copper West. Before we could secure the scene of our last engagement, we got a call from the Colonel that UAV assets had spotted a large group of men pushing across Route Grizzlies to assault the Talibiyah apartment complex on the very bottom corner of our battle space. Since the fight kicked off, some men from the 4th ID had been holding out there against incredible odds. After a few hours, however, the militia's attack was a success, and for a first time they had actually secured a solid foothold into Ur. More importantly, it was within pissing range of the Copper West checkpoint and positioned perfectly to fold our entire line through the district. Now that they controlled two flanks on our southern elements, Captain Bradford was sure that a synchronized attack was soon to follow. If we didn't do something to stop it from happening, the entire border would be lost.

"One-Six, this is Bull-Six." He called up our platoon with a new batch of orders. "I want you to push the southern limit of your patrols southward. I need you to keep an eye on the Talibiyah apartments and make sure we don't get overrun from the south. Over."

"Bull-Six, One-Six." Sergeant O'Brien called him back. "Roger."

We continued our roaming patrols, skirting up and down Route Rolling Rock. This time we pushed across Copper West and came into contact with the apartment complex at the southern edge of town. We took fire at every corner on the way and paid back with interest every round they shot off in anger. Finally, on our last run down Rolling Rock, we got ambushed in the middle of a dirt intersection surrounded by three story houses. It was quick and dirty. They didn't stick around to gloat or see if we were satisfied. All of a sudden RPGs were in the air, bathing us in light flakes of shrapnel yet missing us all together.

"This is Six!" The radio blared. "All squad leaders, give me an up!"

Every vehicle in the platoon responded in sequence.

"This is Two! We're good!"

"Three's good!"

"Six, Seven! We're good here!"

It was a miraculous fact that nobody got hit. Charred blast craters had baked into our surroundings, yet not a single new scratch could be seen on our Strykers.

"You know," Sergeant Dukes said with a shrug. "I expected a lot better than that. These guys would be in much better shape if they took a second to aim."

We all chuckled at the jest, refusing to accept that the day was fast at hand when the militia would finally take his advice to heart. Bravado is the rule of thumb when you're in the Shit. You cheer and sneer when you're up, and you pray to your god when you're down. We got plenty of both for the rest of the day. Eventually it was our turn to head back to COP #329 for a short respite of our own. It was the first time we'd get to sleep since the fighting began.

Bull Company fought in Ur for five days. That was five days of fighting, knowing that it wouldn't be over until the job was done. And these memories, the memories of what happened there, they're just a fog in my mind. A mix. A tangle of old roots. I dig back into the seeded grounds of my past and this is as far as I can get. It's too thick and thorny to dig deeper – and doing so would kill the very thing I want to show you.

I have memories of standing in a hatch. Waiting. "Swiss-cheesing" a car. Saying "wrong place, wrong time." RPGs blowing up all around us. Kids playing in the mud. Lying down on a stretcher for some short period of quiet, staring up at the stars and trying to see if I can find the Big Dipper. White-knuckle fear. Throwing on my headphones and raging out to music while mortars hit the ground on the other side of a thin wall. Insane delirium. Succumbing to dysentery. Heat stroke. Teaching my buddy patty-cake while guns blazed away outside the truck. The sickening realization that even the birds flying overhead were an agent of the enemy. Holding my life in my hands and calling it a machine gun. Taking the time to properly classify the terms 'dusted,' 'ghosted,' 'misted,' 'merc'd,' and 'waxed.' Staring death in the face. And finally pulling my feet out of my boots to pick off the flakes of dead and rotting skin.

They are all there. They are the most important ones. They are as vivid as any story I might tell – more important, as a matter of fact, because they are the real substance of war. They are markers in time. Well-taps to deep veins of emotion and substance. They are the things I really remember, not just the verbs and nouns I use to show you what happened. They are filth. They are pain. They are everything ugly and evil in man. They are confusing, haphazard and random. They are the thousand words I can never write, because they are illiterate. They are not stories but memories. Fog. Things that will die with me.

That night we rolled into COP #329 was the first time that the madness ever stopped. More importantly, it was the only chance we'd get for days to lay down and get some rack. At the time we didn't know how long it would last but the wisdom was to make quick work of our needs and be ready for a brawl. Weapons maintenance, supply runs and sleep were the names of the game.

"Go ahead and ground your gear." Sergeant Dukes barked to the squad. "Take a shit. Eat some chow. Do whatcha' gotta' do."

I carried out his orders to the letter. When I got back to the truck, I barely had time to sit down before he had another task at hand.

"Ludwig," he called over. "Go with Peterson, Hutchens, and Santiago to get some ammo."

"Roger. Where's it at?"

"Back in the west corner of the COP. A supply convoy just dropped off a load of it."

"Moving!" I set off to track it down.

"Hey, Ludwig!" he shouted. "Get with the XO! He's the one in charge of issuing ammo!"

"Roger!"

When I got to the ammo holding area, I spotted a dark mass before me about five feet tall and more than fifteen feet wide on all sides. It was more ammunition than I'd ever seen in one place outside of an ammo storage bunker. I clicked on my red-lens flashlight and scanned over the pile. It had everything you could imagine — literally every type of thing that goes boom. You name it. If it was meant to be fired from the ground, to kill something dead and to do it well, we had it.

"XO!" I shouted into the darkness for our company's executive officer — the guy in charge of the logistics.

"Yeah!" he shouted back.

Instead of playing a game of Marco Polo, he turned on his white-light headlamp, confident that the Iraqis couldn't see through the 15 foot tall concrete barrier that surrounded us on every side. I hustled over to him with my requested count in hand and he greeted me with a wave.

"What's up, Ludwig?"

"Hey, sir! We're here to load up on ammo. Here's our count."

I held out the thin strip of paper explaining what we needed to get back to combat strength. He brushed it off and scribbled some numbers on his clipboard.

"Whatever. I don't need a count. Just tell me what you're taking and how much you think it is."

"What?"

"Just grab what you need."

I'd been expecting the typical, anal retentive counting and signing that always goes with getting ammo from the Department of Defense. This was different. It didn't feel like the Army I'd known.

"I don't need to sign anything?" I asked.

"No. Don't worry about it."

Ian laughed and we dug in like school children. We could barely walk under the weight of it all. We carried backpacks of belted ammo, slung anti-tank rockets over our shoulders, and cradled boxes of grenades and bullets in our arms like babies. After trudging across a hundred feet of gravel, we came up with a better idea and left our assistant gunners behind so we could go get the Stryker.

"Fuck it!" Ian shouted. "Let's go get the whole damn pile!"

We met up with Staff Sergeant Dukes and explained the situation. At first he seemed fed up with our shenanigans, but then he just nodded his head and let out a smirk.

"Well hell," he said. "Why not?"

We fired up the Stryker and got back to our teammates before charging over to the massive resupply point to pillage it again for everything it was worth. All said and done, I think we left with twice as much ammo as we'd tried to carry away on the first go. That was easily four times as much as we'd been sent for — but that's also how it was. Past a point it didn't matter anymore. We went days without shaving. Days without showering. Days without sleeping or getting a full meal. The only thing we had was aggression, as if men could live off of brutality alone. Violence as sustenance.

It didn't take long for us to settle down and get some rack. We'd already filled up with ammo, water, and food. All that was left to deal with was the issue of prolonged sleep deprivation. I went through the motions of getting ready for a king's slumber. With calculated determination and a whole mess of field resourcefulness, I managed to rig up a stretcher under an overhang of camouflage on top of our Stryker. But when I finally lay down I couldn't sleep. I just stared up at the sky in awe and with envy.

Dancing up there in the heavens, a pair of helicopters did their thing: raining down fire on some unsuspecting victims far below. That's the thing about Apaches. It really can rain fire. I've seen it. In that way, I guess, helicopter pilots are like gods. From the sky they peer through the night to watch us mortals scurry about on the Earth. With the flip of a red switch and the twitch of an itchy finger, it's all done. It's all in a day's work. They hear the rattle of the cannon and watch little snaps like firecrackers blow gray pictures of gingerbread men to pieces. But down on the ground, we look right into the face of Armageddon.

It might sound like we're not in it together — the pilots and us. We're all American. We all wear the same goofy gray and white Tetris patterned camouflage. The power of thermal vision isn't unique to pilots and the accuracy of mechanically assisted aiming is a feat that we also have to our name. There is no count of how many white blips, once men, became a tuft of dissipating radiation at the hands of our vehicle commanders — but if there was, it would be a joke when you held it up to the number of kills an Apache pilot might rack up in a tour.

What really separates us — any of us — isn't the body count, it's the persistence. When a pilot clocks off his shift after wiggling the joystick of Fate for a couple hours, he gets to fly back to his pad for a long chill-out session at the chow hall and an afternoon in the officer's club. He writes an e-mail and puts the war out of his mind. He goes to bed that night, ready to wake up tomorrow refreshed and ready. These things are necessary. When he's up in that bird there are a million things he has to think about, and way too many lives are at stake for him to fuck up because he's tired.

But there is no "day's work" when a grunt is in the Suck. We don't have a comfy cot or tasty chow waiting for us back in the rear. When the Shit kicks off, we take it. We give it. We fight in it. We die in it. We call the choppers in and tell 'em where to shoot. And when they've rained down a quarter ton of hot lead, we get to clean up what's left behind. We drive amongst the dead and dying. We get up close and personal. I haven't killed a man whom I haven't seen with my own two eyes — and that's something else that I'll take to my grave.

But the point is this: it was five days. It felt like five months. It didn't stop because we were tired. It didn't follow our own ebb and flow of motivation. It didn't die down when we needed it to or get any easier because we were at the end of our rope. We were in the Shit. It was a fact. It was a state of being. It was unforgiving, and tomorrow it'd be more of the same. So when that rotation out at COP #329 was over, we packed it in and got back to the fight — because when the world burns it's the Infantry who has to put it out with blood.

- Chapter Six -
THUNDER RUN

That whole night I didn't sleep. Not a wink. None of us did. I might've been running on fumes, but I couldn't get myself to pass out. Not that it mattered. I didn't care about sleep. I was thinking about home. I was thinking about that small suburb town, nestled in the foothills of Los Angeles, on the far side of the world. A small town with everyday people, going about everyday lives, which had never known war and probably never will. A town I once belonged to, but now it felt as alien to me as another planet. My world was upside down. I had a family back home. I had parents.

Christ — My mom!

The realization took a chunk out of my side.

I had given up on fear a long time ago. At least on a conscious level, it was totally out of my mind. Sure, there were the shakes and the panic and all those other chemical reactions that are an unavoidable, physical byproduct of shock and anxiety, but on a spiritual level I was ready to die. I'd accepted it as an inevitability.

But my *mom?*

I don't ever want to know what she went through back then. It must've been the kind of terror that only a mother can fathom. From around the globe, through the molten depths of the earth and all logic, I knew it was there. It was poisoning her heart and feeding on her emo tions, squeezing her until she cracked. I could feel it all the way on the dark side of the planet — the connection between a mother and her son.

Oh God! Please come home safe! Please, dear God! Don't take my son!

My heart sank at the thought of it. That was my fault. I was hurting her. From the other side of all humanity, I was tearing her to shreds. Just like that flight attendant's son, I was going to get blasted away in a puddle of shit and it was going to destroy her.

You hear that? I could feel my heart clawing its way up into my throat. *That's on you.*

It was like God himself had connected me to a one-way line, just so I could listen to her cry.

"Tell her I'm fine," I begged Him. "Let her know that I'll be home soon."

But there was no response. No booming voice or burning bush. I didn't hear angels open up a chorus or reach down to soothe my soul. All I heard back from the heavens were deep impact sounds of mortars and explosions. Gunshots and murder were the only things out there waiting for me. People killing each other because that's what we do. We're human. And where was God? Where were the hands of that far away being, tending to the needs of man? Where was that wisdom and omnipotence, giving me a lesson in life? Where was that creature I had been trained to imagine, whose face cannot be drawn but in the patched cracks of a human soul? Where was God?

He was silent.

And in that silence, some other voice picked up the mic to chime in.

It doesn't work like that, kid, the voice whispered into my ear. *You gotta' go tell her yourself — and you gotta' make it outta' here alive if you wanna' do that.*

I could feel my heart break. I was eating the flakes of it for breakfast. I was paying the price of terrestrial real estate with a yard sale on my soul. I had tapped into the bottomless well of human brutality to balance the deficit of human emotion and keep my flesh and blood intact. But I was dying from all the hate. There was only so much more that I could take before my heart was a void and I had nothing left to give.

What then? How much longer could I survive? How was I supposed to make it out of there when the whole world seemed to tear at the stitches of sanity?

Let her know that I'll be home soon?

What a crock of shit. How did I know if I was going to make it out of there alive? I had no control over Fate. Hell, I wasn't even in command of the battle. I was just a grunt. A man with a machine gun. A kid with a fuck load of fear, swimming through his own little Hell and waiting to die.

I wanted to close my eyes and clear my head but all I could think about were my mother's tears. I knew she knew where I was and what was happening to me. Tears whenever she watched the news. Tears that would be shed when the Army gave her that dreaded call. And tears dripping over my casket when I finally came home. I knew what that would do to her if I didn't come back alive. I couldn't let that happen. It didn't matter if I was afraid of dying, or if the cost of my survival came down to my very soul.

I had to keep her son alive.

Not for my sake, but hers.

While everybody else racked out, I fished through my gear and pulled out my journal. It was on those pages that I had written a thousand final words. With scars of black ink I had confessed my sins a hundred times and moved on. In just holding that book, I still get a sense of its weight, as if the sheer volume of my soul crammed into its bindings was enough to add a couple of ounces to the scale. But this time it was different. This time I reached into that book and I made a vow. I vowed to survive. I vowed to see my mother. I vowed to stay alive and make it home. If all I had was a machine gun, so be it. That much I could handle. As a matter of fact, in that regard I was a fucking expert. So I finished up my vow with a prayer to a long forgotten god of war:

Valkyries guide my wicked hand, I wrote in blood-red ink. *To kill all those who stand before me.*

I remember chuckling at the line. No atheists in foxholes? Whoever said that wasn't expecting me to call on a bunch of forgotten gods. But that close to death, it was the only god that made sense. So that's exactly what I did. I put my faith in the power of a heathen deity, and swore to Odin that I would kill as many people as it took to get home safe.

It was only then that I could fall asleep.

For the first time in years, American forces were now in a full-pitched battle against the heart of the Jaish al-Mahdi. What I didn't know at the time was that on the first day of fighting, the Iraqi Army had made a push into Basra in order to secure the city — since the Brits had abandoned it. That push and the ensuing battle for Basra was the first independent military operation to be carried out by the Iraqi Army. As such, it was a landmark not only of strategic importance but Iraqi independence.

The uprising we now faced was the militia's response to that push. Overnight, fighting had broken out in every major city that the Jaish al-Mahdi called home. Just like the spring fighting four years prior, they had managed to seize ground in every one of those places within a day. And now, the fight that I was right in the middle of — the fierce battle over a little known district and downtrodden slum called Ur — was part of an emergent scenario that threatened the entire occupation. It was a conflict tearing across half the country. Absolutely everything we had worked for was now at stake, and if we couldn't get the situation under control, all of that would have been for nothing. The six months we had spent shoveling shit to help Ur. The 20,000 men we had sent here as part of the surge. Even the hundreds who had died fighting the Jaish al-Mahdi back in 2004. As long as the Jaish al-Mahdi was a force in that country, Iraq would never be free — and after letting them fester for half a decade without a check or control, it was time to serve an eviction notice and show those bastards who was boss.

In the middle of the night, a new dispatch came down from higher. The game had changed. After all the Shit we'd been through in the past few days, it was decided that we were going to take the fight into militia territory and go on the offensive. A mechanized infantry unit was on the way to relieve our foothold at COP #329 so that Bull Company could sweep around the south western flank of Sadr City and join the rest of our squadron on the outskirts of Thawra.

"Operation Stryker Denial," which was the official name for the next phase of battle, was nothing short of an all-out attack. The orders were to assault into the city and bring the fight to our enemy. Our first objective was to establish a foothold on Route Florida, just a few hundred meters into the city. After that, who knew. We'd have to figure it out as we went.

It took a few hours for each platoon in the company to get briefed on the plan of attack. Once we were all ready to go, Captain Bradford handed over command of COP #329 to the commander of Alpha Company, 1-21st INF. With that transition, so too went the entire conflict in Ur. At 04:00 hours, Bull Company broke station and set off to our new arena, never again to set foot in the neighborhood of Ur.

The initial attack was carried out before sunrise. Under the dark of night, our entire squadron advanced into the city and set up shop in our enemy's front yard. To everyone's surprise, the initial push was relatively quiet. I'd even say it was effectively unchallenged. The few militiamen who had been up all night offered little resistance in the face of our entire squadron and those who peeked out for a fight were taken down with ease. By the earliest crack of sunrise, I was already set into my first firing position on the second floor of some unnamed apartment building. At 06:00 we mounted back up for another push to capture a five story office building on the corner of Routes Florida and Bravo. If we could get a foothold in that massive vantage point, we could see clear up one of the main avenues in the city and deep into the heart of our enemy's line.

"Dismount!" Staff Sergeant Moore shouted.

I jumped off the truck and filed in behind 2nd Squad, as they led the way with the company sniper team to clear the building. Our goal was to set up a firing position on one of the top floors, looking east. By the time I settled down into a new position, the sun was already coming out. I looked around to get a hold on my surroundings and saw that we were on the fourth or fifth floor of a tall, derelict structure with clear sight-lines across the city.

Both inside and out, the building was ravaged with evidence that we were in a textbook overwatch — one that had been chosen a hundred times before. The walls had been chiseled away with small-arms fire and gaping holes from heavy ordinance riddled the place. The surface of the floor was littered with rubble and the stairway right in front of me stepped off into oblivion where some unknown chunk of the building had long ago ceased to exist. When I finished taking in my surroundings, I wondered just how many people had done exactly what I was doing, in exactly the same spot. How many men had been where I was? Insurgents, marines, soldiers, Shiite rebels, police... And how many of them had died *right here?*

I was staring out at a panorama of Sadr City like it was my own personal theater, complete with hi-def surround sound and fully immersive 3D technology. It was the IMAX of war. I did what I could to cover my silhouette from the street down below using some of the rubble around me and looked out at the city with a strange kind of serenity in my mind. I had the distinct feeling that morning was the beginning of something big. It was the main event. I looked down at the houses of innocent bystanders and followed the caravans of battered armored vehicles with my eyes.

I couldn't help but think of it like a great stage. A show. Swarming around in that city, thousands of insurgent actors had trained and itched and begged for this very day, as we had slaved and fought and struggled for a different cause. But now we had pushed into the very hostile ground where they had practiced their lines for years. We were the big city boys and this was their shot at stardom. It was their chance to show us what they could do. That morning's silence was as much of a welcome as the dim lights in a theater.

"Come in," they said with a smile. "Sit down. Put your feet up. We've prepared something special, just for you."

Now that we were set, the curtains were drawn and it was time for the show. ACT I was to be played by the part of faux bystanders: men on the streets. Men on the rooftops. Men in windows. Men pointing at us with binoculars. Not a one with a gun or a bomb, but they were bad men, that's for sure. Men that you hide your kids from. Men who wanted us dead, who didn't even try to hide the act of casing us down. But they still played by the rules, so there wasn't a goddamn thing worth killing 'em over — right up until there was and it was too late.

"Hey, Sergeant O'Brien!" Ian shouted out.

"Whatcha' got?"

"There's a guy down there with a bundle of wires. It looks like he's rigging it up to something on the street."

Ian raised his rifle and put the man in his sights. I quickly tracked down the suspect and followed suit. I put my cross-hairs right on his chest. He ran a wire right to the curb from out of the front door of his shop and looked back at our vehicles down the road with a fear in his eyes.

"I have eyes-on," I said. "Looks like an IED to me."

"Alright, brother. Let me call that one up."

Sergeant First Class O'Brien jumped on the radio and got in touch with Captain Bradford. According to the Rules of Engagement laid out by the Colonel that morning, we had strict orders to request clearance for a kill — clearance which had to come from him, personally, on a case-by-case basis.

"This is bullshit," I muttered.

The man finished wiring up the road and kicked a fresh pile of trash over the top of the line. He had balls, for sure. I flipped my safety over to "fire" as we all waited like good little minions to get the kill-order and take him out.

"Sarn't," I continued. "He's concealing the wire. I've got him zeroed in. Can I take the shot?"

"Hang on, brother."

Just when I thought we were running out of time, Ian cut in. "I got another one!"

It was the same story. Another man came out of another building with a heavy package in his hands, looked down the road to make sure it was clear, and set it into position with a bunch of rubble on the street.

"Sarn't, are we good to engage these guys?"

I heard Ian flip his safety over to "fire."

"Not yet. We're still waiting on the Colonel."

"Son of a bitch," I snarled. "Come on, Sarn't! My guy's almost done with the wire. He's heading back inside. I've got a clear fuckin' shot."

"I know, brother. Just hold your fire for now. We don't need you goin' to jail over this shit. You'll get the clearance soon enough."

I gritted my teeth and flipped my selector switch back to "safe." Even if I got the call, it was too late. My target was already done setting in the bomb. He ducked back inside the building and the call never came. Ian's target finished up like mine and darted back inside so he could run up to the rooftop and watch the street from above. It was a brazen act and the guy was obviously waiting for us, but we never got the go-ahead. Instead, they told us to call up the IED and hope to high hell our buddies could spot it when they got on the road.

"Where is it?" Sergeant O'Brien asked.

"It's down on the street, right side of the road, in front of the store with a lime-green awning."

Sergeant O'Brien relayed the description to Captain Bradford.

"How far down the street?"

"I don't know... 400... Maybe 500 meters?"

"Do you know what it looks like?"

"Yeah, it's a concealed wire leading right into the curb."

"Alright, brother. Keep your eyes open."

Up the street, from deep within the city, a blue National Police pickup truck barreled around the corner at top speed. The driver, passenger, and gunner were all dressed in plain clothes with no escort, no allies, and no reason to be there. It was all wrong.

"Sergeant O'Brien!" I shouted.

"Yeah, I see it."

He was already on the radio.

The truck slammed to a halt in front of an abandoned police station just a few hundred meters away and the three men stepped out of the truck. One of them grabbed a weighty duffel bag while his buddy grabbed a couple of empty RPGs, and they disappeared into the station, leaving the driver right outside of the gate to stand watch with his cell phone. In a few minutes, a fourth man came outside with an AK-47, wearing the disheveled blouse of a local policeman and the pants of an Iraqi soldier. The uniform was unbuttoned, evidently thrown on in a hurry. Half of its collar was folded under the top of the shirt, and it was clearly the wrong size. When he gestured over to the Strykers down the road, a large bloodstain came into view.

Like I said, it was all wrong.

The gestures explained the whole scene as the uniformed man chewed out the driver for his piss poor positioning and obviously shady character.

The Americans are down there, he motioned, *and they'll be coming up through here. So get the fuck out of the street. They can see you.*

During the altercation, the driver made his own signs of dissent.

So what?! He threw up his arms. *I'm not doing anything!*

But the uniformed man was persistent.

Get the fuck inside.

The driver looked down the road, flipped our Strykers the bird, and stormed inside. If they weren't militia, I didn't know who the hell was.

"Goddammit." Sergeant O'Brien was pissed.

He put down the radio and raised his voice to make an announcement to everybody in the building.

"I just heard back from Bull-Six. The Colonel has ordered us to hold all fire. We are not to engage anybody unless we can positively identify a weapon in their hands and under no circumstance are we to engage anybody in a uniform."

"Even one with blood all over it?" I snarled.

"Yes, Ludwig. Even one with blood all over it. What the fuck are you going to say when they pick up the body? Huh? He was already covered in blood when you shot him?"

I flared my nostrils and shut my mouth. Sergeant O'Brien wasn't the bad guy here — the Colonel was.

"I know it's bullshit," he said. "But hold your fire."

That was the call and we were obedient little minions. We stood by as they carted in a full load of supplies and tossed a couple half-naked corpses onto the truck. All we could do was stand by and call it up to Captain Bradford once they got back in the truck themselves and took off down the street.

Don't get me wrong, I wasn't excited about shooting innocent people. There was more at stake here than a bunch of itchy trigger fingers and some bloodlust. When we set into our overwatch that morning, 3rd Platoon pushed forward to conduct a roving patrol and 2nd Platoon was pulled back to a nearby outpost for a rest cycle. That meant we were the only platoon on the front and those fucking insurgents were sealing that city shut, bomb-by-bomb, with our buddies trapped on the far side of the brand new wall of fire. And for what? To stop the BBC from getting a juicy shot of some bullshit "noncombatant" taking a chunk of lead to the face? So we didn't look bad on TV? Fifty friends of mine were out on those streets and our Colonel was more worried about how all this would look back home than about the lives of his own men. That was a hard pill to swallow, but there was nothing I could do. Not until the action kicked off and we had to fight for our lives, but by then it would be too late.

Despite everything that was happening out there in the city, I had a whole new set of problems coming my way. In the past few days we had been fighting like hell through all kinds of shit and it didn't take long for that to start wearing down our health. Just a few hours into the morning of our overwatch I felt a sharp pain in my side. It was like somebody had slugged me in the gut and I could barely move. There I was, scanning the rooftops, and bam — Nature was on the line and she was fucking pissed. Without a single ounce of explanation to the guys, I scurried off to find a peaceful corner so I could take a shit without being troubled by the risk of getting shot by a sniper. Twenty minutes later I was back for more.

"Ludwig! What the fuck is going on in there, brother?" Sergeant O'Brien shouted from back at our overwatch.

I was way too preoccupied to answer him. The first time I had crawled off to my own little corner to take a shit, it wasn't too bad. The second time however, things got a little messy. Actually, I had managed to use up the last of my little packets of MRE toilet-paper trying to clean the scene, and now that the third volley was well on its way I had no idea what I was going to do. I didn't even know if I'd make it there in time — it felt like I was holding back the ocean with my asshole.

As soon as I tore off my pants, shit went everywhere. It sprayed on the walls and deflected off of my blouse. It dribbled down my legs and spilled onto my pants in pasty brown globs. With every shift and stammer of my legs, I was sucked dry by another surge of diarrhea. After a few minutes, my knees gave out and I tried desperately to cling to the wall as I was drained of my insides and cried out in pain.

"Ludwig!? What the fuck?!" One of our snipers shouted back.

It kept coming. It wouldn't stop. I tried to stand up, but the flexing motion of my legs and abs wrung out another blast of liquid. After a fourth or fifth surge of shit, I got lightheaded and couldn't even stand. I fell over backwards into my own little lake of what was once inside me and gave in to my plight.

"Ludwig! What's up?!" Sergeant O'Brien repeated himself. "Go check on him," he barked to one of the snipers.

The spotter hopped up onto his feet and made his way around the corner to see what was going on. At that point I was semi-delirious. I probably couldn't have recited my own name.

"Is he okay in there?!" Sergeant O'Brien asked.

"Oh man," the spotter muttered back. "Well... he's *alive.*"

"What's going on?!"

"Man, he's taking a massive shit."

"What?!"

Sergeant O'Brien seemed surprised that I had made all that noise for a simple dump, but it was so much more than a massive shit. I was losing vital fluids here. I was even more lightheaded than before. I was on the border of losing consciousness, for Christ's sake. I was weak and my vision was getting fuzzy. Out of nowhere a massive migraine split through my skull like somebody had smacked me in the head with a warm ball of heavy clay. I hurt all over. My abs convulsed and sent another stream of shit spraying out of my ass. I cried out in pain. Another wash of fluid followed. I seriously thought I was going to die. The stench was unbelievable. I leaned over to puke, but when my stomach flexed nothing came out of my mouth. Instead, another half-gallon of water poured out of my ass. I took a step forward and fell back to my knees.

Sure, I'd felt this coming for the past couple of days, but back then it was just a mild fever so I ignored it. I was getting sick — *whatever.* A couple mushy dumps and the flu isn't an excuse to throw down your weapon and leave your buddies hanging. So I sucked it up. I drove on. I pushed through the pain until I hit the wall and shit the bed.

At first I didn't realize how bad my situation was. With bare hands I tried desperately to wipe the shit off my ass. There was nothing I could do about my pants, so I grabbed a rock to scrape away the bigger globs of shit and rubbed some ashy dust into the fabric to cover up the smell. I was completely out of toilet paper. I had no idea what I was going to do.

I turned around to look at the damage. A modern art exhibit of human feces had been smeared and sprayed all over the place. Solid brown chunks dribbled down the walls and piled up at my feet. A thick, deep brown lake of fluid covered the ground and small light yellow speckles and spots littered everything in sight. My hands were filthy. I grabbed some more dirt and tried to rub them dry, thinking I could absorb some of the mess with the dust, but it didn't work. All it did was get my hands dark and sticky. That's when I noticed the dirt on the floor wasn't dirt at all, it was some long forgotten catastrophe, hidden under a thin veil of dust which I had freshly uncovered with my unknowing.

I looked around and saw the details, which I had failed to notice when I first stumbled into that room: the tiles on the wall, the porcelain lined holes in the floor, the exposed plumbing. Of all the horrible coincidences, I had actually found a restroom. Hell, it was a bona fide bathroom. Of all the places I could've taken a dump, I had actually stumbled into whatever was left of an Iraqi high-rise shititorium. The dirt on the floor wasn't dirt. It wasn't mud. It wasn't oil or tar. It was a cocktail of human waste from the broken sewage pipe right over my head, which some air strike had busted open, sending two floors of backed-up and stagnant shit all over the floor. There were sedimentary layers of it — tan dust covering dark-black ashy muck. I was surrounded by it. Swimming in it. It was all over me.

Shit.

I couldn't believe it. After everything I had been through, now I had to deal with this? What the fuck was I supposed to do?! I wanted to scream. I wanted to give up. I wanted to strip down naked, walk outside with my hands up and yell, "That's all, folks!" I was done. Broken down. Finished. Fuck the two-weeks notice. They could keep the final paycheck. I quit. In fact, after everything I had been through, it was the first time I wanted to cry. Something inside of me had snapped — and that's when I spent more time than I'd like to admit kneeling in a lake of shit and staring at a rock without moving or thinking.

And then I just didn't give a fuck.

Really, what was the goddamn point? I was out there in the middle of a war. In the heart of the darkest form of human interaction. I was a soldier in the Shit — and I guess they call it that for a reason. Who cared about some arbitrary idea about the quality of life? Who cared about anything anymore? I was just stuck along for the ride. I was in it for the kicks. There was nothing for me to do now but suck it up and move on — unless I wanted to get shot sitting there with my pants around my ankles. So, ass still leaking, still covered in shit, and still weak at the knees, I forced myself up and looked around. And you know what? It was pretty damn impressive, if I say so myself.

"Well that's that," I chuckled.

I smacked my hands together, miming the act of dusting them off. There was no more hope of being "clean." The best I could do was look like I'd tried. I took my knife and sliced up my right cargo pocket so I could have some kind of makeshift rag. First I wiped off my hands, then I went for the shit on my ass and dribbling down my legs. I did what I could about my pants and boots, but when the rag was too soaked and stained to do any more good, I dropped it to the floor. For a second I considered going for my other pocket, but foresight took the upper hand on that decision. I had no idea if I was going to get to change any time soon, but I was damn sure I'd be back to shit out my brains again, and you can only cut up so much of your uniform before people start to notice.

I pulled up my trousers and set out to get back to work, taking note of my condition. My symptoms were bad, that much I knew: intense vertigo, nausea, lightheaded, spewing diarrhea, and a splitting migraine? I had no idea what the hell was wrong, but it was definitely an all-inclusive illness. Worst of all, there was really nothing I could do about it. I couldn't wash my hands. I didn't have any baby-wipes back on the truck. We had run out of toilet paper on the Stryker, except for the measly thin squares packed into every MRE. But I wasn't the only person who needed those, and you only got about two or three wipes per pack.

"Damn, brother," Sergeant O'Brien cracked up when I walked back to the gun. "I can smell that from out here."

"Yeah" I smiled. "I just had a conversation with God. You can go check it out if you'd like, Sarn't."

"I think I'm fine right here, thank you."

As I settled back down I took another couple of minutes to wallow in my own pity before I could forget about the mess and move on with my life. As if it wasn't enough to be facing everything we were going through, I just had to get some kind of fucked up bubble-gut along the way. Now I'd spend the rest of my time in that battle shitting out my brains with a high fever and nothing to clean up the mess. In that moment, I thought back to a little gem of wisdom I had once heard from my brother, retelling the tale of a hard-ass group of men.

"You'd be amazed what you can do when you don't have a choice," he said.

Well, I shrugged, *it's time to put that to the test.*

Eventually, noon came and went. ACT II, it seemed, had been played by the idle-minded Americans who stood by and did nothing while the militia settled in for the final push. At 13:30 hours, the Colonel dispatched a heavy Route Clearance element to wipe the slate clean of the multiple IEDs we'd seen them set into place throughout the day. Captain Bradford assigned two of our Strykers to help escort them down the road. I'm sure that sounded dandy to the Colonel and his men, but all that really meant for us was that two tanks with two of our own Strykers were going to drive down that street and hope they could shoot at bombs they couldn't see before the Jaish al-Mahdi could set them off.

"Alright, here we go." Sergeant O'Brien grabbed our attention when he heard the news. "Ludwig, Peterson... stay sharp."

We watched from overhead as the two Strykers fell in behind a pair of tanks and crawled forward slowly down the road. They scanned every window and alleyway for a trigger-man, but there's only so much to scan before you're right on top of the bomb. We all knew it was coming, we just didn't know when.

Barely a few dozen meters into the operation, a massive explosion ignited a hot blast of dust and debris that engulfed the first tank in the convoy and sent chunks of shrapnel deep into its armor plating. They had driven right on top of one of the bombs we called up to the Colonel, but there was no way to pick it out from the rest of the trash. As we expected, all they could do was get hit with the first roadside bomb of the mission. When the dust cleared, the tanks rolled on. A minute or two later, another explosion rocked the street and swallowed another tank in dust, debris, and flame.

"Well there's number two." Ian shook his head with disappointment.

When the dust settled, I noticed the tattered lime-green awning on the side of the road and realized that all this could've been avoided if I had just pulled the trigger and called it a day. Luckily, the tank's crew quickly recovered and carried on down the road. Their saving grace was that both bombs had been nothing more than a pair of "conventional" IEDs — nothing but a few artillery shells buried in the earth. To the Abrams tank, a hearty blast is no big deal, but it only took one more explosion for the militia to turn their attention toward the Strykers driving behind it.

2nd Squad's vehicle was the next truck to get hit. It rolled right over an EFP. The blast was huge. Nobody saw it coming. I didn't even know it was there. When the dust cleared, the Stryker idled forward out of control and my heart stopped cold. The hatches were empty. The street was silent. From the looks of it, everybody was dead. That was my old squad's truck — a whole squad — and I suddenly realized what those men meant to me.

"Come on... Move." Ian whispered.

I knew he was feeling what I was. Everybody we cared about was on that Stryker. Everybody I had known since Day One. Bryce was on that truck. He was driving that truck. But it wasn't just Bryce; Gonzo was down there too. Kaz and Steve. Sergeant Lilly and Staff Sergeant Benjamin. Memories. Experiences. Fuck, my whole life was on that Stryker.

"Move," I whispered.

We waited in horror.

"Move."

There wasn't a sign of life to be seen. The vehicle below me didn't back up, it didn't turn, it didn't drive forward or honk. It just sat there with its engine humming away and its hatches devoid of life.

It was still.

Quiet.

Dead.

"Come on..." I choked on my tears. "Come on.... Come on..."

Behind me I could hear Sergeant O'Brien calling into his radio and waiting for a response.

"Two this is Six... Two... this is Six."

Nobody answered.

"One-Two-Victor... this is Six... What's your status? Over."

Nothing.

"One-Two-Victor... this is One-Six."

That's when we saw it.

It was the tiniest movement in the back hatch. There was hope. The truck kicked into gear, the rear air-guards stood up, and the radio cracked back with a reply.

"Roger." Sergeant O'Brien spoke into his radio. "Good to hear. Six, out."

I let out the longest breath of my life. A serious fucking heave. It was the first muscle I had moved since the bomb went off. It's one thing when you're willing to die. It's something else entirely when somebody else's life is on the line. When it's your friends who are about to pay the price. That was 2nd Squad. My old squad. My first squad. No matter where I went, that squad was always home to me, and there wasn't a single vehicle in that whole goddamned war with a denser population of people I give a shit about.

And right behind them?

Another Stryker, packed full of another group of eleven guys who I knew better than my family. I wouldn't give them up for the world. These were my brothers and all I could do was watch them drive down that street to their deaths, knowing that I could've done something about it before they even hit the road.

That's when it hit me — and things don't get any clearer. I'd gladly die for each and every one of them. Put me in that truck. Switch me out with one of them. Take me. Kill me. Just let them go. Let them live. Any one of them. I don't care who. Me instead of them. No doubt. No questions. It's a fair trade. Just don't make me sit there and watch them get blown around like dandelions.

I wasn't the only one who felt that way. Since that day, I've learned that every single one of us had a moment like that. Every single one of us would've made that trade at some point. Every one of us would've rather been in that truck, in that situation, down on that road, if it meant that somebody else would be spared. Bull Company was a family. We were in it together, going down together, and we would die together if it came to that. But we all had jobs to do. Sectors of fire. Responsibilities. You did what you were told to, because even if you didn't know how or why, somebody's life was in your hands.

I watched them drive the rest of the way down that road, getting farther and farther away from safe territory, and deeper into the Shit. With every passing hunk of debris, I thought of another memory shared with the men on those vehicles. It felt like that whole city was about to clench its jaws around them and eat them whole. I felt like I'd never see them again — these men for whom I would gladly die.

Against all my expectations, they made it all the way down to the next major route — just under a kilometer away — before 3rd Platoon linked up with them at the intersection down the road to guide the heavy Route Clearance element farther to the east. Our two vehicles turned around to come back, going slowly at first, but picked up the pace like they had something to prove. By the halfway point of the run, they were heading full-throttle back to the line. Even when small cracks of gunfire came out from passing alleyways and bounced off the road around them, they didn't bother to deviate from their course and respond. They didn't dare to stop. They pushed on, driven by the pure force of fear.

Before they made it back to the line, another array of EFPs hit 3nd Squad's vehicle and sent it careening off to the side of the road. Once again the world stopped turning and we waited for them to get back to us from inside the thick cloud of smoke and fire. Through the settling debris I could see that they had been hit hard. The ballistic glass beside the squad-leader's hatch was nearly shattered through, and every left tire was blown out and running flat. The antennas were nowhere to be seen. Dark streams of motor oil, water, and Gatorade poured out of the storage racks along the side of the truck.

This time they didn't bother calling us back. When the driver regained consciousness, he hammered back down on the gas and broke like hell back to hallowed ground — burning rubber and all. The Stryker rolled past us and I could tell right away that it was out for the count. When the crew pulled up behind cover to assess the damage, it looked like somebody took a giant shotgun to its side. The outer layers of armor were littered with gaping holes where globs of molten copper had burrowed into the steel plating, stopping just shy of killing everybody inside.

"Good thing we're lookin' out for bad guys, right?" Ian scoffed.

"Yeah." I shook my head with frustration and got back to my gun.

About an hour later, we heard some commotion on the far side of town where 3rd Platoon was supposed to be. At first it didn't sound like much. It was just a few pops, here and there, without any rhyme or reason to its form. But when the explosions kicked in, I realized ACT III, the final showdown, was now upon us. We listened from up in our perch as all Hell broke loose.

The thing is that firefights have a way to them. Sometimes they're like a conversation. A fierce argument. They have ebbs and flows. They go back and forth. Some volleys are fired, others are returned. Men run around from here to there until some more gunfire breaks out and they look around for something else to shoot. Hell breaks out for a bit and then everything goes quiet.

Whatever was happening to 3rd Platoon on the far side of that town wasn't a firefight at all. It wasn't even combat. It was something I never wanted to know well enough to define. Something I hadn't experienced since that first raid — only this seemed even harder than the night I faced my own death. It grew, it evolved, and it didn't stop. It got bigger and bigger until it was all we could hear. From my perch in that building, far off from where our brothers were in Hell, I could see the dust rising up from sheer volume of gunfire. And with that, I realized the real battle for Sadr City had begun in full.

As the pulses of gunfire grew louder and more intense, one of our snipers sat up and leaned back in his nest. His jaw hung open with disbelief at the sight and sound of it all. We were so far away that it echoed like a storm in the distance and there was nothing we could do but take it in. When he finally uttered "woah," he had voiced the complete spectrum of thoughts in my mind. I was dumbfounded and blank-faced. It was massive. All of a sudden it was raining. I was listening to a hail storm from a mile away. The gods were taking a shower. A million tiny firecrackers were going off in the distance. Anything you could imagine – but that wasn't a fight. There was no pattern. No give-and-take. No breaks of silence. No sense to the madness. It just kept coming. Whatever the hell it was, 3rd Platoon was stuck right in the middle of it.

We listened to the commotion unravel as reports of contact spread back to the line. Enough time had been wasted sitting around in that building. Now it was time to act.

"Let's go!" Sergeant O'Brien shouted.

I jumped to my feet and followed everybody down the stairs and into the Strykers. When I loaded up, the details of the situation blared over the loudspeaker. 3rd Platoon was in a bad spot. They had set into an overwatch nearly an entire kilometer into enemy territory when the fighting broke out. After a short exchange from the building they were in, their platoon leader, Lieutenant Elgort, moved his men across the road to secure a larger building and set into a base of fire to identify and engage the enemy. That's when their platoon sergeant's vehicle was knocked out by an EFP and before the dust even settled a close-quarters ambush was in full-force. Their vehicles were now right in the middle of the kill-zone with absolutely no cover or concealment. The entire platoon had been enveloped by a force of enemy combatants easily twice their number. Time was running out and if we couldn't think of something quick, nobody was going to make it out of there alive.

With the remainder of our company decisively engaged, Captain Bradford didn't have time to wait for 2nd Platoon to get back from the nearby Outpost. He got on the horn with the Colonel and called in another platoon of Strykers from Apache Company to help us out. In just a few minutes they were on-site, charging into Sadr City for the assist. Not even halfway to 3rd Platoon, however, they got hit with a roadside bomb and found themselves pinned down under their own heavy volume of enemy fire.

I couldn't believe what I was hearing over the radio. It sounded like something right out of a movie. With two platoons in heavy contact, our company frequency was littered with accidental transmissions of gunfire, shouting, frantic commands, and bone-chilling cries for help. The men in those streets were too concerned with returning fire to watch out for a stupid transmit switch and, as they bumped up against the gear on their Strykers, outbreaks of madness overpowered the legitimate command decisions being made on the ground.

Back on Route Florida, 1st Platoon and Headquarters shuffled around our manpower to put together an ad-hoc element and take a shot at another rescue operation since Apache Company's 3rd Platoon was nowhere near our own. In that time, our guys had managed to maneuver their vehicles into a tight perimeter and use them as cover for the self-recovery. For the second time in our deployment, a single squad of soldiers found themselves tasked with hooking up tow-bars under heavy fire — only this time their efforts were thwarted by a number of close-range and well aimed RPGs. As they worked in the middle of all that shit, gunmen poured bullets down on them from every window, rooftop, and alley.

"Bull-Six, Three-Six!" Lieutenant Elgort shouted over the Net. "We are making the hook-up now! Over!"

Captain Bradford called him back. "Bull-Six. Roger."

Another voice rang out in the background of an idle transmission.

"RPG! Get the fuck down!"

When the blast hit, the radio cut out.

Captain Bradford ordered our platoon to split in two, load up extra men and head into the fight alongside the two Abrams tanks from the Route Clearance element that had just returned from the end of their mission right down the road.

"Three-Six, Bull-Six," he called Lieutenant Elgort back.

More interference cut in when he hung up. It was the voice of a light machine gunner laying waste to whatever he saw.

"Get some, mother fuckers!" The transmission came with a flood of automatic fire.

"Bull-Six, Three-Six!" Lieutenant Elgort called back when it was over.

"Roger." Captain Bradford squeezed in a word between floods of transmissions. "This is Bull-Six. 1st Platoon is moving to your position with a section of Abrams tanks. Break—"

He let go of the transmit switch and another voice rang out.

"Fuuuuuck!!!"

Captain Bradford continued with his transmission. "Let me know when they get to your location. Over."

Another radio chirped in to cut him off.

"Are you hit?!"

"I don't think so, Sarn't!"

"Then get back in the fucking hatch!"

Before Lieutenant Elgort could call Captain Bradford back, the platoon leader from the Apache Company recovery element cut in.

"Bull-Six, this is Apache-Three-Six! I have taken heavy contact—"

The radio cut off into static and then silence. A massive explosion rang out from the far side of town, like an echo from what we'd heard over the loudspeaker. The bomb went off and his radio went dead.

"Bull-Six, Apache-Three-Seven!" His platoon sergeant filled-in. "Apache-Three-Six just took an IED! They've lost communication over company net! Over!"

"Apache-Three-Seven, this is Bull-Six. Roger. Relay messages for me until they get that radio up and running."

"*—Ahhhhhh!*" Another voice cried out.

"Apache-Three-Seven. Roger. Out."

The men in the vehicles did everything they could to stay alive — but they were burning through ammo and our communications were getting worse. As more of our vehicles took severe battle damage, their radios stopped working. Many of those who could still speak could no longer receive any transmissions from the outside world. Unrequited pleas for help filled up the airspace until there was almost no room for a legitimate order to be conveyed. Try as we might, there was no way that we could keep track of what in the hell was going on and every moment we spent talking was another moment we pissed away.

Amidst the chaos and with great effort, a plan was assembled and we set out to save our brothers at any cost. Already fighting with an undermanned platoon, Sergeant O'Brien was forced to leave a tank behind to hold the line with Weapons Squad while he charged in. His primary objective at that point was to fight like hell to 3rd Platoon's Stryker where he'd set up a perimeter and cover their escape. As soon as that was done, he'd cross back over his infiltration route and traverse the southern district of Sadr City to link up with the Apache Company element and drive out together.

It took all of a couple minutes for that plan to go to shit. Despite the fact that 3rd Platoon had been in deliberate contact for much longer than anybody in the field, the Jaish al-Mahdi had thrown a lot more weight behind that second ambush of Apache Company's men. Now they faced what appeared to be twice as many militia fighters, with much more damage to their vehicles, and their perimeter was on the verge of getting overrun. Surrounding our boys on all four sides, the enemy had collapsed the range of the ambush to within ten meters of each vehicle — a fighting distance literally close enough to see the whites of their eyes. Fearing the worst might happen if our company failed to act, Captain Bradford ordered Sergeant O'Brien to change course from the original intent and link up with the Apache Company element first.

Sergeant O'Brien's element never made it to the new objective. Just a few hundred meters into their maneuver, an EFP array sliced through the back-half of the second tank in their formation, leaving a massive hole in the back of the vehicle through which gallons of fuel were gurgling out into the street. Unwilling to find out what would happen if that tank ran out of gas, Sergeant O'Brien ordered it back to Route Florida where it could hold the line without putting everybody at risk. At that point, raging infernos had broken out across the battlefield, which had quickly swallowed up entire neighborhoods of the city. With a staggering quickness, the scene before us had degraded from a quiet afternoon to an outbreak of Armageddon. Even though they were armed with just two light armored Strykers and an Abrams Tank, Sergeant O'Brien and his men drove on with the mission.

Within the next few dozen meters, those men came into contact with a wash of small-arms fire, RPG teams, and grenadiers that could've — and should've — pounded them into oblivion with ease. Rather than hunker down or run, Sergeant O'Brien pushed our boys deeper into the fray, where they quickly disappeared in a thick cloud of smoke and were cut off from the outside world. According to the digital readout on our navigational equipment, Sergeant O'Brien's element was practically right on top of the ambush, but their visibility had dropped to just a few meters and the communication equipment on every truck was either blown to shit or barely working. The only good news was that 3rd Platoon had just announced a successful hook-up of their downed Stryker and began their exfiltration to friendly ground — but as it turned out the momentary implications of that recovery were very bad for the rest of our men.

As soon as the Jaish al-Mahdi realized there was nothing to be gained by continuing their ambush on 3rd Platoon, they consolidated their efforts onto our two remaining elements just a few blocks away. With that sudden surge of manpower they had escalated the point-blank ambush into a hopeless situation. By the time the call came through that 3rd Platoon had crossed back into friendly territory, it was overshadowed by the knowledge that everybody we had sent in after them was still in the Shit.

Out there at the ambush site, Sergeant O'Brien was at the crux of a serious problem: none of his men could get eyes-on the Apache Company element through the smoke and gunfire obscuring the street. He was hesitant to push right into their line of fire without knowing where the hell they were shooting at first. Charging headlong into a clusterfuck filled with .50 cal machine guns is an easy way to get all the wrong people killed. Facing his own life-or-death crisis, the Apache Company platoon leader didn't have time to think about what had to be done. Something had to give. As soon as they recovered their damaged vehicle, he charged his men southward through a heavy screen of smoke hoping to emerge on the far side of the blaze where they could find their way back to Route Florida and far away from the ambush. As Fate would have it, their lead vehicle drove right by one of the Strykers in Sergeant O'Brien's formation.

"We have eyes on the Apache element!" A voice cried out.

Before another word was spoken they came to a halt right in the middle of the kill-zone for another ambush. Far more than some bullets and a few explosions, what they saw next was a sight that nobody would soon forget. As the Apache Company Strykers stopped in formation to secure the scene, the militia detonated a three story apartment building right beside them, unleashing a cascade of rubble down onto two of their Strykers. At the same time, a squad of insurgents armed with armor-piercing RPG-7s engaged the other two Strykers from rooftops on the far side of the road. In a matter of seconds, an entire platoon came within an inch of their deaths. Three of the RPGs that were fired hit their targets dead-on. The explosions rocked through the streets and blew gaping holes in the outer slat-armor of both trucks, yet somehow the men inside remained unharmed by the whole ordeal. Across the board, this attack was considered to be the highlight of the battle. It showcased the true extent of the Jaish al-Mahdi's control and determination and just how far they would go to take us out. Far more than that, however, it was yet another sign in a growing body of proof that some higher force was doing it's best to keep us alive.

It wasn't long before the militia ground troops from the initial ambush caught up with Apache Company's Platoon and began a new assault from a building to the east. This time, however, both of our elements had linked up and settled in. Their response was lethal force. As the militia maneuvered toward their location, a river of .50 cal rounds flew back in their direction. When they took cover, the Abrams Tank stepped up to silence the outbreak with a single 120 mm HEAT round. The entire structure was leveled, killing everybody inside.

Undaunted by the event, the number of insurgents fighting our men still grew by the minute. The final drag to safe territory ultimately called for yet another Hail Mary run through their main line of defense. In order to maximize firepower while they escaped, the two elements split up into two columns and drove down both sides of the avenue leading out of hostile territory. With both sections now driving abreast of one another,

Sergeant O'Brien directed the tank to pull rear security on the way out. If they got hit on the way out, the plan was to fill the landscape with as many bullets and explosions as they could until the last truck made it back to the front line on Route Florida. After all, there was nobody left on the benches to jump in and get them if they failed.

On the last leg of their escape, our final convoy of six heavily damaged Strykers and a fire-spitting Abrams tank proceeded south across 800 meters of open road, which led back into friendly territory and out of our enemy's domain. Along the way, their column was hit with more than six IEDs and took fire from literally every direction. The main gun of the Abrams tank, running screen behind them, swiveled back and forth to pump round after round into each building as they went. Out of every window, around every corner, and down every street, hundreds of insurgents waited for them to pass and unleashed Hell when they got close enough to shoot.

When the convoy finally made it back to Route Florida, their vehicles were littered with bullet holes and shrapnel. I remember thinking they looked like an old set of toys that'd been chewed up by a dog. Each one of them had deep gashes where hot shrapnel had torn into heavy armor plates. Little holes were punched through everything up top. I don't remember seeing a single inflated tire in the bunch.

"Bull-Six, this is Bull-One-Six." Sergeant O'Brien called up Captain Bradford when it was all said and done.

As I drifted back into consciousness his vehicle rumbled past our truck.

"This is Bull-Six. Go ahead."

"Yeah we have six Victors with massive battle damage and a couple ambulatory casualties. We're going to need to bring these vehicles back to the rear and get some of these guys checked out by the medics. Over."

The call back was a mixture of pride, relief, and fear. Nobody knew what the hell that meant and nobody expected the news to be pretty.

"This is Bull-Six. Roger that. Leave the tank with your element on Route Florida and take your section back to JSS Sadr City for vehicle maintenance. Have your platoon medic screen people for treatment at the Aid Station and take a breather. You did good. Out."

For the first time since the fight broke out, there wasn't a single gunshot on the horizon.

At 16:00 hours, 2nd Platoon finished up their rest cycle and came back out in sector to relieve us. As instructed, we pulled off Route Florida and cut back to JSS Sadr City where the discards of the squadron had been gathered. When we got there, the helicopter landing zone and vehicle staging areas resembled more of a graveyard than a place to park. Every company in our squadron had a similar story to tell.

We went into that city and they sent us packing. They hit us hard and made us pay the price for our hubris. Yet somehow, none of us died. Bullets flew everywhere, RPGs filled the streets and skies, and massive craters were carved into the roads. But our body armor did its job and Lady Luck had a strong hand in the mix. I heard that one squad had stepped off their vehicle to assault a building and the next second an EFP went off, splitting a massive hole in the troop compartment of their truck. Sure, everybody on the ground was fucked up by the blast, but if they had stayed in that Stryker they'd all be dead.

In another case, an entire platoon had set up shop in a building on the line to discover that it was already rigged with explosives from tip to toe. If only by the grace of God, the cell phone wired up to the detonator had dropped the call. Everybody inside was saved. From what I heard, the worst human casualty sustained all day was a major shrapnel wound from a roadside bomb. A chunk of copper from an EFP had punched through his Stryker's armor and lodged itself into some poor guy's hip. The hole was about as big as a softball. Now, that's already some fucked up shit — but it could've been worse. Just a few inches in any other direction and it would've taken out his entire spinal column or burrowed into the soldier standing right beside him.

Everybody on the ground was in bad shape. For starters, that sickness I had gotten turned out to be an outbreak of dysentery that swept through everyone in Bull Company. Other than that, we had concussions, shrapnel wounds, scrapes, swollen joints, broken arms, burns, cuts, and gaping wounds. The list went on, but there wasn't a man out there who was ready to give up. The medics had to fight to get us into the Aid Station. Nobody wanted to get pulled off the line. After forcing myself to stand and act like I was fine, I cut a deal with Doc for the rest of the battle. He'd pump me full of pills and I'd keep going for the rest of the week. The one rule was that I'd let him know if my condition got worse.

"Easy." I said. "I just need some meds."

"You sure?" He didn't look convinced.

"Yeah, man. Don't even worry about it."

It was a bold-faced lie and he knew it. The only reason he let me stick around was that he also knew what I was feeling. I didn't care how sick I was, nobody was going to leave me back at the Aid Station. I'd be damned if one of my buddies was going to get fucked with a double shift, and there was no way I'd forgive myself if somebody died because I didn't have their back. So he handed me a Ziploc bag of medication and let me wander off to check on our friends.

When I showed up at 1st Squad's vehicle, they were busy pulling mangled supplies off the top of their truck. The boxes and bottles, once stacked two feet high behind every hatch, were riddled with bullet-holes and shrapnel.

"Motherfucker." My buddy Cardona lit up a cigarette and called me over when he saw me standing there. "I'll tell you something: when you go past that line, man, the ROE goes right to shit."

He sucked down the back half of his smoke like the damned thing was a respirator. He had another one lit before I could even think of something to say.

"Dog, you don't even know," he rambled on. "Swear to God. Pray you *never* know."

His eyes were open, but he wasn't looking at me. He was looking into the memory — into a moment he was still trying to escape. He was in his own little world, still stuck in that city, and it looked like it would take him a while to believe he even survived.

"There was a breeze, dude," he continued. "Like, wind blowing in your face. But it wasn't a breeze. It was bullets whizzing by your head, and fuckin' explosions everywhere you look."

As he recited the things he'd seen, every muscle in his body was rock solid. There was zero secondary movement to his mannerism. It was pure intensity. He was zeroed into the moment.

"All I can say is this, brother: these guys are for real. This shit is for real. This ain't no fuckin' Ur. Ur was fucking piss compared to this. This is fuckin' Sadr City. It's the fucking home game."

His ramble was broken with a burst of fire from the other side of what little territory we'd earned. 2nd Platoon was now caught up in another fight of their own and Headquarters was still in position and holding the line. That day wouldn't be over any time soon. For the next twelve hours, 2nd Platoon was going to face down the Jaish al-Mahdi all by themselves, doing everything they could to hang on to Route Florida and keep our frontline intact. And wherever they stopped, barrages of mortar fire would rain down on top of them from all throughout the city. It would be a long night for them, as it had been a long day for us and tomorrow it would be more of the same.

Bull Company was in the Shit for eighteen hours of deliberate and relentless combat that day. Our role in that gunfight wasn't over until 04:00 hours the following morning, when 2nd Platoon was finally called off the line to take a breather and get some rest. Even as the sun was setting behind the horizon, you could feel in the air that we had barely scratched the surface. After linking up with most of the guys and hearing their accounts of what happened, I got back to my own squad to drink some water and nurse my headache.

"Hey, Doc." I pulled up next to him and parked my ass with the rest of the men. "I need a fucking cigarette."

He looked at me with a tired gaze. "You for real?"

"Yeah."

"Alright..." A faint smirk cracked through his exhausted expression. "But this is how it starts, Ludwig. Next thing you know you'll be a full-time smoker."

He tapped out a smoke, lit it with his own, and handed it over with a smile. I thought back to those two kids we had once been so far away in a different life and lingered on the memory.

"Nah, Doc." I took a drag, letting it tear into my lungs so it could sooth my nerves with nicotine. "It's just one cigarette."

We sat there for a couple hours and zoned out to the sounds of war. Every drag of that knock-off American Spirit was exactly what I needed. It was a wildfire, filling my lungs with pain and filth – reminding me that I was still alive.

Eventually, the call came down for 1st Platoon to crawl back into our Strykers and get ready to roll. This time it was to drive back to COP Old MOD, where we would lick our wounds and get ready for tomorrow. Before we could leave, Captain Bradford flagged down our convoy and made his way to the back of our Stryker. He came right up to the ramp and glanced around with a humble nod. It was one of the many moments under his command that I got to look at him face-to-face – the man behind the magic. He was Bull Company's fearless leader and he knew us all by name.

"Hey Ludwig," he said, turning his glance to make eye contact with each member of my squad. "Peterson, Sergeant Dukes, Sergeant Montero, Hutches, Santiago, Doc Jones..."

It was an awkward greeting. Clearly he had something to tell us, but Captain Bradford wasn't the kind of man who had a problem with whatever was on his mind.

"Bring it in, guys." He waved us all towards the back of the troop compartment. "I've got something I need to say."

If you saw him there and didn't know who he was, it would've been easy to mistake him for any one of us. He was filthy and exhausted. His face was fuzzy with a five-day scruff. His eyes were weary and down to earth. Even his rank had been masked by stains of sweat and grime. But what stood out to me the most was the weight of his gaze. It was something I'd never seen in him before. An uncharacteristic kind of empathy. It was almost guilt. As though he was holding back tears and ready to cry. His voice cracked with the smallest quiver when he spoke.

"Listen, guys... with everything that's been going on I haven't had a chance to let you know how much of a difference you're making and what a great job you've been doing out there. This is the first time most of the company has been in one place, so I just wanted to say... ah..."

He choked on his words as he struggled to carry on.

"I wanted to say that you guys have been doing an amazing job out there. Really. You guys, your whole platoon. The entire company."

He paused for a second to complete the thought.

"It's amazing what we're up against and... well... you guys are doing an outstanding job. I don't know what else to say. You're doing amazing out there and I want you to hear it from me."

He wasn't blowing smoke up our ass. He meant it. He was reaching into his soul and pulling out the very meaning in his heart – grasping for words as he went. This wasn't just some bullshit speech he prepared for the sake of tradition. It was everything inside of him. Everything he had given. Everything he had.

"I'm proud of you guys, really." Tears welled in his eyes. He took a breath and tried to keep them inside. "I've never been more proud of anything in my life."

I felt goose bumps crawl across my skin. It was a feeling I hadn't felt since I was a kid when I got in a fight in the first grade and my dad picked me up from school to take me home.

"Who started it?" my dad asked.

I told him what happened: some other kid was picking on a girl and I told him to stop. That's when he pushed me and it got out of hand. The next thing I knew, I had this kid up against the fence and I was kneeing the shit out of his gut.

"But it was his fault!" I shouted. "He was picking on a girl!"

"And who won?" My dad looked down at me with a poker face of authority.

It was the only other thing he asked.

"Me," I muttered.

I knew just how much trouble I was in. After all, that's why they sent me home and not him: because I kicked his ass. But for some reason my dad just smiled and patted me on the head instead of shoving me in the car and raising Hell on the way home. And then he said something that would stick with me forever.

"Alright. Let's get some ice cream."

That was a lesson I never forgot. That sometimes there are people who need help and it's your job to step in and make a difference, even if that difference is a knee to the spleen. He was proud of me because it was *his* kid who stood up for what was right. And that feeling? That knowledge that your father is proud of you? That's the most important feeling in the world — second only to being proud of your own son, I imagine. But that's what it felt like, sitting in the back of that Stryker while Captain Bradford spilled his guts and choked on his tears to let us know that we were doing alright.

He was proud.

Not in that way that an officer gets when his men are making him look good, but like a father looking down at his little boy and feeling a fire in his heart. It was *his* son and nobody else's who stepped up to that asshole and made a difference — and he had the honor to be that kid's dad. It was that kind of pride. He was humbled to be our commander, instead of expecting it to be the other way around.

Keeping firm in his demeanor, Captain Bradford reached up to wipe the tears out of his eyes with the filthy thumb of his left hand and took a deep breath to power through with his speech. Like I said, he wasn't the kind of guy who has trouble saying what's on his mind and there was something he hadn't said — so it was time to come out.

"I wanted to make sure you guys knew that everybody made it out of there alive today, alright? I wanted you to hear it from me. Nobody got left behind. And that's because of you guys. Because of each and every one of you. I don't know how the fuck we did it—"

He choked on another wave of tears and I stopped to think about how it must've felt to be in command of everything that we'd been through, to know that everything that happened was in his hands. All I had to do was fight. He had to keep us alive.

"This is the best company in the whole goddamned squadron." He clenched his teeth and drove on. "You guys have been proving that all week. Now, I've worked in a refit for you guys back at Old MOD, so go ahead and get some good chow, okay? Take a shower. Do some personal hygiene. Call your families. Alright? Call your families, and let them know you're still alive. Let them know you're doing fine. Then come back here tomorrow morning and let's kick some ass."

We murmured a "roger" and he moved on to the next Stryker down the line. From what I could tell, he made his way through the whole company. He took his time and spoke from the heart to each person under his command. And through all the Shit we'd seen, I was more ready than ever to follow that man to my death. In fact, if there was ever a doubt in my mind that he was the greatest commander I'd met, he wiped it clean right there.

"Load it up!" Sergeant Dukes shouted.

We started up our trucks, raised the ramp, and filed out of the outpost. It was just after nightfall when we got back to COP Old MOD and locked up the trucks for a twelve hour refit in a bunk I hadn't touched for a week. And for the first time since, I pulled the rounds out of my machine gun and stripped down to a pair of shorts. It was the most forgiving sensation I could imagine — even more forgiving than our air conditioned room. There was still work to do, and tomorrow we'd be back out there like today, knowing every breath could be our last. But for now I didn't need to worry about that. For now I could look forward to a belly full of chow and a couple hours on a box-spring mattress.

For now, I was safe.

- Chapter Seven -

The Assault On Objective #608

I don't remember exactly when I first heard about the mission. I do remember that it was dark. Staff Sergeant Moore told one of our guys to hold the flashlight while he traced over the satellite photo of the objective with his pencil and gave us the run-down of what to expect. By no later than 08:00 hours, Bull Company would depart JSS Sadr City and maneuver up the road to the friendly limit of advance on Route Florida. From there we were to push deep into the hostile territory and assault "Objective #608." Upon capturing the objective we would settle in for a counterattack and hold our ground until they gave us new orders.

"How long is that?" I asked.

He looked up at me with a featureless expression, relaying exactly what he had been told himself.

"As long as it takes."

Tactically, Objective #608 was nothing more than a very large and wide open collection of soccer fields surrounded by high-rise buildings and a sea of shanty structures. As a strategic location, however, it was the perfect staging ground for mortar and rocket attacks onto any American position in Baghdad. From deep in their own home, the Jaish al-Mahdi could reach all the way over to the Green Zone and hit every big-wig in command of the city. To us on the line, those chumps in the rear weren't even the issue. Objective #608 was also the primary staging area for rocket and mortar attacks on our own guys across the southern border of Sadr City, which made it fair game.

Throughout the night, the militia ramped up their mortar attacks from Objective #608 onto 2nd Platoon and rained Hell down on JSS Sadr City where our supplies and reinforcements had staged for recovery. Casualties from the ongoing mortar strikes were mounting and the threat of highly-accurate indirect fire loomed over us wherever we went. Even if we got a leg up on the militia in a firefight or muscled them out by sheer strength of arms, they could just back off and let the mortars do the work. As long as Objective #608 was under enemy control, it would be impossible to push deeper into the city.

The heart of the objective was a large walled-in compound to the north, into which the foot-soldiers of the Jaish al-Mahdi would run when our Apaches came around. All the militia had to do was take cover in the compound. As soon as the skies were clear they could come back out to launch another volley of mortars at our troops on the frontline. The icing on the cake was that the compound in question — the stronghold they had established — was a goddamned school, and for all we knew it was still chock full of kids, so we couldn't just blow it up and call it a day.

A ground assault was the only option. We needed to go in there on foot, take the compound by force, and keep it out of the hands of the militia until the rest of the squadron could push up through the city and establish a new frontline at Route Gold. Bull Company was the clear choice. We knew the enemy and the terrain better than anybody else and we'd proven ourselves against the militia dozens of times.

"So get some sleep." Sergeant Moore folded the imagery back into his pocket. "Tomorrow's gonna' be a big day."

We got the official briefing first thing in the morning. Line-by-line they laid the plan out before us. It was a badass mission but I didn't know of a single person who was eager to go. In fact, it reeked to me of suicide. Don't get me wrong: when I looked at the plan, it was clear that every wrinkly detail had been worked out to a shine. In fact, it was a textbook assault — and not in that bullshit "by-the-book" kind of way. They had called up every asset, considered every contingency, and plugged the remaining holes with an extra gun just to make sure. But there are still times when no matter how you play with the numbers they don't add up. This was one of those times.

Looking back at the Thunder Run, every one of us knew that we had lost the fight. We'd come in with our chest puffed out and our feathers preened, but we crawled back home with bloody fingernails and our tail between our legs. It was embarrassing. We were a full squadron of trained killers and every one of us could shoot a butterfly in the balls at 300 meters. We could move as a team in the depths of the night, infiltrate a building we had never seen, and extract its inhabitants with little more than a grainy photo to guide the way — and we got worked into the ground by a bunch of part-time soldiers with makeshift weapons.

That wasn't the worst part. The worst part was that we could've won, and we should've won, but every time we had a chance to get the jump on those bastards our own commanders pulled the punch. The only time we got a shot off was when the towel-heads in the street had already gained the upper hand. The enemy in the field didn't defeat us, our own leaders defeated us by their hesitation to engage when we had every reason to kick some ass. Some guy with a black and white feed of a high-speed camera thousands of feet above my head had drawn semantic lines in the sand between combatants and non-combatant civilians.

To the militia anything and everything was fair game.

It didn't matter if we had every toy in the Army. The problem lay squarely with the Rules of Engagement. The problem was that we couldn't shoot first. Hell, we couldn't shoot at all — at least, not without flirting with a life sentence for murder. In the courtrooms for war crimes, you're guilty until proven innocent. That's just the way it is. It's how *the People* want it. They're high on the headlines and caught up in Hollywood portrayals of war. The only thing they know about the ethics of killing is what they learned about in a classroom by some hippy who doesn't have a clue.

What the fuck do they know?

That was all I could think about. It wasn't like they had ever run into a room full of bad guys waiting for you with fully automatic machine guns. It's not like they know what goes down in the split second that it takes to sprint through a door with three guys right behind you, assess the situation, and make a snap decision of who lives and who dies. It's not like they've ever felt that fear in your gut — and God knows they have no idea how easy it can all go sideways.

Hindsight really is a 20/20 picture. By the time that story hits the news, you better bet that everything you could've never known will be out there in the open. Timelines, transcripts, photographs... They'll bring everything out to hang you. Unless you're out there scraping up shell casings and dusting the scene for prints in the middle of a firefight, your story will never make it through all their bullshit — and Lord knows they won't show mercy when it's over. And you better be thinking about that at 04:00 in the morning, when it's time to hand-write four copies of a five page sworn statement about the play-by-play of the raid and how you knew for a damn fact that every person in the room had to die.

Sure, they tell you all you've got to say is that you felt your life was threatened, but that's a load of shit. The only thing that matters to them is if it's going to look bad on the evening news. And the only way it's going to get to the evening news is if some reporter can make it look like the Army didn't come down hard enough on a war crime. And the easiest way to make it clear that they're cracking down on war crimes is to slam somebody's ass for murder. So you better have a damn good idea of exactly what it was that put your life in danger, and exactly why the only choice you had was to pull the trigger, or you'll be spending your better years in prison for what you did during the war.

Of course, war crimes and military tribunals only mattered to us. The only thing that mattered to the Jaish al-Mahdi was a body count. They didn't give a shit if a roadside bomb killed a dozen civilians. They couldn't care less if their rockets missed their target by a mile. Hell, these guys were holding out in a fucking schoolhouse. They were dropping mortars on everything that moved. They were forcing families into the crossfire and using women and children as human shields.

Whatever works.

That's the freedom fighter's motto. They tracked down every loophole or weakness in our codes of honor and fucked us in the ass with our own rules. They hid among women and children, stocked up weapons in hospitals and mosques, and bunny-hopped unarmed from building to building right in front of our eyes, so they could settle down and wait for the perfect moment to strike. When they finally struck, we were powerless to stop them. They even mocked us for it. They treated us like children playing a grown-up's game. We were the ground troops of the American Army, the best trained soldiers in the world, the saints of a brave new modern warfare — and we played right into their hands. We were fighting for hearts and minds against people who were fighting to kill. We could've called in the goddamn Death Star and it wouldn't have changed a thing. You name it: there isn't a weapon in the world that's worth a half-baked shit if you're not allowed to pull the trigger.

I wasn't the only one who was forced to watch the Jaish al-Mahdi set up for the fight on the morning of the Thunder Run. It wasn't just me who was ordered to hold my fire when I could smell the blood on their hands. We sent up dozens of calls. Scores, even. Every time, we were ordered to stand down, keep our eyes on the target, and hold our fire. We all saw it coming and every one of us begged to have a fighting chance — and then it was supposed to be some great mystery that the back half of the day was spent eating our dicks because we weren't allowed to fight.

Well those rules hadn't changed a bit. In fact, they tightened down even harder. Now they were telling us to push in deeper than ever — after everything that had happened — and go back up against the full force of the Jaish al-Mahdi with our hands tied and our balls in a vice. The only addendum that morning was getting the word that our own UAVs would be watching us from the sky — and when I say "watching us" I don't mean "watching out." They were watching our every move to make sure that nobody engaged a thing without calling it up and getting clearance from higher.

"So that's it?" Cardona was furious. "Same fucking shit? Just like yesterday?"

"Same fuckin' shit." Flemming ground the sand in his teeth between drags of a cigarette.

"They really expect us to 'call up every suspect?' Man, don't they fucking get it?"

Flemming let out a sarcastic chuckle as he exhaled the smoke through his nostrils. "No, man..." He crushed his cigarette against the barrier and flung its remains over the wall. "No, they don't get it. Of course they don't get it. What the fuck do they know? They're over in an air-conditioned office with leather lounge chairs and big-screen TV's! No, they don't know shit!"

We were expecting a pat on the back. A "job well done." A consolation for putting our lives on the line for a bad call. But we got a warning instead.

"Now, I'm supposed to tell you to be careful," Sergeant First Class O'Brien said. "According to brass, the media is out there watching us and they don't want all this to get out of hand."

Out of hand?

'Out of hand' was a couple hundred bodies ago. 'Out of hand' was when we had lost every checkpoint in Ur. 'Out of hand' was right about the time that tens of thousands of fighters rose up across Iraq and sent Coalition forces packing for the hills. This wasn't about the tactical situation getting 'out of hand.' It was about saving face in the headlines.

Our Colonels and Generals were more concerned with how the western world would respond to the liberal use of force than our own lives. At best, they seemed to have a vague idea of how intense the battle really was. Or maybe they knew exactly, but in either case they were too concerned with their careers. They were terrified of the political fallout that was soon to follow. Even if it was an unspoken subtext where the orders were cut, down on the ground it was a stab in the back. Out there on the line we were tired of getting shuffled around like defenseless sand bags. We were tired of being questioned, doubted, and threatened while our lives were at stake. Dissension had grown steadily and we were openly talking shit. Every man in the company, every line soldier in the squadron, and even the sergeants on the ground had a fair share to say about our officers on the other side of the radio. If they had spent just ten minutes with their own men it would've been hard to miss the bullet-point list of why our morale was at an all-time low.

"So let me get this straight." Cardona knocked me on the shoulder when the briefing ended. "Some West Point, cherry-ass officer, sitting in the TOC, listening to a fuckin' radio, thinks he has a better idea of what's going on out here than me?"

"Exactly." Flemming said, thrusting his index finger firmly into the center of Cardona's chest. "Ex-fuckin-actly."

"This is a nightmare, brother." Cardona said.

I couldn't shake what it was like to watch a truck full of my best friends get blown up and damn near burn to the ground by a roadside bomb that I could've stopped. I had the bastard right in my sights: zeroed dead-in, and safety off. I had him, but I followed my orders and my buddies got hit. So the way I saw it, if they had died that would've been on me. I made my choice. I let it happen as soon as I flipped that selector switch back to "safe" and let him run inside. But I'll tell you what: the moment that first bomb went off, a lot of foggy and complicated shit got real simple, real quick. I knew right away that I'd rather die by lethal injection than know I could've done something to save a single one of those men. That's what it meant to "have somebody's back." But even then, I had learned my lesson too late. They still got hit and it was still my fault. I could've done something but I didn't.

This time it would be different.

"You know what?" I had been quiet all morning, but after hearing that briefing it was time to speak up. "Fuck that. Fuck the ROE. I'm not going to die today like some fucking idiot because a bunch of officers have no idea what they're talking about. We're the ones who are out there in the Shit, not them."

Flemming and Cardona nodded along with every word of what I said. After all, I was preaching to the choir. There was an unspoken thing going around; I just wanted to come out and say it. To make it clear.

"If I see some shady motherfucker, I'm not asking for permission. I'm going to fucking kill him. They can sort this shit out when I'm in jail."

Flemming pulled out another pack of cigarettes and handed one over to Cardona, who shared his last match to get them lit.

"You do what you've got to do," Flemming said. "And you know what? We've all got your back."

"That's what I'm talking about." Cardona exhaled and looked us both dead in the eyes. "That's how this is gonna' go down. I got your back and you guys got mine."

"Roger that," I said. "No questions."

Let me make this clear: I believe in the laws of war. I believe in discretion of violence. I believe there is something vital and essentially human preserved in the Rules of Engagement. They are a form of chivalry — perhaps the last remaining remnant in this modern world. But these rules do not define some vague form of justice. All they do is define our sense of honor. They are a standard of our culture. They represent the fundamental ideal of our society: the existence of and adherence to law.

When we venture to the ends of the earth to vanquish the enemies of our ideals, we keep those ideals close at heart so we can return as their champions. That's why we have them. Were we to otherwise gain victory by force alone, purely for the sake of winning, having abandoned the very values for which we have waged a war, we would achieve nothing. We would be nothing more than brutes. In the end, these ideals are a personal challenge we set for ourselves: proclaiming that we can win a war without losing our honor. Having the skill and the discipline to beat an enemy single-handed on the field of battle, all while protecting the innocent and fighting for justice.

But there is no set of ethical truths from which these guidelines are derived. There is no collection of natural laws somewhere, defining some ethereal justice on the battlefield. Their creation is not supported by any kind of causality or evidence. They are nothing more than a shallow costume, which we use to dress up something inherently sinister. Something we make up to mask the malevolence inside of us. Once men have turned to murder as the solution to their grievances, they have embraced Evil as their vanguard. They make her an ally and in return she grants protection to whoever inflicts the most suffering and death upon the field. The only real line between what is and is not acceptable in war, the true border between right and wrong, the very divider between moral men and monsters, is that of the battle-line itself: the declaration of war.

Once that happens, the only watchword is death.

I had all morning to think about these things, to throw them around in my head and analyze them, because the mission was put on hold as soon as we showed up at the outpost. After a couple of hours of stand by, I wandered off to find out what the hell was going on. Eventually, I made my way to 2nd Squad's Stryker and crawled inside to have a chat with the guys, where I ultimately found the answer to my question.

"Hey, Sergeant Benjamin, what's going on with this mission?" I asked.

"We're standing by." He didn't even bat an eye.

"Do you know what's the hold up?"

"Yeah, some big-wigs apparently showed up and they're in a meeting right now with Captain Bradford."

That was exactly what I had heard on the 'Joe Network,' which meant the gossip was right. But it was nice to hear the facts from somebody else who really mattered. Word had gone around all morning that some General stopped by right after we left for Old MOD the day before. For whatever reason, he'd elected to come to the most forward hard-point of the battle to get a full report of the situation instead of reading about it in a brief with the morning paper and some biscuits. According to the story, there wasn't any room inside the JSS for his pilot to land — on account of all the disabled Strykers marooned on the landing zone — so his pilot had to park the bird out on the street.

"So Captain Bradford gets the word," a fellow 'Joe' from headquarters keyed me in to the story, "and he double-times it over to the entry control point so he can intercept the General."

"Then what?" I asked.

"Then he spills his guts, man. Right there at the ECP. Cap'n Bradford tells him everything."

From that point on the story was give-and-take. Everybody put their own spin on what he actually told the General. I have no idea what they talked about in specific, but I know this much is true: whatever Captain Bradford said to that commanding General at the gates of JSS Sadr City, it changed the fate of the entire battle.

I made my rounds to sift through the facts and fantasy. I'd gathered that the two of them talked for a good while before Captain Bradford escorted his new VIP to the Squadron TOC. There they met up with the Colonel and got down to business. According to my friends in Squadron Headquarters, the General seemed to have already made up his mind and he addressed the Colonel like it was nothing but a formality.

"Man, for every single thing the Colonel said," my TOC buddy told me, "the General would turn to Captain Bradford for a second opinion."

"So what'd they talk about?" I asked.

"You know, man. It was a fuckin' situation report. They told him what was going on but it was like the General knew everything that Colonel was going to tell him before he even opened his mouth. Man, he knew all the right questions to ask. And I'll tell you what: next to Captain Bradford, the Colonel looked like a fucking idiot."

That's my man, I thought.

"Then what happened?"

"Nothing, man. The General just showed up, talked to the Colonel for like – maybe a half an hour? Then: *boom.* He was gone. Just like that."

The next morning, shortly after we arrived to stage for our mission, a large convoy was seen pulling into the gates. From out of its vehicles, a small constellation of shiny stars – damn near every General within a hundred miles – filed into the TOC to have a little chat about what the hell was going on. Apparently, they asked for Captain Bradford by name and right before we could roll out on our mission he got sucked into an office behind closed and locked doors.

"I wonder if they're talking about the ROE," I thought aloud.

"I'm sure they are," Sergeant Benjamin replied. "But I don't think it's going to change anything."

"No way." Our buddy Specialist Oaks joined in.

"You know what we need?" Sergeant Benjamin cracked a smile. "We need to commence with 'Operation Black.'"

It was an old joke, but he was spot on the money. "Operation Black" was the kill-order. It was also known as "doing the whole village." Killing everybody in sight. No quarter. Its etymology came out of the phrase "black on ammo," which was the code word for when you've got no more bullets left to shoot. For the past eight months we'd joked about conducting "Operation Black." We dropped the name here and there whenever we got fed up with the Iraqi Army. It was especially valid for every stone-cold liar who was obviously affiliated with the Jaish al-Mahdi.

"Come on, sir." Sergeant Benjamin looked totally serious the first time he said it. "We know this whole neighborhood's in with the militia." He pulled out his handgun and playfully cocked the hammer.

"Give the order," he smiled.

"What order?" Lieutenant Savage asked.

"You know. *The* order. The last order you'll ever give: *Operation Black.*"

Everybody but Lieutenant Savage and the man we had spread-eagled up against the wall laughed at the whole thing. That's how the name stuck: Operation Black. It was a textbook example of the morbid humor you'd expect from a bunch of men who are accustomed to violence and stress. There wasn't any way Lieutenant Savage would ever give the order to kill everyone in sight. Even if he did, none of us would seriously consider it — not back then. So we'd pull it out every once in a while as a playful joke in our own twisted, violent way. But now the joke had taken on a whole new meaning, and this was the first time I really noticed how much I'd been changed by what we were going through. I could feel it. I knew deep down inside of me that while I still didn't necessarily want to, I was more than capable of doing it — and if it came down to it, I probably would. That was a terrifying thing to discover: that the only restraint keeping me from killing everybody I came across was my own conscious state of mind.

So what happens if I lose my mind?

The idea sent a shiver down my spine, but it was lost to the numbing effects of hate and fear. I didn't even know who I had become. I didn't care anymore. The very substance of my reality was dissolving into ash and the only thing on my mind was survival.

We settled into a downtrodden silence until Oaks spoke up with a glimmer of hope.

"Who knows," he said. "Maybe they'll change the ROE."

"No way," Biaz muttered back. "This is the Colonel we're talking about."

"I can still hope."

"Well that's your problem. I ain't holdin' out for shit."

The truck filled with the silence of men who knew they were going to die. Nobody wanted to jinx it with words. Rather than sit there and pout about what might or might-not happen, I pulled out a roll of medical tape and wrapped my butt-stock with a white band to replace my frustrations with fiddling.

Whatever, I told myself over and over. *I don't give a damn about the ROE and I'm not going down without a fight.*

In the back of my head, something had been nagging me all morning — something other than the ROE and the knowledge that I would die. During our rest cycle, I caught a glimpse of the date on Facebook. It was my birthday. The 29th of March: twenty years to the day since I took my first breath.

At first I thought it was poetic that we'd be storming into the city on the exact same day I was born. It was like Fate, in the flesh. But the more I thought about it, the more it pissed me off. It was my fucking birthday. I was turning twenty. That kind of thing is usually accompanied with getting drunk and eating cake, not a face full of shrapnel from a roadside bomb. And knowing for a fact that I was going to die, that I was going to get killed by some towel-head with less than a tenth of my own soldiering skill on the morning of my birthday? It was infuriating. At a minimum, I wanted to believe that I had a chance, even if it was an empty hope.

I crawled out of the Stryker to go look for a better conversation, but there were none to be found. Wherever I looked our boys were sleeping, smoking, or bitching. The only ray of hope we had was the idea that Captain Bradford could somehow change the ROE and give us a fighting chance from that point on — by then the sagas of his intervention had reached inhuman proportions. I was about to head off and take a shit when I heard a loud voice cry out from the end of our column. It was Sergeant O'Brien, ordering the squad leaders to report.

"Hey, Sarn't Benjamin," I stuck my head inside the truck to echo what I'd heard. "The platoon sarnt's calling for the squad leaders."

"Moving!" he shouted back.

I watched him grab a hand-hold on the Stryker and swing himself up to his feet in a single motion. Despite his cool and collected appearance, the sudden snap-to betrayed how eagerly he'd been waiting for the call.

"Where's he at?" he asked.

I pointed down to the first vehicle on the line and he immediately set off, disappearing with the rest of the squad leaders into the back of another Stryker. Once they vanished out of sight, a few of us gathered at a distance to stare at the truck and cram in some last-minute bets on what had happened behind the closed doors of the TOC. It was a crapshoot either way, but it was worth it to numb the wait. Nobody knew what to expect until they stepped back out of that huddle and all you could see were smiles and laughs. The only person with a straight face was Sergeant O'Brien — but he always wore that somber mask of leadership.

"1st Platoon!" Sergeant Benjamin shouted. "Bring it in!"

We gathered around to listen and pulled out our pens and notepads in case he had notes to copy. Sergeant Benjamin turned to Sergeant Bitolas and asked him a question.

"So, do we want to do this by squad or as a platoon?"

"Go ahead, man." Sergeant Bitolas waved him on. "Do your thing."

"Alright!" Sergeant Benjamin turned back to the crowd. "Listen up, maggots!"

He changed his tone and spoke to us jokingly, like we were space cadets in some bad Hollywood war flick. In his own way, that's how Sergeant Benjamin worked when he was chipper — so whatever the news, it had to be good.

"Here's the deal," he said. "Prepare to take notes!"

We all listened intently and readied our pens.

"It's the same plan as before. Very little has changed. We're going to head down Route Florida to Route Cat, Route Cat to Route Tennessee, Tennessee to Charlie, and then we'll hit the objective — just like you were briefed. As for the major changes, the company's vehicles will be in the same order of march, but we're going to have more air support and a couple of tanks up there with us. The new hit-time is set at 12:00 hours, so mark your watches."

He waited patiently as we rushed to take short-hand notes of everything he'd said. From the looks of it, that was the end of the briefing but everybody knew that something else was coming — something big. There had to be some kind of reason for all those smiles and cheers when we were about to die.

"Oh yeah," he paused for dramatic effect. "One more thing. There's a change in the ROE."

Everybody stopped what they were doing and looked up with anticipation.

"Come on," one of the men next to me muttered. "Say it!"

I couldn't believe my ears when he finally blurted it out.

"You are now clear to engage all military aged males."

He hung on that last word. We waited for the conditions, for the natural follow-up like "who are shooting at you," "who are setting in bombs," or "who are wearing body armor and a bloody uniform."

I waited for him to finish the sentence, but it never came.

"Wait," my buddy Wagner asked. "Is that it?"

"That's it," he smiled back.

My jaw hit the dirt. It had to be a joke. It sounded like a joke. But he was serious.

"So what does that mean?" Wagner egged him on.

"That means if you see anybody running around, you're free to engage them at-will. Of course, don't go shooting women and children — but if you see them participating or assisting the militia in any way, you are still free to engage."

In the excitement and commotion that followed, the reality sank in: this was Operation Black. It was really happening. We just got our wish.

"Oh my God." Cardona was in shock. "These fuckin' assholes don't even know what's coming for 'em. It's fucking *on*."

He was right: they had no idea. I got goose bumps just thinking about it.

"Now, here's the deal." Sergeant Benjamin continued. "The complex is pretty deep in and we're not sure when — or even if — a resupply can make it out there. We also don't know how long we'll need to hold out, so don't waste your ammo on somebody who doesn't need to die. That goes especially for the machine gunners — Peterson, Ludwig?"

I nodded in bewildered confirmation.

"Yeah brother," Cardona said. "Leave some motherfuckers for us."

I felt a few smacks on my back from the men to my left and right, but I still couldn't believe a word he was saying — and I wasn't alone.

"No, no, no." Flemming chuckled lightly and motioned for everybody to quiet down. "This is bullshit. Come on, they didn't say that. You're just tryin' to cheer us up. What's the real ROE Sarn't?"

"No bullshit." Sergeant Benjamin answered him.

Flemming was adamant.

"No!" he shouted. "That's bullshit! There's no way the Colonel put that out! He's a fuckin' pussy! Come on! What is it — really?"

He turned to the other squad leaders, who simply motioned to Sergeant Benjamin, who skillfully managed to look as if he could just as easily be joking as telling the truth.

"Come on, Sarn't." Flemming looked at Sergeant O'Brien. "This isn't funny. *All military aged males?* Come on, Sarn't."

As much as I wanted to believe it, it didn't make sense. I couldn't help but agree with Flemming. There's no way.

"That's it," Sergeant O'Brien answered him. "No bullshit."

His reply flared up another wave of commotion and excitement. Sure, the squad leaders could pull a prank like that, but if it came from the acting platoon leader's mouth it was the real deal.

"Now, this doesn't mean you should just go out there shooting people for the fuck of it. Use some goddamn discretion, okay? But if you see some shady son-of-a-bitch out there, light him up. Don't wait for these assholes to shoot at you first."

We stood there debating amongst ourselves the finer implications of the facts at hand. The game had changed, that was for sure. We had the initiative now and they'd have to fight like hell to get it back. The only question was how many bullets and how many men it would take before we really did go "black on ammo" and get overrun for good. While that was still a distinct possibility, I was invigorated by the notion that my life had fallen back into my own hands, even if it was at the expense of somebody else. Maybe I wasn't back home getting drunk with some friends at a party, but that seemed distant and unreal anyway. If this was the best I was going to get, so be it. It was a damn fine way to go.

"Alright!" Sergeant Benjamin stood up on the ramp to look out at the men. "Get your shit ready! Let's mount up! We've got thirty minutes!"

We rolled out of the wire just before noon and made it to the front line within a matter of minutes. What we expected to be a fast-paced charge from there, however, turned out to be a slow and methodical push against an iron wall of resistance from the militia.

After a few hits from a couple IEDs, the lead tanks started pumping the curbs full of .50 cal rounds to neutralize any more bombs that might've stood in our way. Following closely behind them, our lead Strykers scanned every window and side street for shooters, coming into heavy contact with the dozens of machine guns and RPGs. The Apache helicopters flying overhead escorted us with a curtain of destruction. The screaming roar of jet fighters carved through the sky, waiting for the word to drop thousands of pounds of explosives. When we turned onto Route Cat, a hailstorm began. Small arms fire spewed out of every gun we had, flooding the streets with the same torrent of fire we'd faced just 24 hours ago.

It was complete suppression. Total domination. A massacre — whatever you want to call it. With every passing meter the fight grew more intense, until the overwhelming volume of the struggle seemed to flat-line. Pretty soon it sounded like white noise in the background of a quiet conversation.

"Just listen to that," Doc said. "This is insane."

He was right. It was exactly that.

When we turned onto Route Tennessee, the tanks of 1-30 INF called up a shot to Captain Bradford.

"Bull-Six, this is Punisher One-Six. We have a built-up enemy firing position in a three story building towards the market to the east. Requesting permission to engage with the main gun. Over."

Captain Bradford called him back with the answer.

"Bull-Six. Roger that. *Hit 'em.*"

A terrifying roar from the main gun sent forth a high-explosive round and reduced the structure to rubble, killing everybody in and around the site of the blast. The sound echoed through the streets. It rocked the entire neighborhood, announcing our arrival like all the bull-horns and marching drums of wars past.

We're here, it cried, *and we're here to fight.*

As I closed my eyes to listen, I couldn't help but think that the noise outside was a kind of symphony. It was a twisted drum-line of bullets, bombs, and rockets. The engine of our Stryker screamed out dissonant chords with the beeps and chimes of radios and electronics. The pulse of the fight was a rhythm, led by a brutal mixture of chaos. I was determ-ined to take in every sound.

"What I like to do," a conductor once told me when I was a little boy, "is close my eyes and imagine a beautiful story. I make every song a kind of soundtrack to a play inside of my mind. So when you hear this, I want you to try that. Go ahead and close your eyes. Make this music your soundtrack and see where your imagination takes you."

He was dazzling and he knew his audience. I was just a first-grader on a field trip back then. When the music filled the concert hall, I let my imagination go wild. Through the blaring trumpets and wailing violins I saw the most amazing spectacle of magical drama. A theatrical production impossible to upstage. It was an ancient battle between angels and demons — an endless struggle of epic proportion.

"Well, what did you see?" My teacher asked us when it was over.

But I couldn't explain the details. I couldn't convey the amazement. I couldn't captivate her as I had been captivated. It would've taken the most skilled and poetic writer a thousand pages to explain what a half hour of music had shown me.

"A battle!" I told her with giddy excitement. "Between good and evil!"

She smiled as I gave her my childish explanation of the struggle: sirens and saints, the pure and the unclean, the twisting magical play over the souls of man. I did my best but I was only a child. I didn't have the words or the skill to scratch even the surface of what I felt. And she gave me that patronizing smile I always got when I was powerless to convey what I was feeling and thinking. It was a smile that boiled my blood, because I wanted her to know. I wanted so badly to share what I'd experienced.

Now, in the midst of all this madness, the same vision was streaming through my imagination. It was as though that battle raged in tandem with ours, on the far side of whatever thin membrane separates life and death. There we were, delivering an army of souls to that distant afterlife over which the God and the devil were fighting. This was the missing movement of that long-lost symphony: a theatrical composition of violence.

"What did you see?" Her voice rang out from my past.

This.

A storm of emotions so profound, it seemed to have rippled backwards through time. *This.* Yet once again I was at a loss of words to explain it. You could feel Satan himself, breathing down your neck as your soul packed up its things to leave.

Eventually we got to the objective and the systematic clearing began. 3rd Platoon moved into a staging position and assaulted a large apartment complex near the open field, still littered with rails and mounts from rocket attacks past. It only took one bump with a tank to breach a hole in the wall. After that our squads filed in. But as soon as they took up positions inside, the militia broke out with a wave of fire from three separate fighting positions.

"Bull Six, Punisher One-Six," the tank commander called Captain Bradford for clearance.

Captain Bradford keyed up his handmic to interrupt. "Roger. Hit 'em."

Within moments all three fighting positions were decimated by 120mm Tank rounds and sustained .50 cal fire from the Strykers nearby. When the coast was clear, 2nd Platoon moved in with 3rd to help with the assault. Once inside, they found a cache of weapons and captured two insurgent fighters.

Although the fight had gone well, it was clear to Lieutenant Elgort that the structure was far too exposed to serve his platoon as an effective base of operations. The windows spanned practically floor to ceiling, the flanks were unguarded, and the sight-lines were terrible. He called up a report to Captain Bradford and the decision was made to conduct a final assault on the schoolyard to the north. The hope was that we could find some better cover from there and set in for the duration.

The battlefield was another scene ripped straight from a movie. A clear and sunny sky had been swallowed by what could only be described as the true fog of war. A thick haze of smoke and dust hung dead in the air all around us. All we could smell were the fumes of burning tires, scorched trash, and detonated munitions. Visibility was getting worse and the entire city seemed to have fallen into rubble. Eerie outbreaks of silence would echo through the streets, broken by long strings of ricocheting bullets and explosions. Frantic shouts cried out in both Arabic and English, muffled by distance and dwarfed by the immense volume of warfare.

In the unfolding chaos it was difficult to organize the assault. Small arms engagements were unending and the shuffling of forces was hindered by the growing number of obstacles and smoke screens. But the breach was made, the cordon was established, and our two dismounted platoons maneuvered into the schoolhouse uncontested. By 17:00 hours the bulk of the fighting was over and Bull Company reconfigured its positioning to hold out against the inevitable counterattack. 2nd Platoon mounted up, the Abrams set in and after five hours of sitting in our Strykers, 1st Platoon finally got the order to set up in the schoolhouse and join the main effort with the ground assault.

"Get ready!" Sergeant Moore shouted down from outside the hatch.

Our Stryker bounced around wildly as it climbed over rocks and downed power-lines. Pfister gunned it through a lake of chopped up mud. The 20 ton beast whipped around to drop its ramp and spit us out.

The call was made to dismount and I wrestled out of the back of our Stryker. My cramped legs struggled to keep me standing under the intense weight of my gun, ammo, and gear. I'd brought over 600 rounds of linked 7.62mm bullets. Fifty of those were hanging right out of the feed-tray of my M-240B machine gun. They hung ready to be consumed in a fiery blaze at a moment's notice. Ian also struggled under the weight of everything we'd brought. Just to make sure we had plenty to shoot, he left his own machine gun on the truck and carried an overloaded assault-pack with thousands of rounds packed in and ready to go. The rest of our squad had all brought an extra heavy load with full magazines and surplus strips of rounds shoved into their pockets. Nobody was eager to run out.

When my boots hit the ground, they sank into the wet earth. With each step, more mud clung onto my soles and dragged me down like iron running weights. The sun was about to set behind the buildings and it looked unreal through all the dust on the horizon and smoke in the air. Tall pillars of black soot crept up into the heavens to celebrate the unspeakable name of whatever god had overseen all this violence. Glimmers of light bounced off the cockpits of aircraft overhead. I struggled to keep up with the file as I took it all in and we made our way up through the breach in the wall.

"Friendlies coming in!" We shouted as we passed through the hole.

"Friendlies coming in!" The sentries echoed down the line.

We sprinted through an outer doorway and rushed through the seemingly endless maze of hallways and rooms — each one leading into the next with a trail of soldiers, like breadcrumbs to guide us.

"Friendlies coming through!"

"Watch out! Friendlies coming through!"

I ran across a carpet of empty shell casings. It was everything I could do to keep myself from tripping as they rolled out from under my boots. It felt like walking on a floor covered with marbles. The distant enemy gunfire was muffled through the outside air but the blasts of our own rifles echoed off the countless angles of hard concrete walls and floors all around us. They pounded through the hallways, amplified with every blast. As I walked past a soldier pulling guard out of a window, he fired a shot at some target off in the distance. The resonance alone shook me to the core. I kept hustling down the halls as he fired two more times behind me. With each blast, my ears felt like they were about to burst.

"I got him!" He cried out.

But with all the gunshots my eardrums had already swelled shut. The call sounded distant and muffled.

"Friendlies coming through!" I shouted ahead of me as I ran.

"Watch it! Friendlies!" Voices in the shadows echoed back.

Guided farther into the compound by the flow of men, we were ushered deeper and deeper into the darkness. I booked it around some more corners, pushed up some stairs, and found myself leading the last file into an empty room with nothing but a barrel and some trash to set up shop and get in the fight.

"Ludwig, Peterson," Sergeant Moore came in behind us and ducked down on the far side of the room. "Get in that window!"

As I took a knee to scan, he came up behind me, pointed out my sector of fire, and disappeared back into the hallway to check in with Sergeant O'Brien. I had nothing but the window sill to hold my machine gun, but I did everything I could to stay out of the line of fire. After a few seconds of staring into the sun, however, it hit me how big of a window it really was.

"I don't like this," Ian whispered.

"I don't either," I whispered back.

"We're exposed as fuck."

"Yeah."

There was a long silence before we spoke again.

"I don't like this," he said.

"I don't either," I whispered back.

I glanced around to look for anything else to use as a support or cover, but the room was completely empty and the unfinished window in front of us spanned floor-to-ceiling and wall-to-wall. The bottom of it was at an awkward height: not nearly low enough to go prone, but not quite high enough to take a knee. I was stuck in some kind of strenuous crouch with no real idea of what I was looking at.

The more I scanned around, the more it became obvious that the complex we'd assaulted was barely half-constructed. Piles of dirt and gravel were amassed in the courtyard below. The whole site was littered with masonry tools. Every one of the walls had been freshly painted with a bright white luster so it didn't matter where I went or how low I could get. Killing me would be quick work for any man with half a brain and a steady trigger.

I heard some commotion in the hallway. Sergeant Moore appeared again to order us into another exposed and empty room. It wasn't much of a difference but at least we had the sun to our backs so the light didn't blind us.

"I need you lookin' across the way," he said. "Watch the windows."

I flipped over my safety and scanned the half-dozen buildings in front of me. Now that I could see what was going on, I noticed that the structure we had taken was in the middle of the block and one of the tallest vantage points around. I was looking north-east out of a second story window, from what was clearly supposed to be a classroom – though it was devoid of any tables and chairs. Barely a hundred meters out, a row of tract houses formed a kind of wall that ran along a road I couldn't see, behind the single story structure to my front. The rest of the two story building to my left and a smaller two story compound to my right ran along this road as well, masking the earth underneath them. It was a nerve wracking scan, sitting there silently in the time it took for the sun to disappear behind our backs. Eventually the gun fighting died off and by nightfall the entire compound was quiet. We had moved in, assaulted the objective, and set up shop. Now the ball was in their court.

When it got dark enough, I hooked up my night vision optics and switched on my gun's infrared aiming-laser to continue scanning across the road. Through the eerie green glow of my night-vision monocle, I could now see what had been invisible to the naked eye. There were dozens of bright green lasers like mine. Illuminated cones of infrared light scanned back and forth across every window to shine in the shadows. Other streaks of green lasers traced the border between the rooftops and the sky, darting in and out of pitch-black recesses into which even our NODs were powerless to see. After a long stretch of silence, a sudden explosion of .50 cal fire caught me off guard.

"It's all right, Ludwig," Sergeant Moore whispered with a giggle. "That's us."

I smiled back at him and laughed at my propensity to flinch, but I could tell I wasn't the only one who wasn't expecting the blast. You could've cut glass with the tension in that room.

"Sergeant Moore!" A loud whisper reached around the corner from the hallway.

"Moving," he whispered back, disappearing into the darkness.

"Alright," I heard Sergeant O'Brien explain to him. "We're going to be picking up and pushing into that smaller building right in front of us."

"That one right there?"

"Yeah, that one. It looks like an older building, but it's significantly more defensible."

"Alright."

"So pick up your guys and move out."

"Roger."

He came back in and we got up to file out the door and back through the compound. This time I was lost in the darkness. I could barely make out the way ahead and not a single turn was familiar to me.

"Come on!" Sergeant Moore whispered for us to hurry up.

We made it back down the stairs and through a couple of long corridors before I finally emerged on the ground floor. I was at a loss to identify the terrain. All I could see was a long, covered walkway extending out ahead of me, which opened up into an empty street that I just knew in my gut was "out of bounds."

"This isn't right," I murmured.

Sergeant Moore probably thought the same thing. He stopped for a second to ask a nearby sentry if we were heading in the right direction.

"Down there?!" He asked.

"Roger, Sarn't — right down there." The sentry waved his arm towards the road.

"Okay," Sergeant Moore's voice was thick with apprehension. "Let's go."

After shuffling along for a few paces, the walkway spit us out into the final patch of dirt that spanned a short stretch to the curb. I clutched my machine gun as we drew closer to the open road. I didn't have a map and I only had a vague idea of where we were going, but when you spend a long time living on instinct you can feel when something is bad. That's exactly what I was feeling. We were being watched. I knew it. When I looked across that road, I felt an unspeakable fear that if I carried on much farther we'd get caught in an ambush and eaten alive. Little did I know, I was standing right on the edge of our perimeter. One more step and I'd be out there on my own.

"Hold up!" Sergeant Moore whispered from behind me as I stood on the border of oblivion. "It's right around this corner."

I looked back and saw him crawling over some rubble through another hole in the wall to our right. It looked like the breach led into the front yard of the smaller two-story compound, which I soon realized was the very same two story structure I had noticed from my firing position just a few minutes before. Now that I was looking back at the structure, I got my bearings and realized where I was. Much to my dismay, I also realized that you could see every soldier we had up in those windows with the naked eye from down on the street.

"Come on!" Sergeant Moore shouted.

I raced to catch up with the squad and followed him through the breach where I caught a glimpse of Ian sprinting around the north-most corner of the building inside. That's when I came face to face with the devil himself. I could swear the front of that schoolhouse looked down at me with a grin. That timeless structure watched me with its open windows as if it had known since the day it was built that we were coming. It welcomed me with its empty doorways. It beckoned me onward like it knew me already, waiting to soak our secrets into its walls. If I had ever seen a haunted structure, a truly soulless and evil entity that should've never been created, that schoolhouse was it. It was alive, and welcomed us with open arms.

"Friendlies coming in!" I shouted under my breath.

"Come on in!" A voice called back.

I ran up to the threshold of the building and dove into a darkness so thick that even my NODs blacked out.

"This way!" Somebody called from down the hall.

I couldn't see shit. All I could do was listen to the rustle of the men ahead of me, and hope I was heading in the right direction.

"Where?!" I cried out.

"Down here!"

The ghastly words cut through the darkness and right into my skin. *Down here* — through the gateway into Hell. I figured it would take about one more turn before I saw the doorway to some forgotten crypt below and a warm glow of fire shining up from around the bend. But the voices guided me farther until I ran by an open courtyard and finally re-introduced myself to reality. I looked up and saw the sky underlit with the faint glow of distant fires still raging throughout the city. The faraway sounds of gunfire and mortars echoed across the memories of where I was. At that point I calmed my nerves and accepted the fact: I was already in Hell.

"Look out!" The darkness whispered back. *"Stairs!"*

It was too late. My foot hooked on a ledge and I stumbled headlong into the stairwell in front of me. As I got back on my feet, a pungent stench pierced my nostrils and I gagged.

"Hey!" Sergeant Benjamin called out with a whisper from overhead. "That stairwell is covered in bird-shit! Be careful!"

I tried to brush it off with my hands but it was all over my uniform — there was nothing I could do.

"Goddammit!" I shouted. "Everything's covered in shit in this fucking country, isn't it?!"

"Hey!" Sergeant O'Brien stuck his head out of an unseen doorway. "Quiet the fuck down! Ludwig, do you need some light?!"

"No, I'm good!"

I grumbled in frustration and made my way up the stairs, carefully placing one foot in front of the next. When my eyes finally adjusted to the darkness, I made out the banisters and hallways of the second floor walkway. It was much better lit than the first.

"Over here!" Sergeant Moore stuck his head out of a door on the far side of the courtyard and waved me over to join him in the room.

"Moving!"

I dove inside and took another moment for my eyes to adjust. The rest of Weapons and 2nd Squads had gathered in a northward facing room with a large pair of windows that were covered over by a thick steel mesh. The floor was littered with benches and chairs. A heavy metal cabinet leaned against the back wall of the room with its door wide open and nothing inside.

It's hard to explain why, but I felt safer in that room than anywhere else I'd been all day. The windows were large, but the bottom sill was a full three feet off the ground. We had plenty of room to duck down and take cover. With the moon to our back I knew it was impossible to see us from the street. I approached Sergeant Moore by the window and could see that we had a clear view all the way down the street ahead of us. It seemed like we had found the perfect firing position.

"I want you to set up your gun right here, looking down that road to our front." Sergeant Moore stood in the spot and used his hands to signal a sector of fire. "If you see any movement, light 'em up."

I barked a quick "roger" and found a hand-cut hole in the wire mesh through which I could rest my gun and peer out at the street down below. It was forged out of some serious steel, which gave me a stronger platform than I had expected.

With a quick glance, I pieced together the general lay of the land, but it was clear that I wouldn't know more of the specifics until sunrise. The road running across the front of our new outpost was cut in half by a "T" intersection right in front of me. The street in question, which had now become my sector of fire, stretched out into the darkness as far as I could see. Though I could barely make out 200 meters of the road, it was obvious that a plethora of walkways and tertiary routes branched off in all directions. I knew right there that I was staring down one of the primary avenues of approach onto the schoolhouse. That meant if the militia mounted a counterattack on our position, they'd be coming down my sector to make it happen. What I didn't know was that every other avenue was already plugged with an Abrams or a Stryker, so that alley was going to be the main event all week.

"Hey!" Sergeant Moore smacked me on the shoulder. "Do you see that corner down there, on the right?"

I flipped on my night-vision floodlight and scanned down the right side of the alley where he was pointing, but right away I could see three or four potential "corners" that he could be talking about.

"Which one?" I asked.

"The end of that second building right there," he continued. "There's a cross street on the right side."

I scanned a little farther down and made out the corner he was talking about, steadying myself for the shot as soon as he gave the call.

"Yeah, I see it."

"There's somebody peeking his head out at us. Can you spot him?"

"Negative." I whispered.

While Sergeant Moore was looking through a set of hand-held thermal optics, all I had were some NODs. I could see the corner but the minute details were practically invisible. There was no way I'd see a figure unless he came all the way out into the street.

"Okay." Sergeant Moore came over to my side to get a better look at what I could see. "Give it a burst and I'll walk you in."

It occurred to me that opening fire would just chase the man away and fuck up any chances of a solid kill, but that's when the thought hit me that it didn't really matter. The end-state was the same: stop him from peering around the corner and gathering intel on our position.

I let out a short string of rounds and they hit dead center on the wall, skipping down the road and well out of sight.

"Bring it left a bit."

I followed his advice and the next burst skipped off the corner, landing in just the right spot to kill anybody who may have been standing on the far side.

"Perfect! Now you just keep a bead on that location and I'll let you know when he comes back."

I glued my eyes to the spot and did everything I could to make sure my machine gun didn't shift or move to point off-center. It seemed silly to stand up there waiting for the chance to shoot, especially since I couldn't make out a target even if it was there.

"What makes you think he's coming back?" I asked.

"Trust me," Sergeant Moore was clearly speaking from experience. "He'll be back. They always come back."

We waited in silence for the man to stick his head back out so I could shoot him in the face and after a minute or two of waiting I noticed the faintest glimmer of light through my nods.

"There he is!" Sergeant Moore whispered. "Shoot him!"

Without batting an eye, I jammed down the trigger and littered the corner with rounds. I did everything I could to hold my machine gun steady against my shoulder, despite the wire mesh that rocked back and forth with every shot. When I let go of the trigger, I could see the figure of a man fallen limp on the ground with half his body still concealed around the corner.

"Nice one!" Sergeant Moore smacked me on the back. "You got him! Good job!"

I couldn't help but think about the implications of what I had just done. It was the first time I had ever fired without being fired upon. The first time I had ever shot a man without confirming for a fact that he had a weapon. Hell, I didn't even think he did. But what I knew for damn sure is that we had burrowed deep into enemy territory. We were surrounded by tens of thousands of militia soldiers, fighting all on our own, with no back-up, no resupply, no ammo drops, and no ex-fil until the job was done. We were in it. For real. "Balls deep," as the saying goes. As far as I was concerned, there was no good reason for some guy to peek his head out around the corner and eye us down in the middle of the night. Even if he was just a civilian, he clearly knew what he was doing was dangerous — which meant he knew why. That also meant he understood the implications of the act. Hell, he came back even after I pumped a bunch of rounds into the spot where he had just been standing. So whether it was legitimate force or the theory of Darwin at hand, I didn't really care. He got what was coming for him.

In the other room, a commotion broke out as Sergeant O'Brien linked up with the other platoon leader and sent out word for all the squad leaders to report. Now that we had successfully captured the schoolhouse, it was only a matter of time until they came back with a vengeance and dumped everything at our doorstep. It was up to our leaders to engineer some kind of perimeter defense that could hold out against the horde.

"I'll be back in a bit." Sergeant Moore stood up to find Sergeant O'Brien. "Keep your eyes open."

"Roger," I whispered.

"Hey Ludwig," he whispered from the doorway.

I turned around to find his face in the shadows.

"There ain't nothin' out that window except for a bunch of people who want to kill you."

The words sank deep into my heart.

"Roger Sarn't," I spoke with a flat tone.

Before he disappeared into the night, he spoke one final order that was as much of a warning as it was a command.

"Don't fall asleep."

- Chapter Eight -
Outpost "Gumby"

Staff Sergeant Moore didn't come back for a couple of hours. It didn't matter. Now that I was in position, my job was clear: stay awake and hold the line. By midnight, intelligence had confirmed that a massive counterattack was already in the works. The Jaish al-Mahdi was mustering entire battalions of men from every corner of the city to assault our position. It was a simple matter of arithmetic. We had only used a single company for the assault and months of observation gave them plenty of intelligence about our total size and strength. They knew for a fact that we couldn't have more than 150 men to our name. That didn't count the dozen or so we had lost to the aid station and various guard duties in the rear. They had an army of thousands. Our only leg up in the fight would be the two tanks on our perimeter and the heavy weapons on our Strykers. If they were going to hit us, now was the time.

Of the men who remained organic to the assault on Objective #608, nearly a hundred of them were split across some 20 Strykers, leaving each vehicle with a five man skeleton crew for security. That left about 35 men on the ground with each platoon reduced to the size and strength of barely a single squad. We were down to less than a quarter of our nominal strength. And if that wasn't enough to thin the ranks, 2nd Platoon, was holed up in a completely different building, taking a full third of our combat power to cover the entire southward and eastward facing flanks of the objective.

There couldn't have been more than about 26 men in that schoolhouse. That's counting the two-man sniper team, both medium machine gun nests, and the only dismounted .50 cal heavy machine gun in the compound. Everything else would boil down to three fire teams of five men each to secure the entire northern flank of the building. Our vehicles had been set up in sections of two Strykers apiece, out in the open where they had freedom to maneuver and a clear shot from all sides. By then, the 'ground crew' of Bull Company had done everything we could do to build up the battlements and get ready for an attack.

It turned out that the steel mesh in front of our window was virtually impossible to break free from the steel anchors that'd been bolted into the edge of the window. After about an hour of going at it with our tools, we had barely made it through half of the mounting brackets before calling it quits. We left the entire apparatus hanging awkwardly off the side of the building, held in place by a single point of contact on the bottom right hand corner that we simply couldn't break free. Realizing it didn't have to be perfect, I stepped up into the window and stomped it down as far as I could, bouncing it up and down under its own massive weight until I had bent it far enough out of the way to give me a clear shot across my sector of fire. The rest of our crew took turns cutting small holes in the mesh with a pair of heavy duty bolt cutters. By the time they were finished, the blades were destroyed.

It was a long time after we settled in before anybody had a reason to take another shot. In that silence which followed, I had plenty of time to think about what I had done. Each time I traced my infrared laser across the body of the man I had killed, the sight of it hit me with another wave of second thoughts.

Out there in the Shit it was kill or be killed. We had no choice. So I took aim at my enemy, pulled the trigger, and didn't think twice. Nobody did. It was an act of survival as much as aggression: locate the shooter, take aim at his chest, pull the trigger, and move on. Do not pass "Go," and do not think twice. But this time it was different. This time it was intentional. This time it was quiet, reserved, and deliberate. He didn't even see it coming. He just stuck his head out to get a good look at our position and saw a short burst of fire in the moonlight. Now he was dead. He bluffed and I called.

I waited for him.

I *wanted* it.

As convinced as I may have been that he was "the enemy," and every bone in my body told me he was a soldier pulling reconnaissance for the Jaish al-Mahdi, I couldn't shake the fact that I had seen a man, speculated on his intent, and made the conscious decision to kill him without warning or violent provocation. It was the calculated act of shooting an unarmed man because of probable cause. Something devoid of "in the moment" justification and beyond the quid-pro-quo nature of combat. No, this was cold blood — right to the bone. Something I wasn't quite ready to know I had inside of me. Yet there it was, splayed out on the dirt below, and I knew for a fact there would be more of it to come.

This was going to be the grand finale. The final act. Nowhere in the country had the struggle become as bloody and bitter than in the streets of Sadr City. This was their last stand and the entire war was at stake. If they lost a footing in Baghdad and the two million voters who came with it, al-Sadr's regime would become a thing of the past. Once we got control of their city, nothing would save them. It would be the end of the largest organized resistance to the Coalition's mission of establishing a free, independent, and secure Republic of Iraq. With that, so too would go the strongest hand of Iranian influence spreading corruption and terror vicariously with the ongoing support and training of the Jaish al-Mahdi. All we'd have to do is clean up shop and dust off the rubble.

As long as they could hammer our lines with accurate and consistent indirect fire, a victory in Sadr City would be a pipe dream for the Coalition. Their fire missions would continue as long as they had control over Objective #608. Sure, there were plenty of other fields to launch smaller and more diffuse attacks on our assault. But none of them were as big or close enough to give them the kind of consistent opportunity, on such a diverse set of targets, and with such a wide array of munitions. It was the fulcrum of their resistance. As it turned out, the fate of the entire battle — and with it quite possibly the war itself — had boiled down to a muddy soccer field just a few hundred meters away from my position. If they could not send us packing before the rest of our boys pushed the front line up to Route Gold, the Jaish al-Mahdi would lose a full third of their city in a single blow. There was no way they'd let that go down without putting up a hell of a fight. So after running all of that through my head, it was easy to conclude that there was no room for the benefit of a doubt when it was time to pull the trigger — but I had yet to understand the full weight of what that meant.

In the dead of night, a single blast rang out through the schoolhouse. It echoed down the halls and ripped my heart into a flutter. In the room to my right, the company sniper team had set up right beside our dismounted .50 cal machine gun nest. It wasn't long before they spotted another hostile target right across the street. Without warning anybody or calling it out, they took aim at the suspect and blew his head off with a well placed round.

"Got him!" I heard the gunner cheer.

Fearing the start of the impending counterattack, I doubled my efforts to scan down the road but I couldn't make out a single target across my sector of fire. Next door, the spotter caught sight of another target and passed the word to his buddy on the gun.

"There's somebody else down there. You see him?"

"Yeah."

He pulled back the bolt and slammed in another round.

"Go ahead. Pick it up. I dare you."

Another loud blast rang through the halls.

"Ha! Got him!"

Silence gripped the battlefield and Sergeant Moore entered the room to check on our status.

"What do you see?" He asked.

I scanned back over the scene. "I got nothin'."

"Alright."

He peered through his thermals, joining me in the search for another target. I looked over at his shadow and broke the silence with a question.

"What were they shooting at, Sarn't?"

"Some guy looking through the window across the street. He was holding an AK-47 and casin' us down."

All I could do was grunt. There wasn't anything else to be said. We settled back into silence and I scanned my sector. On my fifth or sixth pass, we heard a blood-curdling scream from inside the house across the street. The door swung open, and a frantic woman ran out into the alleyway, wailing and shouting hysterically into the darkness.

"What the fuck is her deal?" I asked Sergeant Moore.

"I think that's the missus," he answered.

She paced back and forth down the street, screaming curses and waving her arms towards the sky. The sputtering, ululating Arabic vowels echoed into the darkness for miles and hard, guttural consonants of pure rage flung out of her mouth like a thick paste. She heaved, she moaned, and she sobbed — and when it was finally over she simply started again.

I sat there listening to her and it occurred to me that we had probably just killed the only two men in her family. If that was the case, we might as well have killed her too. Out there, in the real Arab world that everyone back home is so scared to call on its shit, a widowed woman without a male heir is more useless than a ravaged scrap of trash. She was now free to get raped and abused by her neighbors, forbidden to venture out into public, and doomed to spend the rest of her days wasting away with no man to provide for her and no future to look forward to.

We had seen it all a hundred times before. Children chained to stakes in the ground because they were born with 47 chromosomes. Men beaten to death for a crime they couldn't have possibly committed. People left in dungeons to rot in their own shit. An old man primed and ready to fuck his two little boys as soon as we left. After months of turning a blind eye to all the ugly truths about their culture, it was an easy thing to write off whatever fate was in store for that woman. They were trash and it was none of my business — even if I still cared. The only thing I really felt sorry about was that she had the misfortune to marry a fool.

As a general rule of thumb, it's never a good idea to act shady around a bunch of guys with guns who are convinced they are in a war of some kind. The best thing you can do is get the fuck out of sight and hide in a corner like everybody else in that god-forsaken city. The last thing you should do is grab an AK-47, peer out of the window with a scowl, and hold your gun like you're looking for a fight.

Those two guys knew exactly what they were doing. More importantly, they knew exactly who they'd be leaving behind and exactly what it would mean to her if they died. And all of this could've been avoided if al-Sadr and his fuckbag militia put their guns down and obeyed the law. So as far as I was concerned, the hopeless fate of that poor woman was just another casualty of a backwards society.

With every passing moment of her annoying and never-ending stream of bullshit, I found myself caring less and less about what happened. It wasn't long before it gnawed my brain into an apathetic mush. We had bigger fish to fry and bigger problems than hers. By sunrise, every bad-guy in that whole goddamned city was going to flood in from every direction and they were going to do everything in their power to kill us all. I wasn't even half convinced we'd last more than a day against the full brunt of the Jaish al-Mahdi — not on their turf with nothing to back us up.

To Hell with her, I figured.

If she stuck around long enough, she might even get a chance to take a shot at my cold, dead balls.

"Shut the fuck up!" Somebody finally cried out.

There was a short cheer in agreement but she didn't heed the call. One of our Iraqi interpreters, Marshall, was roused by the screaming and found his way into our room.

"Hey, Marshall," I asked. "What the fuck is she yelling about?"

He leaned towards the window to listen and translated for us. "She's ahh, saying you guys are evil and ahh, you're the devil." He dropped back away from the window. "You know," he laughed. "Typical bullshit."

Her screams flared up and our man cried out again. *"I said shut the fuck up!"*

Marshall got back to the window and carried on with his translation. "Now she is saying you have shoot her husband and her only son."

He turned to us with a shocked expression. "Is this true? Did you do this?"

I could tell he assumed there was a good reason.

"Yeah," I explained. "The snipers spotted a guy in a window with an AK-47 and so they capped him in the head. Then another guy picked up the rifle and they shot him too."

"Oh," he said. "Then she had family of idiots."

The shrieking continued, now pushing the better part of a half hour without pause or intermission. Down the way, our man got fed up with the noise and yelled at her for the third time with a cold-hearted ultimatum.

"Shut the fuck up, or I swear to Allah I will fucking shoot you!"

As far as I was concerned, he was saying out loud what every one of us was thinking. Since we had an interpreter right there, I decided to put him to good use.

"Marshall, tell that bitch to shut the fuck up," I said. "She's getting on our nerves."

Eager to help out and pretty annoyed himself, Marshall leaned over to the window and cried out in her native tongue that she needed to go inside right away. Rather than acknowledge the plea, however, she ignored him like he wasn't there at all. He spoke up again but she screamed louder to drown him out, and that far into the commotion, I was fed up with the task at hand.

"You know what? Tell that bitch that if she doesn't stop, I'm going to shoot her myself for giving away our position."

He abruptly stopped what he was saying and looked back at me with surprise. "You would do this?"

Putting my money where my mouth was, I stopped for a second to think it over. At first I had just meant it as an empty threat — but then I realized I might just do it, depending on the circumstance. Banking on his compassion and desire to keep an innocent woman breathing, I spoke in a somber tone with the threat of following through with what I hoped was a bluff.

"That depends on how long I have to listen to this shit."

The words came out cold and mean. He knew that I could be serious. We were all serious. It was pretty hard to miss the signals when we weren't. In this case, something about the way I said those words drained the chipper tone from his voice and he nodded with conviction.

"Okay. I will tell her this."

He turned to the window with renewed zeal but despite his every attempt to dissuade her, she carried on with her fits of shouting. He finally stepped right up to the window and shouted at the top of his lungs to make it clear that he was serious. Upon receipt of this message, she turned back at him with a string of curses and addressed him in person for the first time.

"What the fuck?" He leaned back with surprise. "That stupid bitch better go inside."

Changing tones, he stuck his entire torso out of the window and screamed at her with an all-out rage, flinging his very own gestures out the window like a mad man. I almost thought he was about to pick up a gun and shoot her himself, but a group of young girls sprinted out of the house to grab the woman and drag her back inside before more damage could be done. She kicked and screamed and fought them the whole way, right up until the door slammed shut and there was nothing left to see.

"Finally!" Our man in the other window cheered.

"Thanks Marshall," I said.

"These fucking people!" He turned at me to catch his breath and calm down. "They are fucking idiots!"

"What'd you say to her?"

"You know. I try explaining her what is happened — that her husband and son are idiots who deserve to die — but she was not listening. So instead, I tell her that you are all mad, derange, bloodthirsty infidels who were going to kill her and cut her into pieces if she is not going inside. She listens to me then."

Marshall had this way about him. It was a little weird, but it was funny. He was crazy — and it worked. Especially in this case, where it was obvious that we weren't going to win any hearts and minds. Personally speaking, I didn't mind the impact of a little hyperbole to get a woman out of the line of fire.

"Awesome, man," I said.

"Is my pleasure."

He bowed and took a seat on one of the benches in the room, ready and waiting for another chance to serve.

The rest of the night passed without a single gunshot. In the growing light of the following morning, I finally got to see the entire range of my sector of fire. Down on the street in front of us, what I'd previously taken for an awkwardly parked car turned out to be a trashed hunk of metal. It was riddled with gaping holes and packed full of corpses. On the ground, at the nearest corner where I had engaged my own target, a dark pool of blood had soaked into the earth – but the body was gone. In the middle of the night, right under my nose, somebody had grabbed the half of his body still hidden behind the corner and dragged him off to discard the remains. Evidence of the previous afternoon's engagement was hard to miss: bullet holes, craters, ricochets, blast marks... nothing was unscathed.

At the crack of dawn a group of five Iraqi men and two boys came out with some makeshift white flags and rugs to pull the bodies out of the car below us and carry them off to – wherever. Since they were clearly doing their service to the dead, we let them pass by without a fight. As they struggled to wrap up one of the bodies in a blanket, Flemming walked in with his breakfast MRE and gave me a smile, checking in with the situation. I let him know what was going on below and then it hit me that I had survived until morning.

"Hey!" I smiled back. "Did you know that yesterday was my birthday?"

"No shit?!" He shook his head with surprise. "Well happy birthday, man!"

"Thanks!"

"How old are you now?"

"Twenty."

"Ha! You're still a kid, man!"

We laughed together as I passed him a chunk of crackers.

"Damn. I wish shit like this happened on my birthday."

"Yeah. I know, right? Just think. Next year I'll be allowed to buy a beer."

I looked down at the men in the street and locked eyes with the one who was waving the white flag. He must've wondered why I was smiling so much at the sight of them wrapping a cold corpse in a rug. It was hard to miss the fear in his eyes. Something gave me the distinct impression that he knew about the new Rules of Engagement. I did my best to make it obvious that he was "safe" but that didn't change a thing about his demeanor. Not that I blamed him for the lack of trust.

The morning continued, and the street in front of us slowly packed full of civilians who went about their daily lives and ogled the damage all around them. There wasn't any hiding from the masses since we were in plain sight and the sun was up, but for the most part they knew the drill. They averted their eyes, avoided looking at us directly, and we scanned over the likes of them for any sign of hostile threat. For all intents and purposes, we might as well have been invisible.

As for the militia, it couldn't have been any easier to spot them out if they were wearing clown suits. Among the hundred or so civilians scurrying about, a dozen or more scowling onlookers analyzed every detail of our perimeter. They were men who clearly wanted to kill us and were literally taking notes on how to get the job done. They even communicated with hand signals and gazed around conspicuously at the crowd, calling up details on their cell phones whenever something changed. All the while, we just waved and smiled back at them. Everybody knew the time was fast at hand that we'd get back to killing each other, but for now we respected the *de facto* ceasefire declared by the meat-shield of innocent bystanders. As I lined up my belts of ammo and did a check of all the equipment, Sergeant Bitolas cut the tranquility with a foreboding nod.

"Just wait," he said. "You'll know when it's about to go down."

I knew better than to doubt him, even though it seemed to me like any one of them could've simply pulled out an RPG and hit us right there, when it would hurt. It didn't make sense to me that they would wait until later or make it clear that we'd get hit. But like most of our leaders, Sergeant Bitolas had seen his fair share of fighting and I knew he was right.

Among our NCOs we had plenty of veterans who had been on the streets of Fallujah, spearheaded the invasion of both Iraq and Afghanistan, and gone head-to-head with the insurgents south of Baghdad back in 2006. Hell, some of the older guys had experience from Panama and the first Gulf War. There was a lifetime of combat experience between them, so when they felt inclined to share that wisdom I listened up. This was one of those times.

"Yeah," he continued as his eyes swept the crowd below. "The streets will clear out first, then the Shit will kick off. You'll see it coming from a mile away. Don't even worry about it."

At around 09:00 hours, his prediction came true. The only people who stuck around were the ones we had suspected of being militia soldiers, studying our positions and defenses. As I checked out each one, I came across the unyielding gaze of a young boy who had been staring at me for the better part of a half hour. As soon as I noticed him, we fell into a glaring contest and it hit me that I was staring my enemy right in the eyes. It was a personal introduction — face-to-face and in the flesh. He gritted his teeth and clenched his fists at the sight of me. I stared back at him in turn with a firm resolve and blank stare.

On the outside, he wore the skin of a twelve or thirteen year old child but his face was laden with a scowl of hard-earned age. His eyes shot darts of hatred into my heart, thick with loathing and disgust. His features were sandblasted with time. He had fingernails like mine that had been caked over with dirt, grime, and carbon. The clothing on his back was tattered and stained. He stood there unmoved by the nature of our introduction, beyond the urge to kill me where I stood. You couldn't make a harder man if you chiseled one out of stone — but he was still a boy and that was all too clear to me.

I couldn't help but think that he was too young — that I was too young. We didn't belong there. It wasn't right. When I was his age, I was frolicking around Berlin and stealing free train rides from the municipal traffic authority. Back then I was addicted to TV and video games for Christ's sake. This kid was supposed to be going to school and playing with puppies or something. I should've been back in the States, going to college and getting plastered at frat parties. He should've been building forts in the junkyard down the way. There wasn't any justification for either of us to be lost in that flux of adrenaline, testosterone, hatred, and violence. There was no reason for the two of us to be fighting a war. We were too young. Neither of us had any business being so willing to kill for nothing and neither of us had any reason to die. Yet there we were, committed to violence and war with every drop of sweat and heavy breath for the cause.

He raised his hands in the shape of an imaginary rifle, took aim at my position and "fired" with an evil smirk. Without shifting my gaze, I looked right back at him and dragged my finger across my neck. Like him, I pointed back and smirked, before cocking my thumb like the hammer of a pistol and miming the kick of a gunshot into his chest

We're coming for you, he told me with his eyes.

Bring it, I stared right back.

And with that, he spat on the ground and disappeared behind a corner.

"Get ready!" Sergeant Bitolas cried out. "It's about to kick off!"

Within a few minutes we were back in the zone and getting ready for a fight, like somebody upstairs was playing "Red Light, Green Light" with the fate of men below. It was instinct. It was electric current. I flipped my selector switch to "fire" and nuzzled the butt-stock of my machine-gun against my shoulder, waiting for a target and the chance to get a shot. I heard one of our men shout, *"Game on!"* from down the hall, and Ian looked at me with a smile.

"I think it's time to kill some motherfuckers. How 'bout you?"

"Yeah," I nodded. "Yeah, that seems about right."

Down the way, a small child sprinted across the street, giving away that somebody was getting ready to start some shit. No sooner had the child reached the far side of the road than another young man appeared from around a nearby corner with an RPG. He took aim and fired right at us. My heart flat-lined. I watched him pop quickly into view, pull the trigger, and disappear in the same breath. By the time it left the tube, the thing was pointed right at his feet. It blew up in his face at point-blank range.

See, the thing about an RPG is that it takes a second for the rocket to actually go anywhere when you pull the trigger. After the click of the firing pin, there's a short moment where the rocket flares up, and then it's off to hit whatever the hell you aimed it at — but only then. The trick is that you have to keep aiming for that entire moment. You have to stare down your target with balls of steel. You have to fight every instinct to take cover, and make sure you hear the rocket fire. I've never stared three machine-guns in the face at point-blank range, but I don't imagine it's an easy thing to do. Like countless others before him, he took aim at us, pulled the trigger, and darted back behind cover without waiting for the rocket to go off. I can only speculate that he died instantly from the wall of shrapnel that followed the blast. Since he flew back around the corner from the shock wave I couldn't really tell. All I knew for sure was that I owed yet another life to the impatience of a terrified man.

From that moment forward, all we did that day was fight. The counterattack was upon us and that single blast of an RPG signaled the start of a larger advance, moving pieces into play that'd been set up all morning. The only good news was that we had enough firepower and positioning to hold out against those odds for about a day, which meant that those who were in charge of logistics had a couple of hours to figure out a resupply. Until then, it was a race to kill as many people as we could and hope to God we got more ammo. I didn't even want to think about the fact that eventually we'd have to work out a sleep cycle for the men who were on guard. As I pondered these nuances, a large group of militia footmen set off on a charge. It was a long haul — hundreds of meters — and we were set in well.

They didn't stand a chance.

Every time they jumped up to sprint towards their next covered position, we mowed them down with three machine guns and a dozen rifles. As they darted across the road, a river of fire shredded them to pieces and forced them into hiding. Where they teamed up in groups near shanty walls and cars, I unloaded on them with my M-240B, inflicting as many casualties as I could until they bunched up behind metal barriers or trucks. At that point the dismounted .50 cal machine gun went to town. It was a hopeless advance. Dead and dying littered the streets until their friends could rush out to save them or drag their bodies around blind corners.

At 09:30 hours, the entire company was engaged. The Strykers on our flanks did their best to ward off rockets and vehicle borne IEDs while keeping the militia troops at bay, but the number and frequency of men crossing the danger zone into the block north of our position was difficult to manage. Despite growing piles of bodies all the way down the main roads into Sadr City, a good number of men still made it through to the other side and quickly reinforced their assault on our schoolhouse. I was grinding through ammo. I had already covered the floor below me with empty casings to the point where it was difficult to walk. Even though I limited my fire to large groups and targets of opportunity, I had already chewed through a dozen belts in just over an hour.

"Hey, Ludwig." Sergeant O'Brien patted me on the back. "You're kickin' ass, brother, but we've gotta keep an eye on that ammo. I want you to hold your fire unless you see a group of three or four of 'em down there."

"Roger, Sergeant," I answered him. "I have been."

He grimaced and smacked my back even harder. "Alright then, but you better not go black on me."

This time it wasn't a joke. He was dead serious. I was cruising through my ammo and we only had so much to spare back on the Stryker. Even then, somebody would have to actually go get it in the middle of all that shit — which meant they'd have to run across a bunch of open terrain in a patchwork of hostile territory; right through the middle of the beaten-zone of a counterattack, to link up with an armored vehicle, grab forty to sixty pounds of ammo, and sprint all the way back to the schoolhouse. All that so I could just piss it away in a hailstorm of fire. Even then, our Stryker would have to pull off the line and meet us halfway there, which would put the entire perimeter at stake.

Hoping that I was wrong, I picked out what mattered and asked Sergeant O'Brien a simple question. "Are we getting a resupply any time soon, Sarn't?"

"I don't know, brother."

The answer was a total firebomb. In the three years I had served, I never saw the day that a resupply wasn't on the books. That's probably our biggest asset: an endless stream of bullets, chow, and creature comforts. What hammered that reality home was the ammo still sitting on the table right in front of me. By the looks of it I figured if the pace kept up, I'd run dry before the sun even set. If the past was a decent marker of their resolve, this attack wasn't about to end any time soon. The cold grip of reality overcame the numbing mask of my adrenaline as I considered the phrase that would mark the inevitability of my demise:

Out of ammo.

That was something I never wanted to say in a real fight.

Ever.

After a few more assaults from down the road, it was becoming clear to me that the militia's only real plan was to use the alleyway in front of us as the high-pressure artery of their assault. Their only chance was to push up that road until we had nothing left to shoot. Even from the nearest outlet, they had to run across seventy meters of totally uncovered terrain and take fire from every kind of ordinance we had, only to come face-to-face with the doorway and say hello to our light machine gun on the inside. But they weren't even coming from the nearest offshoot. They were charging from 200 and 300 meters away with a twenty meter spread between covered positions. It was insanity. I couldn't bring myself to feel sorry for anybody stupid enough to try. So with every futile attempt, we butchered another group of insurgents until they got the picture and gave up. All I had to do was forget that those were human beings bleeding out on the street.

A couple hours into the attack, their plan changed from an all-out assault to a more dynamic attempt to hit us with well-placed RPGs and sniper fire from concealed positions down the road. Clearly, their idea was to work us down using targeted attacks, since they had a pretty good read on our strength and munitions. The battlefield quieted down, the vehicles lost sight of their targets, and those of us in the schoolhouse focused our red-dot optics and magnified lenses on every blind corner we could see. Any of those corners could be the next staging ground for an enemy RPG, and I was positive at least one of those suckers would know how to use it. Despite the fact that we'd been awake for more than 24 hours, I did everything I could to stay alert and stay alive.

After a few false-starts, I noticed a familiar face peeking around the nearest corner of the road. It was the sandblasted gaze of a child, masked behind a hard scowl. He was the very same boy from earlier — the one who didn't belong in that fight. But now he was back, and through my scope I could read him like a book. I could see his shaking nerves. I could smell the terror on his breath. I knew that he had no idea why he hated me but I could still see that hate in his eyes. He wanted to kill me. He was ready to do it without hesitation and he was begging for that chance. Itching to kill me — just like I was for him. The only difference was that I'd practiced for this moment for years. I had been mowing people down for hours. Where he was trembling with anxiety, I was steady as a rock. Where he was crying prayers to God, I was fingering my trigger and frothing at the mouth. As I locked him in, I made out the tip of an RPG poking around the wall and chuckled lightly at his fate. It would be an easy thing to kill him before he got that shot off, especially now that I had him zeroed in and I was waiting for him to try. The whole battlefield seemed to fade away and I realized he was staring right at me — right through my scope. His time had come. This was it. And it was personal.

"It's your turn now," I muttered.

I exhaled slowly and pulled the butt-stock of my machine gun tight against my shoulder. I waited patiently for him to take the shot. I was betting that I could shoot him first — but I didn't want to miss my chance. I asked myself if he even knew how to shoot that thing. Truth be told, I was unhappy with the idea of his own incompetence snaking my kill. My heart raced with anticipation. I took a deep, deliberate breath to calm it down. I steadied my aim. I let go of my conscious thoughts. I drowned out everything but the two of us, so that I'd be ready when the time came.

As soon as he stepped out — the very moment I saw him move — I jammed down the trigger and fired off a tight burst of rounds. They hurtled through the air and slapped square in the middle of his chest. They pierced his lungs and blended his insides. They shattered his ribs and tore gaping holes in his back. His body went limp and he hit the earth before he even had a chance to aim. He was down before he knew what hit him. I tagged him and he was out. A flash — that's all it took. It was that simple. Immediately a smirk sliced across my face and I filled my lungs with fresh air.

"You lose." The words dribbled out of my mouth with contempt.

But it wasn't over. It was far from over. In that moment when I pulled the trigger, I had done something I will never forget. And now everything was lost. There wasn't any war. There weren't any politics. There wasn't a cause. There wasn't a mission. It was just me and him. It was a young man and a soldier. It was an RPG and a machine gun. It was a split second that didn't belong and a moment that never should've happened. My smirk disappeared. My heart sank.

I just killed a little boy. I watched him gurgle on his own blood. I saw his insides pour into the streets and soak into the dirt. I studied his hard exterior as it washed away and all that was left was a kid — a dying, crying, and helpless little kid. I could almost hear the air hissing out of the holes in his chest. I could all but smell the bubbling acids and half-digested food gurgling out of his stomach and pooling around whatever mush was left of his vital organs. I could taste the dry grit in his mouth and see him writhe in pain. I could feel it when he surrendered. I could've told you the very moment he crossed over.

I watched him die — and it killed me.

This time I didn't cheer. I didn't feel a wave of excitement. I didn't point him out to anybody and I didn't pat myself on the back. I wasn't relieved. There wasn't any pride. I just took it in because I had no choice. When I pulled that trigger, I'd stripped off both of our hard veteran faces and left us naked for the world to see. Now, we were just two boys in a battlefield. We were playing war and one of us got hurt. We started a game of tag and somebody tripped. We ran with scissors until somebody's eye poked out. We were boys. He should've been in a playground and I should've been doing homework. Now he was dying in a gutter and I was the one who killed him.

I don't know how long it took. I wasn't keeping track. What I did know was that I wasn't just watching him die, I was watching whatever was left of the young boy in me die too. With every moment that his heart was still beating, with every cough, with every gush of blood pouring into the street, I felt another cold grip steal an ounce of my innocence and claw at the insides of my soul. That was the bottom of the barrel. My heart had been sucked clean. I lost something that day, something that I can never get back. And I took something from him, something that can never be returned.

"What's up, Ludwig?" Sergeant Benjamin asked me. "Did you get somebody?"

"Yeah." I told him.

"Where?"

"Right there."

I pointed out the stiff lying beside the wall, and the RPG just a foot or two away from his hand.

"Nice one!" He smacked the back of my body armor and cheered me on.

"Fuck yeah," I grunted — and it was all over.

I didn't feel anything after that. I didn't care. I'd found that great shield of apathy and rolled up in it like a blanket. He wasn't a young boy anymore, he was the enemy — he always had been. He was just another body, lying right beside a locked-and-loaded RPG with my name on it. He was all that was left of a man who was trying to kill me: a dead body and a couple of empty casings. I was a Grunt, and he was a corpse. I was living and breathing because I was willing to kill. Because I was good at it. Because I was better than him. And from that point forward, my soul had nothing to do with it.

They made two more attempts to hit us with a potshot RPG before the directed assaults picked back up and the morning thunder returned. After a few more hours of solid fighting, the militia finally seemed to be running out of steam. Teams dwindled into pairs and they left longer intervals between attacks on our position. Finally, we entered into a long respite of keeping our enemies hiding behind corners with a low rumble of gunfire dragging on well into the afternoon. In the middle of an uproar, Flemming, who had taken over as the radio guy some time ago, stepped away from the window so he could hear the communications traffic over the fight.

"—This is One-Six-Romeo!" He spoke into the hand mic, slowly and deliberately, making every word clear over the chaos. "Roger that! ... Good copy! ... It's goin' steady, over! ... Roger! ... One-Six-Romeo, out!"

He hung up his mic and turned back to the room, passing on what he heard to the rest of the men.

"Alright guys, here's the deal! Squadron has a level-four intelligence hit that the militia has brought in special group snipers with special orders to target our machine gunners in the windows. So keep your eyes open, watch for snipers, etcetera, etcetera."

"So, same shit?" Sergeant Moore asked with disdain.

"Yeah, same shit."

"Okay, go make sure Sergeant O'Brien knows what's up."

"Already on it."

Flemming went off to find Sergeant O'Brien while the rest of us had a little chat about the message. It wasn't really news — we had been dealing with snipers and marksmen all morning — but the fact that Squadron Headquarters had a reason to call it up was enough to put me on edge. As far as your typical Iraqi went, a "sniper" could be any hot-shot with the brains to keep his rifle on semi-auto and the patience to actually aim at a target. But if the higher ups were getting "positive hits," that meant the snipers they were talking about were the real deal. They were crack shots with excellent training and some of the highest body counts in the country. Resolved to get a solution up and running before it was too late, the squad leaders divvied up a detail and cleared out the room to go find anything we could use to block out the windows and make it harder for our enemy to see us.

Snipers were bad news. Really bad news. I couldn't care less about a bunch of lunatics trying to charge up that street. As for the rocket-men with RPGs, we were doing well enough at keeping their heads down. But snipers were a different story. I'd been using a wall of bullets to protect myself that day, but I could only shoot what I could see — and there was a slim chance that I'd ever see a sniper. There were a lot of windows out there, a lot of dark places for a man to hide, for him to take his time, for him to line up a shot and give me a healthy dose of what I'd been dealing all day. Hell, I was an easy target too: just one dude in a window, sitting in the same damn spot with a machine gun and a purpose. I didn't really have any cover to speak of. I didn't have any tinted glass or camouflage. It was just me and the open window, clear as day.

Thankfully, the relative lull in the fight lasted long enough for us to set up some curtains and barricades before another barrage broke out. In fact, we had enough time to completely upgrade our fighting position into a full-blown machine gun nest. Before then, I'd been using a box of MREs to support my machine gun and sitting on a little kiddie bench out in the open. We'd moved the overturned metal cabinet to rest in front of me where it could act as a platform right inside of the window. In order to provide a better support for my machine gun, somebody hauled in a heavy, old-school projector that was still in its case. The rest of the benches were either stacked up to form shelves and concealment or set up as reclining areas to sit and relax. Across the width of the setup, we had lined up a plethora of rifles and magazines. Where the setup really shined were the windows, which we had draped over with tarps and tapestries. These were all things that were once discarded, scattered throughout the compound to be repurposed for war. But when the fighting kicked back up, we found ourselves facing off with shooters in every window across the way who had likewise used the brief respite to set up some barricades of their own.

This time the engagement was nowhere near as one-sided as all the attacks that had failed before. With the sun still high in the sky and the light tan bricks reflecting the bright light of a cloudless summer day, it was virtually impossible to see into the rooms where the shooters were hiding — not unless they came right up to the window and flagged themselves in the light.

"Do you see where they're shooting from?" Sergeant Moore shouted over to Ian.

"Yeah, I see one!" Ian popped off some rounds. "Got 'em!"

I saw another shooter come into view. A flood of small-arms quickly gunned him down. I could've sworn that every soldier in the schoolhouse took a chunk out of him. It was the first target of opportunity in a long time.

"Dusted!" Somebody cheered.

But the volume of fire was wholly disproportionate. The flood of incoming rounds — as inaccurate as it may have been — was a steady stream of fire while our own response was limited to small outbreaks of highly accurate shots. Just listening to the gunfire told me everything I needed to know: our men were itching to get a round off, but the only ones who presented a target were the morons that didn't have the sense to stand back in the shadows.

Finally, one of our guys rallied a cry to lay down a blanket of suppressing fire into every nook and cranny of the neighborhood. Whatever the hell the original message was or who sent it didn't really matter; the end result was an outbreak of fire so thick and senseless that it put the whole morning to shame. In just a few minutes we filled every window, car, and alleyway with a full magazine of rounds. We even peppered some of the walls of buildings we knew for damn sure had at least one or two shooters inside, on the blind hope that it would punch through and find a target.

There were cheers. There was laughter. When everybody finished up their blind-firing rage, the streets fell silent and the windows stayed clear for a full two minutes. As for me, I couldn't afford to waste any more ammo, so I just spotted targets where I could see them and passed on the word to the surrounding men. This was a rifleman's fight now. A single-shot engagement. It was about accuracy, not volume. Somewhere in the middle of it, a small team of men scurried across the street, hoping to make it across unnoticed with all the fighting. They had no idea that every machine gunner we had was itching for a target, and before I could react, Wagner laid down a carpet of rounds with his light machine gun and tore them to shreds.

"Come get some!" He cried out.

Another gunman stuck his head out from behind a car and Wagner leveled him with an extra long burst of rounds. The tight group tore into his chest and neck, and riddled him with holes. He fell limp behind his cover and out of sight for good.

The situation went on like that for a long time. For most of it, I just sat there and watched it unfold, with strict orders not to let anybody but Ian take a run on my gun — not that I wanted to anyway. As I scanned down the road looking for another target to call up, I noticed a single bright flash from the muzzle of a rifle, shot from damn-near all the way down at the end of the street. It was a single flash — that's it. I couldn't even hear the crack of the gunshot over everything else that was going on.

Even through my scope, I could barely make out the shooter. From the looks of it, he was lying in the prone firing position on the top of a half-finished balcony. Between us, I could make out two or three houses obscuring the line of fire. As I dialed him in, I noticed that another balcony was jutting out from one of those buildings. He had perched himself behind a sort of horizontal slit of cover from my vantage point in the school. Moreover, the clutter of makeshift power-poles and flag-posts strewn all the way down the street created a kind of bracket on both sides of his position. From any other angle he'd be wide open, but from where I sat it was like shooting into the front slit of a bunker through a forest of trees.

Knowing that it would take too long to talk somebody else onto a target I could barely see, I opted to zero him in myself and test my skills with a long-range shot. By the book, my M-240B machine gun had an effective "point target" range of about 600 meters — if you have a bi-pod and steady aim. In training, I had confirmed that countless times. And while I wasn't quite sure how far away he was, I knew for a fact he was close enough to hit. As long as I stuck to my fundamentals, there was no good reason I couldn't shoot him. Eager to score another kill, I sucked in my machine gun tight and jammed down on the trigger to send a quick burst at my target, but the rounds either skipped off the wall or slammed into the balcony, missing him completely. As if in direct response to my fire he took another shot. I saw another flash, like before, but this time I heard the crack. This time, I felt the round snap right past my head. This time, it grazed my ear with a gentle tuft of wind that I hadn't felt in a long time.

Holy fuck! I was gripped with shock. *He's shooting at me!*

My heart took off like a racehorse out of the stall at the Derby. It wasn't hard to piece together that he was one of those snipers we had been warned about and that I was the target of opportunity he was looking for. Trying desperately to tighten up my group, I squeezed the butt-stock harder against my shoulder and flung another burst of rounds down range.

He took a third shot. I saw the flash and heard another crack. Another snap as a bullet tore right by my face, and my mind went blank.

Again, I squeezed harder against the butt-stock and did everything I could to tighten my cone of fire. When I let off the trigger, I watched the last few rounds slam into the scenery all around him — my tightest group yet. There was a short moment of silence. I thought I may have hit him, but the silence was broken by another crack of his rifle. As soon as I saw the flash, I flinched. My eyes slammed shut uncontrollably and I could feel every muscle in my body shaking with fear. Instead of opening my eyes to return fire, I squeezed down on my machine gun like a teddy bear and waited for that final round. I would've cried if I had tears left to do it.

I heard another crack, and the next round rapped right by my head like the others. With my eyes closed, I could feel the warm air graze the hairs on my neck and leave a faint tickle that seemed to spare my life by little more than the width and tangibility of a nightmare — as though it had graced me with a faint kiss and moved on. A line of goose bumps rose up around the left side of my neck and I screamed at the top of my lungs.

"Fuck this shit!"

For the second time in my life, I couldn't shake the image or sensation of getting shot in the face and feeling my body go limp as it fell to the ground.

This is it, I clenched my teeth at the thought of it. *This time it's really happening.*

I knew I had been lucky that night of our first raid and I didn't expect to repeat history and survive, but something else took over in that moment which I've never been able to explain. It was a strange kind of determination, if only to die with my eyes open and doing something to survive. Without thinking much about it, I ripped open my eyes and picked him back up in my sights. My knuckles still white with terror, I held my breath, jammed down the trigger, and let out a long, drawn out, desperate flood of rounds. I can't even tell you what I was thinking. Maybe something along the lines of *"If it's my turn, I'm going out with a bang,"* and *"Everything with a beginning has an end."* Then again it could've just as easily been the lowest form of human instinct that can ever be conveyed. A thought barely higher up on the totem pole than basic motor function, yet far down below the lowest bar of what we esteem to be an intellect.

The fact is that I sprayed the walls, I sprayed the upper and lower extents of the balcony, and I sprayed back-and-forth along the width of that little slit through which he was shooting. I prayed to the gods that at least one of those goddamned bullets would hit him. I held down that trigger until my throat went dry and my voice cracked. It seemed like forever. The barrel of my gun heated up until it warped the very air through which I was looking and the cycling action peppered my face with a dozen hot, black drops of carbon. Burning gas of exploding cartridges seeped into my tear-ducts and stung my eyeballs. Blood curdling fear reached in and pulled the life right out of my lungs. All I cared about was sucking in that grouping and putting as many rounds as I could into the smallest cone of fire imaginable.

When I let my finger off the trigger I saw the smallest glimmer of relief. A rifle dropped off the ledge and tumbled down to the street below. I was heaving and panting like a dog. My vision was pulsing and my fever was flaring up. But even through the fuzzy haze of stinging tears and gasping breaths, I could see his arm hang limp off the edge of the balcony, his body inert and unmoving. His head dangled down to the ground at a singularly lifeless angle. He was completely still — deader than a rusty nail.

"I got him!" I sat upright and cradled my face in my hands. "Holy mother of God!"

My fingers muffled the words. Suddenly all of my fear became an amazing wash of glee. The adrenaline shivered across my skin. I looked back out at the scene, slapped my leg, and cheered.

"That was fuckin' wild, man!"

I didn't figure anybody knew what the fuck I was talking about, but I didn't care. That was for me. That moment was all mine. How the fuck was I even alive?

Before I could gather my thoughts, I felt a light tap on my shoulder and turned my head to meet Sergeant Moore's dumbstruck eyes. Sergeant Bitolas and Sergeant Benjamin laughed alongside of him and cheered wildly at the scene. Everybody else joined in. Still convinced that nobody but me had seen the shooter, I figured right away that I must have missed something important.

"Hey, uh... Ludwig," Sergeant Moore said. "I think you should probably look at this."

He motioned that I should turn around and check out the wall behind me so I could see what they were laughing about. Right there — I mean right fucking there — three fresh bullet holes had slammed into the wall a few inches away from my silhouette. It was a tight group. Each one had whizzed right by me and buried deep into the hard plaster. They missed my face by a matter of inches every time, and while none of those guys had heard the rounds fired from down the street, every one of them took cover when the bullets cut through the window and slammed into the wall. At the sight of it, I reached up and touched my ear; it was still tickling from the tufts of air.

"There's another one right outside," Sergeant Moore continued. "It hit around the window somewhere, but we don't know exactly where."

"Ludwig!" Sergeant Benjamin was dumbstruck. "Holy shit, man!"

I grunted back at him, only half convinced that I was alive. Now that I wasn't almost dying, I had time to realize how close I had come and the glee of adrenaline morphed back into an uneasiness at the prospect of an early death.

"Wait," he said. "Did you actually get him?"

"Yeah," I said.

"Of course he did," Sergeant Bitolas cut in. "He's still here, isn't he?!"

"Where was the sniper?" Sergeant Moore jumped down beside me, giddy with excitement.

"You see that balcony down there?" I tried to point it out.

"No. Where?"

I talked him in, but even I had only seen it from the flash of his muzzle.

"Right there. About... 400... maybe 450 meters down, on the right side above the white car."

I could still see his arms dangling down. I could still spot the small dark stick that only I knew was a rifle, that only I'd seen drop down to the street below.

"You see him?" I asked.

"No, but fuck Ludwig. That ain't no 400 meters. Hey, Benjamin, come check this shit out!"

Sergeant Benjamin was already behind us, looking for the balcony I had described. Sergeant Moore took over to talk him in.

"You see it, man?"

"What — by that car way down there?"

"Yeah."

"Where's the stiff?" Benjamin laughed.

"You can barely see it," I told him. "His arms are dangling down there off the edge of that balcony."

Again I tried to point it out, realizing how far away it really was. They looked it over some more but gave up in short time.

"Ah, whatever. Good job, man!" Sergeant Moore got up.

"Haha! Yeah, good thing he didn't zero his rifle or you'd be fucked right now." Sergeant Benjamin nodded.

I looked back at the wall and felt a tiny shiver still rumbling in my knees and hands. I tried to calm myself down and turned back to my machine gun.

"Well shit," I laughed nervously. "God loves the Infantry!"

"Yeah, right. You're one lucky son of a bitch, Ludwig. Let's just hope that was their best sniper."

Yeah, I thought, *let's fuckin' hope.*

At some point we gave up on keeping track of anything but expended ammo counts. Our firing position had become a kind of self-serve buffet of lethal force. Every kind of weapon was available for anybody to step in and use. From an M-14 rifle with a long-range Leupold scope to a few M-4 assault rifles with both red-dot and 3.5x Acog optics — we had it all.

Throughout the day the men in our platoon cycled through the room, watching and participating, picking up different rifles, and having their own go at the madness. I didn't even bother getting up to take a break. The way I saw it, I didn't have anything better to do than sit there and enjoy the show. We had trained for years and I was finally living the dream: all-out, kinetic warfare. Real war. Force-on-force.

Even if I took a break, what was I going to do? Sit-down and stare at a wall? As I had found out from my sickness, I couldn't exactly eat anything without shitting my brains out thirty minutes later, and most of the furniture in the schoolhouse had been piled up in the windows to serve as cover and concealment. Unless I wanted to go sit on my ass in an empty room while everybody had a blast playing Army, the only place in the world for me was right there behind my gun. So I sat and I watched it all happen, taking part when the going got rough. I think that was the first time I really stopped to listen to the nearby mosque with Marshall, my favorite interpreter.

For days we had listened to the mosques on the front lines of the battle shouting commands at the insurgency, masking it under the guise of "daily prayer." That alone wasn't a surprise; we learned on day one in-country that the militia used the mosques for command and control of their forces. What was different this time, however, was the message — and how it betrayed the worn out condition of our enemy.

"They are saying... ehh... *'Stand up!'*" Marshall listened in with a smile. "Ehh... *'Fight the American devils!'*... yes... they are saying this."

The loudspeakers carried on unabated and after deciphering the message he felt obliged to spread the word.

"Now, they are saying we are almost defeated! Yes! Ha! They are saying that they have killed almost all of us! That we will be dead by nightfall! Ha!"

Marshall shouted some curses from the window as we scanned our sector to watch for snipers and RPGs. It was different for the interpreters. We were just soldiers. We were fighting because we had been ordered to.

Because we were shanghaied and sent to Hell and the only way out was to kill our way to safety.

But the interpreters?

This was their home. These were their people. Every one of them had some reason to be here and it was always something personal. Maybe their family had been tortured and murdered. Maybe they just needed the cash. Maybe their father had died in the Shiite revolution against Saddam Hussein or the chemical weapons massacres in the mountains to the north. Maybe they didn't qualify for their own military or they felt safer with the Americans. Sometimes they were adrenaline junkies. Sometimes they'd been beaten damn near to death. Sometimes, they were double agents for the militia. But Marshall?

He just hated the fuckers.

"They are just shit!" he'd say, frantically waving his arms and shouting, "I hate the militia! Kill them all! Every last fucking one of them!"

"Why do you hate them so much?" I asked him once.

"Because they are fucking assholes!"

That was it: *because they were fucking assholes*. He never elaborated on the subject because he didn't need to. He was one of us in that regard: fed up with their bullshit and determined to see them die. Like I said, they all had reasons to be there, but I liked Marshall's the best. It was simple. It was clean. He might've been a little crazy but I always felt like we had that much in common and the entire afternoon he had run steady stream of slapstick humor as he took in the sight of all the carnage.

"They are fucking done!" He shouted out the window. "Listen to them! They are probably all fucking dead!"

Without warning he slipped right back into Arabic, flinging huge globs of spit out of his mouth, shouting at the top of his lungs so his message could be heard all the way down the street.

"Marshall!" I shouted over him. "What are you yelling now?"

"I am telling them to hurry up! That we are bored! I am saying '*If we are all dead, why do all the dead bodies look like Arabs?*' I hate these fucking assholes! They are dogs!"

"You're fuckin' crazy, Marshall!" Wagner shouted.

"Thank you." He bowed.

"What's all this commotion?" Flemming walked into the room with a mockingly stern look on his face and a fresh sweet-roll in hand.

"Where'd you get that honey-bun?" I asked.

It seemed unreal to me that such a luxury could be found this far forward and out in the Shit.

He looked down at the snack with a shrug. "I don't know. I think somebody night-hawked a couple boxes from the chow area at JSS Sadr City right before we rolled out."

"What?"

"Yeah!" Wagner smacked me on the arm. "Dude, we've got a whole box of them in the break room."

"The break room?! When in the fuck did we get a *break room?*"

I felt like they had kept me out of some epic conspiracy to settle in and build a home. I mean, a *break room?* Out there? What else was I missing out on? A jacuzzi and wet-bar?

"Man," Flemming said. "I think you've been sitting behind that gun a little too long."

"Yeah, man." Wagner pulled a crumpled honey-bun out of his cargo pocket and waved it in front of me.

"Here, you want one?"

Looking down at the sugary treat in front of me, it was hard to imagine anything else in the world that I wanted more, but I knew that as soon as I ate it I'd spend the rest of that day writhing in pain and confessing my sins to the porcelain goddess.

"No, man." I waved the treat off. "I've got a pretty bad case of the bubble-gut, but thanks."

"Well they're right outside if you change your mind." Wagner shrugged.

"So what the fuck is going on?" Flemming asked again.

Marshall was still going at it.

"Ask him," I said.

Flemming tapped him on the shoulder. "Hey Marshall, what are you saying?"

"I ask them where the fuck are all their men! I say we have fucking cook them like falafels! I tell them you are here, eating fucking honey-bun while they eat our bullets! These fucking assholes! We will kill them all!"

By then it was high in the afternoon. The sky was deep and clear without a cloud or blemish to be seen. We couldn't even see smoke on the horizon. Bright floods of light reflected into our eyes against the tan bricks of the buildings across the way and heat waves shimmered off of every surface. Out there, the sun baked the landscape to a crisp, but up in our shaded firing position we might as well have had an air conditioning unit. We lived like kings in our own little castle, and for the first time since I'd set foot in that country I found myself feeling pretty okay. Who cared if we were deeper in the Shit than we'd ever been before? I was high on some kind of traumatic addiction. It was like Stockholm Syndrome for bloodshed. Something deep inside my brain had switched over and I was having a blast.

The three of us cheered Marshall on like a gang of soccer hooligans doing our best to pick a fight. I suppose the hope was that some Iraqi would get fed up with all the insults and charge into the open, filled with rage. Instead, Sergeant Moore came in the room and jerked us up short.

"Hey!" He shouted. "Stop fucking around! This shit isn't over! Scan your fucking sector!"

Like a bunch of whipped dogs we barked out a "roger" and got back to our weapons, doubling-down on our efforts as though it would make up for fifteen minutes of goofing off.

That's when I saw it.

It was a tiny, diamond-shaped, green hunk of metal, sticking up behind a berm and bobbing along the length of it, getting into position for the right time to strike.

"I've got something!" I shouted, getting myself ready to take the shot.

"What?! Where!" Sergeant Moore asked me.

"Down in that courtyard!"

When it stopped moving, I got a good look and knew exactly what it was.

"RPG!" I shouted. "Right-side of the road! 150 meters!"

"I don't see it!" Sergeant Moore shouted. "Where's it at!"

"In that walled in area! It looks like a garden! I think there's a berm in there! I just caught it for a second!"

"I think I see it!" Wagner cried out. "But I don't have a clear shot!"

I had the RPG locked in dead-center but the shooter himself was still hidden from view.

"It looks like he's crawling behind the berm," I said. "I'm going to have to wait for him to take the shot."

I locked him in and tried to get a good look at what he was hiding behind, but from my vantage point all I could spot was the rocket. It occurred to me that he had found the perfect spot. He could've been watching us the entire time. I never once saw the shooter until it was too late. I saw a spark, I saw a flash, and I saw a rocket flying right at my face. He knew exactly what he was doing. He had timed the shot to perfection. He got into position, pulled the trigger, and in that single moment of pause, hopped up and took aim at our position. The rocket started flying as soon as he had us in the cross-hairs. By the time I saw his face and pulled the trigger, it was too late. I watched the back half of his head and neck explode and a third round lanced his shoulder, ripping off a chunk of flesh as he rolled back behind the berm — but there was nothing I could do about the incoming RPG.

Somebody called out a warning. It didn't even register in my brain. I couldn't believe it. That bastard had finally shot off an RPG and it was flying straight at me — right at my face. It was such a good shot that I could still see it through my scope. It just hung there in the air a couple of mil-dots to the left of my cross-hairs, getting larger and larger until it crept out of my field of view. I couldn't even move. I was totally blank.

I felt the blast and the heavy rumble that shook me to the bone. It all happened in an instant — a split second that seemed to be an eternity. It felt like something had jarred my internal clock. The shock wave of hot gas smacked me in the face and singed my hair. A hundred tiny flakes of shrapnel bounced off my vest, tore holes in my uniform, and lodged into my skin from point-blank range. I felt a million tiny pinpricks of pain and for a split second I could've sworn I could feel every living cell in my body.

Then it was over.

Stunned, I brushed my filthy paws across my scruffy bearded face and felt a dozen jagged flakes of metal stuck in between the follicles of hair and the wrinkles around my baggy, tired eyes. I looked down at my hand and noticed a single smear of blood wrapping around a larger chunk of shrapnel, neighbored by little shreds of jagged copper that hadn't quite managed to break skin and do any damage. Feeling a sharp pain lingering on my chin, I ran my finger back across the spot and felt a fresh gash, oozing blood through a week's worth of dirt and grime. I grasped at straws for my brain to start working but I was stunned. Shocked. Stuck on one idea.

How the fuck am I still alive?

The ringing in my ears subsided enough for the sound of my surroundings to overpower what had just happened. The room filled with the rustling sounds of Wagner, Marshall, Flemming, and Sergeant Moore pulling themselves up from the ground and doing their best to assess the situation. I braced myself for the horror that was about to unravel because there was no way that none of us were hit.

"Holy shit!" Flemming shouted out as he stood up. "What the fuck was that!"

"Ludwig!" Sergeant Moore said. "Why the fuck didn't you get down?!"

"What?" I was still in shock.

Flemming grabbed my shoulders and looked me straight in the eyes. "You okay, man?"

"Yeah." I was only half convinced.

We glanced around the room and got a count of everybody and their status. To my dumbfounded amazement, not a single one of us was seriously injured and there was no sign of where the RPG had gone off.

"Ludwig," Flemming continued. "Why the fuck didn't you get down?"

I had no good reason. The act of taking cover hadn't even occurred to me. In fact, I was rather shocked at the thought of it.

"I don't know," I said.

As I regained my senses, I noticed a jagged chunk of shrapnel, which had lodged into the ballistic lens of Flemming's shades and come to a stop within a quarter-inch of his eyeball on the far side. When I pointed it out, he crossed his eyes comically to focus in on the projectile and we all reveled in the near-miss that had somehow spared us from what we all accepted as certain as Fate.

"Where the hell did that thing go?!" I finally asked.

"I swear to God," Wagner said. "That thing was heading right for us."

"Oh yeah," I chuckled. "Yeah, that's definitely true."

We scoured the room and the scenery outside, searching for a crater or a blast, but none of us could find anything that resembled the remnant of an RPG. Before we could get too far, one of the snipers ran into the room in a panic, with a trauma kit in-hand.

"Holy shit!" He shouted. "You guys are alive?! Where the hell did that thing hit?!"

"I don't know," Sergeant Moore said. "That's exactly what we were trying to find out."

"I guess it missed us," Wagner said.

"No man." The sniper shook his head with his jaw slack. "I watched the whole fuckin' thing. I swear to God I thought you guys were all dead."

Struck with a sudden sense of immortality, I stood up and walked over to the window so I could stick my head outside and look back at the outer wall of the schoolhouse. I was looking for some kind of evidence that what we had all seen was even real. All I could make out were a bunch of bullet holes and tiny chunks of missing plaster.

"I don't see anything," I said.

"Let me check that shit out." Sergeant Moore stuck his head out after me.

As more people filed in to make sure we were all okay, somebody passed around the idea to pat each other down and double-check for injuries that might've been hidden behind the layers of our uniform and the numbness of shock. It wasn't until I looked down at my own clothes that I realized how lucky I was. At first I noticed a flake of copper that had melted into the Velcro on my right shoulder. Then I saw another chunk had sliced through one of my pouches and shattered the screen of my camera. Larger pieces had lodged into my ammo pouches and helmet cover, and my uniform was covered from head to toe with tiny holes where shrapnel blasted through the fabric and cut through my skin. Thankfully, none of them had punched through to my vital organs inside, but it was still a terrifying sight. We continued our search for the impact zone and I couldn't find a single trace of an RPG beyond a room full of minor flesh-wounds and flakes of mangled copper.

"Dude," I said. "Where the fuck did that thing hit?"

Wagner shrugged and pointed to Flemming. "Well it looks like he was staring right at it. Let's ask him."

We all turned to him for an explanation.

"I don't know." He shrugged. "The last thing I remember seeing was an RPG comin' right at my face. I was already hittin' the dirt when it blew up. I mean — I swear to God it must've blown up right in front of me."

"That doesn't make sense." Wagner protested. "RPGs. don't just blow up. It had to have hit something."

"Hey, check out that pole right there!" Sergeant Moore interrupted us with a grunt and pointed out the window.

"What pole?" I looked down the street.

There were dozens of poles holding up thousands of wires. I had no idea what he was talking about.

"That one right there — right in front of the fucking window!"

I shifted my gaze closer and noticed a cock-eyed metal telephone pole standing just a couple of meters in front of our window. Upon closer inspection I noticed a fresh dent in the side of it and a chunk in the metal where it'd clearly been hit with a heavy projectile. When I walked over to my left a few paces and lined up the bend in the pole with the vantage point of the shooter, it was obvious that our savior was a one-in-a-million shot of dumb fucking luck.

"Fuck me," I said. "I think it hit the pole."

"Yeah, that's what I'm thinking too." Sergeant Moore said.

At first it was too crazy to believe. But there was nothing else we could find to back up the events and explain what the hell had happened. It was flying right at us — straight enough that I could see it through my goddamned scope. It was close enough to pepper us with shrapnel, which meant that wherever it went off was in line-of-sight with every one of us in the room. And it had been close, too. Close enough to singe the hairs on our skin. Close enough that everybody else in the schoolhouse was convinced that we should've been dead.

By our best reckoning, the RPG in question had slammed into the metal telephone pole and deflected into a spin before the charge went off in mid-air and sent the meat of the blast in a "safe" direction. The only other legitimate theory, given the shrapnel marks on the pole and the kill-radius of such a weapon, was that God himself had reached down to shield us from our fates. Either one could've been true, because it didn't really make a difference.

We were alive, and that's all that mattered.

"Alright." Sergeant Moore threw up his arms. "Fuck these guys. I'm getting Sergeant O'Brien. Let's see if we can't do something about all that cover and concealment they've got goin' on down there."

Half an hour later, an Abrams tank rolled up in front of our window. The only sound I could hear were the screaming turbines of its engine as it settled into its new position.

"Well, would you listen to that." Sergeant Bitolas set down his rifle and leaned back in his seat.

The alleyway was completely devoid of enemy fire.

"Yeah," Sergeant Benjamin said. "You bet your ass I'd be hiding too if they showed up with a fucking tank."

Sergeant O'Brien called up the tank, and I could hear the response crackle through his hand mic.

"One-Six this is Punisher-One-Four. Go ahead."

"Yeah, One-Six here. Listen Punisher-One-Four, We've got a couple of things down there we need you to go ahead and take care of for us."

"This is Punisher-One-Four. Roger."

"Alright, the first thing we need you to take out is that cinder-block wall down there, just beyond that first building on the right."

"Stand by. Let me see if I can spot it."

The tank commander pulled the trigger of his heavy machine gun that was mounted right beside his main-gun. He squeezed off a three-round burst at the corner of the nearest building.

"Punisher-One-Four, Bull-One-Six. Negative. Bring it left a little. Over."

Another burst went off, blasting chunks out of the cinder block wall in question.

"That's it! Right there."

"Punisher-One-Four. Roger — Standby."

We stood patiently and waited. He fired off another burst and the radio crackled again.

"Bull-One-Six, Punisher-One-Four. Stand by for main gun. Over."

"Bull-One-Six. Roger."

"Main gun!" He shouted for all of us to hear.

"Main gun!!!" we all echoed the cry in unison.

At first nothing happened. After a minute or two of suspense the radio crackled again.

"Bull-One-Six, Punisher-One-Four. Sorry for the delay, we had to double-check with Bull-Six. For real this time, stand by for main gun. Over."

"Bull-One-Six. Roger." He turned back to shout the warning. "Alright guys! Let's try this again! Main gun!"

"Main gun!!!"

We cheered for a second time, shouting taunts at the scene unfolding. We cursed our enemy and joked about their plight, as a bone shattering shock wave blasted through the streets. Everything in front of us disappeared behind a thick cloud of dust. All I could see through the haze was a hot tongue of fire, reaching out from the muzzle of the gun and engulfing the wall with an inferno. The schoolhouse flooded with cheers. I was surrounded by a wild commotion of clapping hands and raspy cries of celebration. We might as well have been watching the final touchdown of the Super Bowl. When the dust cleared, a massive chunk of the wall had been reduced to rubble, and every car that had been close to the tank lit ablaze.

"Damn." The radio crackled. "Bull-One-Six, it looks like the round punched straight through the wall. We're going to have to knock that sucker down manually. Over."

"Bull One-Six. Roger."

The tank commander inched forward down the road to knock it down with his treads, but stopped just a few feet from the nearest corner. That's when the tank commander second guessed the act and called us back.

"Hey, One-Six this is Punisher-One-Four. *Eh*— This is a little sketchy down here so we're going to try to do this as quick as possible. Over."

"One-Six. Roger. Do whatever you gotta' do, just take care of that wall."

"Gotcha. On it."

The tank crept forward and approached the wall with caution. Back then, I couldn't understand why a fucking tank would be so scared of a couple bad guys on foot. Thinking back on it, you couldn't pay me to drive down that street in a battle cruiser. There's no telling what the militia had waiting for them around all those blind corners and back-alleys, but that didn't stop them from driving right up to that wall and ramming it to pieces like it was nothing.

"Hey, Bull One-Six, Punisher-One-Four. Is that what you wanted?"

"Yeah," Sergeant O'Brien called back. "Just go ahead and knock down as much of that wall as possible and come on back."

The tank wiggled back and forth, rotating and grinding the bricks and mortar into tiny chunks. It drove forward and tipped over more of the wall, then backed up and dragged pieces of rubble along with it. It came to a stop once again right below our window.

"Okay. Bull One-Six, Punisher-One-Four. What else needs doing?"

Now that the main obstruction was clear, it was time for a little fun.

"Punisher-One-Four," Sergeant O'Brien said with a smile, "How many rounds do you have in that thing?"

"As many as you need." The tank commander chuckled.

Eager to take advantage of the situation and maximize our return on calling him in, we had him obliterate everything that looked remotely akin to cover. They punched gaping holes into the houses that'd been used as firing positions and peppered the windows with .50 cal rounds. They unloaded high-explosive projectiles into trucks and cars. The shock wave of each successive blast was enough to shatter the windows, blow in the doors, and crumble brick barricades along the length of the road. By the time it was all over, an already war-torn alleyway of bullet holes and shrapnel scars was blasted into a stretch of desecration fit for the cover of Time Magazine. It was a canvas of wretched details. A mosaic of shattered glass. Heaps of crumbled bricks, twisted metal and burning trash. In less than a day, I'd watched a typical Baghdad back-alley become a showcase of wanton destruction and I couldn't be happier. But as soon as that tank left, the militia made another jab on our position. It was clear that no matter what we did, they were Hell-bent on coming down that goddamned road.

By nightfall, our engagements with the enemy had subsided into shadow games and secret whispers, broken occasionally by a random burst of rounds into the darkness. At that point we had struggled with the militia for nearly two straight days so we had no choice but to draft up a guard roster and take turns doing our best to fall asleep. Even after twelve hours of warding off countless attempts to dislodge our hold on the schoolhouse, there was still no end in sight and we had no reason to believe tomorrow would be any easier than today.

I knew that I wouldn't be able to get any sleep if I tried, so I didn't bother. Sitting in that window, behind my gun, was the only ounce of control I had over my own fate. It was the only place I wanted to be. It was the only way to keep my life in my own hands. So I sat there behind that machine gun until the sky went black and swallowed our world in silence. Throughout the night, two-man guard teams filed through the firing position and sat beside me to scan the streets and listen to the crackling radio, waiting for the militia to make another move.

"Here's the deal," I whispered to every shift when they showed up. "I can't sleep, I'm not going to sleep and we only need two people to be on guard, so you guys can take turns getting some rack while the other stays up with me."

"Are you sure?" They usually asked.

"Yeah. I've already run it by the squad leaders. They're cool with it. You two pick who goes first. I don't care what kind of rotation you use. I'll be here all night."

I want to make this much clear: I wasn't staying awake out of compassion. I wasn't doing it just so my buddies could get some extra rack-time. I wasn't trying to look like a badass or earn some kind of kudos because I had the balls to stick it through. I sat there because I couldn't shake the shiver in my bones. I stayed there because every time I walked away from that machine gun, I felt stripped, naked, and gripped with fear. I did it because every time I closed my eyes I couldn't stop thinking about the thousands of militia foot soldiers in every direction who wanted us dead. I stuck around because I was terrified. Because I didn't have a choice. Because I didn't want to die in my sleep. I watched every hour of that night tick by in silence and waited for tomorrow like a child hiding under the sheets. I scanned every shade of darkness and listened to every scratch echo as deeply into the corners of my soul as it did into the depths of the night. I was compelled to, even though I knew it was wearing me down to the bone, because I was too damn scared to fall asleep.

Late that night, our sentry on the east side of the schoolhouse spotted movement in a back-alley and held his fire to observe and report. As it turned out, he was looking at a militia reconnaissance patrol, and just a few minutes later a two-man probe snuck up on us from the same position he had been watching. This time, he unloaded on the crew. An hour or so later, another reconnaissance patrol was spotted to the west. We even caught sight of a man taking long-exposure photos of us with his digital camera.

All throughout the night we played "hide-and-seek" with the militia. Inch by inch they tested the limits of our outpost's blind-spots. Deep down I knew it was only a matter of time until they found a weak spot in our perimeter and exploited it for all we were worth. When they got too close, we cut them down. All throughout the night, the silence was shattered by loud cracks and rattles of machine guns and sniper fire to the point where I even wondered if I had missed out on any sleep. When the daylight returned, it felt like we had entered some kind of twisted Groundhog Day of killing and violence. Throughout the morning, civilians took to the streets and the militia gazed over every inch and detail of our fighting positions, and by 10:00 hours the first round was fired.

Once again, they came at us with everything they had. They poked here and prodded there. They fired a couple of RPGs and brought up a sniper to see if they could pick us off one at a time. They charged a few men down the main drag and leap-frogged buddy teams across the rooftops of buildings down the road. It struck me that we were like some kind of bloody Rubik's Cube to them and every failed attempt to match up our corners cost them in human life.

Some time in the afternoon we got another call on the radio with a warning about a confirmed intelligence hit on an elite group of snipers moving in to take us out. This time the TOC even had a description of the make and model of the vehicle they were driving and a stern warning that they'd be swinging by ahead of time to get a good look at the schoolhouse before setting up down the road to take the shot. According to the call, if anybody spotted a silver, four-door, Opal sedan with tinted windows, five passengers, and a missing front hub-cap that was moving southbound towards the objective house, we were clear to engage. The unspoken warning, of course, was that if we gave those guys time to set up, we'd never know what hit us until we were dead. The obvious conclusion was that it would be better all around if we could simply spot the car and pump it full of hot lead with all five of the shooters still inside.

Less than twenty minutes later, a silver, four-door, Opal sedan rounded the corner down the street, creeping forward down the road at a snail's pace. It looked as shady as could be, as far as I was concerned. Without so much as a second thought, I took aim at the car, counted the number of silhouettes through the lightly tinted windows, confirmed my suspicions, and laid into that bastard with a long burst of rounds. As soon as he saw it coming, the driver slammed his foot on the gas and spun his wheel over to the side, doing everything he could to round the nearest corner and get out of my line of fire.

He was too late.

I pumped about a hundred rounds into that car. I littered the windows and side-panels with holes. Round after round. A solid ten to fifteen seconds of gunfire. In the dwindling afternoon daylight and faint overcast of an incoming sandstorm, it was difficult to see for sure if they were dead — so I cleared any doubt with another burst into the side-panels as it rolled idly to a stop, now half concealed around the corner of the intersection down the road.

Damn, I thought, *he almost made it.*

It was obvious the driver was dead. I would have been surprised if anybody survived the barrage, so I chuckled lightly with smug pride in what I had done. Then the rear passenger door cracked open and a young boy fell out into the street. He tried to walk, but his blown out shin crumbled under his first step and he flopped down to the earth in a bloody, half conscious pile. It was like a sack of mush coming to rest on the floor. I scanned back over the car. Now that it wasn't moving and the tinted windows were all shattered, I could get a better look at the people inside — people who I had just mowed down with a smile.

I steadied my aim to scan the car through the haze of dust and darkness of the sandstorm rolling in. Counting the boy in the street, I could see five bodies from the car. And as I looked closer into the wreckage, I faced the true horror of what I had done.

I had just killed a family. An innocent family. A family of people who had no good reason to die. Their blood was splattered everywhere. They were riddled with bullets. Their bodies hung from seat belts, lifeless and maimed. There wasn't a single sniper among them. Just a family. A family who was in the wrong place, at the wrong time, with the wrong fucking car.

I sat there groping for a justification for a very long time. A thick tumor of horror in the back of my throat. I couldn't breathe. I couldn't think. I felt sick to my stomach. I wanted to die. I wanted to undo my existence. I wanted to be no more, rather than live in a world where my own hands had just done this horrible, horrible thing.

I killed them.

All of them.

For nothing.

There was no justice in that. There was no reason to celebrate what I had done. As I ran it over and over in my mind, it hit me that they were probably just trying to escape. He was probably creeping that slow because I was there and he didn't want to provoke the very wrath I had unleashed. He did everything he could to make it clear that he wasn't a threat — and I pumped a hundred rounds into everybody he loved because of it.

I knew immediately that I'd never forget that sight: five mangled corpses that had been chopped into mush by my own two hands. Of all the things I had done in that city, that single act of barbarity would stain my soul for the rest of my life. But I was too far gone at that moment to face what I had done. I was too much of a machine. Too burnt out and ruthless to let anything linger in the foreground of my mind for very long. I swallowed the colossal guilt in a single gulp and it shot straight into the empty crevasse where my frayed and distressed soul used to live. I knew that any attempt at reconstruction would always be tainted with the knowledge of what I did. Deep down, if my soul ever returned from whatever refuge it may have found, it would never again fit inside of me as it had done before that day.

And then I heard myself say something that I will also never forget.

"Better you than me."

That was it. What was done, was done. There was nothing I could do about it now. They were dead. And you know what?

Okay.

I scanned the car and confirmed the signs I had been told to watch out for: silver Opel, one front hubcap missing, four doors, sedan, tinted windows, driving slow, five passengers. It was all there. I hadn't missed a thing. For all I knew, that could've easily been a car full of snipers, a caravan of bad dudes, or a vehicle-borne IED. And if it was any of those, I'd be dead right now — or soon to be, at least.

So, *whatever.*

I had once accepted collateral damage as a fact of life — back when I had no idea what the hell it really was. Back when it was an academic discussion. I simply acknowledged the fact and moved on. Now it was right there in front of me: an innocent family in a bullet-riddled car. A man, his wife, and his kids. People who did exactly what I would've done if my entire neighborhood went to shit like theirs. I'd get the fuck out. I'd say, "Honey, get the kids and get in the car."

But that's what all of this was about, right? The difference between thinking and doing. How things change when you have blood on your own hands and you smell the shit on your own fingers. How things get murky when you're the one who's out there, fighting for your life and the lives of your friends. How *you* change. How everything goes out the window and you're forced to see the true evil in the world. How sometimes that evil is the only way to make it right. How we make a deal with the devil every time we decide to kill, and it's times like these when he takes a cut.

In the end you have a choice. You can pull the trigger. You can *let 'er rip*. You can pepper that fucking car until there's nothing left but splatter marks of meat and bone. And sometimes you'll be right. When you search the car you'll find bombs, guns, intelligence — the works. You'll see the fucker explode just far enough away to keep you and yours out of the kill-zone. You'll go home and tell the story about how crazy those fucking towel-heads really are. How they push the limits every fucking day. How they bank on your compassion and abuse it as a weak spot. But you didn't fall for that weak spot. You killed that motherfucker and you're here today because of it. You're alive because you didn't think twice — because you didn't bother with doubt.

Then again, sometimes you'll be wrong. You'll see a family of five in a Swiss-cheesed car that's sprayed with blood and guts. You'll find a businessman who was hurrying to work, or an anxious husband rushing to the hospital with his pregnant wife. You'll realize that you just unloaded on some kids going to school because they had a toy gun. And these won't be the stories you tell at a bar. They'll be the ones you keep inside. The ones that drink you to death when you're all alone.

But like I said, you have a choice.

You can hold your fire and wave them by. You can clench your teeth and pucker your asshole because you know there's a chance that it can get you killed. But you're rolling the dice because innocent lives deserve protection. And you know what? Nothing will happen — not the first, or second, or third, or maybe even fourth time you let them go. And you'll start thinking you're doing right by the world. You'll start thinking you can go the whole deployment without ever taking the shot. But one day, sure as the sunrise, some car will pull right up to your squad and one of the kids inside will smile at you and wave. He'll show you his favorite soccer ball and you'll give him a stick of candy just to see him smile.

And then boom.

Now you and everybody you care about is dead. They'll ship home twelve empty boxes because there wasn't anything left to bury. A whole squad of your friends — all of them fathers, sons, husbands, and cousins — they'll all be dead because of *you*. Maybe not today. Maybe not tomorrow. Maybe never.

But *maybe*.

So you've got to decide if those people you might be saving are more important or less important than the men to your left and right. You've got to realize that you're not betting your life, you're betting everybody else's. And you've got to ask yourself what right you have to risk all that on a bullshit wager that you can trust people you don't even know. You've got to think about all those people who depend on you, and who are going to die because you *didn't* make the call. And when you make that call, you better turn off all that shit up in your think-box about ethics, doubt, and anxiety. You just shut the fuck up and pull the trigger, because nobody's going to do it for you. And yeah, you might be wrong. And yeah, innocent people will die. And yeah, it'll be a horrible thing to face. And you know what? It'll be your fault. Because you had a choice. You chose "us" over "them."

And that's war.

So now I owned it. It was all mine. Just mine. My bullets. My kills. My call. I pumped a hundred rounds into an innocent family who was running for their life. I even laughed when I did it. So if there really is a Hell, that's how I know for sure I've earned my place. But none of that mattered out there. We weren't playing some sport with a referee calling fouls and throwing flags on the field. Nobody really cared if some civilians were killed in the crossfire — the militia least of all. And that was the true nature of collateral damage. It was the whole point of the phrase. It was right up there with "acceptable losses" and "fair trade." So I shook it off and drove on. I brushed it off and got back to work. And years later, in the middle of the night, when I was all alone with my thoughts and a gun, I'd remember that car, that kid, and his family, and I'd come to terms with what I did. But I still had a job to do. And that job meant the difference between life and death. That job was about me and my own. It was to make sure nobody made it down that fucking road, and to pump round after round into anybody who was stupid enough to try — especially if they were in a silver, four-door, Opel sedan with missing hubcaps, five passengers, and tinted fucking windows.

After all, I'd have my whole life to live with the things I had done, but only if I earned it.

The Jaish al-Mahdi made one last-ditch attack on the schoolhouse. They threw in the towel right as we burned down to the bottom dregs of our ammunition. Hell, they probably could've had us if they were stupid enough to try it again, but after one last pot-shot with an RPG a peaceful silence broke through the fray which would last for hours to come.

By sundown, word had made it around the schoolhouse that somebody had finally come up with a name for our new stronghold. We were now holding ground at the newly christened "Outpost Gumby" — named after Staff Sergeant Gamboa who we'd lost back in Ur. When I got up to take a break, I was starving, aching, and trembling. I could barely stand under my own weight. For the first time in days, I walked away from my gun and grabbed an MRE to gorge myself on two thousand calories of snacks and dried foods. I mixed every sloppy chunk of sun-boiled, pasty condiment into a packet of radiation-proof jambalaya and swallowed it whole. I even got my hands on the last honey-bun that side of Route Florida and ate that too. The pleasure was short lived. Now that I was completely ravaged by dysentery, it only took twenty minutes before I was downstairs with a chem-light in hand, shitting myself in the dark to the soundtrack of snoring soldiers enjoying a hard-fought rest.

As I bit through the pain and drained myself of fluids, I couldn't help but think about home. Ten thousand miles away, my friends and family were about to embark on another typical lazy Sunday in southern

California. It was right about time for mom and dad to come home from church. I figured my sister was probably on a run and my brother was out for lunch somewhere. And all my old friends? Two words: "Spring Break." My understanding was that college was a hell of a place right about that time of the year, which meant they'd be out for another hour or two at least before stumbling home with a pounding headache. At least in that respect we had something in common. But how in the hell was I supposed to tell them about days like today? About the young boy I had shot? About the RPG that should've killed me? About the sniper who should've zeroed his shit? About the family I had killed — just like my own — and the words I muttered right after the fact?

"Shot!" the snipers cried out.

"Shot!!!" I heard some men echo the call.

They fired off a round and the shock wave rippled all the way down into the bathroom to box my ears — ears that had been blasted into nothingness since the fighting began. In that moment I took a deep breath and really listened to everything that was happening around me.

What a strange sensation, I thought.

Not the sensation of a gunshot or the musky, dank hot air, but the experience as a whole. The utterly strange sensation of being at ease in all that shit. Of living in a world where everything I knew was upside down — where a kid like me had done the things I had done. There I was, in some God-forsaken bathroom, stilted up on the half-broken frame of a toddler's stool, taking a shit in the middle of a nightmare, with every reason to believe that I could be dead by morning.

"Did you get him?" Somebody shouted.

"Yeah!" A voice called back.

"Fuck yeah!"

"I see another one!"

"You see him? Take him out!"

"Shot!"

"—Shot!!!"

The second shockwave was louder than the first. It hurt. It rang in my ears like a period marking the end of a sentence. We were paving these streets in blood — us and the Jaish al-Mahdi. We were tearing the place down with every gunshot and explosion, leaving bodies of lost loved ones to rot in the minds of those who survived.

I caught myself wondering how all of this would be remembered when the blood soaked in and was buried with time. It hit me that the whole world was probably watching. They were probably sitting on the sidelines, calling out plays with color commentary and stadium seating. Would there be headlines? A centerfold editorial? A presidential debate? Would that car I destroyed and the shredded bodies inside make it to the nightly news? Would it be the last thing my parents saw before they clicked off the lights and went to bed? Would they know I was the one who did it? Would they know why? Did anybody tell them what all of this is for, or did they have to dig for the truth through a mirage of bull-shit?

This was the end-game. It was the last stand. In a few miles and a couple thousand bodies there'd be nothing left of the Jaish al-Mahdi but a splinter-cell and a footnote in a book somewhere. Once that happened, there'd be nothing stopping the new Republic of Iraq from taking its place in the world as a legitimate democracy after six hard years of struggle and war. So once again I found myself considering the nature of collateral damage, the cost in innocent lives, and the price paid by every-body there.

There wasn't any room to back down now. If we were to quit now, we might as well have never pushed across the Tigris. All that death and destruction would be for nothing. It would mean the Jaish al-Mahdi would have won because we quit when the going got tough — because we didn't have the stomach to kill them when they had the guts to die. It would prove that whenever we get down to the meat of it, the American military will turn its tail and go home. That was the lesson we taught the world when we lost the war in Vietnam: that ultimately our military is at the mercy of a frenzied mob of college kids, soccer moms, and stay-at-home pussies who live in a paradise with no idea what the world is really like. That all you have to do to send us packing is score some late-night footage of the "true face" of war. We've been that way ever since — standing watch against the realities of the world to placate the sensitivit-ies of a sheltered society.

Out there in the Shit it didn't matter why we started the war. The only thing that mattered was our obligation to see it through. We were responsible for the Jaish al-Mahdi who now threatened the fate of our entire cause. After all, we created the void they used to gain power. We legitimized their agenda and handed them a victory when we negotiated a ceasefire back in 2004. Then we stood by and watched them become a dominating force in the country until they were too big to simply be eradicated from the equation. We let them murder, torture, and racket their way into power because some duly elected politicians back home didn't have the stomach to let the grunts do their job when they had the chance. They tried to cut corners and avoid the bloodshed. But that's not how the world works. All that got us was a pile of shit. Now that pile blowing up in our face and the only choice we had was to see it through or walk away. And it was faced with that reality, I finally understood the back-half of why I had signed up to serve my country in the middle of a God-damned war.

I was right when I knew it wasn't good enough to stay at home and watch the world unravel on TV — not when I could go do something about it and stand up for what I believed in. But there was something else that I had missed entirely: that it isn't good enough to go out there and "do the right thing" if you aren't willing to take responsibility for all the good, the bad, and the God-awful that comes along for the ride. That sooner or later — no matter what the cause — you're going to find yourself in the pit of some fucked up shit without a map or compass, and nobody there to show you the path. And once you get to that point you can either be the guy who drops the shovel, walks away, and tries to wash your hands clean of what you did, or you can be the one to knuckle the fuck down, pick a direction, and get to work fixing what you started.

That's what we were doing out there. The only way any of this was going to end was with the obliteration of the Jaish al-Mahdi once and for all. The only way out was to go up the middle and kill every person who stood in our way. To clear a path through the rubble so the only legitimate force with some clout in that country was the government we had stepped in to help create: a government elected by the people to serve the people. Everything else was immaterial. Anything less and we might as well have never tried. We were in it for the long-haul — total war — and I was ready to take it all the way. So with that conclusion burned fresh in my mind, I finished up my business and made my way back upstairs, wandering through those dark halls which had felt so terrifying just a few days before.

These were the very same corridors I had thought capable of eating me alive. The same dark halls through which I'd blundered like a fool. Now, just two days later, I trusted them with my life. They comforted me with understanding. They stood mute with forgiveness. They were devoid of judgment and bound to an eternity of silence. But it wasn't them who had changed, it was me. It was the man inside of me. It was who I had become.

That was the farthest I've ever been from any kind of god. The devil himself could've shown up to play cards and I would've taken it in stride. Hell, I would've given him a cigarette and asked him to stick around. You know, get to know him a little before we became roommates for eternity. Of course, he's a pretty busy guy. I'm sure he'd have more pressing appointments to attend. Still, something gave me the distinct impression that if he was there, he'd pat me on the back and tell me to keep up the good work. He'd shake my hand like a gentleman, thank me for my service, and reassure me that I was in good hands.

"Don't forget about that RPG," he'd snicker. "You owe me."

And I'd just laugh it off and give him a wink.

"You got that right, buddy — I owe you big."

After all, he didn't need to drag me to Hell.

I was getting there just fine by myself.

- Chapter Nine -
Terms And Conditions

When I got back upstairs, I made my way over to the infamous "break room" to find a place where I could lay down on my back, close my eyes, and get some sleep. The room was right in the middle of the schoolhouse, on the second floor between the two courtyards of the structure. Its window faced inward to safety. The only door opened to a hallway behind the sniper's lookout and .50 cal machine gun nest. Our overhead cover was a thick ceiling of shoddy concrete. It was the safest place we could find, but the acoustics were terrible.

Every surface of Outpost Gumby was made of brick, stone slabs, or cheap tile. Every corner of the structure was a hard, ninety degree angle. Sound echoed through that building like an amphitheater. You could drop a pin in the back room of the compound and it would bounce around until it flooded into the break room and snapped like a firecracker next to your ears. Whenever somebody took a shot it sounded like it had gone off right next to your face. When a bomb went off it hit you in the gut like you were in a bar-fight with a ghost. But at that point I wasn't worried about the creature comforts of the outpost. I just wanted to get some fucking sleep.

I walked into the room and looked for a place to pass out in the shadows so nobody would kick me awake or disturb my slumber when they switched guards throughout the night. The only illumination came from a single green chem-light that had been thrown into the corner of the room, but it was still bright enough for me to find a cramped opening on the ground where I could settle in for the night. Still drenched with sweat and wearing all of my gear, I unclipped my helmet, took it off and wedged it right behind my back to serve as a support for the ceramic plate of my body armor. As I had done a hundred times before, I leaned back against my helmet, undid my armor, and set up my rack of ammo and equipment in position to throw it on in case of an emergency. When everything was arranged, I slid down onto the ground to rest my head on the carefully constructed pile of gear that would now act as my pillow for the remainder of the night. It might have been made out of hard ceramic and heavy-duty Cordura fabric, but I'll be damned if it wasn't enough to get the job done. Back then, it felt as good as a Temper-Pedic mattress and I'll tell you: even dead babies don't sleep that well.

Hours later my buddies told me that I slept through so many gunshots and explosions they were a little worried that I was in a coma. Squadron had sent a supply convoy out to our location, which got ambushed within a hundred meters of where I was sleeping, and even when a couple of IEDs hit them and ripped everyone awake, I snored on without pause. I slept through it all. I slept through the sniper fire and Ian's stretch of wrath when he got his own M-240B, "Lizzy," up in the window. I slept through another night assault and a run of Apaches pissing lead for the better part of an hour. I even slept through the sunrise, through another daylight attack, and right up to mid-morning when an RPG went off somewhere and shook me awake. After eight and a half hours of unconsciousness, I finally stumbled back into the room to see our boys laying waste to another outbreak of resistance.

That third day at Outpost Gumby was the last day of hard fighting, but the real meat of it only lasted a couple of hours. It was clear that the militia had simply given up on the attack and by mid-afternoon the situation settled down into occasional, irregular bursts of action. While many of us regarded that to be the real "end" of fighting at Outpost Gumby, small pockets of armed militia still made a few more attempts to break our hold on the objective over the next couple of days. Each of these assaults, however, was far less committed than any previous engagement and they all shared a similar fate.

At that point, Bull Company had been up against the Jaish al-Mahdi for ten days. In that time, we had racked up a recorded body count well into the triple digits of confirmed hostile kills. While I'll admit that number was highly contested because it had all but excluded dismounted contact that had never been called up, its impact on our enemy was unmistakable. Forced by blood to accept our hold on the schoolhouse, the militia now turned their full attention to our friendly positions and support networks back on the line. While the symptoms of this new effort were far less acute than the full-on assaults of days past, the inherent dangers of our position were hardly at bay.

Between snipers, RPGs, scouts, and the ever-looming threat of indirect fire, we still had our hands full. There was no stopping the militia from launching another attack on short-notice with the wisdom of lessons learned. The fact that we had barely slept in days wouldn't help. But the real Achilles' heel in our position were the supply convoys who had to brave unsecured hostile terrain just to keep us shooting, pissing, and shitting as the battle continued.

With our entire squadron dug in and well entrenched, the convoys had become the weakest link in the operation. Both sides diverted substantial resources to a growing fight over freeze-dried entrées and 24 oz water bottles. The only solution was to run a heavy clearance operation along the precarious journey out to the objective on a nightly basis. The militia took every chance they could get to set up an IED or attack a passing convoy with all the firepower they could muster. These engagements were almost never within direct line-of-sight for anybody in our company, but they were still well within earshot and served as a steady reminder of what we'd be in for if one of the convoys was pushed back or overrun altogether.

During the day we laughed and cheered as a group, keeping each other going with a cocky kind of winner-takes-all attitude, convincing ourselves that we were invincible and refusing to face that we could be wrong. But each night we retreated to our minds, scared and alone, sitting and lying in silence, waiting for the hammer to drop. We left a third of our number awake on four-hour guard shifts so everybody who wasn't critical to our survival could pass out and wait for their turn to stand watch into the night.

It was a generous schedule, given the situation, but the problem was that the fighting never really "stopped." It was never "over" and "done." There was always something: a gunshot here, an explosion there, air weapons engagements that never seemed to end. When we closed our eyes to sleep, it came with the guarantee that we'd be shocked back awake within a few minutes of settling down. The best we could get were a couple of cat-naps between the ongoing events of the battle. Correspondingly, our biggest threat was now the inevitability of falling asleep on guard, which opened the door for any member of the militia to sneak in and hit us wherever and whenever he'd like.

Those cat-naps became the front lines of my own personal battle with fear. It was easy to laugh through the madness when I had a four foot machine-gun in my hands and I was sitting in a room of violent and merciless companions. But as soon as I walked away from that firing position to wrap myself in the quiet and empty hours of nightfall, everything changed. I struggled to clear my mind of the shivers that had worked their way into my bones. I lay there for a half hour or more, staring at the ceiling to work out the fear from my mind. It was hard to fall asleep when I knew exactly what was waiting for us. More so when I had to listen to our only lifeline get pummeled from behind.

No matter how well we'd stood up against the hordes of insurgents, there were still thousands of men out there working on a plan to kill us all. I knew exactly how easy it could be to toss a grenade through a window or sneak through our back door. In fact, I could think of a dozen little tricks that could kill an entire fire team or more. All it would take was a clever man. A man with some guts. Just *one* and we could all buy the farm together.

I found myself thinking about these things every time I tried to sleep. I fought them out of my head whenever I laid down. I struggled with them every night and the smallest sound would jolt me awake so I could start all over. Eventually the only reason I could sleep at all was the physical inability to stay awake.

"Shot!" Somebody would shout.

Or they'd just pull the trigger first and call out the shot when it was done. Either way, when the shock wave hit me it felt like a flashbang. They tore me awake in an instant. They left me ravaged and panicked on the floor. My only comfort would come in figuring out that the gunshots were out-bound and that an attempt on our perimeter had just been repelled. But that also came with the knowledge that a gunfight in those very halls would be indistinguishable from the daily grind. So I'd wait for another shot, settle down, close my eyes, and restart my ongoing struggle with psychology until my eyes fell shut and another round went off.

After three more days of shuddering terror, the chemicals in my brain simply ran dry. I had nothing left at that point. I was numb. A zombie. A drone. I just stripped out of my gear and stumbled down to the ground. Within seconds I'd be unconscious. My eyes wouldn't even close. I'd slip into a trance and fall deep into a dream — but those dreams were a far cry from childhood memories. They were fractals, the echoes of my final conscious thoughts. They were the most distilled versions of my greatest fears. They were living nightmares of every horrible terror that'd gripped my heart in the last seconds before I checked out and surrendered to unconsciousness.

When I was awake it was easy enough to know what was real, but when I was asleep it was impossible to tell the difference. My bouts of unconscious made more sense than the life I was living, so it was useless to search for absurdities in the extravagant chaos of events. Both were lucid, yet in those dreams I was never saved by lucky shots or telephone poles. Even when I had every reassurance that I didn't just die in some horrible catastrophe, it was hard to believe. A gunshot would rip me into consciousness. I'd fall back into sleep a moment later. I'd scream for my life with my guts spewed out on the floor in front of me and the next thing I know someone's kicking me awake to let me know it's my turn on guard. After a long day of playing jack-in-the-box with a machine gun, I'd fall back down to the ground and the cycle would start all over — only now with a fresh batch of nightmares and a brain full of fears.

It was a torturous existence, shared by everybody there, and the fact that we had seemingly and inexplicably stalled our advance didn't help at all. We had grown accustomed to our perpetual state of violence. We no longer feared the prospect of taking pro-active steps to die for something worthwhile, but waiting around for the enemy to strike was a completely different story.

Combat is assertive. It favors aggression. It demands action. To assault something is to fight for an upper hand. It is to force yourself into a better position while depriving your enemy of his own firm ground. It is to take something that will not only hurt him, but help you. Should any side succeed in such an advance and know that they've dealt a strong blow to their enemy, the clear follow-up action is not to sit around and gloat about the victory, but to build a footing on new ground, pick another target, and attack again... and again... and again.

This is why we call it the initiative: it is the power to pick and choose where and when we fight. It forces our enemy to be defensive and split their reserves across an entire line so we can have free rein on the battlefield. It means we can push those reserves out into the fight as a single, aggressive force, thereby maximizing and further securing our initiative instead of holding fast and waiting to react. In fact, the initiative is such an important key to victory that we train it into our minds until it's second nature. We live it to the letter. We even have cute little mottos like, "In the absence of orders, set the conditions and attack," and, "It's better to die making a bad decision than sitting on your ass." It's a common practice to heckle bystanders until they get to work on a detail instead of standing around and jerking off. Initiative is everything — and so far it was still ours.

So why aren't we pushing forward?

The thought was on everybody's mind. We had done well to interdict the sustained and deliberate indirect fire-missions that had been pounding down on the front line for days, but our hold on Outpost Gumby was a stop-gap measure at best. We were still deep behind enemy lines with a tactical disposition that was hardly sustainable, and once the militia was done licking their wounds there would be nothing to stop them from coming back with a vengeance. Right now we were winning. The freedom for American forces to maneuver, assault, and hold territory without suffering indirect fire was a decisive advantage. Combine that with the overwhelming reduction of our enemy's fighting strength in the past few days, and there was no reason we couldn't force a total victory within a month.

What were we waiting for?

To those of us on the ground the next step was obvious: press on with the attack. Mount a follow-up push to clear the dead-space between the front lines and Objective #608. Lay on the pressure to keep the initiative in our grasp. The way we saw it, we were at the crux of the conflict and there was no better time to push up the middle and drive it all home. Why not? We could end it now. Deal the final blow. Get rid of the Jaish al-Mahdi once and for all.

But the politicians in the rear disagreed with us completely.

Just a few kilometers away, on the outskirts of town where all of our higher-level officers were still holding out at JSS Sadr City, the evidence of an ongoing battle had long since passed. Just two blocks away from where the Thunder Run had pitched our entire squadron all-in against the Jaish al-Mahdi a week prior, the ravaged streets around the TOC were as calm as any other part of Baghdad. The only evidence of how bad it got was the rubble in the blood-soaked streets leading up to our men on the front. From the sidelines — without a context — the fight could easily be taken as nothing short of a senseless massacre and pushing forward in the face of such a one-sided body count would've seemed egregious in the headlines.

In just nine days, the uprising of Sadr City had already claimed thousands of lives and left behind a catastrophic wake of collateral damage. Regardless, we had barely managed to secure a single quadrant of the city. All we'd done so far was clear out the lower section of the town — a section that was projected to be a cake-walk compared to the real heart of our enemy's holdings. It wasn't until we crossed over Route Gold, two kilometers into enemy lines, that the fight was originally expected to get "hard."

To the growing swarm of anti-war journalists now granted safe passage out to the JSS on the border of town, the ends hadn't justified the means. To them, violence meant that something had gone wrong. It meant there was a gaffe to be uncovered. It meant the next big scandal, and with it, the rest of their career was waiting somewhere around the corner to be uncovered and exploited. It meant there was somebody to blame for the death and destruction. Until that happened, none of this made any sense. The question on their mind was "When is this all going to end?" But for me, my buddies, and everybody else in the Shit, the answer to that question was a no-brainer:

When they're all dead, dying or surrendered.

"Yeah? And how long is that?" they'd probably ask.

As long as it takes.

"So what's your plan?"

Go up the fuckin' middle — and kill them all.

What can I say? We were in the Shit and that's all that mattered. It was us, our enemy, and the fight. It was fighting for as long as it took. It was doctrine, training, and rage all wrapped up into one. "The mission of the Infantry is to close with and kill the enemy by means of fire and maneuver to defeat or capture him, or to repel his assault by fire, close combat, and counterattack." That's what it says in the field manual for an infantry rifle platoon. I know it by heart — it's fuckin' scripture. Giving up wasn't the job. The job was to show up and fight, to fight until the fight was over. After a week and a half of intense, personal combat, that's all we had left to rely on.

But the Generals in the rear could never be so candid — even if they understood and shared our point of view. Condoning that kind of mentality would be political suicide for a commander in the modern military. After all, the days of Patton's Army are long dead. These days Americans are looking for Gandhi to call the shots. So with each morning's sunrise there was a new press release about some non-existent lull in the fighting, and every day we got a corresponding gag-order with an updated set of engagement procedures to keep a lid on our brutality.

"One-Six here," Sergeant O'Brien was on the horn for the first of these calls. "Say again?"

The shock on his face was unmistakable.

"He does realize that's the only thing keeping them from blowin' us all to Hell, right?"

His demeanor with our commander was enough to clear the room of conversation and pique the curiosity of the men.

"Isn't that the whole reason we're out here?" he continued. "So what are we supposed to do? Just sit here and wait for him to get back to us?"

A long transmission came back over the Net as Captain Bradford elaborated on the situation at hand. Sergeant O'Brien was clearly annoyed, but he kept his cool and called our commander back with his receipt of message.

"Alright. Good copy. I'll let them know."

When he hung up the handmic, he took a second to himself to shake off the frustration and don the mask of leadership. After all, no matter how he felt about our orders, he had to spread the word with the voice of authority.

"Listen up!" He announced to the room. "New ROE: we are no longer authorized to engage spotters with cellphones or binoculars unless they are actively walking in rounds on our current position. Make sure everybody knows."

"What?" Sergeant Bitolas protested.

It seemed like a random decree. Only a moron would make it. Indirect fire was our biggest threat and "spotters" play a key role in making that happen. But the more I thought about it, the more it made sense from a political perspective that we'd get a gag order on shooting men with cellphones just because of the suspicion that they might be aiding such a cause.

The average civilian has no idea how indirect fire really works. They just think you drop some mortars in a tube or load a two-foot shell that'll fly off in the general direction of your enemy and kill something bad. Everybody has these iconic mental images of artillery crews shoving shell after shell into the back of a giant Howitzer. That's where all the action is so that's what packs the theaters. But the real magic of the whole thing is how those guys at the gun don't even have to see their enemy when they load up the rounds. Some other dude with a radio has eyes on the target, and he's telling them where to shoot.

Indirect fire is a team effort. That goes for everyone. The most important member of that team is the spotter. Without his eyes on the target, shooting off mortars and artillery is just another waste of precious ammo. If you can stop the spotter, you can stop the rounds. At a minimum, you can make sure they don't actually land right on top of you. That might sound simple enough, but it's a lot harder to do in practice. Harder yet is that you have to get the bastard before sends any corrections to the rear. If you can't get him by the third or forth round, you might as well grab some cover and kiss your ass goodbye — they already know where to shoot.

Our solution was simple. Every time we saw a shady looking bastard talking on his cell phone and leering at us from any kind of vantage point, we took him out. Depending on the situation, we might've fired off a warning shot to make sure he knew that we meant business. But if he didn't put away the phone, we killed him. Period.

Obviously, it sounds a little fucked up to blast a guy for talking on his cell phone — even if it's completely legit. That's probably why the gag order came down from the Colonel in the first place. But any doubts we may have had about the process had long since faded with each new day that we didn't take a single incoming mortar or rocket from afar. Based on what I knew, that made us unique throughout the battle. Telling us to wait until the incoming rounds were "actively walking in" was like telling a cop to wait until the robber is actually shooting at him before pulling out his gun to shoot back. It was absurd. But the real chap in our ass was that we had been sent out to Objective #608 with specific orders to engage and suppress the indirect fire capabilities of the militia so they couldn't lob any more rounds back at our guys. So if we couldn't shoot the spotters, what the hell was the point of assaulting that goddamn schoolhouse to begin with?

"I want to make this clear," Sergeant O'Brien continued. "We are no longer clear to engage anybody we might suspect to be a spotter until the rounds are currently incoming and we are actively taking indirect fire."

I listened to the words but couldn't wrap my head around them in the slightest

"You've got to be kidding me," Sergeant Moore said. "Let me guess: we have to call that shit up, too? Right?"

"Yep. We clear it with Bull-Six and he clears it with the Colonel."

"—and meanwhile we just sit here and take it up the ass?"

"Those are the orders. Make sure everybody knows."

"How does that even make any fucking sense?" Sergeant Benjamin said. "That motherfucker's supposed to positively identify a spotter from back in the War Room? Hey I've got an idea: why don't we just call this shit up to the Pentagon and see what they say?"

"Yeah I know," Sergeant O'Brien said. "I brought all that up. It's bullshit."

"And what did Captain Bradford say?"

"He explained the new engagement procedures, as he was ordered, and wanted me to make sure everybody was aware of the change. Then he told us to keep up the good work and make sure we continue to call up targets as we see fit, in accordance with the ROE."

"So, that's it?" Sergeant Benjamin asked.

"That's it. Make sure everybody knows."

"You hear that, Ludwig?" Sergeant Moore shouted over to me on the gun. "What are you gonna' do?"

"If we take rounds and I see a spotter," I glanced back at him with a snarl. "I'm gonna' call it up and wait for approval. Otherwise, I hold my fire."

I wasn't stupid enough to mutter what I was thinking, but I wasn't on board with the orders in any case. We were out there on our own. Nobody was coming to the rescue, nobody would be trooping our line to keep our act in shape, and nobody else's lives were at stake. I'm not saying that I was out there to break the law. We weren't in the slightest operating under pressure to violate the Rules of Engagement. But I'll admit that after everything we had been through, I also didn't give a damn. Knowing about the official change did squat to effect my discrimination of targets. After all, who the hell would know the difference if we called it up or not? We hadn't called up shit since I set up my position in that window. To the guys back at the rear it wouldn't look any different from the days before, and I knew from experience they'd just say "no" regardless. There was only one way out of this alive and I wasn't going to settle for anything less.

We weren't the only unit in the fight, we were just uniquely poised to ignore the command if it really came down to a life or death scenario. Everybody else was still subject to the immeasurable scrutiny of modern warfare. Their adherence to that order marked the first step backwards on our road to victory. We could hear it unfolding over the radios, in the skies, and out on the ground all around us: returning fire was becoming a case-by-case luxury. Everyday engagements were being made into examples of excessive force. IED strikes were becoming more and more common. Even the Apaches, having done their part to keep the militia in hiding for so long, were going entire missions without firing a single shot.

Big Brother was out there, watching us with his UAVs and spreading his gospel through the radios. It took the Jaish al-Mahdi all of twelve hours to adapt to our new Rules of Engagement, and for the first time in days mortars could once again be heard pounding away on our buddies. We had lost the initiative, only this time it was our own commanders who were to blame. They gave it up freely to the enemy by confusing politics with the mission, thrusting us once again at the mercy of our enemy when we had every reason, every right, and every desire to win.

It was late one night when the seeds of insurrection took root among the ranks of the men and began to grow out of control, until they spread across the battlefield and poisoned every aspect of the battle. Long past were the days of talking shit about our orders because of our obligation to follow through. None of these events, however, came close to rivaling the most famous act of insubordination, which was broadcast across the entire city for anyone listening in to hear.

During another late-night convoy to clear the route up to Outpost Gumby a large IED went off. It effectively disabled one of the vehicles and forced the entire column to a halt. Capitalizing on the situation, the militia was quick to envelope the entire element. After the second or third RPG of their ambush, the Apaches flew in to the rescue.

"Sadr-City-Six, this is Skyhawk-Two-Three." We picked up their call to the Colonel from our forward position. "I have eyes on seven military aged males engaging your men from a rooftop due west of the schoolhouse. Request permission to engage."

"Roger." The Colonel replied. "Hold your fire. Over."

Those of us listening in were dumbfounded by this response. So was the pilot. Another flood of gunfire rang out through the streets until a fifth RPG marked the end of the latest volley. By the faint sounds of return fire, it was clear that the convoy was vastly outnumbered.

"Uhh... Sadr-City-Six," the pilot continued. "I say again: I have a positive ID on multiple enemy targets. They are actively engaging a nearby friendly convoy with small-arms fire and rocket propelled grenades. I have them zeroed in with a clear shot at the target.... What's your problem?"

His voice rang out like a challenge to the gods.

"Skyhawk-Two-Three this is Sadr-City-Six," the Colonel replied, "I say again: you are not clear to engage. There is too great of a risk for inflicting collateral damage on the surrounding area. You are to hold your fire until I give the go ahead. Over."

With an earthshaking shudder, one of the Apaches raked over the schoolhouse. He was buzzing right over our heads with his throttle jammed to the max in order to minimize the risk of getting hit with an RPG. It was the basic strafing configuration, with the gunner at the floorboards while the wingman stays up high to pull a bird's-eye-view on the target, but it only works for a short amount of time. After that they'd be rolling the dice.

"Hey, Sadr-City-Six this is Skyhawk-Two-Three." The pilot snapped back. "I'm not going to sit around here and wait for you to get the warm-fuzzies about putting some rounds down on-target. We have eyes-on a convoy of American soldiers who are decisively engaged by a number of hostile enemy combatants. My gunner has a clear shot at the target and we are weapons-hot. All I need to know from you is if the engagement area has been cleared of ground forces so I can light these guys up. I say again: Am I clear to engage?"

"Skyhawk-Two-Three, this is Sadr-City-Six. You are not clear to engage." The voice on the radio drew the phrase out to make it painfully clear that our man in the sky was well out of line. "If you open fire, I will not only consider it a violation of the ROE, but as disobeying the direct and lawful orders of a commanding officer. You are to stand down and maintain visual reconnaissance on the objective, but under no circumstance will you open fire without my express permission to do so. Over."

A volley of fire rang out at the engagement site as the chopper buzzed by for another shot. He called the Colonel back, this time clearly fed up with the situation.

"Hey, Sadr-City-Six... What's your rank?"

I glanced over at Wagner. His eyes were practically falling out of their sockets and his jaw was agape in shock. In my three years of service I had never heard such a blatant lack of disrespect on such a wide scale with such a massive audience.

"I am a Colonel in the United States Army," the Colonel snapped back. "And I am in command of this mission!"

I chuckled at the phrase — people didn't say that shit in real life.

"Oh, is that right?!" The pilot replied. "Well I've got another full-bird Colonel and two Majors up here who say that you're not! Now, we have eyes-on hostile forces, engaging American soldiers with a clear line-of-sight. One of my pilots is now taking fire from the men on the ground. This is a clear-cut case of hostile intent. Break.—"

The Colonel cut him off before he could continue.

"Skyhawk-Two-Three this is Sadr-City-Six, I say again: You will hold your fire and maintain overwatch on the objective."

Another string of rounds echoed through the streets. Out of the window, I saw a stream of tracers flying high into the sky as the insurgents took their shots at the low-flying pilot. The ambush still raged down below, where a small group of vehicles were fighting tooth-and-claw to make it through the night. I wondered if they were also listening to the exchange and what that must've been like for them to hear. As much as I agreed with the pilot and I wanted him to act, I couldn't believe how sideways that whole conversation had swerved. It was poor form by any standard.

"Sadr-City-Six, this is Skyhawk-Two-Three." The helicopter made another pass overhead and another burst rang out into the sky. "I'm not here to be a fuckin' UAV. I'm an Apache pilot with the most advanced weapon system on this entire battlefield. If you're not gonna' let me do my job, I'm returning to base."

"Skyhawk-Two-Three, you are to remain on-station until I say otherwise! Break—"

"Negative, Sadr-City-Six." This time the pilot cut him off and carried on with his call. "One of my birds has just taken extensive battle damage, it is in need of repairs and we are almost out of fuel. I am returning to base. If you have a problem with that, I invite you to bring it up with my commander. Skyhawk-Two-Three, out!"

For weeks there had been a constant drone in the sky. It was the sound of circling angels with box-fed Vulcan cannons raining down hell onto the earth all around us. But now the air weapons team who had been our skyline protectors since our first day in action were fed up with the bullshit and left us out there on our own. When I was done laughing at the smack-down, I realized what it meant to lose our only real backup with teeth in the fight. As the pilots turned tail to fly home, Captain Bradford jumped on the net for some final words.

"Skyhawk-Two-Three, this is Bull-Six..."

"Hey, Bull-Six! This is Skyhawk-Two-Three." The pilot responded like he was greeting an old friend.

"Hey, I wanted to thank you guys for all the help. You make a huge difference down here on the ground. Seriously, thanks. And good luck patching up that bird. I hope you guys make it back in one piece."

I listened to the transmission, wondering why the hell Captain Bradford wasn't the commander making the call. I prayed to God those guys up in the sky would stick around just for him. I mean, they were bailing on us and he was saying *thank you*. That kind of respect is the sign of a real leader — not just some asshole with a badge and a voice of authority over the radio. He knew it. And he knew the only way to get those guys to stick their necks out for the likes of us to was give them the recognition they were due. Nobody on the ground was as important as those officers and their guns.

"Don't even worry about it, Bull-Six." I could hear the remorse in the pilot's voice as he faced the men he was leaving behind. "We'll be okay. Listen, you tell your boys down there that they're doin' a damn fine job."

"Hey, they can hear you Skyhawk-Two-Three, but I'll spread the word."

"Alright. Good to hear. I'm gonna' go see what I can do about this bullshit. You can bet your ass that I'll be right back out here as soon as I can. Keep up the good work."

"This is Bull-Six. Good copy. Thanks again."

"Skyhawk-Two-Three. Out."

That was the end of it. We were all alone now. Just us and the Jaish al-Mahdi, with the thin line of law wedging us farther and farther between a rock and hard place. And if the stage played out as it had been doing for days, we'd be fucked five ways from Sunday. We had not only lost the initiative but also everything that had given us a leg up on our enemy. If they hit us now there was no telling how it would all pan out. That was my fleeting thought as I drifted off to sleep that night. Something deep inside had changed, and all my confidence disappeared.

I don't know what it was that I was dreaming about or what it was that woke me up; all I remember is the vivid, shattering jolt of reality, followed by an instant blast of terror.

Where's my weapon?!

It was the first thought in my mind. I reached for my pile of gear and tore it apart in the darkness.

My gun! My mind screamed out. *Where the fuck is it?!*

It was nowhere to be found, and some part of me knew that I wasn't going to find it, but that didn't stop me from groping frantically for something else to fill in for its role. I shuffled through my gear three times before I noticed a faint glint on the shiny metal blade of my bayonet. I lunged for the handle and pulled it in close, hugging it like a teddy-bear. It was the only thing I could find, but it was enough. I laid my head back down on the hard tile floor and waited intently for whatever was coming. Slowly, I turned onto my side so I was facing the door and, with some shifts of weight, I readied myself to spring up at whatever was coming and kill it with my own two hands. Every muscle in my body was frozen solid. My heart was pounding.

Come on, Ludwig, I drilled myself for answers. *Where the fuck are you?*

I had no idea.

Keeping my mind on the door, I scanned the room for some comforting detail, but there was nothing to be found. The only light was a dim green glow from a dying chem-light in the corner and the window above my head that barely cast a shadow on the wall. The floor was littered with unconscious bodies and I was at a loss to recognize a single one. As the shock of waking up in such a hurry wore off, my first truly conscious realization came to mind: I was cold — very cold. It felt like I'd been shivering for hours. When I tried to figure out why, I realized the night air had taken with it the sweltering heat of the day and the tile floor — once so invitingly cool — had leached the warmth from out of my veins.

Where am I?!

I drilled myself again, this time awake enough to have answers.

I was at Outpost Gumby.

Where's my gun?! — At the firing position in the window...

Who's on guard?! — Either Wagner, Flemming, or Ian...

Why am I awake?! — Something is wrong...

I took a deep breath and gathered my senses.

"No matter what," I whispered to myself. "You're gonna' die fighting."

A commotion gathered in the courtyard outside the window. As a series of whispers and some shouts of authority cut through the cold air, I knew that something was wrong. The rustling of footsteps and the sound of shifting equipment had pushed me to the razor's edge.

"Sergeant Moore!" I heard Sergeant O'Brien whisper loudly through the halls.

From there I made out the words "breach" and "secure" with some garbled instructions about our "perimeter."

Oh God...

I squeezed my bayonet and glued my eyes to the door.

What the fuck is going on?

The idea crossed my mind that some militia fighters might've worked their way into the compound and that our perimeter was breached, but I shoved the idea out of my mind as soon as it formed. If that was the case, somebody would've already fired off a shot. The next thought to cross my mind was that we were conducting some kind of recon or covert attack, but that seemed just as unlikely, since they would've woken everybody up, either to join in on the mission or pull security while they were gone. I looked back around the room and figured that at least half of our strength was still sleeping, which did wonders to calm me down. If it really was that serious, the first order of business would've been rallying the men.

So why am I awake?!

The question hung in my mind. A few moments passed and I couldn't settle on a single reason. All I knew was that something was going down — something serious — but I had no idea what it was.

"Alright, put that down right there," a calm voice directed the action.

The large thud of a box hit the ground and that same voice carried on with the instruction. After about a half-dozen impacts, the instructions changed.

"How many are left out there?" the voice continued.

"Just a few more, Sarn't."

"Alright. Put those MREs up with the rest of the chow. The ammo goes in the room with the gun. Put the water in the hall."

"Roger, Sarn't."

I let go of my knife and drew in a deep breath of relief.

"It was just a detail," I whispered, trying desperately to reassure myself. "Just a detail."

I don't even remember what happened next. The world went black and I fell back down to the earth. I don't even know if I fell back asleep. If I did, I couldn't have been out for very long. The next thing I remember was another terrifying rush — this one far more intense than the last. Whatever it was, this time I had a damn good reason to be scared.

Where am I?!

My mind raced through the routine.

I'm at Outpost Gumby, I told myself again in silence.

Where's my gun?! — At the firing position in the window...

Who's on guard?! — Wagner, Flemming or Ian...

Why am I awake?!

There was a lasting moment of silence as I struggled to listen in. A few seconds later, a bone-chilling cry sounded out into the night.

"Incoming!!!"

The phrase barely made it into my groggy skull before the distant sound of a muffled explosion echoed through the halls. It was relatively faint compared to the IEDs we were used to hearing, but the nature of the explosion was what I feared — far more than a wayward bomb on some back-alley in Sadr City. It was a mortar, and it had landed close enough to rattle my cage for sure. The next one landed even closer than that. The third hit closer still.

All I could think was, *it's finally happening.*

I was shivering from the cold and something was clawing at my mind. It was a paralyzing fear that I can't even explain. I lay there staring at the ceiling and waiting to die. The rounds walked in, one after another, and I didn't know what to do. In the silent pauses between explosions, I could hear the radios blaring through the halls of Outpost Gumby. The company searched for the spotters, but there was little hope that we could find them in time.

Another round came in.

Another call on the radio.

The building shook.

"Fuck me!" Somebody whispered in the dark. "That was close!"

Every one of us was wide awake by then. We all knew that if one of those rounds hit the ceiling over our heads, there was a good chance we'd get killed in the blast.

A moment passed before another round went off, kicking up the dust in the room.

"Fucking Iraqi construction," somebody else murmured. "If that thing hits, we're all going to die."

"Shut the fuck up!" Another voice spoke up with authority.

Another round came in. Then another. Each landed closer to our position as some spotter out in the city barked up corrections to his boys.

"Just a few more rounds and they'll be right on top of us," yet another person whispered.

"Everybody shut the fuck up, put your gear on, and stay the fuck down!"

I didn't bother with the gear. If that concrete roof caved in, body armor wasn't going to do shit. The room fell back into a cryptic silence during a pause in the volley as we waited for the next set of rounds. When it came, I almost cried. Each round was now crisp and clear.

"They're almost on top of us!" The radio crackled.

Another round went off.

"Somebody find that fuckin' spotter!" First Sergeant's voice was easy to pick out through the distant hand mic.

Nobody in the schoolhouse spoke another word.

Another round landed.

"Target spotted!" A voice on the radio crackled.

A .50 cal machine-gun let out a long burst of rounds. The shock wave pounded through the schoolhouse like a jackhammer — and another round came in.

"Goddammit! Hit him again!"

Another chain of .50 cal rounds rang out.

"Again!!!"

The final volley of machine-gun fire was a broken set of ten to fifteen round bursts. When it was over, the battlefield froze. Nobody moved a muscle. The tension in the room wrapped around my neck like a noose. Every one of us waited for that final round — that final blast. We clenched our butt-holes for the direct hit. The "Bingo." The one round that brings with it a flood of Armageddon.

"Fire for effect." It was a phrase we all knew well. It's the code-word for throwing mortars in the tube until there's nothing left of the target. They were close enough, too. But the rounds never came. Seconds passed. Then minutes. It must've been an hour before my heart stopped racing. In those first few minutes, I strained my ears to overhear the ongoing radio transmissions as our leaders assessed the damage and checked our ranks for emergent casualties. After Sergeant O'Brien made his rounds and got a count of his men he called it up to Captain Bradford.

"Yeah, Bull-Six this is One-Seven. We're up. Everything is good here. No hits... Roger... Yeah... Roger. One-Seven out."

I could hear Ian's voice flag him down through the halls. *"What's up, Sarn't? Where'd they hit?"*

"3rd Platoon. They were gunning for one of our Strykers out on the street."

"Everybody okay?"

"Yeah. Everybody's fine — it was just closer than shit."

I tried to go back to sleep, but I couldn't muster up the courage. I couldn't believe that another volley wasn't coming or that they didn't have a second spotter on standby to pick up where his predecessor had left off. At a minimum, there was a mortar tube that had been zeroed in to within a hundred meters of our position, which might as well have been a loaded gun at my face. That was the most terrifying night of my life.

The next morning I woke up for another run on the gun, but it was an empty gesture. That was our first day without a single hostile round — in or out — and it wasn't very long before the civilians took to the streets and carried on with the daily grind. While we took this as a sign that nothing was going to happen that day, the mosques still preached on with their sermons and cries for the local people to rise up.

"They are saying," Marshall translated. "Allah himself is watching our sin."

"So much for separation of church and state," Flemming chuckled.

"Now they are saying," Marshall continued. "That by allowing this... eh... your infection... to be staying here... where we are, we are helping evil and... Allah will be forgetting them and... eh... Hell is wait on them."

The message was in vain. Nobody came. It was the first true sign that we had practically won: when God's very own mortal voice on Earth couldn't muster them up for a fight.

"You know what that means?" Ian looked at me with a smile.

"What?"

"They're more afraid of us than Hell."

It was a comforting thought. Back in the rear, the prisoners were telling our intelligence officers everything they could think of. They were terrified of what we'd become — of what they'd stirred up and we had brought to bear.

"We never thought you'd fight like this," one of them told our interrogator.

"Like what?" she asked.

"Like us."

When I heard the story, I laughed. He was right. Dead on the money. Fighting like we're actually in a war. Fighting like there's something at stake. Fighting like we actually want to survive. Actually fighting — just like them. Not driving around in circles for the cameras. Not only did we fight like them, we were starting to live like them too. In the face of all the disease, the dirt, and the shit, we hadn't showered or shaved for days. Our stench was horrible. I couldn't even notice the smell of my own leaking asshole — it had been masked by a cocktail of everybody else's. Our uniforms had wilted down to t-shirts, vests, and helmets. Our faces were grown over with scraggly beards. Hell, some of our guys were walking around in sandals and workout shorts and nobody gave a damn.

Discipline, in the uniform sense, was a far cry away. Our military bearing had become nothing but sludge. Rank was all we had left — and that was just a matter of knowing who was making the calls. We had been left to our own devices and cut off from the rest of the world. On more than one occasion, I mistook the lot of us for a well armed band of renegades. We were the antithesis of everything a modern commander admires and we were proud of it. Our thick layer of grime was proof of who we were, where we had been, and the things we'd done. We wore it as a badge: the blood, the sweat, and the filth.

After the second straight day of silence, our senior officers got the balls to come out front and troop the line. It was finally time for the age-old cock-shake and waggle. It was time for the "atta'-boys" and a mock Q&A. It was time for the Colonel to come out and feel like part of the fight — which meant the fight was officially over and everything we had earned in the way of "common sense liberties" was about to die with it.

"It's time for you grimy bastards to shave those mugs," Sergeant O'Brien said with a smirk. "Grab yourself some razors and get to work."

He pointed out the supplies in the hall: a giant pile of UNICEF care packages loaded with single-serving hygiene kits. They had been carted in through the night with the expectation that we needed supplies to get back to inspection standard before the Colonel would arrive.

"You know," I reached in the box and grabbed a bag. "It's a bad day when the Army sends us UNICEF care packages instead of letting us go get our own goddamned hygiene equipment."

"Yeah. You'd think we'd at least get more than one refit back to the rear," Gonzo said.

"Hey!" Sergeant O'Brien shouted. "Cut the shit! You got your refit six days ago, remember?!"

I laughed. "Yeah, Sarn't. I remember."

"I don't remember shit!" Gonzo pulled out his knife and sliced open the plastic wrapping. "My ass was passed the fuck out the whole time!"

"Sarn't," Wagner was in the corner, double checking his kit. "Where the hell is the shaving cream?"

"What shaving cream?" Sergeant O'Brien laughed.

"They don't have shaving cream?" I asked Wagner.

"No man! And check out these razors!"

He held up a plastic handle with a single bladed face and shook his head with disapproval.

"Man, there is no way in hell I'm scraping that shit across my face," Gonzo said.

On the far side of the room, Ian was splashing his face with water and getting ready to dive right in.

"Come on guys!" he shouted with a crazy look in his eyes. "It can't be that bad!"

"I don't know man." I walked over to a box and readied myself for the project.

Ian held up the razor, dragged it right across his face, and let out a blood-curdling scream. "Oh my God!" He blew off the razor for another go, screaming with every swipe. Tears swelled up in his eyes as he worked.

Now that it was my turn, I scrubbed my face with a handful of water to clean off as much grime as I could. When I looked at the razor in detail, I was even less amused by the sight of it. Not only was it a bad razor by design, but the craftsmanship was even worse. Of the five razors in the package, three of them had poorly seated blades and all of them were chipped and dull.

"Here we go," I laughed.

Ian screamed again as he scraped another patch of skin. I steadied the razor on my face and resolved to take it in tiny scrapes instead of streaking it across my face. With the first yank, I was convinced I'd sliced off a patch of skin. I pressed it down, dragged it a half-inch, and it carved right in.

"Holy shit!" I shouted. "Who's got a mirror?"

Everybody looked at me like I had a dick growing out of my forehead.

"Are you kidding me?" Gonzo said.

"Fuck, man! I think I just sliced off a chunk of my face!"

He looked over and laughed. "No, man. You're good."

"For real!"

I dabbed over the spot with my finger, but there wasn't any blood.

"Yeah, you're fine."

"Fuck, man."

I reached up for another swipe and took a deep breath. I pulled through the burn. It literally felt like I was tearing skin off my face — like I was going to look down at the razor and find a four-inch chunk of flesh dangling off it. By the third swipe, tears poured down my face.

"This is unbelievable!" I cried out.

It was the most barbaric attempt at hygiene I have ever witnessed — like a ritual of some masochistic satanic cult, in fact.

"Squad leaders!" Sergeant O'Brien shouted.

They filed in and laughed at us before Sergeant O'Brien cut them off.

"Sure. Laugh now, but you're next. I want everybody with clean shave and back in uniform."

"What's up with the care packages?" Sergeant Benjamin asked.

"The Colonel is coming out to troop the line and he's supposed to be bringin' some reporter bitch along with him. But before he gets here, we need to clean this place up."

"So what?" Sergeant Moore said. "We gonna' straighten up these boxes n'shit? I mean, the battlements are all straight. What else do we need to do?"

"No, brother. I mean the Colonel wants it *clean*."

They gazed back at him, bewildered by the news.

"Now, personally I don't see what the problem is but you know fuckin' brass. There's no such thing as common sense."

"What does he expect?"

"Apparently, we're supposed to sweep and mop the floors — and they want everything dusted down, too."

"What?" Sergeant Moore's jaw dropped.

"Yeah, I know. Listen, I don't care what the fuck he said, we're not mopping the floor. Still, we've got to sweep down the stairs, clean up all these shell casings, and pack away all the trash. They even shipped out some cleaning supplies for us to get all this done. Also — like I said — the uniforms need to go back on."

On cue, a soldier walked past the door behind him wearing body armor and a pair of boxers, to which he simply threw up a gesture and got on with the briefing.

"You bet your ass that shit isn't going to fly when the Colonel shows up. And no more of this t-shirt and vest bullshit either. Everybody on guard needs to be in full kit and uniform. Blouses go back on. I want boots laced up and pants tucked in all the way. As for those of us who are on a rest cycle, he wants everybody wearing body armor at all times... even in here."

"—but this is the break room!"

"I know. Still, everybody suits up — at least until he's gone."

"What about the guys who are sleeping?"

"Oh, that's another thing: I want everybody awake, starting now."

"What?"

"Yeah. Apparently the Colonel went out to some other patrol base on the line or some shit and lit them up for sleeping. I want everybody awake until he's gone."

"And how long will that be?"

"I don't know. But he should be showing up in a couple of hours so we've got some time to get everything straight. Remember: we've got to get everything as close to inspection standard as possible. I don't feel like getting my ass chewed because we actually look like we're earning our paycheck."

As soon as we finished shaving, we got to work getting ready for the parade. Every room was cleared out and cleaned. Empty boxes were filled to the brim with casings and the bags of trash were hidden in the closet. We even squared away the desks in the empty classrooms in case he went exploring. Every one of the guard posts doubled up on manpower and we even added one or two extra men just for the shit of it. Technically, we were padding our numbers back up to regulation strength, but the real reason we put so many people on guard was that nobody wanted to hear the man talk.

The few of us who hadn't been assigned to some extra duty were designated to be his audience and briefed on the conduct expected. Our job was basically to sit there, shut up, and nod. In absolutely no case were we to talk about the fighting in specifics. When he got to asking questions — which officers always end up doing — we were ordered to stick to a specific set of topics. It's not an unusual thing to expect during one of these meet-and-greet shenanigans, but I had no idea what we were supposed to talk about if we weren't allowed to bring up the fight. What else was there to say? Was I supposed to ask him about my life insurance or something?

Of course, it was hours before he actually showed up and by the time it happened, the reporter was nowhere to be seen. One of the Colonel's entourage explained to us in passing that nobody was too keen on having some hot reporter out there in the Shit, so she had been "voluntold" to stay behind. After all, Outpost Gumby wasn't exactly the kind of place he wanted plastered all over the nightly news.

Fair enough.

When it came down to it, the inspection was more of a pep-talk. At first, he stuck to praising us for what we'd done. Then, as though we weren't the ones doing it, he briefed us on the play-by-play of what happened.

"You see," he said. "We pushed you guys up here and had you take this objective because they were using it as a hot-spot for indirect fire-missions on the whole city."

We nodded with blank faces as the speech dragged on.

"And then — men — they threw everything they had at you."

We know, I wanted to bark at him. But I shut up and listened like a good little boy.

In my mind, men like him were a false idol — a mockery of a god. As far as I was concerned, somebody like Captain Bradford or Sergeant O'Brien should've been running the whole goddamned war. After all, they were up front and center. They knew exactly what needed to be done.

This guy? He was a crock. A POG. A pussy. He was the kind of officer that expects somebody to mop down the floors of a commandeered outpost for the sake of discipline. The kind of guy who tells the men on the line that they're not allowed to shoot their enemy. For a while I wondered if we were even fighting the same war. I just swallowed his bullshit whole because that's all I could do. But when he finally got to his point, it was the final straw.

"And you know what?" He smiled. "You did it. You accomplished the mission. You guys came out here and put a stop to their rocket attacks on the Green Zone. They're safe now — because of you. Good job!"

It was unbelievable. Did he have any idea who he was talking to? Any idea at all? We'd been out in the Shit for eight goddamn months. We'd been sucking in these streets every goddamn day. We'd gone at it a hundred fucking times with the Jaish al-Mahdi and everything had finally come to a head. We worked our asses off. We ground ourselves down into dust. We pushed those bastards out of Ur, Adhamiya, and New Baghdad. We spent the better days of our youth hawking the leftovers of our soul on the corner of Miller and Pabst, and I'd be damned if all that was in the name of some non-combat fuckwads in the Green

Zone. Seriously, who gave a shit about some POGs in the rear? They could go fuck themselves — them and their "Salsa Tuesdays" at the on-post nightclub. I wouldn't have given a half-gallon of piss for the sake of their security. The way I saw it, in fact, they could've used a reminder that we were actually in a war.

No, we were there because the city was literally up in arms. We were there because the world was going to shit. We were there because half of the Iraqi Army in Baghdad had deserted their ranks and the militia was going nuts. We were there because of almost three million people who were living in fear for their lives and ruled by an illegitimate tyrant with his own private army. We were there because men like him had settled for a ceasefire the last time the Jaish al-Mahdi was on the verge of destruction, and after five years of defunct bullshit it was our job to make it right.

For Christ's sake, the uprising of Sadr City wasn't about the *Green Zone.* All this killing wasn't for the sake of some Morale Welfare and Recreation Center fifteen miles away. Nobody in the Shit gave a damn about the rear — nobody but the politicians. And now this fucker had the nerve to come all the way out here and tell us "good job" with a pat on the back like he knew what the fuck it was all about?

Sure, I knew that's why the orders were officially cut — and it was bullshit. He should've fucking lied. He could've told us anything but the truth. I would've cheered like a champion if he had told me the whole battle was fought because some stripper in Reno thought it would be a good idea — better that than discover everything we had been through was for the sake of the status quo. That the reason we lost a brother, killed so many people, and spent weeks in the Shit was because some pussies sending e-mails back in the safest district in Baghdad were finally getting hit with something hard. That we had to wait four days for air support and almost a week for a goddamn tank because it wasn't a big deal until the Green Zone was hit. But he kept going. He kept singing our praises with a long-winded speech. He had his half-facts and assumptions all lined out in play so he could hear himself talk and hang out with *the Men* — if only we gave a shit.

"Alright," he finished up his speech and put his fists on his hips like some kind of sailor from a cartoon. "Are there any questions for me?"

No, there weren't. There was nothing but a quiet room and judging eyes. Nothing but a room full of soldiers too familiar with the drill. Nothing but bit tongues and sealed jaws – and I couldn't let that stand.

"Yeah," I raised my hand.

I knew immediately that everybody's attention had turned to me. I could feel the heat coming from every direction. I was breaking the most fundamental rule of talking to a big-wig and they all knew I wasn't about to tread through the flower patch with a gentle touch.

Oh well.

The way I figured, he shouldn't have asked the question if he didn't want to hear an answer. For a second he was stunned by the candor, but he quickly recovered to hear what I had to say.

"Go ahead."

"When are we driving north?" I asked.

"What?"

"North, sir." I pointed out the window towards the heart of the city.

I took care to stay as chipper as possible while I played a dangerous game with the ever-looming voice of the man upstairs.

"Oh," he awkwardly chuckled. "You mean deeper into the city?"

"Yes sir!"

I eked out a motivated smile. To those who knew me it wasn't much of a disguise.

"Well, that's a complicated question to answer." He stumbled over his words, careful not to stray into territory unbecoming of a politician. "You see, uh, we're actually working out a plan with the Iraqi Army to take over the assault as part of a greater, large-scale ceasefire agreement with the militia."

Of course, I thought.

Trying desperately to keep my eyes from rolling I stared right back at him and answered with a chipper jab. "But we're winning, sir."

"Right..."

It was obvious that I was flirting with fire, but as far as I could tell, I was just asking what was on everybody's mind. I honestly wanted an answer, too. Ceasefire? That didn't make any sense.

Up the fuckin' middle.

After a few seconds he geared up to give me an answer.

"Well the truth is," he replied, "we've managed to wipe out just about every one of their special weapons teams. On top of that, we've inflicted some very substantial casualties on their conventional forces. So yes, we are definitely winning, but now it's time to talk about a ceasefire. We want to put an end to the violence."

There was a brief moment where I simply stared at him and considered my next move. Before I opened my mouth again to speak, he gave me an out.

"Does that answer your question?"

The tension in the room eased a bit as everybody expected me to drop the issue but he hadn't answered my question at all. I'd be damned if I was just going to drop it; this was my only chance to hear it from the horse's mouth.

"Sort of, sir."

I knew my words hit the mark when the man sitting next to me on the sofa cleared his throat and shifted his weight away from the general direction of an impending ass-chewing. In my defense, I was just being honest. The Colonel had just regurgitated what I already knew — granted, with far better access to the facts at hand. But we were winning. We had victory in our grasp. We had the militia in our clutches. We were writing the history about their end of days. So what I wanted to understand was why we were quitting when we should've been pressing home with the attack. I straightened my back and leaned forward, careful to maintain as much tact and respect as possible as I did my best to drive a hot iron into his side.

"It just feels like we should be demanding a surrender, sir — and not a ceasefire."

There was more at stake than a simple issue of semantics. It was the very heart of what I couldn't stand about the war. By every standard,

Muktada al-Sadr was a criminal and his organization was a legitimate and fatal threat to the success of the entire occupation.

Ceasefire?

A ceasefire is what you declare when you're tired of fighting and elect to go your separate ways. When you leave dust to dust and move on from the madness. A ceasefire is not a solution. It's not even an answer. It's just a two-way white-flag. And from what I could tell, there was only one motherfucker in that whole room who was the kind of man to call it a truce and walk away — so it makes sense that he didn't see the difference.

"Well that's... That's what it is..." He stumbled on. "A ceasefire. Right now we're just focusing on putting an end to the fighting, alright?" Without a single pause to hear whatever else I'd come up with, he turned to the rest of our group. "Any other questions?"

I felt the heat brush off me as everybody's eyes turned on to my successor.

"Yes, sir!" Gonzo raised his hand.

"Specialist... *Gonzales?*" The Colonel shamelessly read the name of his tag before glancing up to meet him eye-to-eye.

"When is our next refit comin' up, sir?"

I did my best to stifle my laugh along with everybody else in the room. If we weren't allowed to talk about the fighting we might as well bring up the basic necessities of a soldier. The fact was that no matter where he looked, the Colonel wasn't going to get any easy questions from the likes of us.

"Well," he sighed. "We're working on that. As soon as we can work something out we'll get you back to the rear. Alright? In the mean time, you just hang in there. If you think it's bad out here, we've got some guys back in the rear who haven't showered in days. Hell, I haven't even set foot on a FOB, myself, in about a week — so you're not alone."

At that, I could feel my jaw fall agape. Resentment oozed out of the pores of the men to either side of me. It was like the whole room had been shanked with a rusty blade.

A week?

We hadn't seen a FOB in month and a half. But Gonzo wasn't asking about a FOB, he was asking when we'd get back to our own outpost for a full night's rest and a cold shower. He was wondering when we'd get some hot chow that hadn't been heated by the radiant power of the sun. He was asking when we'd get to take a load off and not get shot at for a day.

Before Gonzo could get in a reply, the Colonel cut him off and looked around for another hand. Either way, that's when our NCOs stepped in to hush the crowd. The interview was over. We'd blown our wad with a two-hit knock-out and there was nothing left to be said and the Colonel wasn't winning any points with the likes of us.

"Alright then!" He glued a smile on his face. "Keep it up, men! You're doing great things!"

The words were as hollow as the man. He just said them as a catch-phrase. They had no meaning or conviction. They were nothing more than an idle force of habit. An insult to the things we'd accomplished. A strike at our pride.

Two days later Outpost Gumby was abandoned.

- Chapter Ten -
Operation "Gold Wall"

According to the world, the first official ceasefire of the 2008 uprising of Sadr City stood on its own from the 1st to the 5th of April. If you asked the leaders of the Jaish al-Mahdi, they'd tell you that a strict gag order on violent activity was issued out of respect for the peace. Our commanders declared it to be a mutual agreement made in good faith on both sides of the line. To the media, there were no hostilities to report.

I can tell you right now that was all a load of shit.

Hardly a day went by during that week of "non-violent solutions" — much of which we had spent fighting at Outpost Gumby — that our men on the ground didn't endure some kind of deliberate attack from an organized insurgent militia still determined to carry on with the fight. Of course the militia decried these attacks as "renegade criminals" but we knew exactly what was going on. They were taking advantage of us — again. As our leaders met with theirs to discuss the intricacies of a bogus arrangement, the militia foot soldiers continued the battle and got free hits in whenever they could. It was kindergarten level shit that a boy's supposed to learn how to deal with on the playground, yet somehow our ranking commanders were still caught up with the politics.

From down on the line, these attacks were no different from any other militia sanctioned activity. They were carried out by the same men, with the same weapons, in the same neighborhoods, using the same tactics and logistical support as any others that had come before. It wasn't until a year later, from the comfort of my own home, that I read about the short-lived ceasefire in the official report and I confronted the notion that somebody actually believed it was a *thing*. Out there on the ground, there was never an end to the fighting; it was just a short lull while our command took lunch

On the 5th of April, Bull Company packed up our camp in a single day and drove back to Route Florida where we rejoined the rest of our squadron just in time for the next wave of shit to kick off. Despite all of our efforts and sacrifices over the past week, the frontline hadn't moved an inch since the fateful afternoon of the Thunder Run, and there still weren't any plans in the works to push it forward. Now that we were shoulder to shoulder with the rest of our brothers on the battlefield, Bull Company had no choice but to set into a new structure and call it home.

Our new building was quickly dubbed "Patrol Base Bull," which would become ground zero for the next phase of the battle. Our new mission was to work part-time at night as a high-value raid element on targets of opportunity and secure the neighborhoods on either side of Route Florida with daily foot patrols and neighborhood-wide search operations. The overtone of our mission was to hunt down and decapitate the smaller "renegade" forces of the Jaish al-Mahdi while maintaining a low enough profile that our fledgling "ceasefire" would remain in effect. The end-goal of those efforts was to clear a buffer zone between the militia's domain and us without provoking another outbreak of violence.

It took a single day for that plan to go to shit. Around one or two in the morning, on the 6th of April, high-level intelligence verified the existence of an active insurgent group working in the vicinity of our patrol base. Now that we had a bead on their commander's outpost just a few blocks away, a snatch-and-grab raid was put together as quickly as possible. 1st Platoon was the main effort of the operation. We maneuvered onto the objective quickly, but the building was already deserted by the time we got there. We didn't get much out of the raid, but it was clear to all of us that the Jaish al-Mahdi was still an active and aggressive force in the area.

By sunrise, the Iraqi Army's 11th Division, with the rest of 1st Squadron in tow, had formed up to push deeper into Sadr City and establish forward positions in accordance with the terms of the ceasefire. Their goal was to secure some of the remaining indirect firing positions still serving the "renegade" militia as staging areas for ongoing rocket and mortar attacks across half of Baghdad – an operation that fell well within the limits of the ceasefire. But it wasn't long before every militia fighter in the area banded together to attack our advancing troops and kick-start a pitched firefight that lasted well into the night. By the time the mess was over, heavy casualties had been inflicted on both sides of the line and the ceasefire was in shambles.

That morning's engagement was much larger and more prolonged than any other in the past few days. Much longer, in fact, than any one of us could have foreseen. But simply coming into contact was hardly an unforeseen risk of such an operation. The real surprise came when Muktada al-Sadr himself claimed responsibility for the actions of the so-called renegades, and confirmed our suspicions that he had been calling the shots all along. The political hat trick was that he had erroneously declared us to be the aggressors who had allegedly stormed into his territory without cause or consideration for the truce. And according to him, we had betrayed his "noble attempts at peace" with an unprovoked attack – a lie which he knew for a fact everybody listening would be more than happy to believe. So, rallied now behind the flag of vengeance, and bolstered with wide-spread public support, the foot soldiers of the Jaish al-Mahdi began a well-prepared campaign to gain the upper hand using the familiar tactic of 'shock and awe.'

Throughout the day the militia had taken to the streets with the full force of their conventional army. The militia's objective was to envelop the Iraqi division and force them to surrender. At the same time, however, special groups across the entire front had launched a widespread indirect fire operation onto our positions along Route Florida. By the time it was all over, three American and 20 Iraqi soldiers had been killed in action, with 31 wounded casualties ex-filtrated back to the hospital. I have no idea how many of "them" were killed in the fight, but it was obvious that the Jaish al-Mahdi had used the one-way ceasefire to consolidate their efforts and dig in for the long haul. Little did I know, that would be my last night on the front line of the battle for about a month.

On April 7th, a select crew of Bull company soldiers was given special orders from much higher up the chain than anybody expected to detach from our unit and report for duty back at COP #329 in Ur. Our assignment was to use a high-tech observation platform, which each of us had been trained on in the past, and maintain surveillance of militia operations in the northern corner of Sadr City.

As ordered, I gathered up what few things I had and made my way out to the front gate of the patrol base so I could meet up with my compatriots and catch a convoy back to our old home. On the way out I stopped to say goodbye to the few of my buddies who were still awake and I took some time to bitch about my orders. The general consensus was that I'd be back as soon as I could work it. I made a special stop to remind Kaz, Sergeant Lilly, and Staff Sergeant Benjamin that I was still looking forward to our next game of dominoes. We had found the only complete set in the city and I'd be damned if I missed out on some genuine entertainment.

"Well, I guess we'll see you later then," Sergeant Lilly smiled.

"You too, Sarn't."

That's the last thing I remember saying to him before he died. I've wracked my brain for years to uncover that single memory. I don't even know if it's real. I could've easily made it up, but it's all I have: the vivid recollection of him saying goodbye as I walked out the door of Patrol Base Bull to serve my time on the far side of town, running a $4,000,000 video camera. That was the last time I'd ever say goodbye.

The explosion caught everybody by surprise. To this day no one really knows what happened. All we know for sure is that Kaz and Lilly were hanging out by the front door of the building when the blast rang out. Over the years I've only heard parts of the story. Nobody really wants to tell the tale; it's not exactly the kind of thing they like to remember. Little by little, I learned about a danger-close explosion that rocked the entire platoon awake. They came down the stairs to find our buddies gurgling on their own blood, barely hanging on to their lives.

"You wouldn't believe Doc," Ian told me. "He was like a machine. He just got to work doing everything he could. We tried to help him..." His words trailed off as he hung up on the memory. "There was so much blood."

Ian was never the same after that. Nobody was. To this day I can see the cold stare in their eyes when they think back to what happened in that courtyard. A part of them is broken inside and I don't think it can ever be fixed. In a strange way I wish was broken too, if only so I could have been there with my buddies. But since I wasn't there to see it for myself, I did my best to paint the picture of what happened in the wake of anguish that followed. I dug for the answers because I needed to know what happened.

Doc gave me the gritty details from a medical point of view, and told me what it was like to clean up the mess when it was over. Wagner told me step-by-step how they teamed up to track down some stretchers and sprint our buddies out to one of our Strykers. Before either one could get picked up by a helicopter and raced back to the rear, somebody had to drive them out of the no-landing-zone where they'd be at risk of getting hit again. We always knew that would be the case but I don't think anybody ever entertained the idea of how long that would take. Flemming let me know what it was like to call up a medevac for his own guys. That had always been my fear when I was on the radios, knowing every second of delay could be the difference between life and death. He had to live it. The doubt. The fear. The anger.

They all did.

Everybody pitched in. The whole platoon got their hands bloody. When Kaz and Lilly were finally flown out of the city, all of 1st Platoon mounted up on their vehicles and raced over to the hospital back in the Green Zone where they were taken. Our boys died in the air. They didn't even make it back to solid ground. And then some fuck had the stones to give the rest of our platoon some shit for lighting up a pack of smokes right there on the lawn. Some fuck who had no idea that Hell was right across the river. One of the very same fucks we had been fighting so hard to protect in the first place.

"The truck, man..."

I'll never forget Ian's face. It was like he could crawl into that moment and be there again. Like he was torn between worlds.

"Everything inside of it was covered in blood. It was all over the floor and the seats. We had to replace all the pads and trim."

I could see him reliving the moment again and again. He was grasping at straws and vomiting details without sense or connection. To him, it was all at once. It was a flood. Every time he went back to that memory it was to pick up something new and try in vain to put it all in place.

"Everything in the truck was slippery. Like water. Like when you're gutting a fish and there's that slimy blood and shit. And the smell... God it was awful. I'm never going to forget that smell."

I hate myself for being anywhere else when it happened. Not that I could have done anything to change it. Not that anything would be different. But those guys were more than family. They were more than brothers. They were men I was walking through Hell with, who had held my life in their hands and watched over it like their own.

All I could think was that I should have been there to help. I should've been there to see it happen. I should have suffered the memory, if only so the rest of them could have another buddy at the bar whose eyes glaze over and go back to that horrible place in their minds. If only so I could help them carry that moment — because it will never go away. I wish I could've been there because none of them have ever really left. Because I was gone when it mattered most. Because I'm an outsider now, in this fundamental way. Because I was pulling recon duty for some tanks when two of my closest brothers died. That was the one thing I was there to do: keep my buddies alive. It was a burden we all shared. A duty that we all shared. A mission we had all failed.

And I wasn't even there to help.

Just two days later, the rest of the men in Bull Company teamed up with a force from the Iraqi Army to assault into the city and push all the way back up to Route Gold. There would be no respite for those men, my brothers, who had gone back to the rear to find out our buddies were dead. There was no grieving to be had but in revenge. In that respect they were determined to get their share, but no matter how many of those bastards we killed it wouldn't bring back the men we had lost.

Don't get me wrong: I'm not overlooking the fact that for every one of ours who died in that battle, a dozen more of them were killed by the likes of us. But nobody gave a shit about that. When you're in combat, it's about you and your own. The enemy is just a target. Feeling bad about his fate is a luxury afforded only to the victor. Back then, our boys had bigger things to worry about than ten-to-one ratios and the peril of second-guesses. Their next assault was going to bring them right up to the farthest northward position any American had ever held before or during the battle. The only thing on their mind was how to accomplish that mission and make it out of there alive. Everything else was just a distraction.

That morning, on the 9th of April, Bull Company was ordered to escort a barrier emplacement crew from the 4th ID who was going to construct a blocking position for the Iraqi Army out at the intersection of Routes Bravo and Gold. According to the brass, it was high time for the Iraqi Army to start pulling their weight so they could finally claim a victory as their own. Taking over the front line was the best way to make that happen, but that also meant Captain Bradford was going to be forced to take a backseat role and let his Iraqi counterpart call the shots.

Try as he might, Captain Bradford's advice fell on deaf ears until it was too late to turn back. Rather than take advantage of the back-alleys and side-streets leading up to Route Gold, the Iraqi commander insisted on moving the bulk of his light infantry unit across two kilometers of open road, with virtually no support from the heavy weapons and vehicles we had in tow. Needless to say, that hubris was exposed when his men got hit with a number of IEDs and suffered heavy casualties within the first kilometer of the assault.

To my knowledge, that was the first time the Iraqi commander and his men had ever gone face-to-face with the Jaish al-Mahdi on their enemy's own turf. To be frank, they had no idea what they were in for. What we considered to be a day's work in the streets of Sadr City was about to become the hardest fight those men had ever faced. In the height of the operation, the Iraqi commander turned to his men and called for an all-out retreat from the fight. Thankfully, Captain Bradford convinced him to hold his ground and called up our Strykers to fill in the ranks with heavy weapons, and I've been told since then that the sight of our Stryker's driving calmly into the fray with their guns blazing was all it took to rally the spirit of our Iraqi counterparts and keep them fighting to the end. Having beat the streets on my own two feet and felt the pressure of enemy fire for myself, I can speak to the truth in those words.

By midday, a perimeter at the intersection of Routes Bravo and Gold was established. The emplacement effort took all of two hours from start to finish — an amazing feat in the middle of combat. Each segment of the concrete barrier was a little over 5 feet wide and 16 feet tall. They required an up-armored crane and a full crew of workers just to haul them off a heavy equipment transport trailer and stand them upright. Combat engineers had to lay down their weapons and guide each barrier into place by hand. Once a section was in place, an engineer had to climb up an aluminum ladder to the top of the wall and detach the metal hauling chains — all under live fire, without a weapon.

When the wall was complete, Bull Company and their counterparts in the 4th ID fell back to their old front line on Route Florida, and the Iraqi Army stuck around to hold out for the duration. Bull Company's mission was to carry out regular patrols throughout the nearby area and maintain a lifeline out to the Iraqi unit they had left behind, and for the next week they held the line.

I watched this unfold from our reconnaissance platform out at COP #329 back in Ur. For weeks, a horizon of smoke billowed up from the far side of Sadr City as a river of updates flowed in from the front. That far into the battle, the three platoons of Bull Company had been operating largely as individual units with synchronized agendas against vastly larger numbers of militia troops. The establishment of Iraqi troops up on Gold did little to change their fate. It was an easy thing for the Jaish al-Mahdi to skirt around the Iraqi positions and set up shop on our side of the line. By the time our boys could react, it was too late to make a difference. Rocket and mortar strikes had reclaimed their fame in a big way, and there was nothing we could do to stop it.

In those first few days after the blocking position was constructed, 2nd Platoon had moved back to their original firebase from the days of Outpost Gumby. From there, they reacted to militia patrols and attempts to launch rockets onto our positions from the familiar territory of Objective #608. Meanwhile, 1st and 3rd Platoons maintained a steady flow of dismounted operations just north of Patrol Base Bull, escorting an EOD Route Clearance convoy along Route Bravo on a daily basis to rid the road of IEDs and EFPs. They carried on like that for about a week, coming into heavy contact with militia ambushes every step of the way, but nobody was about to complain about their fate.

Up on Route Gold, the Iraqi Army had suffered a relentless onslaught of mortars, small arms fire, RPGs, and sniper attacks, dwindling their number to less than half of their original strength. Unlike us, there wasn't a single piece of modern weaponry among them, and aside from the basic requisition of water, MREs, and bullets, they had nothing to go on but courage. No matter how undisciplined and unskilled we thought they were in the past, and no matter how many of them threw down their arms and deserted the ranks, it was hard to ignore the courage of those few Iraqi soldiers who stuck around to tough it out. The trial they faced out there was just as hard as any we had faced on our own journey, and it was only getting worse by the day. We knew they couldn't hold that ground for much longer, so unless some change was in the works our claim on the southern districts of Sadr City wasn't going to last very long.

On the 15th of April, 23 days into the battle, that change came to bear. Way up the chain, some general had come up with the bright idea of constructing an impregnable blast-wall along the entire length of the frontline. The concept was pretty easy to understand: by walling them in, we could forcibly contain the Jaish al-Mahdi inside their own hostile territory and create a defensible obstacle to keep them from sneaking through our front lines and wreaking havoc on our rear. As an added kicker, building the wall along Route Gold put their rockets right out of range of the bigwigs and VIPs back at the Green Zone. More than anything, however, a wall along our front line would give us the chance to divert much-needed aid and reconstruction efforts to the neighborhoods in which we had been fighting, who had suffered three weeks of warfare without food or fresh water.

At first glance, the newly christened "Gold Wall" was a great idea. Upon closer inspection, however, it was sure to be a clusterfuck of unmatched proportion. The wall itself was going to be made with the same type of barrier that we had set into place at the blocking position of Bravo and Gold. When completed, it would run the entire length of Routes Aeros, Gold, and Grizzlies — all three flanks of the southeast, southwest, and northwest borders of Sadr City. That's a distance of more than fifteen kilometers, working two meters at a time, under what was sure to become a never-ending flood of enemy fire.

It was no secret to any of us that the Gold Wall was an insane plan. I would've much rather charged into that city with our guns blazing than embark on the tedious task of hauling piece after piece of concrete into place, under a constant hail of gunfire. The militia wasn't stupid. They'd see that we were walling them in as soon as the first barrier went up. And once they figured that out, you bet your ass they were going to do everything in their power to stop the project dead in its tracks. But orders are orders. All I can say is that I'm happy I wasn't chosen for the task. When the Colonel wants a wall, you build a fuckin' wall. And that's exactly what happened.

Originally, the job of setting up the barriers fell into the hands of an engineering brigade from the Missouri National Guard. They began work first thing in the morning at the intersection of Routes Aeros and Gold. Covering their ass was a heavy escort of Apaches, Abrams tanks, and Strykers, pulled from every unit in the area who had a platoon to spare. The first order of business on the project was to work westward along Route Gold — the most critical front of the battle. The rest of the wall, two more sections cutting off the northwestern and southeastern flanks of Sadr City, would have to be dealt with in due time. Route Gold was the priority of the operation.

In all, the barrier construction escort drew from "Team Steel" of Charlie Company, 1-68th CAB; the "Death Dealers" of Delta Company,

4-64th AR; and a fellow Stryker unit known as the "Bushmasters" of Bravo Company, 1-14th INF. While they built the wall on Route Gold, our very own 1st Squadron of Strykers, with the 11th Iraqi Army Division still fighting beside them, established outer security across the remaining front of the city to keep the militia from circling around and enveloping the entire operation.

As we had suspected from the very start, that first barrier of the Gold Wall brought with it a stern response by the Jaish al-Mahdi. No matter what our Squadron did to hold an outer cordon for the fight, they were powerless to stop the militia from pounding away at the barrier emplacement crew from the Jaish al-Mahdi's turf directly north of the wall. It was a brutal fight, but piece-after-piece and meter-by-meter that wall went up. Each day the militia came out in the morning to voice their disapproval with lethal force, and each night the barrier crew sent them packing to lick their wounds and try again. It wasn't long before the sheer volume of collateral damage reduced the buildings on either side of them to rubble. No matter what they did, the barrier crew was at the mercy of our enemy and flirted with death every step of the way.

On the second day of construction, a sandstorm rolled in from the desert, which forced every Apache, UAV and fixed-wing aircraft to the ground. That far into the war, the militia knew all too well how much a sandstorm limits our abilities on the ground, and jumped on the opportunity to retake what they had lost. By nightfall, the Iraqi Army was finally routed from the line, leaving our squadron to fill in across the entire three-kilometer breadth of the city. And if that wasn't a bad enough omen for the coming days, the construction crew up on Gold had a genuine outbreak of insurrection among their ranks.

Based on what I've gathered since the battle, a militia sniper hit one of the National Guard engineers during the blood-drenched sandstorm that shrouded the city in chaos for more than two days. As a direct result, the ranking leader of the construction crew backed out of the fight and refused to put his own men in the crossfire of such a ridiculous operation. According to him, the job was too dangerous for engineer work — let alone for a bunch of part-time soldiers from Missouri. Apparently, he was more than willing to drop off supplies from behind the cover of what little they had constructed, but it was the grunts who would have to put the rest of the wall into place. In any case, the task of constructing the Gold Wall fell into the hands of a small crew from Charlie Company 1-68th CAB who had never been trained on the equipment or the process, and had to learn it as they went.

When the sandstorm was over, the men from 1-68th CAB settled in for the rest of the job. A few days later, they had worked out the kinks in their operation and come up with a system to get it done as fast as they could. By then it was obvious that the Jaish al-Mahdi was getting bottled up inside of their city, and unless they went back on the offensive they were going to lose it in the end. On the 28th of April, a second major sand storm rolled in from the horizon triggering another massive outbreak of fighting across the line.

At the time, Bull Company was right in the middle of a high-action raid to hunt down three brothers who had filled in as Jaish al-Mahdi commanders after their predecessor was killed. It was easy for them to tune out the gunfire on the horizon, but as they finished up with the objective it was hard to ignore the growing volume of fire just a few hundred meters to the east of their position. A few minutes later, a massive volley of rockets was fired off at the Green Zone from an open field situated well south of the Gold Wall, proving that the lines had been overrun. Contact reports flooded into the TOC from every corner of the city, prompting Captain Bradford to maneuver the company back to Patrol Base Bull where they could hold their ground on defensible terrain.

In the following hours it became clear that the bulk of the attack was focused on the barrier crew up on Gold. By then they had finally worked their way up to the intersection at Route Bravo, which marked just 500 meters of the 15,000 meter plan for the wall. They had been working as fast as they could for thirteen days, only to get slammed with another wash of deliberate contact without air support to cover them. Progress on the wall crumbled to a halt. For the first time, the incoming fire was so intense that construction became a hopeless cause. The men on the ground were busy enough just trying to stay alive and hold their own. In 24 hours of fighting, you could count on a single hand the number of barriers they put up. But even then, the grunts in 1-68th CAB adapted to the circumstance of the fight and drove on with their mission. The militia's attacks on our positions throughout the city lasted eight more days after the sandstorm ended. Regardless, by the 3rd of May, the wall had grown by another 500 meters to the intersection of Routes Charlie and Gold. With the first kilometer completed, they had four kilometers to go before construction could start on the next three sections of the wall.

By that time, Bull Company had been forced to change their position and assume a more aggressive role in holding the line against our enemy. The militia had already destroyed our squadron TOC with a coordinated rocket attack, and it was necessary to set up a new patrol base at the intersection of Routes Bravo and Florida to provide improved security behind the wall. This was a far more favorable position for the men, who lovingly nicknamed their new home "The Fortress" because of its clear sightlines and defensive posture.

With the growing ferocity of the engagement, however, and the fact that the men of Steel Company had been fighting danger-close engagements on a daily basis for three weeks, none of my buddies had any time to settle in. Once again they were ordered forward into the fray, to clear the path ahead of the barrier crew and soak up bullets while the wall was built. The cornerstone of this operation was an abandoned police station on the corner of Routes Gold and Delta, which had served the Jaish al-Mahdi throughout the battle as the cache for insurgents and equipment. By every measure, the assault of that police station was expected to be a bloody fight, but to everybody's surprise there was virtually zero contention by the militia. In fact, our boys had settled in within the span of a few minutes, and were able to cover the barrier crew with ease.

For the first time all year, the infinite well of manpower and supplies that our enemy seemed to posses was finally starting to run dry. The assaulting element in our company hardly found a platoon's worth of supplies in the belly of that structure and the counterattack that followed was laughable at best. That afternoon our company began a daily rotation to cover the construction efforts on Route Gold for the remainder of its advance. At the same time, the second phase of the wall's construction kicked off as "Chaos" Company of the 10th Mountain Division's 2-30th INF Battalion began erecting their own barriers along Route Aeros. By nightfall of the assault on the outpost of Delta and Gold, American and Iraqi troops went back on the offensive to pick a fight with the militia on all three fronts.

After two months of combat, the end of the battle was in sight. Bull Company carried on like that for another week, running regular raids on high-value targets and pounding dirt into dust throughout the neighborhoods just south of the wall. Every two days, another platoon from our Company cycled up to Route Gold to clear the road and suppress the enemy so the barrier crew could pick up the pace on the race to Route Grizzlies. Eventually, progress on the wall crossed over to the west of Bull Company's blocking position and into the hands of our 1st Squadron brothers in Comanche Company.

At this point I had once again assumed my rightful place behind my machine-gun with 1st Platoon. I have to admit that from the ground it had all melted together into an undecipherable stew of fighting and chaos. It was only in hindsight I picked up the details and put it all into place. By the 11th of May we had systematically purged Sadr City's southern district of Jaish al-Mahdi commanders and special groups. After 47 days of fighting, Coalition generals sat down with what was left of the Jaish al-Mahdi's leadership to propose another end to the hostilities. To their credit, the second attempt had far better terms than the first.

It was only in the face of such a resounding defeat that Muktada al-Sadr begrudgingly agreed to demilitarize his movement and let us into the city without contention for the first time in the history of the war. To those of us on the ground the new "fourteen point plan" was far from perfect, but at least it allowed the Iraqi Army to set up outposts north of Route Gold. As for the Coalition, our job was to finish the Gold Wall and get to work rebuilding the lower third of Sadr City.

Our new mission from that day forward was the cliché battle for hearts and minds. Occasionally, we'd have to pick a fight with the Jaish al-Mahdi whenever they made a ruckus and set up an outpost south of the wall, but for the most part our daily grind was helping the locals get back on track. We rebuilt homes. We paid for damages. We offered interest free micro-loans to entrepreneurs willing to take a chance and set up shop. For the first time in decades, the inhabitants of Sadr City were free to do as they'd like without getting murdered for speaking out. It wasn't a wonderland, but at least they weren't getting tortured and killed for wearing short skirts and playing billiards at a local club. Right in front of my eyes, markets opened up with forbidden luxuries that had been outlawed by al-Sadr during his reign.

In just a few weeks, the city south of the wall sprung to life as if nothing had ever happened. Burned down tanks became relics of the past. The prominent scars of our conflict, the rubble, craters and the holes, all faded into dust. After a month, they had become little more than obstacles in a child's game of tag. For a long time I felt as if the world had fallen victim to a powerful amnesia, in which everything evil had been forgotten.

In the months that followed, we got back to the daily grind of pounding dirt and working with the locals to make sure we had more to show for our time in Sadr City than a bunch of bullet holes and freshly filled caskets. At first I found it hard to imagine that we'd be forgiven for what we brought into those streets, but the truth was that most of the people there were thankful for what we had done. It wasn't pretty, it wasn't clean, and there was plenty of misplaced bloodshed for us to atone for, but even they knew why it was worth it in the end.

In time, we earned the trust of the people in our district, and made good on the promise of a better tomorrow. Ironically, our best ally in this campaign had become the Jaish al-Mahdi themselves, by dint of their abysmal track record and the fact that every neighborhood north of the Gold Wall remained as downtrodden and derelict as it was before the battle. I couldn't help but draw parallels with Berlin and the DMZ in Korea where American influence had made all the difference in the world. There was a clear and unmistakable line between *us* and *them* — a barrier more visible in the disparity of circumstance on either side of it than by the concrete walls that ran the length of the divide.

But the going wasn't easy. We were still at war, and the Jaish al-Mahdi was still a threat. They had even reestablished an outpost south of the wall, despite our best efforts to ward them off. As a byproduct, daily run-ins with EFPs and IEDs were still a commonplace fact for Coalition troops in and around the former battlefield of Sadr City. We had been on high alert since the fighting began, and part of me wondered why the hell we didn't just roll in and finish what we had started. Everything south of the Gold Wall was all the proof I needed to know that it would be worth it in the end, and part of me couldn't stop thinking that the best thing we could do about the Jaish al-Mahdi was push north and kill them all.

The thing was that simply guarding our new outpost, had spread our numbers dangerously thin. Nearly half of our company, myself included, were cooped up on the Strykers and left out in the streets on the perimeter. Another quarter of our company was put on guard at gun positions and lookouts within the building. Even after we'd stripped every guard position and Stryker team down to the bone, barely two squads of dismounts could be spared for a patrol.

Our corresponding "rest cycle" in all this was about six intermittent hours of sleep for every eighteen hours on the clock, only a slight improvement from the weeks prior. It was a crucible; sheer will against the basic forces of biology. No matter how much we accomplished there was always more to come. One day the Colonel came out to troop the line and review our security, which only added to our resentment of the entire situation.

"I want one more man on every one of these positions," he told us after a slapdash analysis of our perimeter.

I heard a soldier behind me mock the command under his breath to one of his buddies who had just come off patrol. "You think he realizes that putting one more guy at every window would take more men than we have in our entire company?"

His buddy scoffed and snapped back a reply that was hard to miss. "You think if he knew what the fuck was going on they'd put him in charge?"

"Good point." They both laughed.

To the best of my recollection, we didn't change a damn thing when he left. We just drove on, as we had done before, and forgot about the details. Our living conditions had yet to improve, and with summer falling down upon us, a very human and humid stench dripped off of our very essence. Whatever we drank would leak out of our pores and soak into our clothing. Whatever we ate would dribble out of our ass and run down our legs. Both bodily functions went unnoticed outside of a general assessment of "sucking." The food that failed to fall into our mouth when we ate would get lost in a crevice or crack of the floor-panel and feed the armada of flies fucking and puking all around us. The dust of the endless desert would wash into the city and carpet everything with a fine grit. "Clean" was a few flaps of a hand and the "ten second rule" had no jurisdiction — everything was fair game.

Not a man among us could claim a clean bill of health. My own symptoms of dysentery had passed but it still raged rampantly throughout the company. My feet throbbed with months of untreated athlete's foot and my crotch could've been mistaken for a new breed of venereal disease. All of us had puffy-red cultures of fungus growing somewhere on our skin. Moments of relief were few and far between. Refits to our Combat Outpost came at best once a week, and on average every two. For some of us, the clothes we were wearing were the very same ones we donned on the first day of fighting. The sores on our skin had a long way to go before they could be considered "healed." In that world, where showers were a pipe dream and your toilet was a trash bag, a fresh pair of socks became a gift from the gods and a pack of baby-wipes was a solid brick of gold.

We went on like that for weeks. We dragged our brains into mush. It felt like a long, time-lapse video of a life being lived before my eyes. I could've died and never noticed. It's a black hole in my past into which vital details and crisp memories have been lost. Yet amidst it all, there are occasional snapshots, violent reminders that I was alive and in a war.

A wall would explode.

A sniper would take the shot.

The whistle of an in-bound RPG or crisp blast of a mortar would rip me back into reality.

A rush of adrenaline would flush through my body and reanimate its idle extremities.

I was reduced to primordial goo. For just a few moments, an hour, a breath, or a day at a time, I was awake and alive. We reacted. We fought.

We killed – and I only knew that I was human because I had a programmed will to survive. Other than that, days of my life were disappearing into the mist. Everything else – the endless broken cycles of sleep and deprivation – just felt like rapid-fire blinking in my mind. Time passed before my eyes without pause or reflection, trekking through the fog of deprivation at random intervals to imprint a broken and fleeting memory onto the meat of my brain.

It was a full month into that amorphous flux that Sergeant Duke's voice came across the radio with an unexpected call of the long forgotten administrative variety. At the time, Ian and I sat on top of our Stryker during a shift while our truck maintained another weeklong blocking position on a main road leading into Sadr City. Even though one of us should've been sleeping, it was impossible to get any rest during the day. Both of us decided to cram away at our studies for the promotion board we had been promised – though it never came.

"Hey, Seven, this is Four," Sergeant Dukes called us up from The Fortress.

"Four, this is Seven," Sergeant O'Brien replied.

"Yeah, so apparently General Petraeus is going to be showing up at JSS Sadr City to give out coins n'shit. The Colonel wants Bull Company to send some guys over. Bull-Six says he wants every platoon sergeant to pick one soldier from each platoon and have him report to the ECP."

It was a noteworthy statement. Not only was Petraeus heading out to the JSS, but a select few of our rank and file were about to be selected to receive "coins" from the man himself. This is a special kind of award that floats somewhere between a pat on the back and a full-blown medal.

"Alright..." Sergeant O'Brien took a second to think. "I'm sending Ludwig."

My ears tuned in carefully as soon as he said my name.

"Roger," Sergeant Dukes called back. "Have him come into the building. He'll be riding back with Headquarters."

"How long will this take?"

"Not that long. They should be back in a couple of hours."

"Good copy. He's getting ready now. One-Seven, out."

Ian stopped and glanced over at me with a dumbfounded look of surprise.

"Did you get that, Ludwig?" Sergeant O'Brien shouted back at the hatch.

I hopped down so I could answer him directly. "Roger. I'm just going inside?"

"Yeah."

"Roger!"

I turned to unlock the hatch.

"Hey!" Montero shouted. "Get all your shit straight before you go!"

"Yeah," Sergeant O'Brien continued. "Make sure you've got all your fuckin' shit straight. We don't need you lookin' like an asshole in front of the General."

I searched through the truck to find the kneepads I'd once discarded and strapped them around my ankles so I wouldn't forget.

"You probably need these too." Montero tossed me a pair of elbow pads.

"You have your nut-flap and neck protector, right?" Sergeant O'Brien asked.

"Yeah I got that, Sarn't." I reached under my vest and let the nut-flap hang free underneath it.

"Throat protector?"

I pulled it out and clipped it on. "Yep."

"Eye-Pro?"

I held up my sunglasses and put them back on my face.

"What about clear lens?"

I pulled out my extra pair of ballistic eye protection and showed him the clear set of lenses.

"Gloves?" he snapped back.

I sighed and pulled them out of my pocket.

"Be sure to blouse your boots, too. And find your fuckin' hat."

I went through the motions and put on all the crap I was supposed to be wearing. None of it had done me any good in the fight. Its only purpose was to be seen by a bigwig. I took a moment to thank the gods for the small grace that our unit was exempted from wearing the "duck flaps" — a pair of huge Kevlar shoulder pads that really made us look like a bunch of morons.

Once I was geared up to go, I grabbed my rifle and hopped out of the troop door, walked casually to the front of the Patrol Base and met up with the other two soldiers who'd been picked for the detail: Nickolai and Manganella. It was a quick ride back to JSS Sadr City — much faster than I expected. During the battle it felt like we were a hundred miles away from the rear. Now I realized it was practically right down the street — a grand total of less than two kilometers away from The Fortress.

This wasn't like our usual supply runs to the JSS where we filed out with specific jobs to grab as much shit as we could carry and make it back to the front as soon as possible. Instead, Headquarters Platoon pulled right into the motor pool, powered down, lackadaisically wandered out of the back of their Strykers, and dropped their gear like they had done it a dozen times. As soon as they were settled, a runner was dispatched to find out the specifics of what was about to go down. It was obvious they knew something I had missed.

"Hey," Nickolai chuckled. "Maybe we'll actually get some good chow, eh?"

"Yeah, right." I scoffed.

"No really!" He looked at his watch. "It's 10:00 — and these guys have a chow hall."

"You're buyin' a dream, man." Manganella shook his head.

Our scout came back in a hustle to give us the lowdown on where we'd be meeting up with the General. As soon as we got there, some two-dozen underlings scurried about to make sure everything was perfect. They went over the layout, double checked the events, whispered little speeches, and set up camera angles for the world. High-ranking officers gave commands and eyed us down judgmentally. All I could think was that we were about to be *coined* — not promoted, not awarded, not even presented with a certificate of achievement. No, he was giving us a *coin*. Back on the front, in every one of our Strykers, somebody was fucked over with an extra-long guard shift so that we could be given a lousy hunk of metal for the sake of military tradition.

He won't even know why, I thought.

Hell, I didn't even know why.

After a brief moment of standing around, the Colonel came over and settled into command.

"Alright guys," he signaled over to us. "Go ahead and put your gear down over here. The uniform is going to be ACUs and soft-caps only."

"Of course," Nickolai grunted as he pulled out his cap. "I don't have any rank on my hat."

"Whatever," I said. "Fuck it."

"Yeah," Mango joked. "What are they going to do? Send us back to the line?"

The three of us laughed and undid our gear. Scanning over the crowd, it was obvious that we were the only group with somewhere else to be — us and the other grunts we had found in the corner. Even if it was nothing more than staring at the street and fighting like hell to stay awake, we had a job to do. This was nothing more than a distraction. Besides, infantrymen don't play well with others.

"Hey! You there!" Somebody shouted out in my direction.

I had long ago learned not to look unless I was addressed by name.

"Hey! Specialist! Specialist... what the hell is that... *Lub-wib?*"

But apparently he was talking to me.

I turned my head to address the voice only to discover it was the voice of some Major, glaring into my eyes with disdain.

"It's *Ludwig*, Sir."

"Yeah. What's up with that uniform?"

I looked down to inspect myself and make sure that I was tight. None of my buttons were unbuttoned and none of my patches had been ripped off.

"That shit's all jacked up!" He shouted. "And what's with your goddamned face?"

I was dumbfounded and silent with absolutely no idea what he was going on about.

"Well?!" He pressed on.

I looked for assistance, for some sign of what I was missing, and that's when I noticed a chubby white chick standing next to one of my buddies. Her light gray camo uniform looked damn-near bleach white next to his ratted and filthy scraps. I looked back at the Major and then to myself, immediately making the connection. The juxtaposition warmed the cockles of my heart. It showed the difference between our two worlds: Grunts and POGs, fighters and clerks, swords and pens. Call it what you like. We were two clans on the opposite ends of the spectrum. Two different cultures in the same set of clothes. They had iron-pressed creases of flattened and freshly starched fabric; we had large stains of dirt-soaked sweat from head to toe, bordered by months of crusty salt stains and polka-dotted carbon globs. We reeked of gun cleaning solution and shit. When I reached up to brush my face, I felt a week's worth of scruff on its way to becoming a beard, and no matter how hard I tried, I couldn't hide the smug grin stretching cheek to cheek across my face.

"Do you even know what's going on?" The Major drilled me even harder.

"Roger, Sir." I snapped back.

"What?"

"We're meeting General Petraeus—"

"That's right." He cut me off. "So why are you wearing that fucked up uniform, Specialist?"

His emphasis implied that I should've known better than to show up looking like a scrap of mulched asshole. I looked him dead on and told him the truth.

"It's the best one I have, Sir."

"Bullshit!" he shouted. "You've gotta' have something shoved in some bag somewhere! Come on! You smell like dog shit! When was the last time you took a shower?!"

"About six weeks ago, Sir."

Now I was full pomp and decorum, standing tall — Parade Rest and snapped to. I figured I'd let discipline speak for my character; my uniform was doing its job with the experience. He scanned over me again and his expression shifted to something else — something almost cautious in nature. Sure I looked like some fucked-up dirty private, but I wasn't acting like one, and my attitude practically accused *him* of being the fuck up.

"What unit are you in?" He squinted his eyes with hesitation.

I couldn't hold back my smile. I barked out the answer like I was picking a fight.

"Bull Company, sir — of the 1st Squadron, 2nd Stryker Cavalry Regiment."

A while back, some interrogations had turned up a string of intelligence including our nickname among the militia: *The Dirty Forces.* We were the spearhead of the squadron. The personal point of interest for a couple two-stars back in the Green Zone. We were the ungloved hand in an unfair bare-knuckle boxing match. How did that General put it when he came to visit? Oh, that's right: *"All I ever hear about is Bull Company."* Even if this guy had just the foggiest idea of what was going on, he would know exactly where I'd been. As I expected, he abandoned his inquisition all together.

"Alright," he awkwardly stammered. "If that's all you got then I guess it's all you've got. Carry on."

He turned away to bark at somebody else about the configuration of some equipment. I considered our two lives. How long had it taken him to get where he was? How many dicks did he have to suck? To what lows had he gone to get the job he had? One of the personal entourage to the most powerful and highest ranking commander in the entire theater of war — or maybe just an underling of one. Or an underling of an underling. He'd gone to school, earned a commission, shuffled shit for years to get his golden leaf of power, and all he really earned was the right to bark at me about a uniform.

I wanted to stare him in the face and say, "We're at *war,* sir." But a lot of people forget that. They get lost in the bullshit — bullshit like getting a coin when there's a fight down the street. Shit like duck flaps and knee pads when there's work to be done. But it wasn't worth the strings he could pull on me for disrespecting a superior, so I just shut my fucking mouth and settled in for the ceremony.

Military rituals like the one I was about to endure are not without a recurring pattern. In fact, it's a rare thing that a soldier even needs to pay attention to what's going on once he's mastered the basics. First, they usher those-to-be-recognized into a line. Some people of lower rank will make some corrections, and then some higher-ranking officer will come around with his two cents on how it should've been done. The lower ranking officers will then reinforce and expand on those corrections until another, even higher ranking officer comes around to contradict the first. Somebody will bark a command like "hats on!" and once they see that somebody's hat is missing or fucked up, they'll tell us all to take our hats back off for the sake of uniformity. Then, somebody won't have a haircut or someone else will say we look like shit regardless. They'll try to find a loaner for the soldier without a working hat before moving on to boots, blouses and rifles. It's always the same story. Always the same pattern. You'd be amazed how different people can look when they're all wearing the exact same goddamned clothes.

In the midst of finding out how to make us fit for a recruitment poster, some higher ranking officer will step forward with a piece of paper and explain the order of events. In this case, it was the Colonel. The public announcement, however, isn't so much for us to have a better idea of what's going on as it is for him to finally put into words what he's been penciling and plotting for the past half hour. With that, some kinks in the plan will be worked out and a footman will come out of nowhere to tell them the VIP is en-route. That's the first time we'll be told to "look sharp" and "get straight." Meanwhile, whoever is coming has barely set foot in their helicopter on the other side of Baghdad. We all know what's in store and we've all seen it a hundred times: whomever we're waiting on won't show up for at least another thirty minutes. So after a short while, we'll be told to stand at rest. Sooner or later we'll get back down to smoking and bullshit, and before a single cigarette is finished, they'll bark us all to attention as the next status update rolls in:

General Petraeus has taken off.

It was bullshit.

When General Petraeus finally did get there, he took a shotgun to the poor Colonel's plan. With complete informality, he walked right up to us and gave it a go.

"Listen up," he announced. "Everybody relax. I know this is a big deal and everything just because I'm a general. I just wanted to stop by and hand out some coins, and let you guys know that you're doing a damn fine job. So everybody just relax. This is gonna' be real informal."

Then he spoke a few words of wisdom, which felt like a carbon copy of what I had always thought about the battle, yet with a much better picture of what the hell was going on.

"That's why this guy's a good leader," I mumbled to myself. "He fucking gets it."

After a short speech he got right down to business, walking up to the first man in line with a hand shake and the words, "So what's your name, son?"

For the first time since Captain Bradford came up to the back of our Stryker, I was impressed by a commanding officer. More importantly, I was proud. He was the first glimmer of common sense leadership I'd ever seen with a solid stack of rank.

Among the field of awardees, not many of us there were from 1st Squadron. There were three of us from Bull Company, one or two from Apache and Comanche, and a couple more from the Squadron TOC. Everyone else — over a dozen in all — were from either 4th ID, the 10th Mountain, or some other admin unit I had never heard of. Of the units I had seen out in the shit with us, it didn't look like a single one had sent a grunt to get coined. It didn't matter. We were all the same to him. When it was my turn, I got my coin, shook his hand, said "Thank you sir" like everybody else, and he moved on to the next person down the line. A few minutes later he was out of sight and back on his bird. While we gathered up to leave, a short and stubby Army photographer handed out business cards and announced that we could get copies of our photo with the General if we wanted. All we had to do was e-mail the address on her card and she'd send them out as soon as possible.

"Right," Nickolai chuckled as he glanced over the card. "A lot of good this will do me back on the line."

He crumbled the card and shoved it into his pocket.

"Hey," I asked her as she handed one to me. "Are you like, an Army Times photographer or something? Like, how did you get this job?"

I was always curious about how somebody in an Army uniform could end up playing football, driving a racecar, tooting a tuba, or doing anything else that doesn't fall into the list of military occupations. I had never been so close to one, so I had to ask.

"No." She sneered and literally stuck her nose in the air. "I'm the personal photographer to General Petraeus *himself.*"

I shot her a snide look. "Well, *excuse me.*"

She blew us off and turned around, handing out business cards to the other half of the crowd.

"Yeah, you're also a bitch," Mango muttered.

"Excuse me?!" She spun back to face us with a gasp.

Rather than make a minor engagement into a real fight, we rolled our eyes and made our way to the grill where some dude was flipping burgers to the songs on his iPod.

"I told you!" Nikolai smiled. "12:00 on-the-dot!"

"Hey Sarn't," I asked the guy at the grill. "Can we get a couple of those burgers before we go?"

"Sorry guys." He slapped a thick layer of barbecue sauce on the patties with a smile. "Ain't quite ready yet."

"Ah, come on, Sarn't! They look good enough to me."

"Nope. They gotta be perfect!"

Before we could haggle him down, a runner showed up from our company to get us back to the trucks.

"Ah, fuck." Nikolai smacked me on the shoulder. "Hey, Ludwig, we gotta' go."

"Damn!" I looked back at the runner. "I could've really used a burger."

"Hey," the cook winked at us. "Maybe next time!"

But there wouldn't be a next time. That was the last time I would ever set foot in the combat outpost of JSS Sadr City.

We hadn't been there for very long, but when I mounted back onto the Stryker I discovered that something inside of me had already changed. It was like I had been rattled out of an illusion and faced with a startlingly lucid fact. For the first time since the battle began I felt like I was staring through a looking glass at my own life. I scanned over the men around me and my heart sank at what I saw. There were no more brothers among us. No husbands or sons. We were monsters, with sweat dripping down our brows and hatred burned into our scowls. Our smiles were the twisted smirks of soulless jackals. I was revolted by the stench of it all. We accepted Fate. We lusted to suffer. We were proud of what we'd become. And there I was, eager and willing to get back to my fucked up little corner of Sadr City.

When we got back to The Fortress I was resolved to think things over, so I settled down in a corner and worked my way through a plastic bag of mushy chow. I set up my armor as a reclining backboard and reached into my pocket for some old crusty peanut butter that I had been keeping safe for a couple of days. As I prepared my instant meal, a squad of grunts filed in through the doorway from their most recent patrol. I watched as they set down their gear and collapsed to pass out within seconds. I couldn't help but notice that they didn't give a second thought to the ever-looming reality that we could all die at any moment.

That's when it hit me: we were no longer alien to this strange and desolate world, but a part of it. We were organic inhabitants of the apocalypse. We were a stitch in the seam of the landscape. So long had we lived amidst the ruins that we were now a part of them, as naturalized as any other artifact in the city. Or maybe we had become the ruins ourselves, as battered inside as the scenery we had scarred. In either case, I was a different person now: broken, hard, and aged. I had no idea how that could be undone. I had no idea how I could ever change back. I couldn't even remember what it was like to be that boy I had once been — that kid who took a $20,000 check as compensation for everything I had been through.

That kid didn't know shit about the world except that it was his turn to pay the price for the American dream. He thought that you could just roll an army into a far away country and make things better. He honestly believed that as long as your intentions are noble and the bad guy was bad enough, it would all turn out okay. In other words, he didn't know shit. What I had really learned since then was that my life boiled down to the men around me and the machine-gun locked into the back of our armored vehicle. All I cared about now was making it through that night and the following day. My entire life had become a never-ending chain of "carrying the one" in a simple equation of kill-or-be-killed until it was all over and I was finally dead.

I didn't have some cushy job in the rear. That kid who signed my contract didn't even give me the chance. He signed away my life thinking he knew how it all worked. Now I was paying for it with my soul and learning the hard truths about the world. I had seen first-hand what was going on "over there." I was making a difference with belts of bullets and cries for war. I was pushed to the brink of a world that I could never have seen on my own, and I was doing things nobody should ever have to do. But most of all, I finally understood what it takes to be one of those hardened vets on the far side of oblivion, fighting for a cause, and lost in the Shit.

I glanced over at the men pulling guard through the window. They were joking about prostitutes and blowjobs. The radio crackled on behind them, echoing small talk from the trucks. A single pillar of smoke billowed up into the sky behind them. Far off down the street, a burst of rounds fired off. At the sound of it I chuckled with hope. Hope that the militia would start another ruckus. Hope that they'd be stupid enough to try again. Hope that we'd go all the way into that fucking city and wipe them out for good. Hope that we'd stay there as long as it took. Hope that we'd never leave. Hope that we'd wallow in that Shit until the war was won, because after everything we had been through, that was all I had left.

I didn't care about suffering. I didn't care about the squalor and the filth. I didn't even care if I made it through all of that alive anymore. All I cared about was finishing the fucking job. I wanted to see that goddamn country stand up on its own two feet and be better off because of what we had done. I wanted to know that we made a difference, and if that difference would be worth it when this was all over.

"Ludwig!" Sergeant Benjamin shouted my name from the bottom of the stairs.

"Yeah?!" I shouted back.

"Get your shit, brother! We're rollin' out!"

Another burst rang out in the distance. Sergeant Benjamin's voice echoed up through the halls, taunting his foe to "come out and try." Outside, a Stryker backed up to the front door of the Fortress to pick us up for our next mission. We'd be heading north today. Pulling a dismounted patrol just south of the Gold Wall.

"Roger that!" I shouted back to my old squad leader.

As I had done a thousand times before, I flung my gear over my head and donned the wardrobe of a soldier. I felt the weight of it in my back and knees. I tossed my head from side to side and worked out the kinks in my neck. I wiggled the straps and fabric of my vest into their rightful places. I picked up my rifle and checked it over to make sure it was loaded and ready to go. I watched my hands drift over the handles and levers, manipulating the weapon with ease.

I couldn't help but think back to that first day Uncle Sam issued me my first bulletproof vest and a rifle. They had felt so awkward and encumbering back then. True symbols of the weight and burden of war. I chuckled lightly at the thought of how much things can change.

This vest was so much different than my first. It was a part of me now. But it wasn't the vest. It was me. The weight of it had rebuilt my very frame. From the dead nerves in my numb shoulders to the twisted shape of my aching bones, I had been changed into something different from what I was. And that rifle, which had followed me from my first days on the radio, had become an extension of my person as much as any prosthesis for a missing limb. Its movements and functions were wired into my brain like it had always been a part of me. Its function had become as natural to me as any other tool.

I was a soldier. A killer. A man who can be trusted to do what needs to be done. There was nothing left of the boy I had once been. He was dead, and in his place stood the man I had become. A man who wasn't afraid of what waited for him in the abyss. A man who didn't care if he lived or died. I thought back to my mom and dad, and all the people I had left behind. For the life of me, I couldn't think of a single reason to go back. Not yet. Not until I had finished what I started or died trying in the end.

"Ludwig!" Sergeant Benjamin shouted up at me again, reminding me that I needed to hurry up.

"Moving!" I shouted back.

When I reached down to grab my helmet, a strange sensation crept into my heart. I looked out at the men around me who had become more of a family than any other. In that moment I finally realized something more real than the ground under my feet.

When all this was over, there was no "home" for me to go back to.

I was already there.

- Epilogue -
Unfinished Business

It starts with a blast.

I'm on patrol with the guys. We've been walking around for hours. I crack a joke that I'd rather be jacking off. We mount up and drive a couple feet forward.

Then everything goes black.

The next thing I know, I awake, gripped with panic, and crawl out of a neatly folded bed somewhere. By the feel of it, I've been unconscious for days. I have no idea where I am. I have no idea how I got there. My head is pounding, my ears are ringing.

"Where's my gun!" I shout frantically, ripping apart the sheets for a weapon.

There's no answer. I hear nothing but stillness. I find myself wrestling to my feet with adrenaline surging at every corner of my body. I leave my instincts to fend for me while my brain boots up — and they have one thing in mind.

"Where is my goddamn gun!"

The words blast out of my mouth as I stagger away from my bed and clench my fist into a club. I'm ready to jump at the first person who crosses my path. I hope it happens just so I can tear his face to shreds. When I stop to take in my surroundings, my eyes scour over the corners, cracks, and shadows. I have no idea where I am. I don't recognize this place. I don't know these walls or this bed. There is no sound of roving generators, no droning night of fellow snores. The air is crisp. It's cold. It bites against my chest. The open window in front of me becomes my only point of focus. I take it all in. A gust of cold slaps against my chest. I quiet down and listen.

So much for my gun, I think to myself.

I'll have to find that later. Right now I have to focus on survival. The first thing to register is the door. I rush over to check the locks. They're dead-bolted shut from the inside. This gives me a second to think.

I need to find out where the fuck I am.

The light that's shining through the blinds comes into focus and I make my way to the darkest corner in the room. By now, the clean and well-constructed nature of things becomes apparent. I'm not at the outpost. Not even close. Hell, even those long-forgotten barracks back at Camp Taji aren't this nice.

Built-in air-conditioning?

Real tile floors?

Hardwood furniture?

No, I've gotta' be in the Green Zone somewhere.

Somewhere safe.

If that's the case...

I run my hands across my skin to check myself over for missing limbs and jagged scars. I find nothing. Nothing but ten toes, ten fingers, and a bunch of goose bumps as my body begins to shiver.

So where the fuck am I?

As silently as I can, I creep over to the window and peer outside to get a fix on my surroundings. I make sure to keep my profile low so I don't flag myself to some shooter out on the street. Creeping closer, I get a good look at the world beyond.

"This can't be real," I murmur.

My brain finally kicks in and I start to analyze my surroundings, but nothing makes sense. I shouldn't be this cold, not unless summer somehow disappeared, but out that window there's a parking lot full of cars and a carpet of dew on everything in sight.

I make another futile scan of my surroundings. It's only now that I realize I'm not going to find my gun. I don't have one. That sends me deeper into a panic. I scramble for anything sharp to take its place and find a broken chunk of plastic to hold me over. I grip it in my hand and cower in a corner where it's safe to stop and think. Just a moment ago I was back with the boys. I was in the hatch of a Stryker. It was a hot day in Baghdad, on the corner of Miller and Pabst. We were almost done with our patrol cycle. I could tell you exactly who was there. Exactly what we were doing. I cracked a joke about jacking off, and Kaz said he can't wait to go home to his fiancée.

Kaz is dead.

The thought smacks me right across the face and makes me sick to my stomach. That was three years ago. It was a world away. It was a different lifetime. It's like a bad dream. A dream I can never forget. A bad dream that's real until it turns back into a memory.

Kaz is dead. He died with Sergeant Lilly on the line. They were blown away and I wasn't even there to help. I swallow the fact with the renewed sorrow that I'll never see them again in my life.

But he was just there.

And I was talking right at him.

We were talking about home and the lives we left behind.

That memory unlocks another chamber of secrets in my mind. I look around the room and start to notice familiar shadows and pieces of life. Bit by bit it all comes back: the end of the deployment, flying back to Germany, getting stationed in Texas after post-deployment leave. I drop my jagged shank when I realize that the room I'm in is mine. It's my own goddamn Barracks room. This is my stuff. My life. It's supposed to be home, but it doesn't feel right. Not anymore. I can't help thinking it never will.

I'm crouched in the corner, in the biting cold, far away from that world I once knew. I can still feel the grit and sweat on my skin. I can still taste the salt on my lips. My throat is dry and my lips still chapped from the sun. My chest can't stop itching, right in the middle of that heavy-ass armor-plate, right in that spot that I could never quite scratch. I can still hear the pounding drums of combat on the sidewalls of my heart and I'm still waiting for the final blast when it's all going to be over. But in a strange way I wish I had never left, because over there I had a purpose. Over there I had a mission. Over there I had friends and bonds that were closer than anything else in my life. Over there I died in a mangled heap of rotten memories and fucked up deeds, and now I can't stop thinking that I don't belong here. I can't stop thinking that I never made it home.

I'm stuck in a purgatory where the worlds I've lived in and the two people I've been do battle over who I am. I struggle to regain the footing of my soul and piece together what happened. More importantly, I struggle with "why." Deep down I know that I should've died in that fucking war. It should've been me instead of them. I should never have come back. Now I've got nothing left but debts to be paid for a life I don't want to live. Even with all the memories that come with this newfound consciousness the nightmare isn't over. I'm still fighting the war, and the battle isn't over. It never was. It just moved inside of me, into the ashy pit of my heart and soul. It's in everything I touch, and I'll never forget those days I spent in those Strykers, rotting away into oblivion.

On the 6th of June, 1st Platoon was the first element in Bull Company to fall back to the rear and pick up our new mission on the other end of town. Six days later, 2nd and 3rd Platoons followed suit. On June 14th, Captain Bradford passed the torch and relinquished command of "The Fortress" to the men of 1-6th INF. After 82 days of vicious combat, our struggle with the Jaish al-Mahdi was finally over, marked with little more than a tired salute and new orders to move out.

I wish I could say the story ended there. I'd love to leave you with an image of us riding triumphantly into the sunset with the wind behind us. It would be great if I could paint the picture of our relief swooping in to pat us on the back so we could fly home to our sweethearts and win awards for good deeds. It'd be nice if it was the wrap, with a noble finish and a spiffy narrative, but it's not. This isn't a story about some spit-shined set of heroes rising up above it all, and the war wasn't over because a ceasefire was called.

The guys who relieved us in those streets were just getting started. That was their first month on the job, and they were going to rot in that

Suck like we had done for the next fifteen months of their deployment. They would face the same trials that we had faced and finish the job that we had started, long after the last unit who fought in the battle was gone. But we still had five more months on the clock. Five months of day-in, day-out shit. Five months of pounding dirt into dust and whittling our hearts into nothing until it was time to go home.

A week after pulling out of the Fortress, the bigwigs upstairs gave us a detail to "take it easy" over in the nice part of town. I imagine that was done to limit collateral damage as much as it was a break for the men. We spent two months in Adamiyah, working out of a joint security station with the Iraqi Police until they sent us up to the Logistical Supply Area (LSA) "Diamondback" up in Mosul. For three months we patrolled the wastelands of the northern desert, until our last patrol ended with nothing in sight but sand and sky. After thousands of patrols, hundreds of named operations, a dozen direct action raids into Sadr City, and millions of net-man-hours fought, it was finally time for us to pack up our shit and go home.

But what was that?

For many of us it was just an empty house with a cleaned out bank account. It was a mountain of debt and a goodbye letter from a woman who'd skipped town while we were gone. For the single soldiers like me, it was a barracks room with a liquor store down the street. "Home" was just a finish line. It was something we'd glorified. It was a light at the end of the tunnel – nothing more. Even when I made it back to California for post-tour leave, all I had earned was the distinct feeling that my entire life belonged to somebody else. It was the life of some kid who went off to die in a battle somewhere; yet there I was, sleeping in his bed, living with his family, and hanging out with his friends. I was a trained soldier – a killer of men – sleeping in a bed with plaid sheets under a bookshelf of knick-knacks from life-changing events I couldn't remember. And as I thought back to that war, I couldn't help but ask myself what happened when we were gone.

What about those kids out in the junkyards who used to hang out with us on our breaks? Or that family living on Copper West, whose house we had used on a daily basis to fight our enemy? Or all those people who had taken us in and given us their trust that we'd make things better – only to see us leave in the end and never come back? What happened to all of them when we left? Did some other Americans come in with no idea what the fuck was going on and make enemies of good friends? Or maybe they never came back. Maybe they didn't even try. Maybe the Jaish al-Mahdi got their revenge for every cup of tea the locals gave us, and every patrol that we didn't get hit.

It was hard coming back, not just because of the war and the memories, but because of how they separated me from the people I knew and loved. When I looked at myself in the mirror, there was nothing left of the kid these people had all known so well. The only person I saw staring back at me through the glass was a tired and angry man. A man whose hollow expression confessed a thousand evil things. A man I wouldn't let near my own family out of fear of what I knew he could easily do. But he was me. He was Konrad. He was the person I had become – what the war had made me into. And I couldn't help but wonder what the hell it was all for. Why the hell I had signed up in the first place, and what the hell we were doing for fifteen months in Iraq.

I didn't have the answers when all this started, just a bottle of Scotch. I pounded out my problems. I drank glass after glass of that smoky amber poison until it was impossible to stand. I stumbled around my apartment like a fool each and every night until it was time to face my nightmares. And when I fell asleep, it was always the same story. The following morning, I'd wake up to repeat the process. I'd fight on for another day. Hate and hardness of spirit was all I had left. I had been in conflict for so long I didn't know how to find peace.

That was my life for much longer than I like to admit. I was living in a prison of my own mind, locked away by my own thoughts, waiting for it all to end and knowing I could make it happen. But one night I made a choice: I put down my bottle, I sat down in front of my computer, and I started facing all those memories which I had kept hidden from the world. With trembling hands and tears in my eyes, I set out to tell the story of what we did in Sadr City – if only so my family could know what happened to that kid who left them to go die in a war.

That was the first step, and it's been a long road from there. These days I have the luxury of looking back at what happened in Sadr City with sober eyes and a clear mind. I know what it really means to go fight for a cause. I know what it takes to make it home at any cost. Most of all, I no longer define myself by what that war had turned me into. I've found answers to the questions that almost killed me, and I can only hope that my brothers can do the same.

In the years that have passed, the Final Battle for Sadr City has become a major point of discussion for those who know about it and have a stake in the game. Perhaps the most important questions it raised were at the Pentagon, regarding its insights as to the effectiveness, limitations, and proper application of the "Counterinsurgency" (COIN) doctrine. The COIN doctrine had been the unquestioned cornerstone of the troop surge until the uprising that spring, and overnight American forces were forced to abandon the experimental strategy, committing to all-out "old school" tactics to defeat the Jaish al-Mahdi. At the same time, however, certain elements of the COIN doctrine were still just as critical to their success in the aftermath of what happened. Ultimately, the Spring Fighting of 2008 and the Final Battle of Sadr City played a huge role in bringing the end of the war within grasp, but only after challenging every assertion that had been made about how to finish the operation and go home.

In the end, Muktada al-Sadr and the Jaish al-Mahdi were never totally defeated — but they will also never be the same. What we did in those streets brought an end to their militant reign. It forced them out of the battlefields and back alleys, and into the forums of their republic. More importantly, it brought some concept of peace, prosperity, and freedom to over two million people who had lived under ruthless oppression since long before the war began.

I'm not saying what we did was perfect. It was war. But at least I know now that I can point to a place in the world where something I was a part of made a difference for the better. I can fall asleep at night proud of what we did, even if I'll never forget the price of that victory. I know my part in the bigger picture now. I came back to make sure you know about a place called Sadr City, and what happened there in the spring of

2008. I've told the story of what happened in the streets of that vicious battle, the scars of which still linger in the memories of the people who were there. I've done what I can to make sure those sacrifices are remembered, and that we can learn from our own past. I've done my part.

The rest is up to you.

Bull Company 1/2ND SCR
Battle Roster

Commanding Officer:

CPT. Jonathan M. Bradford

Executive Officer:

CPT. David M. Chichetti

First Sergeant:

1SG. Andre T. Williams

Headquarters (HQ) Platoon:

1LT. Herbert S. Wilmer
SSG. Mark Brooks
SSG. Shawn M. Griffin
SSG. Bryan D. Hailestock
SSG. Ronnie D. Lappi
SSG. Carl W. Stanberry
SSG. Patrick K. Turner
SSG. Kevin T. Vo
SGT. Steven T. Davies
SGT. Timothy W. Duvall
SGT. Johnathan D. Harper
SGT. Nicholas C. Neighbors
SGT. Matthew B. Parsley
SGT. Manu Reece
SGT. Walter C. Stewart
SGT. Derk A. Walter
SGT. David B. Waters
SGT. James T. Wilson
SGT. Vorasack T. Xaysana

SGT. Ricky Zhorne
CPL. Michael L. Billingsley
SPC. Todd Barnum
SPC. James D. Bentley
SPC. David R. Crider
SPC. Kristopher L. Davis
SPC. Alex J. Egan
SPC. Chad S. Fujimoto
SPC. Rob Hanson
SPC. Kraig A. Jackson
SPC. Gabriel A. Kitchen
SPC. Robert E. Raymer
SPC. David A. Rosc
SPC. Phillipe K. Vorhies
SPC. Romie Williams
PFC. Rodney A. Piper
PFC. Jacob B. Smith
PFC. William D. Wakeford

1st Platoon:

CPT. Daniel Savage
SFC. Patrick A. O'Brien
SFC. Geoffrey Dukes
SSG. Jerrad N. Benjamin
SSG. Abraham D. Bitolas
SSG. MarkDaniel C. Brasel
SSG. Michael R. High
SSG. Lee T. Holsker
SSG. Julius W. Moore
SSG. Rey F. Quinones
SGT. Evan D. Bennion
SGT. Michael Lilly (KIA)
SGT. Konrad R. Ludwig
SGT. Nicholas M. McKeever
SGT. Joshua B. Montero
SGT. Christopher M. Oaks
SGT. Ildefonso M. Palacios
SGT. Ian M. Peterson
SGT. Neil F. Tuioti
SGT. Matthew L. Waite
CPL. Jason Kazarick (KIA)
SPC. Steven P. Baiz
SPC. Rene Cardona
SPC. Matthew J. Colby
SPC. Darryl J. Cummings
SPC. Shawn J. Donnery
SPC. Cory W. Dulany
SPC. James E. Flemming
SPC. Allen Gonzalez
SPC. Max M. Haiflich
SPC. Kent T. Hannivig
SPC. Leland B. Heithold
SPC. Daniel T. Hutchins
SPC. Charles G. Jones
SPC. Zachary N. O'Connor
SPC. Brian D. Pfister
SPC. Marcos A. Santiago
SPC. Patrick G. Scalzitti
SPC. Matthew A. Wagner
SPC. Jeremy Wallace
SPC. Leon D. Williams
PFC. Harry L. Keller
PFC. Justin M. Meiers

2nd Platoon:

CPT. Matthew D. Apostol
SFC. David M. Mennig
SSG. Christopher W. Donnelly
SSG. William R. Edwards
SSG. Jose Palomino
SSG. Steven A. Pikus
SSG. Dmitri E. Quist
SSG. Robert P. Wood
SGT. Nicholas L. Dutkiewicz
SGT. Christopher R. Landry
SGT. Casey W. Lyons
SGT. Scott Q. Mauck
SGT. Craig A. McWilliams
SGT. Christopher W. Moody
SGT. Luke C. Palombo
SGT. William S. Pascoe
SPC. Nicholas C. Anna
SPC. Paul C. Danna
SPC. Aaron L. Duncan
SPC. Alex W. Hamilton
SPC. Robert J. Hanson
SPC. Andrew S. Kirchoff
SPC. Brandon D. Lake
SPC. Jerry L. Mcentee
SPC. Janio H. Moreno
SPC. Daniel Navaguttierrez
SPC. Jeffery C. Nikolai
SPC. Joel D. Pearce
SPC. Timothy P. Rose
SPC. Daniel A. Sieczkarski
SPC. Paul W. Thurman
SPC. Jose R. Valencia
SPC. Robert J. Walters
PFC. Randy Dittmar
PFC. Fredrick L. Busch
PFC. Christopher S. Raya
PFC. Jason W. Williamson

3rd Platoon:

CPT. Kenneth Elgort

SFC. Jason M. Kerns

SSG. Derek L. Arnold

SSG. Alejandro Contrerasbaez

SSG. Joseph Gamboa (KIA)

SSG. Scott W. Howard

SSG. Darren A. Leslie

SSG. Paul B. McCully

SSG. Patrice A. White

SGT. Thomas D. Alfano

SGT. Kelly E. Beberniss

SGT. Joseph T. Chamberlain

SGT. Christopher L. Fee

SGT. Nicholas M. Herman

SGT. Daniel C. Hullett

SGT. Aaron M. Lopez

SGT. Anthony J. Lynch

SGT. Richard L. Martel

SGT. Michael L. Mattice

SGT. Brett J. Russell

SPC. Apollo A. Arevalo

SPC. Cody K. Barham

SPC. Dustin R. Bauer

SPC. Michael L. Dameron

SPC. Wade M. Doyle

SPC. Robert A. Farrell

SPC. Michael B. Garner

SPC. Michael J. Gomez

SPC. Reginald T. Jeffress

SPC. Sean T. Kirkpatrick

SPC. David G. Manganella

SPC. Rolando A. McConaughey

SPC. Christopher D. Morgan

SPC. William Otero

SPC. Jonathan E. Patterson

SPC. Edward T. Pineda

SPC. Jesse M. Urias

SPC. Ryaan J. Villagomez

PFC. Michael D. Lopes

PFC. Samuel J. Montalbano

PFC. Frank J. Ruf

Mobile Gun System (MGS) Platoon:

2LT. Charles E. Hoke

SFC. James D. Omalley

SSG. Biden J. Jim

SGT. Jesse J. Jamison

SGT. Ruben K. Ortiz

SGT. David M. Wallace

SPC. Cody L. Davis

SPC. Daniel G. Morrison

SPC. Jared C. Osburn

SPC. Dylan B. Owens

*Note: Due to limited resources, this roster is based on the official documentation of Bull Company's '07-'08 deployment with all ranks and assignments approximate to the end of October. Due to the many personnel changes made shortly after the battle in March, however, official sources failed to accurately represent the "proper" layout of personnel throughout the majority of the deployment and battle itself. Wherever possible, corrections to platoon assignments on this list have been made according to feedback from the men. A number of discrepancies undoubtedly remain. Please submit any additional recommendations or corrections to feedback@roland-kjos.com

Special Contributors

Siri Kjos & Eric Ludwig

Bent Kjos

Kyle Spitznagel

Doug Spitznagel & Cameron Hall

Lance Turner

Daren Leslie

Ed & Felice Lammi

Michael Blaszczyk

Einar Kjos

Teddy Landry

MarkDaniel Brasel

Bryan Hailestock

Chris Landry

Quentin Christman

Aknowledgements

The production of this book was made possible by the amazing generosity and support of over 850 backers who ordered their copies through Kickstarter. Without their confidence in my work, this manuscript would've never made it into print. To all those who contributed — especially to Bent Kjos, Kyle Spitznagel, Doug Spitznagel, Cameron Hall, Lance Turner, Siri Kjos and Eric Ludwig — I am forever grateful for your support. Backing this project when it was just in an early phase of development was far more than a simple book order, it was a gesture of your trust and faith in my abilities. I have striven ever since to deliver on that trust and I hope this work has earned what you paid forward in advance.

This book has been a long time coming. Too long, in fact. It would be wrong of me not to apologize for the many delays in its production. The many setbacks, which have plagued this project, were due entirely to my own egregious miscalculation of what it takes to develop a "zero-draft" manuscript into a fully typeset and published book. Since then, I have come to learn that the original timeline for the publication of *Stryker* was less than a quarter of the average turnaround for a major publisher. Given the small size and limited experience of the team involved, I am blown away at how quickly it was actually put together, and the level of quality reached in that time. I'm sure that we have still missed a few things, but at this point it's time for me to put down the red pen and ship some damn books. There is always room for a second edition, and I owe it to all my backers to make good on what I promised.

On a more personal note, I would like to use this opportunity to thank my father, Eric Ludwig, and mother, Siri Kjos, for their everlasting love, forgiveness, faith, and encouragement. I owe everything good inside of me to my parents who have nurtured me my entire life, from when I was a child to when I went to war, and even to the man I am today. Furthermore, I owe them every ounce of my own credit for this book. If it weren't for their countless contributions, readings, comments and encouragements, this book would hardly be a shadow of what it is today. So thank you Dad, for the many nights you spent reading my terrible prose as I grew in my skills as a writer. And thank you, Mom, for having more courage than I could imagine, and giving me an endless list of reasons to fight on. Let it be known that I have the best parents in the world.

There are two other people who were there for me through the length of this project, keeping me going to the finish line, and I would like to take this opportunity to thank them as well. To Chris Landry: you are a dear friend and such an amazing motivator. This project wouldn't even be close to finished if it weren't for you. Thank you for keeping a fire burning under my ass and showing me that this book is bigger than just me and my own story. To MarkDaniel Brasel: thank you for being there for me when I needed a friend the most. Like Chris, knowing you were there, supporting and motivating me to make it across the finish line is the only reason I made it. I knew you as a great leader when we served together in 1st Platoon, and now I know that extends as much outside of the uniform as in it. Both of you helped me more than you'll ever know, when I needed you most, and for that I am forever grateful.

My highest honor is that I have served with one of the finest groups of men this country has to offer, in one of the hardest battles of Operation Iraqi Freedom. I have never known, nor will I ever again know, such a tightly-knit and disciplined group of soldiers, and I will never be as proud of anything as I am of having been a member of the Bulls. Here's to every man who's ever been a part of that legacy, from the days of the "Deathmasters" to their latest deployment to Afghanistan. I hope that what I've written here rings true to your memory, and is worthy of your praise. It has been an honor to be the voice of so many brave men.

A special recognition goes out to Rene Cardona, Chris Landry, James Flemming, and Ian Peterson, whose photographs of the battle provide a much-needed visual element to the story. Those pictures make all the difference in the world to readers who have never been to Iraq and have no idea what it's like. Were it not for the great efforts, especially of Rene and Chris, I would've never had such an amazing collection. To whomever took the photos I have provided without credit, I hope you will accept my sincerest apology. With so much content shared throughout our unit, it was a difficult task to identify the photographers of each shot. If you recognize a photograph as your own, I hope you will let me know so I can update its citation and give you credit in the next edition.

I'd also like to thank all my former leaders and mentors who guided me along the way, and to whom I owe my life many times over. That goes out to my recruiter, Staff Sergeant Jones, who was always honest and straightforward from the start. To my drill sergeants: Sergeants First Class Johnson, Chapman, and Herring — although it wasn't until years later that I came to realize just *how far* above the standard they trained all us young and inexperienced soldiers. To all the squad leaders and team leaders who kicked my ass and finished the job my drill sergeants started: Staff Sergeants Hailstock, Dukes, Moore, Benjamin, Bitolas, Betts, Clark, and High. And finally, to those leaders we lost, who will be remembered until long after the last Bull Company soldier is gone: Staff Sergeant Gamboa, Sergeant Lilly, and Corporal Kazarick. I have never known better teachers and mentors in my life than these few men, all of whom were masters of a brutal craft, with the most unforgiving test of mastery in the world. Believe me when I say that they could lead me anywhere in the world and I'd follow without question.

A big thanks goes out to First Sergeant Williams and Captain Bradford, who rallied the Bulls through it all and made our company what it was. For as long as we've had an Army it's been common knowledge that a unit can have a good first sergeant or it can have a good commander, but it can never have both. The two of these men are the exception that proves the rule. I haven't met a single man who's served under them that doesn't give them credit as the reason so many of us made it home alive.

For that and so much more, I owe them thanks for what they did. I'd also like to give a special thanks to Captain Bradford for his support in the early days of this project, years ago, when he dumped the motherlode into my lap. As soon as I told him what I was doing, he sent me a draft copy of the Army's official account of our company's involvement in Sadr City. That document was based on every primary resource of the battle and assembled specifically for strategic research and accounting, which gave me a unique ability to conform my own recollection to the reality of events.

As my last "military mention," I want to thank Captain Dan Savage for everything he taught me, the trust he held in me, and the privilege I had of serving as his right hand man for so long. I've come to realize since I left his side that the days I spent as "Bull-One-Six-Romeo" were some the greatest days of my military career. His appearance in my book hardly does justice to one of the finest men I've ever met — a man who gave me the eyes and ears to see things I would never have noticed, the wisdom to take it all in, and the patience to think critically under fire. People have asked me dozens of times how I can remember everything that happened in the battle or how I knew what the hell was going on outside of my own little sphere of the fight. The truth is that what I learned during my time with Captain Savage has found its way into every little detail of this book and continues to guide me to this day. Dan: wherever you go and whatever you do, if you ever need me for anything, I'll be there.

There are, of course, a number of people who have helped me with this project in the civilian world as well. I'd like to thank Bruce Gordon, Gabriel Gordon, Natasha Fried, Frank Rosenberg and Lisa Rosenberg for helping me find a developmental editor to guide me with this project. Without all of you, I would have never met Desa Philadelphia, who was instrumental in helping me make my "zero" draft manuscript into something worthy of a real book. Desa, I can't thank you enough for encouraging me to find my voice, my story, and my mission. I am truly in your debt for all the help you gave, teaching me how to see what needed fixing, and giving me the courage to step into the world of literature.

There have been almost a dozen major drafts of this book, each one better than the one before it, thanks entirely to a dedicated team of people who believed in my project and helped me see it through to the end. Therefore, I'd like to thank the lovely Christina King, whose endless efforts to inspire and support this project made all of this possible. Christina has read this book more times and in more ways than anybody else I've mentioned, and spent many frustrating nights helping me shape every sentence to its proper form. It's amazing how much of a difference it makes to have somebody right there next to you, ready and willing to do everything she can to help. Christina, I love you. But most of all, thank you for inspiring me to be proud of my own work, and confident in my own skills as a writer.

As for the rest of the team, I'd like to put a deep thanks out to Corin Porter, whose diligent eyes gave me a much needed perspective on the project and helped me clean up what had become a mechanical nightmare of a text. To Cody Shea, a dear friend with whom I would be honored to go through Hell, and whose technical feedback was essential to ensuring the integrity of the work. To Kyle Spitznagel, who has always been a source of wisdom and powerful advice throughout my life, and whose later additions and suggestions solved some of our biggest structural issues with the work. And once again, to my parents, Eric Ludwig and Siri Kjos, who volunteered when it was obvious that I was overloaded with work and threw down some extra eyes on the text. And to my aunt Lisa, who went through to clean up with everybody else had missed. If there's one thing I've learned with this project, it's never to release a pre-release copy before I have the six of you look it over and show me what to fix. If this book gets any recognition at all, I owe it to you.

Finally, I would like to thank Anthony Farina for his friendship and guidance as we work together to build a network for other soldiers to publish their own stories about the war. He was the first one to tell me something I will take to the grave: "A veteran without a mission is dead, and a veteran with a mission is deadly." Here's to that mission: giving a voice to those who serve their country in unknown corners of the world and make sacrifices every day so the rest of us don't have to. Congratulations on your new edition of *Angels in Sadr City*, and thank you for letting me be a part of its legacy. Together we will do great things.

It has been an honor to serve with and speak for so many people. I am truly humbled by all the support this book has received from the veterans of Sadr City and the families of those who served. Writing and publishing *Stryker* has been one of the most difficult journeys of my life, due in no small part to my own connection to the subject. I can say without a doubt, however, that putting all this down into words has done more to heal my soul than any pill or half hour session with a shrink, and I am both humbled and amazed that so many people have shown faith in my work.

Thank you all so much!

— *Konrad R.K. Ludwig*
December 1st, 2012

AFTERWARD

In the years that have passed, the Spring Fighting of 2008, and with it the Final Battle of Sadr City, have become critical fields of study among the leaders of our military regarding the way in which we fight our wars. For the first time since the Second Battle of Fallujah in 2004, American soldiers were forced into a ruthless fight for control over a critical piece of terrain. Just as it was in Fallujah, their enemy, the Jaish al-Mahdi, were an expertly trained, highly organized, and well-supplied insurgent organization, fighting from an entrenched position in complex urban terrain. The principal difference between these two events, however, was not the level of ferocity met during the fighting, or the weapons brought to bear, but rather the sheer number of civilians in both cities.

Unlike the Second Battle of Fallujah, where the non-combatant inhabitants were largely evacuated from the city to avoid civilian casualties, the district of Sadr City at the onset of the battle boasted a population that was already roughly twice that of Manhattan, living in roughly half its geographical footprint. And the sheer strength of the Jaish al-Mahdi, combined with the unforgiving urban terrain of the city, had resulted in a five-year standoff, during which Coalition troops rarely ventured inside of the district's borders. By the time the Final Battle of Sadr City kicked off, American troops had no choice but to embark on a ruthless and bloody battle in and among the civilian population, and what followed in the course of that struggle would ultimately challenge every policy and protocol of the war.

The Final Battle of Sadr City was divided into two distinct phases. The first of these two phases, "Operation Stryker Denial," began on the 25th of March as an immediate response to the Jaish al-Mahdi uprising and was led by the men of 1/2nd SCR. The primary objective in this phase of the battle was to regain a foothold against the forces of the Jaish al-Mahdi and put an end to the ongoing indirect fire missions raining down on Coalition troops throughout the city. After a week of relentless combat, however, American forces had barely regained the original front-line of the siege, thanks to the militia's well-stocked reserve of manpower and munitions from inside of their stronghold in Sadr City. By the 28th of March, the Coalition had no choice but to embark on an all-out attack into the heart of the district, meet their enemy on hostile ground, and strike a solid blow at the Jaish al-Mahdi.

What followed were three weeks of vicious combat, during which the American military managed to capture a full third of Sadr City before their advance was stalled. Due to the flexibility and adaptive nature of their enemy's defensive strategy, it was an impossible challenge for American troops to clear a region for very long. Without some kind of barrier, the only counter to the hit-and-run tactics employed by the Jaish al-Mahdi during Operation Stryker Denial was to leave a squad on every corner throughout the city – a task which had depleted the assaulting force of its men, and worn down their effective strength.

The second phase of the battle, "Operation Gold Wall," was launched in response to those hit-and-run tactics, in order to isolate the Jaish al-Mahdi within the northern quarters of the city, thereby securing what had already been captured and allowing a reconsolidation of Coalition troops. This phase of the battle also provided a secure environment for the reconstruction and humanitarian aid efforts launched by the American military to help the civilians who had been caught in the crossfire during the outbreak of the battle. Construction of the Gold Wall, which was carried out by the men of the 1-68th CAB, began on the 15th of April and continued well after the official end of the battle on the 11th of May, though open hostilities would remain a daily routine until well into the month of June.

In all, at least six different elements were on the front lines of the Final Battle of Sadr City. This includes the men of "Team Steel" of the 1-68th CAB (3/4th ID), who built the section of the wall along Route Gold; the "Wild Boars" of 2-30th INF (4/10th MTN), who held the southeastern flank and built the section of wall along Route Aeros; the "Gimlets" of the 1-21st INF (2/25th ID), who took over the northeastern flank along Route Grizzlies; the "Death Dealers" of the 4-64th AR (4/3rd ID), who provided heavy armored support throughout the battle; the "Bushmasters" of the 1-14th INF (2/25th ID), who supported the advance into Sadr City; the "Regulars" of the 1-6th INF (2/1st AD), who took over after the battle was won; and of course the "War Eagles" of the 1/2nd SCR, with whom I fought in the streets of Sadr City.

Beyond the scope of frontline action, I have heard that as many as eight brigades had some involvement with the battle, not counting an unknown number of non-military assets from outside the Department of Defense. This includes the air weapons teams of Apache helicopter pilots, unmanned airborne vehicle operators, and the many pilots of other fixed-wing assets who provided extensive air support to those of us out there on the ground. It also includes EOD technicians who rolled out with route clearance to secure the roads of IEDs and EFPs; the psychological operations operators, intelligence analysts, and communication specialists who orchestrated the flow of information throughout the battle; and a number of logistics support units who made sure the beans and bullets made it out to the men in the fight.

Obviously, it would be impossible for me to compile an account of everything that happened during the battle. Rather, this book is primarily an autobiographical account of my own experience on the ground, intended to provide a first-hand look at Bull Company's participation in the troop surge leading up to the battle, Operation Stryker Denial, Operation Gold Wall, and the months that followed the kinetic actions of the campaign. It is my hope that I can provide a valuable account from what I feel is an underrepresented view of the battle: that of the enlisted infantry soldier who is out in "the Shit."

For those who were expecting an objective account of what happened, it must be stated plainly that the nature of my involvement in the events of that spring precludes any notion of an unbiased telling. Please note that while this is certainly a well-informed look at my own involvement in the battle, I have made no effort to extract my own opinions and natural bias from the work. What I have done, however, is use every available opportunity to ensure that what I have written is as accurate and as honest as possible, while still representing the thoughts and emotions I had at the time.

I have spent the last three years researching the battle, comparing my own account of what happened to the official documentation and other academic source materials. Wherever those reports were either missing or inaccurate, I have sought to fill in the gaps with details taken from informal interviews with other veterans who were there. This book is the product of those efforts, and while I am positive that part of what I have written will differ slightly from other accounts of the battle, I am also confident that it represents the most accurate story I can write. My goal was not simply to provide a dry recital of the events at hand, but to represent the human factor in the face of combat with all the scars and uncertainty of having seen it unfold with my own two eyes. Regarding that uncertainty, however, I am obliged to explain a specific aspect of this story which has undoubtedly ruffled the feathers of a number of people who were involved in the battle and may have projected themselves into specific situations.

I must first assert that a first-hand account of any battle would be impossible without providing an honest interpretation of certain decisions made, orders given, and actions taken by third parties who are often of a higher rank and position. Often, however, such decisions, orders, and actions may have been impossible for the author to have witnessed himself, no matter how profound their effect may have been on his life and survivability in the field. This is due in no small part to the nature of battlefield communication, where orders, information and reasoning are continually conflated and simplified as they are passed down from "on high" — assuming, of course, that they were explained at all in the first place.

More often than not, exactly what was actually said by whomever gave the order is never really known by those who are expected to carry out the task. As a result, it is common to hear a wealth of speculation, rumor, and hearsay among the troops as to why certain orders of potentially questionable merit were ever given, and how whomever came up with whatever plan thought it would be a good idea at the time. And though such hearsay is a natural and unavoidable feature of military life and often serves as the primary source of noncritical information among enlisted soldiers, retelling such rumors in a public setting without due consideration and amendment raises an obvious threat of libel and defamation to any number of honorable men.

The paradox here is that a soldier's actions and interpretations of the current situation are almost always forged in large part by his personal understanding of the "big picture," yet that understanding is almost always exclusively formed by his exposure to this very hearsay and rumor. Simply eradicating any mention of these details is no solution, however, for such an attempt would effectively eradicate any logic in the story itself as well. Without them, the narrator would be unable to convey any higher-order reasoning with his decision making process outside of the most binary requirements of combat. ("I walked here and guys shot at me, so I ran there while more guys shot at me," etc.)

Historically, the solution to this paradox has been to plainly identify rumors and hearsay as second-hand knowledge which may or may not be true, and anonymize the subject of the rumor with a single literary device. This device is most commonly known in our culture as "the Man." In essence, the use of a blanket character or term serves to absolve any target of libel from potentially baseless accusations of malfeasance, while at the same time allowing the narrator to elaborate on what he believed to be true at the time. This allows him to explain why he did what he did, or why he felt a certain way about a given event, while admitting freely that he could've been wrong.

I am not exempt from this technique. One of the most difficult challenges in writing my story was to provide an honest testimony of what I believed at the time and why, while also clarifying that those beliefs may have been the product of faulty information and may no longer represent what I believe to this day. For structural and stylistic purposes, however,

I have modified that long-standing literary device of "the Man" with a new and far more dynamic title to serve my needs: "the Colonel."

Please note: THE COLONEL IN THIS STORY IS NOT A REAL PERSON. "*He*" is nothing more than an amalgamation of various decisions and events of the battle, which I have personified to serve as a tangible, flexible, and mutable device throughout the story. The specific rank of colonel was chosen for no other reason than to represent an anonymous brigade level command structure, which was the primary level of command during the battle. I'm sure there were probably a dozen or more men who held the rank of colonel or lieutenant colonel during the Final Battle of Sadr City. None of those men are represented by this device. When I describe the actions and decisions of "the Colonel" it should be taken no differently than if I were to have referred to "the Man." The fact that "*he*" walks and talks like a real person is nothing more than a literary quirk.

It has not been my intention to defame any person with my story, and I have not set out to list petty grievances or accusations in the public forum. In those places where the content of this book might be critical of my former command structure, I have sought to ensure such critique is legitimate, constructive, and telling of my emotional and psychological state at the time. I do not claim to be an omniscient observer, and am aware that there is a whole body of facts and knowledge to which I will never be privy. All I can do is tell the story I know, as I saw it, from on the ground. Beyond that, a true understanding of this event will only be possible when other soldiers, officers, and civilians come out and do the same.

On that note, I would like to formally recognize Staff Sergeant Anthony Farina as the first person I know of to take up the gauntlet and share his own story of the Final Battle of Sadr City with the world. Taking that first step required an amazing amount of courage, and Anthony's book, *Angels in Sadr City,* provides a much more in-depth report of Operation Gold Wall than my own. He and his men were the very soldiers who built the wall with their own two hands, under a relentless flood of enemy fire. If you are interested in getting a look at the battle from an entirely different perspective, the second edition of his book has been revised to include additional content by two of our soldiers from the 1/2nd SCR, John Isaac Reyes and Chris Violette, who teamed up with Anthony to do their part.

I can only hope that other veterans of Sadr City will come out of the shadows of history as we have done to publish their own stories and help us build a collective account of the Final Battle of Sadr City. Hopefully one day we will have a primary source from at least one soldier in every unit who was there. It is only by working together that we can fill in the body of research related to the war, and honor the courage and the perseverance of the men with whom we have served. After all, the hero's journey does not end in the cauldron of fire, but only when he comes home to speak of his journey through the land of giants.

CPSIA information can be obtained
at www.ICGtesting.com
Printed in the USA
FSHW022226151019
63047FS

9 780985 339807